City in a Park

A History of Philadelphia's Fairmount Park System

TEMPLE UNIVERSITY PRESS *Philadelphia Rome Tokyo*

City in a Park

James McClelland and Lynn Miller

Temple University Press
Philadelphia, Pennsylvania 19122
www.temple.edu/tempress

Photographs not otherwise attributed are by the authors. • Text design by Tracy Baldwin.

Library of Congress Cataloging-in-Publication Data

McClelland, James, 1934–
  City in a park : a history of Philadelphia's Fairmount Park system / James McClelland and Lynn Miller.
    pages   cm
  Includes bibliographical references and index.
  ISBN 978-1-4399-1208-9 (hardback : alkaline paper)   1. Fairmount Park (Philadelphia, Pa.)—History.
2. Urban parks—Pennsylvania—Philadelphia—History.   3. Philadelphia (Pa.)—History.   4. Philadelphia
(Pa.)—Buildings, structures, etc.   5. Philadelphia (Pa.)—Social life and customs.   6. Parks—Pennsylvania—
Philadelphia—Management—History.   I. Miller, Lynn H.   II. Title.
  F158.65.F2M33 2015
  974.8'11—dc23   2015008595

♾ The paper used in this publication meets the requirements of the American National Standard for
Information Sciences—Permanence of Paper for Printed Library Materials, ANSI Z39.48-1992

Printed in the United States of America

9 8 7 6 5 4 3 2 1

Background image:
Early nineteenth-century print
of Fairmount waterworks and
dam. (Courtesy of Frederick
and Margaret Johnson Sutor
collection)

Publication of this book

celebrating Fairmount Park,

which was established to protect

Philadelphia's water supply,

was supported by a grant from

the Watershed Protection Program

of the William Penn Foundation.

Contents

Acknowledgments

The history of Philadelphia's parks leads in many directions and is enriched by this diversity. Equally rich in diversity are those people to whom we are indebted for having assisted us in this effort to uncover and reveal that history.

We are grateful first to the staff at the Fairmount Park Historic Resource Archive. Rob Armstrong, the preservation and capital projects manager, welcomed us to browse about Philadelphia's remarkable archive of the city's parks, guiding us through the files and offering suggestions. Theresa R. Stuhlman, preservation and development administrator, was also helpful. Next door in the Fairmount Park offices, two city officials gave freely of their time. The first deputy commissioner of Philadelphia's Parks and Recreation Department, Mark A. Focht, more than once helped us understand important issues about the park system, particularly in light of the 2009 charter change that radically revamped the administration of the parks. Michael di Berardinis, Philadelphia's first commissioner of the new Department of Parks and Recreation, aided our understanding greatly with his perspective on the city's parks in the aftermath of that change.

Ellen Freedman Schultz, education and outreach coordinator for the Fairmount Water Works Interpretive Center, encouraged us after seeing an early draft of our chapters on the waterworks. The director of the Fairmount Park Conservancy, Katherine Ott Lovell, and the members of her staff, including Sarah Hirschler and Meg Holscher, were gracious and helpful in what they could tell us about their commitment to Philadelphia's parks. Philip Price Jr., in an interview, provided the unique insights of a longtime member of the Fairmount Park Commission and descendant of two giants of that commission, starting from its beginnings in 1872. Adam Levine, historical consultant to the Philadelphia Water Department, provided helpful criticism of our draft chapter on the origins of the Fairmount Water Works.

Among many others who provided access and expertise to our enterprise were Robin Barnes, major gifts officer at the Philadelphia Museum of Art; Ellen Carver, president and co-director of the Schuylkill Regatta; Bruce Laverty, curator of architecture for the Athenaeum of Philadelphia; Michael O'Malley, editor, Pennsylvania Heritage and Museum Commission; James Mundy, director of education and programming at the Union League of Philadelphia; Yuichi Ozama, Friends of the Japanese Tea House and Gardens; Phoebe Resnick, who helped provide us with entrée to historic sites; and Inga Saffron, architectural critic of the *Philadelphia Inquirer*.

We are grateful to photographers Mark Garvin, Ian Hartsoe, Eric Karlan, Rodney Miller, and Michael Murphy for providing us with images of their work, and to Chet Creutzberg, David Martin, Steve Lynch, and Margaret Johnson Sutor for allowing us to reproduce images from their collections.

At Temple University Press, executive editor Micah Kleit has supported our project with unswerving faith and devotion throughout a years-long process. We have also profited from the support of Sarah Cohen, Gary Kramer, Kate Nichols, and David Wilson, among many others.

Finally, we are grateful to the William Penn Foundation for agreeing that our history of Philadelphia's parks deserves to be told. Thanks to the foundation's generosity, we are able to present this history in a form that should allow many who know and love Philadelphia's parks—or who may do so in the future—to appreciate them more fully than ever before.

Your Parks Need Your Greening

The parks of Philadelphia form one of the largest urban park systems in the world. At nearly eleven thousand acres, the Fairmount Park system makes up almost 12 percent of the city's total land area. Numerous nonprofit organizations are dedicated to maintaining and improving the parks community, but their budgets all fall short. Below are those with the largest missions and greatest reach. They are joined by dozens of neighborhood associations, typically "Friends of" particular parks or playgrounds, where support is entirely voluntary.

Association for Public Art
Founded in 1872 as the Fairmount Park Art Association, this is the nation's first private, nonprofit organization for public art and urban planning. The aPA

commissions, preserves, and promotes public art in Philadelphia's parks and throughout the city. 1528 Walnut Street, Philadelphia, PA 19102. 215-546-7550. www.associationforpublicart.org.

Philadelphia Parks Alliance
The organization's mission is to champion the public's interest in outstanding parks, recreation, and open spaces, which are key to making the city one that is healthy, vibrant, and sustainable. P.O. Box 12677, Philadelphia, PA 19129. 215-879-8159. www.philadelphiaparks.org.

Fairmount Park Conservancy
The conservancy advocates for Philadelphia's Fairmount Park system, promoting the message that parks and open spaces can be catalysts for positive and enduring change to the city. The conservancy works as a collaborative partner to lead and support efforts that preserve and improve the Fairmount Park system, to enhance the quality of life and stimulate the economic development of the greater Philadelphia region. 1617 JFK Boulevard, Suite 1670, Philadelphia, PA 19103. 215-988-9335. www.fairountparkconservancy.org.

Friends of the Wissahickon
The group's mission is to preserve the natural beauty and wilderness of the Wissahickon Valley and stimulate public interest and support for this landscape within Fairmount Park. 8708 Germantown Avenue, Philadelphia, PA 19118. 215-247-0417. www.fow.org.

Authors' Note
Defining Philadelphia's Parks

When Philadelphians refer to "Fairmount Park," they usually have in mind the green space of nearly three thousand acres that extends from Fairmount up both banks of the Schuylkill River and Wissahickon Creek in a contiguous stretch to the city's northwestern limits. But from the time that park was created in 1867, its governing agency, the Fairmount Park Commission, also has been authorized to oversee noncontiguous parkland elsewhere in the city. The Fairmount Park system is the term we prefer in reference to facilities not physically part of the Schuylkill-Wissahickon land (the Benjamin Franklin Parkway, for example, is part of the Fairmount Park system).

Yet neither is that more-inclusive term always adequate. Some pieces of what today lie within the Fairmount Park system, the four (originally five) public squares created with William Penn's plan for Philadelphia in 1682, also long ago came under the jurisdiction of the Fairmount Park Commission. Today, one of them, Washington Square, is part of the Independence National Historic Park of the U.S. National Park Service.

Early in the twenty-first century, Philadelphians voted to revise the governance system for the parks, combining them for the first time with recreation in a newly created Philadelphia Parks and Recreation Department (PPR). Other name changes at the time suggest the new reality: the Fairmount Park Commission has become the Commission on Parks and Recreation (PaRC); the Fairmount Park Art Association, created in 1872 to oversee and encourage public art in city parks, became the Association for Public Art (aPA). Although the term "Fairmount Park" is too deeply ingrained in Philadelphia's history to disappear, it seems likely that it will diminish as a reference to all the city's parks over time.

To complicate the picture further, additional agencies today, such as the Delaware River Waterfront Commission and the Schuylkill River Greenway Association, are responsible for creating and improving green spaces in and around Philadelphia. Some increasingly connect with land within the Fairmount Park system. From the standpoint of the public, the name of the governing agency matters far less than the attractiveness and availability of the parkland. While this history focuses strongly on the original Fairmount Park, it also considers both more far-flung pieces of the Fairmount Park system, and other, especially more recent park initiatives that are occurring outside it.

City in a Park

William Penn's 1688 plan
for Philadelphia included
an open square near
each of the town's four
corners and a plot for
public buildings at the
center.

Introduction
Philadelphia and Its Parks

From its genesis more than three hundred years ago, Philadelphia's park system has grown with the city to encompass ever-increasing recreational opportunities, as well as important art and architecture, America's first zoo, and musical performances of every variety. It also has spawned one of the greatest urban planning projects undertaken by any American city. The history of Philadelphia's parks is the story of a project that keeps expanding, as succeeding generations continue to mold and develop it. It is the story of the intimate, unfolding connection between the city's people and its environment.

When William Penn planned his city of Philadelphia in the 1680s, he included public green spaces within the grid of streets. For the first century, those squares were left largely to nature and for citizens to use as grazing and burial grounds. Then, in 1799, the plot at the center of Penn's grid became the site of the pumping station for the world's first public water system. A park with a fountain and sculpture was created on the grounds surrounding that elegant little pump house. Within just a few years, the water plant had to be expanded to larger quarters, and land was chosen beside the Schuylkill River, just beyond the city limits at the foot of Fairmount.

Today, more than two hundred years after that move and the beginnings of a new public park at Fairmount, Philadelphia is widely regarded as having one of the finest urban parks in the world.[1] From the few acres acquired in 1812 to construct a new waterworks on the riverbank, Philadelphia's park system has grown to include some 10,200 acres of parkland encompassing 120 neighborhood parks scattered far across the city. Approximately one acre in ten within Philadelphia's boundaries is now devoted to parks and playgrounds, with more continuing to be added almost annually.

The city created out of the wilderness in the 1680s as a "greene countrie town" connects clearly to our own day, when Philadelphia's mayor has proclaimed the goal of making this city the greenest in America. If that seems a merely rhetorical or sentimental connection, it goes much deeper than that. The ideal of green space for the city across more than three centuries addresses both very different and, at the same time, nearly identical realities. A salutary quality of life is the constant. In laying out his city, William Penn's desire was for houses to rise surrounded by small garden plots and open spaces for the health of the inhabitants. He included five public squares in his plan for the same reason. Today, the vision of a green city is a response to the enormous increase in population—both regionally and across the globe—and that population's consumption of resources on a scale that, thanks to the accompanying pollution, now threatens the very viability of the planet, including the health of *all* its inhabitants, human and nonhuman. The need is the same as in Penn's day, but the issue is vastly larger and more critical.

Penn's hoped-for private plots of green were quickly filled in by dense building in a rapidly burgeoning town. For most of its first two centuries, Philadelphia's enormous growth overwhelmed its open spaces. But a little more than halfway through that period, moving the waterworks to Fairmount marked the start of a new and much greater effort to protect the city's water supply. That required protection of open spaces on each side of the Schuylkill. A long struggle followed against the impact of industrialization on the city's waterways. That effort eventually proved fruitless when the natural resource grew hopelessly polluted from industrial activity beyond the city's boundaries. By late in the nineteenth century, it was clear that Philadelphia's water had to be made safe through greater intervention in its treatment. But meanwhile, a remarkable public park had been born.

By the 1850s, when Fairmount Park was beginning to grow beyond its base at the waterworks, the park idea was spreading across America. The industrial age was making its belching presence felt around urban settlements, drawing unskilled laborers into its maw and spitting out its wastes into what had been pristine air and water. As an antidote, the romantic appeal of nature seemed to grow in proportion to its ever-greater distance from the lives of city dwellers. Alternatives were needed to this shutting out of the natural world. First came the rapid spread of rural garden cemeteries. One of the first was Laurel Hill, which was laid out in 1836, just to the north of what would be an expanding Fairmount Park. The romantic, contoured landscapes of these cemeteries became places both to honor the dead and elevate the thoughts of the living who strolled there. From these, it was a small step to the creation of city parks intended to bring similar uplift and spiritual restoration.

For the early proponents of parks in America like Andrew Jackson Downing, such public grounds also would be good for our democracy. "Much as they would create healthier cities," he wrote, "so would parks bring together all classes of people in the common enjoyment of nature."[2] Where European towns and cities had expansive parks, they typically had originated in the private pleasure grounds of the nobility. Many of these were only coming into the public domain early in the nineteenth century.[3] So, for park advocates in the new world, it seemed persuasive that the cities of republican America should create their own public gardens, libraries, and galleries, which would supplement the education of the masses. In Downing's view, "by these means, you would soften and humanize the rude, educate and enlighten the ignorant, . . . give continued enjoyment to the educated . . . [and thereby] banish the plague-spots of democracy."[4] A number of the early proponents of Fairmount Park took that idea very much to heart.

From the beginning, Philadelphia's Fairmount Park has been inseparable from its place beside the Schuylkill. Soon after the park was created as such in 1855, a decade after Lemon Hill had been added to the Fairmount Water Works on the river's east bank, it began its expansion to larger lands along the Schuylkill's west bank. This Pennsylvania waterway begins more than 130 miles to the city's northwest, flowing past Pottsville, Reading, and Norristown before entering the Philadelphia city limits for its final fourteen-mile course to the Delaware. By the 1870s, some five miles of that route passed through Fairmount Park. That stretch of the river quickly became one of the nation's best courses for boating and rowing. Today, open space continues to be added along the riverbank south of the Philadelphia Museum of Art to extend parkland and hiking trails ever farther downriver. It is now possible to imagine a time when virtually all of the Schuylkill's path through Philadelphia will be a green and public space.

The Schuylkill's tributary, Wissahickon Creek, flows from its source in Montgomery County northeast of Norristown for more than twenty miles to its mouth at the Schuylkill in East Fairmount Park. By 1869, its seven-mile stretch within Philadelphia had been incorporated into the park. Because of its steep descent—it drops more than a hundred feet within the city limits—the creek had been an early site for water-powered industry in eastern Pennsylvania. Once the creek and gorge came under the jurisdiction of Fairmount Park, the park's commissioners moved swiftly to demolish virtually all the mills along the way. That began a remarkable transformation. Within a few years, what had been a valley teeming with industry was returned largely to its wild and rugged state before Europeans settled in North America. In the 1920s, when motor vehicles were banned from the only motorway through the gorge, Wissahickon Drive, the sense of a return to primeval nature was complete. That ban gave the road its popular name since then—Forbidden Drive.

The Schuylkill River, rolling through a wooded landscape and its tributary plunging dramatically through the wilderness, defined Fairmount Park. By the same token, the creation of Fairmount Park defined the Herculean civic effort to provide a clean water supply to Philadelphia while offering public pleasure grounds. Over time, other creeks flowing through additional Philadelphia neighborhoods—most important, Cobbs, Pennypack, and Tacony— were brought into the city's park system to try to prevent their further pollution and provide more green retreats for Philadelphians. Meanwhile, however, the greatest waterway of them all, the Delaware, remained largely beyond the intended reach of the great new municipal park. There, where commercial activity could lead directly to the highway of the Atlantic, commerce and industry ruled.

In the 1920s, what would become perhaps the most iconic piece of outdoor art in Philadelphia was dedicated at Logan Square. Alexander Stirling Calder's *Fountain of the Three Rivers* depicted Philadelphia's three principal waterways as recumbent Native Americans: one male to represent the mighty Delaware, the others female for the gentler Schuylkill and the Wissahickon. While the three were equally beautiful in this allegorical depiction, it would be almost another century before Philadelphians could begin to imagine that this could become a reality. Yet by early in our century, green shoots were being established along the Delaware, that most rugged—and ragged—of the city's rivers. It began to seem possible that Philadelphia might one day claim public greenways linking all three of its principal rivers.

The park's beneficial impact on the city it serves has been profound and, in some respects, unique among urban parks in America. From its earliest days, the development of parkland has been accompanied by the installation of great public art, much of it within the parks themselves, but a good deal of it spilling out to enhance other public spaces throughout the city. For well over a century, Philadelphia has held the distinction of displaying more public art than any other city in America. That tradition began with the establishment of the Fairmount Park Art Association by private citizens only a few years after the park itself was named and began to grow.[5]

The Fountain of the Three Rivers (*Swann Fountain*) on Logan Square is dominated by three reclining figures of Native Americans that represent Philadelphia's three principal waterways: the Delaware, Schuylkill, and Wissahickon.

Early in the twentieth century, the most extensive urban plan in Philadelphia's history came about because of the existence of Fairmount Park. The Benjamin Franklin Parkway was designed to provide a direct and impressive entrance to the park while creating a handsome civic boulevard connecting that entrance to City Hall. It extended a green swath of the park down into the heart of the city at the same time it provided a thoroughfare lined with many of Philadelphia's principal cultural and educational institutions. In the process, it provided a superb avenue where additional works of art and architecture could be presented to the public.

With the creation of Fairmount Park, the city also acquired an unrivaled collection of houses, mostly along the Schuylkill, dating from the colonial period and the first decades of the young Republic. At first, officials tended to regard these buildings as practical assets, to be used to house park offices and personnel. But gradually their historic and architectural value came to be appreciated, and the finest of them were refurbished and opened to the public. While some of these houses have been lost to the ravages of time—fires and vandalism have taken a toll—others now are being maintained by private groups leasing them for their use. Today, the Fairmount Park villas make it unique among urban parks for the number and quality of its examples of eighteenth- and early nineteenth-century domestic architecture in America.

Thanks to its parks, high (and not so high) musical culture lives outdoors throughout Philadelphia's summers. The Philadelphia Orchestra has long provided a summer concert season at its home in Fairmount Park. Ballet, jazz, and other popular fare, musical and otherwise, are presented in parks throughout the city in the warmer months.

More than a century after the Schuylkill stopped providing the city with its water supply because of its ever-greater pollution, the river is once more clean enough for shad to return there to spawn. This was only made possible due to the combined efforts of the Philadelphia Water Department, the Pennsylvania Fish and Boat Commission, and the Army Corps of Engineers. A fish ladder at the waterworks dam was essential to the shad; with them have come striped bass, perch, and other game fish to attract anglers back to the riverbank. For Philadelphians, the restoration of the Schuylkill may be the most satisfying indicator that their beloved park still thrives.

This is also a prime example of how a society's commitment and hard work can overcome the injury human settlement often does to the natural landscape. Unfortunately, however, the sequence of cause and effect more often flows in the other direction. Too frequently the demands of urban life have impacted negatively on Philadelphia's parks. Roads in the age of the automobile are the most dramatic example. By the mid-twentieth century, the nation was consumed with enabling automotive traffic to speed across the country. For Philadelphia, that resulted in building the Schuylkill Expressway right through some of the most bucolic acreage of West Fairmount Park.

More insidious harm to the city's park system has come from the long, slow decline in maintaining it. In the second half of the twentieth century, too many parks and recreation facilities subsided into urban jungles. This was the result of a number of factors, primarily the city's loss of population, in which once-thriving neighborhoods were abandoned to the very poor.

This resulted in a decline in Philadelphia's tax base whereby city services were increasingly starved for funds. Among those services, the parks were perhaps the easiest target since the benefits they provided were widely seen as nonessential. With severe cutbacks in the personnel required to maintain the parks and keep them secure, their decline was so great that some came to be seen as civic liabilities, not assets.

For decades following World War II, the decline in Philadelphia's parks bore the hallmarks of a self-fulfilling prophecy. Where increasingly derelict neighborhoods threatened the attractiveness and even the safety of neighboring parks, park advocates found it ever more difficult to persuade a declining population of taxpayers of the need to maintain them. The more parks declined, the greater the loss of support for them, and vice versa. During the second half of the twentieth century, Philadelphia lost 26.7 percent of its population, mostly in the form of white flight to the suburbs. As a result, while tax revenues shrank, city officials could not afford to make parks a priority for spending.

Happily, as reflected in the current drive for a greener city, Philadelphia may be starting to turn back from that nadir. This is suggested by two hopeful trends: first, the stabilization and slight growth in the city's population since 2006, which had not happened since 1950; second, and more significant, what may be durable, long-term changes in the kind of life and livelihood this postindustrial city is able to offer its citizens. In the early years of the twenty-first century, Philadelphia saw an increase in the number of young people living in the city. Among them were substantial numbers with specialized training and advanced degrees for whom attractive recreational and other green space was an inducement to stay in the city.[6]

As a result, even during the most serious economic downturn since the Great Depression, starting in 2008, Philadelphia's parks were showing new signs of life. Although they remain badly underfunded, almost miraculous signs of their restoration are visible today. Volunteer groups and nonprofit organizations are stepping up to restore and enliven park properties, bringing many back to life that had long been moribund. The Fairmount Water Works and South Garden now beckon as brightly as they have at any time in the past two centuries. Smaller parks throughout the city, such as Hunting Park, have undergone face-lifts and revitalization that make them neighborhood magnets once more. What would have seemed a foolish sentiment not so long ago may be a sane possibility today: The best years for Philadelphia's parks may still lie in the future.

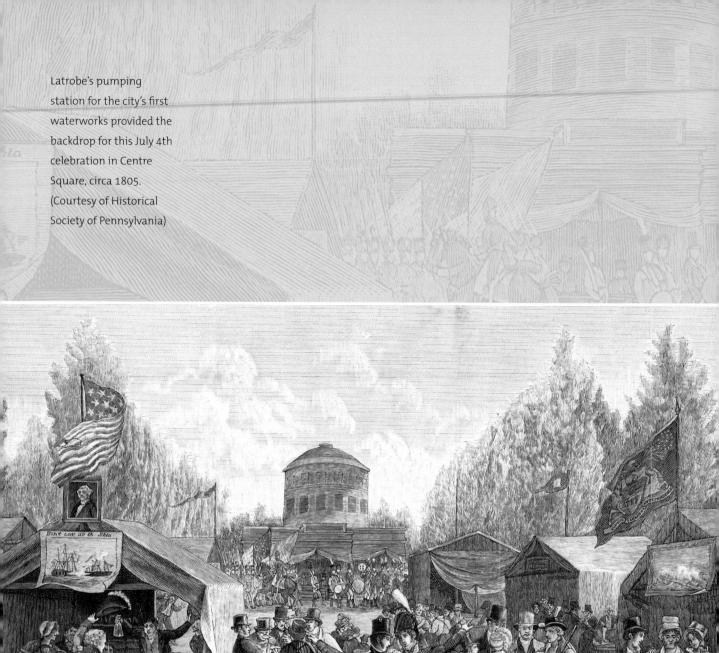

In the Beginning, Clean Water

Three circumstances converged in Philadelphia at the end of the eighteenth century in a way that seems fated from our vantage point more than two centuries later. Their convergence would lead to the birth of the Fairmount Water Works, then Fairmount Park, endowing both with a special character that remains visible today.

The first of these circumstances was the increasingly urgent need for clean water to supply the city's growing population. In addition to frequent outbreaks of various infectious diseases, yellow fever afflicted the city almost annually, with a terrifying scourge in 1793. It again became a plague in the city in 1798. It was not yet understood that the yellow fever virus was carried by mosquitoes. Rather, the odor of rotting organic matter arising from polluted streams was thought to be the source of all these diseases. Slaughterhouse waste that washed up on creek banks was an obvious problem. A study concluded that the city's water supply was contaminated by covered streams long used as sewers, as well as from cesspools that lay too close to the wells providing water to public pumps and hydrants. In 1798, a Joint Committee on Supplying the City with Water (the Watering Committee) was created, its members drawn from Philadelphia's select and common councils. Philadelphia was about to become the first major city in the modern world where it would be a municipal obligation to provide clean water to its inhabitants.

For advice, the Watering Committee turned to Benjamin Henry Latrobe, an English-born engineer and architect newly arrived in Philadelphia. He proposed that with the aid of a new invention, the steam engine, pure water could be pumped from the Schuylkill River to an engine house and pumping

1

station on Centre Square. From there, the water would be distributed through a system of bored-log pipes throughout the city. The Watering Committee accepted that recommendation and commissioned the architect to design and create the new system.

Here was the second circumstance: Latrobe soon employed as his assistant a twenty-three-year-old native Philadelphian, Frederick Graff. That brought together a brilliant architect with a first-rate young engineer who would be profoundly influenced by their association. As style setters, the reach of the older man through the younger one soon would extend to the larger stage at Faire Mount. Latrobe's plan of 1798 called for two steam engines, the first at the foot of Chestnut Street on the bank of the Schuylkill, which would pump the river water through a tunnel to Centre Square, where the second pump would raise the water to a holding tank. From there, it could be distributed to the city.

Latrobe's associate, Nicholas Roosevelt, got to work building the engines. But it was Latrobe who designed the engine house that would act as the centerpiece for the new system. Imbued with the teaching of the great Renaissance architect Andrea Palladio, he conceived the building in a chaste, neoclassical style with strong Palladian influences. Neoclassicism was already Latrobe's signature in the construction then under way of Philadelphia's Bank of Pennsylvania.[1] His impact would be so great that it would dominate the next era of public architecture in America, starting with the U.S. Capitol in the rising federal city in Washington.[2] Graff, whom Latrobe described as his first pupil, would carry on the master's stylistic principles when he was selected as superintendent of the waterworks in 1805.

The new system went into operation in January 1801. Its pumping station in Centre Square (the plot occupied by City Hall today) stood in the middle of one of the original five public spaces laid out by William Penn's surveyor. That plot of land became at last the kind of urban park it had failed to be throughout the previous century when, in spite of its theoretical place at the center of the founder's planned city, it remained at the western edge of the actual eighteenth-century settlement. General Rochambeau and his French army had used the square as a campground in September 1781, on their way to join Generals Washington and Lafayette for what would be a decisive action at Yorktown. Twenty years later, Latrobe's beautiful new engine house, emitting mysterious clouds of smoke from the hole in its dome through all hours of the day and night, was an immediate attraction. Soon, the space around it was enhanced by new landscaping that included walkways, benches, and stately Lombardy poplar trees. In the summer of 1809, a beautiful fountain created by America's finest sculptor, Philadelphia's own William Rush, was installed in front of the engine house.[3]

Here was the third propitious circumstance: housing for a utilitarian necessity became the centerpiece of a sylvan shrine where public art grew within the city. The need for clean water, the arrival of a superb architect imbued with the neoclassical tradition, and the civic vision of a public park all came together to create Philadelphia's first waterworks at Centre Square.

Even though Latrobe's engine house was admired for its proportions and Greek prototypes, the steam engine and pumps fit very tightly in the interior. That was a problem when it soon became apparent that the machines were subject to frequent breakdowns. The boilers were inefficient and the reservoir too small to hold a supply of water for more than twenty-five minutes unless more water was continually pumped into it. Yet an enormous amount of wood was needed to keep the engine running, which proved a great expense. If one engine broke down, the entire system would fail. Fears arose that there would be insufficient water in the tanks to fight fires.

It quickly became clear that the city's population was simply growing too fast to be adequately served by its beautiful new waterworks. Philadelphia's population in 1790 was nearly 29,000. That figure had increased by more than 30 percent by the time of the Centre Square station's first year of operation in 1800, when more than 41,000 residents were counted. By 1810, the population had more than doubled from twenty years earlier, to nearly 64,000.[4]

Latrobe, meanwhile, having made his reputation in Philadelphia, moved to Washington, D.C., in 1803, when President Thomas Jefferson appointed him superintendent of public buildings in the nation's new capital. In 1811, the Watering Committee directed Superintendent Graff and John Davis, Graff's predecessor as superintendent, to study the situation at Centre Square and make recommendations. Their solution was much like Latrobe's a dozen years before. The Schuylkill should remain the source of fresh water for the city, but the waterworks should be reconstructed on a much larger scale on the riverbank below Faire Mount. Graff's rationale was that water could be pumped easily from the vigorous Schuylkill to large new reservoirs at the top of the hill, some fifty feet higher than the highest building in the city, where it would then flow through pipes to the city below. He presented the need for a new engine house at the foot of the hill and a deep reservoir at the summit.

Graff and Davis's plan was accepted, and construction began in August 1812, at the new five-acre site, which included Faire Mount and the river-

Fairmount

This hill was named "Faire Mount" by William Penn when he and his surveyor, Thomas Holme, laid out the new city in 1683. Philadelphia's planned grid of streets ran from the Delaware River to the Schuylkill across a plain criss-crossed by a number of streams, with Faire Mount rising some fifty-six feet beside the Schuylkill less than half a mile beyond the city's northern boundary. Penn considered building his own manor house on the crest, but decided instead on a larger site thirty miles up the Delaware. When the British occupied Phila-delphia in 1777–1778, they built a line of defensive works starting on Faire Mount that extended to the Delaware, thereby blocking a possible attack by Washington's troops from the north, the only city boundary not protected by a waterway.

In 1812, construction began at the foot of Faire Mount for a new waterworks, and reservoirs were dug out of the summit. When work was completed, water was pumped up the hill from the river to flow by gravity down into the city below. The site gave its name to Fairmount Park in 1855, one year after the Spring Garden District in which it was located was incorporated, along with many other outlying districts and townships, into a much enlarged city of Philadelphia. After the waterworks were decommis-sioned in 1911, a city ordinance named the Fairmount summit as the site for a new public art museum. The Philadelphia Museum of Art was completed there in 1928, as the focal point at the end of the new Benjamin Franklin Parkway where it led to Fairmount Park.

bank below. For the new engine house, Graff created a building that both reflected how he had been influenced by Latrobe and paid tribute to the country villas of the rich that had sprouted nearby along both banks of the Schuylkill during the previous half century. What looked from the outside like a wealthy family's Federal-style mansion concealed the boilers, two steam engines, and pumps of the new machinery.[5] The Philadelphia-built engines, one low-pressure, the second a more advanced high-pressure machine, were meant to ensure that one would always be in operation if the other needed repair. A reservoir capable of holding three million gallons of Schuylkill River water was dug out of the top of Fairmount. By 1815, water began to fill it.

Once in operation, the new waterworks greatly increased the amount of water being pumped from the river. But two problems soon became apparent. Water flowed from the new reservoir to the old holding tank at Centre Square to be distributed as before. Yet the small diameter of the city's bored-log pipes allowed no more than one million gallons to pour out into the city throughout a twenty-four-hour period. That situation was improved starting in 1819 by replacing the log pipes with larger ones of cast iron, greatly expanding their rate of flow and eliminating the need for the holding tank at Centre Square. As a result, that facility became obsolete, and in 1829, Latrobe's elegant building was demolished.

The Upper Ferry Bridge was known as the "Colossus of Fairmount" for its immense single span, the longest of its kind in the world when it was completed in 1813. (London, October 1, 1830, published by Jenner and Chapman)

The second problem was economic. In 1819, Graff estimated that each engine cost nearly $31,000 annually to run, since 3,650 cords of wood had to be burned to keep the steam rising. There was a human cost as well; in 1818 and again in 1821, boilers exploded, killing three men.[6]

The solution finally determined was simplicity itself. The city would forego the most modern—and still dangerous—technology involving steam engines and revert instead to one of the oldest forms of energy known: water power. The Watering Committee decided to build a spillway dam a short distance above the engine house that would allow water to be diverted toward

The Colossus of Fairmount (Upper Ferry Bridge)

This engineering marvel, built in 1811–1812, was a wooden covered bridge arching over the Schuylkill in a single, 340-foot span, the longest of its kind in the world when it was built. Designed by a German emigrant, Lewis (Louis) Wernwag, it crossed the river from the lower end of the South Garden at Fairmount at the approximate location of today's Spring Garden Street Bridge. The structure allowed horses and carriages to pass in two lanes in the center, while walkways on each side gave pedestrians views of the river through a series of windows. The handsome structure was world famous, regarded as perhaps America's premier engineering achievement in its day. The bridge was destroyed by fire in a likely act of vandalism on September 1, 1838.*

*Wernwag was among the leading bridge builders in America in the early nineteenth century. After his Upper Ferry Bridge was destroyed, Charles Ellet's Fairmount suspension bridge—called the "Wire Bridge," another engineering marvel—would rise in its place by 1842 on the old bridge's abutments.

new waterwheels responsible for pumping river water to the reservoir. Construction began in 1819 and was completed by 1821, when the last hickory crib was floated into place, then filled with stone and anchored into the bedrock of the riverbed with iron spikes.

The dam was a major engineering achievement, consisting of four distinct interlocked sections of which the wooden, rock-filled spillway was the longest. The dam created a tranquil pool behind it that extended several miles upstream to the natural cascade at East Falls. It was constructed at a sharp diagonal toward the northwest across the river from the eastern bank, so that water directed toward the dam's southeasternmost section would then flow into a new forebay—in effect, a channel dug deeply into the rock behind and parallel to the riverbank. From there, it would be fed to each waterwheel via flumes the width of the wheels, spilling down into their buckets to make them revolve. At the time of its construction, the 2,008-foot Schuylkill dam was the longest in America.[7]

The plan also required the construction of a mill house, again from Frederick Graff's design, between the water's edge to the north of the engine house and the new forebay behind it and parallel to the bank. That meant blasting into the rock so that the roof of the 238-foot structure would be nearly at ground level, or just above the level where the water in the forebay

Historical Blue Staffordshire plate, circa 1830, depicting the Fairmount Dam, Water Works, and Lemon Hill opposite. To the left is the canal and lock that permitted boats to navigate past the dam. (Courtesy of Frederick and Margaret Johnson Sutor collection)

In the Beginning, Clean Water

behind it would pour into and through the mill house. The water would fall first into the buckets on eight wheels, which turned four pairs of pumps to carry water to the top of Fairmount, while the spillover flowed back out the other side of the mill house into the river below the dam. The first pump began operation on July 1, 1822, and additional wheels were added gradually until 1843. On Fairmount's summit, a total of four reservoirs were constructed by 1836 with a capacity of 22,031,976 gallons. What distinguished the new facility aesthetically was that Graff added administrative space by creating two small temple-like structures at each end of the terrace roof of the mill house to form a neoclassical monument in the spirit of his mentor, Latrobe.[8]

With the completion of the dam, including a canal and lock system to move boats up and down the river on the western side, the new pool of placid water above it would become a place of recreation: boating in summer, ice skating in winter. The waterworks themselves were a constant draw for citizens who came to gaze at their power and be dazzled by the sound of water splashing all about them. As Charles Dickens put it when he visited the city twenty years later, "Philadelphia is most bountifully provided with fresh water, which is showered and jerked about, and turned on, and poured off everywhere."[9]

A new public park had been born. The old steam engines were stopped for the final time in October 1822, and were sold ten years later for scrap. That left the earliest building, the engine house, to be turned shortly thereafter into a

This view from the porch of a hotel on the Schuylkill's west bank takes in the Upper Ferry Bridge, Fairmount, and the waterworks on the opposite shore. (Lithograph published by J. T. Bowen in 1838. Courtesy of Historical Society of Pennsylvania)

public saloon, where refreshments were available for decades to follow. A porch was added on the river side in 1835, with columns that gave it a neoclassical appearance in harmony with the little temples atop the mill house.

In 1825, the Watering Committee, whose office was in one of those pavilions (a caretaker was housed in the other), commissioned William Rush to create two pieces of sculpture to adorn the mill house entrances. His *Allegory of the Schuylkill River in Its Improved State (Schuylkill Chained)* and *Allegory of the Waterworks (Schuylkill Freed)* were the result. In 1829, Rush's 1809 fountain, *Water Nymph and Bittern (Allegory of the Schuylkill)* was moved from Centre Square and placed at the edge of the forebay where its high-spouting plume

In the Beginning, Clean Water

added to the aquatic spectacle Dickens would admire a few years later. Also in 1829, a carved figure of *Mercury* by Rush was placed atop an arbor-like gazebo that stood at the top of the hill.[10]

But even while the conversion to water power was under way—and in spite of the appealing design lavished on the remodeled facility—it was far from clear that a more substantial park would grow from Fairmount and its waterworks. Philadelphia initially promoted a plan to build factories south of the area, based on the idea of extending the forebay so that the city might sell water power to new industries there. Graff himself produced a drawing showing how an industrial complex might be accommodated. But legal

A ferry steams toward the lock beside the Fairmount Dam in this early nineteenth-century print. Lemon Hill is at center on the opposite shore, the waterworks to the right. (Courtesy of Frederick and Margaret Johnson Sutor collection)

After extensive renovations between 2006 and 2008, ramps and staircases along the west face of Fairmount again allowed pedestrian access between the waterworks and South Garden complex and the grounds of the Philadelphia Museum of Art on the summit. During those renovations, the long-vanished Rustic Pavilion, a wooden structure dating from the 1860s, was re-created in steel near the top of the slope. The Mercury Pavilion has been reinterpreted in the structure that now stands on the summit, but without the figure of the messenger of the gods. Below, to the north of the waterworks, a circular gazebo was built on the eastern end of the dam in 1835. The carved eagle on its peak is an interpretation of the original, now lost, that was created by William Rush's son John.

issues arose over the water rights of those from whom the city had purchased land; in addition, it was determined that to blast through the rock to extend the mill race south around Fairmount might seriously endanger the existing structures of the waterworks.

These obstacles meant that plans to create an industrial neighborhood below the reservoir were abandoned by the time the first of Rush's sculptures was moved to Fairmount in 1829.[11] The area had become, and would remain, a pleasure site. As the English writer Frances Trollope wrote in 1832 after traveling to Philadelphia, "the vast yet simple machinery" of the waterworks "is open to the public, who resort in such number to see it, that several stages run from Philadelphia to Fair Mount for their accommodation."[12] At the time of Mrs. Trollope's visit, the city already was engaged in developing the South Garden just below the waterworks. What had been a stone quarry there was filled in. Then, between 1829 and 1835, the garden was laid out with walkways and an esplanade. The proponents of an improved public park surrounding Fairmount evidently were carrying the day.

On the north side of the waterworks, a circular, columned gazebo for viewing the falls was built on the stone pier at the eastern end of the dam's spillway in 1835. Its summit was ornamented with a carved wooden eagle created by John Rush, William's son, who earlier had assisted his father in making the Schuylkill allegory figures. Shortly thereafter, the figures of *Wisdom* and *Justice* that William Rush had carved in 1824 were housed in the main hall of the engine house. They had been created to surmount the triumphal arch that had spanned Chestnut Street in front of Independence Hall in honor of the return visit that year of the great hero of the Revolution, the Marquis de Lafayette.[13]

The water-powered waterworks proved to be so efficient and economical that they soon became a prototype for other cities. Over the years, Graff

would act as an engineering consultant to at least thirty-seven municipalities in America and abroad seeking to learn from Philadelphia's experience. In 1844, the Fairmount Water Works supplied an average of 5.3 million gallons of water per day to 28,082 water tenants. The operation cost $29,713, while the city treasury was paid $151,501, a high point for revenues.[14]

Meanwhile, the city and its suburbs continued to expand. For years, city officials had watched with concern the growth of industrial sites along the banks of the Schuylkill to the north of the city. Where the river within living memory had been bucolic and nearly pristine, with only the estates of the landed gentry rising here and there along its banks, by the 1840s, it was becoming a thoroughfare for commercial transportation and power. Worse, with industrial growth, factories were increasingly using it as a sewer. Nor

In the 1830s, the South Garden was laid out on what had been a stone quarry for the creation of the waterworks to the north. The memorial to Frederick Graff is in the foreground; behind it is the marble fountain.

In the Beginning, Clean Water

Graff Memorial and South Garden

Frederick Graff (1775–1847) began his work for Philadelphia as the young assistant to Benjamin Latrobe, designer of the city's first waterworks at Centre Square in 1798. Graff was named superintendent in 1805, and six years later recommended creating a new facility at Fairmount. He remained in charge of the Fairmount Water Works until his death in 1847. As a memorial, a white marble portrait bust was dedicated in the South Garden in the year after his death. Not only had Graff designed all the major features of the waterworks but also had been responsible for creating the South Garden between 1829 and 1835. After filling in what had been a stone quarry, he laid out walkways and lawns, as well as an esplanade accessible by a staircase to the riverbank below.

After years of neglect, the South Garden was restored to its early nineteenth-century appearance between 2006 and 2008. The 1830 marble fountain again functioned after more than a century of disuse, and the Graff Memorial was brought back to its original appearance.

had the construction of the Fairmount Dam helped, for that had produced stagnant water at the dockside entrances to a number of the country houses north of the waterworks. The financial crisis of 1836–1837 further contributed to the decline of this once posh area. All these factors combined to make available land affordable to the city when the forty-five-acre estate nearly adjacent to the north of the waterworks, Lemon Hill, came on the market in 1844.

Once the country seat of Robert Morris, Lemon Hill had been purchased from his estate at a sheriff's sale in 1799 by Henry Pratt. Pratt maintained the grounds as a semipublic garden for the next thirty-six years before selling the property to a New York merchant in 1836. The property deteriorated until the city, now determined to protect the river above the waterworks from further pollution, bought it in 1845.[15] Nonetheless, in spite of Lemon Hill's earlier role as a retreat for city dwellers, its purchase did not immediately prompt Philadelphia officials to improve it as a public amenity. Instead, in 1847, the city leased the property for a period of ten years to P. Zaiss, a German immigrant who operated a brewery on the site until 1855. By 1854, what had been a magnificent greenhouse dating from Pratt's time—its lemon trees had given the estate its name—burned down.

Yet, during that decade of official inaction at Lemon Hill—1845–1855—other forces were at work. Frederick Graff's nearly fifty-year career as the guiding light of Philadelphia's waterworks, from his apprenticeship at Centre Square to his long superintendence of Fairmount, came to an end with his death at age seventy-one in 1847. His replacement as superintendent was his son, Frederic Jr., who, in 1851, recommended purchasing additional land to the north of Lemon Hill to protect the watershed and provide more recreational space.

That recommendation came after the younger Graff had been commissioned by a prominent Philadelphian, John Price Wetherill, to create a plan for integrating Lemon Hill with a twenty-four-acre estate immediately adjacent to the north known as Sedgley. Its villa had been redesigned in 1799 by Benjamin Latrobe in a Gothic Revival style, the first of its kind in America. The estate had then undergone changing ownership throughout the early part of the nineteenth century. For several years, the city ignored Graff's proposal to buy the property, continuing a pattern of official inaction when it came to creating a greater park at Fairmount.

Meanwhile, however, in 1854, the Act of Consolidation brought the greatest enlargement of Philadelphia in its history. That legislation produced new initiatives in every aspect of the city's life, including the creation of Fairmount Park. Yet, by the time the city finally purchased Sedgley in 1857, the house was derelict. It was demolished shortly thereafter.

This gazebo provides a
lookout over the dam and
Boat House Row at the end
of the mill house, which was
built between 1859 and 1862
at a diagonal to the old one.
The eagle ornament is a
replica of the original carved
by John Rush in 1835.
(Photograph by Mark Garvin)

A Park Grows from Fairmount

The 1854 Act of Consolidation transformed the city of Philadelphia as at no other time in its history. Its boundaries were extended to make them coterminous with the entire county of Philadelphia, where they remain to the present day. The new borders embraced nearly half a million citizens—more than three hundred thousand of whom had previously been outside Philadelphia—and abolished thirteen townships, six boroughs, and nine districts. This radical and long-sought change in what constituted Philadelphia prompted renewed energy on the part of those promoting an expanded park. It had been more than ten years since the Lemon Hill estate north of the Fairmount Water Works had been acquired, then largely ignored by the city. But on September 28, 1855, both Lemon Hill and Fairmount were designated as public land and renamed Fairmount Park. Even then, not until angry citizens demanded action were Lemon Hill's tenants evicted a year or more later.[1]

In 1857, the proposal Frederic Graff Jr. had initiated in 1851 to add the Sedgley estate to the park finally came to fruition.[2] Again, citizen action led the way. In October 1856, the Committee of City Property began to investigate land both between the Fairmount Water Works and Lemon Hill and between Lemon Hill and the Spring Garden waterworks to the north. While that proposal languished in committee, a group of determined citizens purchased Sedgley with the intention of donating it to the city. The group raised $60,000 toward the $125,000 purchase price and then deeded the land to the city "as a park, in connection with and as a part of Fairmount Park," on condition that the city take out a mortgage to pay the remainder. The city accepted the offer and annexed Sedgley to Lemon Hill.[3] With that, the new Fairmount Park consisted of nearly a hundred acres. It stretched from the South Garden through the waterworks and skipped a short way along the Schuylkill's east bank to widen out at the crests of Lemon Hill and Sedgley.

The new parklands remained disconnected to the waterworks and Fairmount itself. Since all were now envisioned as a single park, the City Council in 1858 asked for proposals to unite the two sites. The landscape firm of Sidney and Adams presumably won the competition, but—the pattern recurs—most of their plan remained unexecuted. Four years later, however, in 1862, the city did purchase a narrow neck of land west of Landing Avenue that connected the two parcels. In 1869, the city bought additional land known as the Flat Iron, a triangular area north and east of Coates Street and Landing Avenue.[4]

Meanwhile, changes were under way at the Fairmount Water Works. In 1851, a new hydraulic turbine was installed to increase the plant's ability to provide water to the city's inhabitants. There being no more space available on Fairmount's summit, a new reservoir was then constructed at Corinthian Avenue, while a new standpipe at Fairmount, designed to resemble an Italian bell tower, raised the water to a height from which it could flow there. The success of the new turbine inspired the next waterworks superintendent, Henry P. M. Birkinbine, to install three larger hydraulic turbines in a new mill house that was built between 1859 and 1862 into the mound dam at a diagonal from the old one. Its roof also became a terrace, adding to the area available for spectators to stroll. To connect the three new discharge mains from the three new turbines to the reservoirs and standpipe without blasting, Birkinbine designed and built a distribution arch that protected the

"No Hydraulic Works in the Union Can Compete"

"It is impossible to examine [the Fairmount Water Works] without paying homage to the science and the skill displayed in their design and execution; in these respects no hydraulic works in the Union can compete, nor do we believe they are excelled by any in the world. Not the smallest leaks in any of the joints was discovered; and, with the exception of the water rushing on the wheels, the whole operation of forcing up daily millions of gallons into the reservoirs on the mount, and thus furnishing in abundance one of the first necessaries of life to an immense population—was performed with less noise than is ordinarily made in working a smith's bellows! The picturesque location, the neatness that reigns in the buildings, the walks around the reservoirs and the grounds at large, with the beauty of the surrounding scenery, render the name of this place singularly appropriate."

Source: Thomas Ewbank, *A Descriptive and Historical Account of Hydraulic and Other Machines for Raising Water*, 4th ed. (New York: D. Appleton and Company, 1842), p. 301.

This mid-nineteenth century view of the waterworks shows the distribution arch and standpipe which allowed water to be pumped to the Corinthian reservoir. ("Fairmount Water Works," courtesy of the Frederick and Margaret Johnson Sutor collection)

discharge mains and hid them from view. Water could then be pumped into the Corinthian Reservoir, which was on higher ground than Fairmount, and be redirected either back to Fairmount or down into the city.

The new Jonval turbines not only increased the city's water supply but also solved the problem of tidal flows below the dam, which caused the old waterwheels to stop twice daily as a consequence of high tides interfering with their operation. The turbine wheels were mounted horizontally rather than vertically like the old waterwheels, and were encased in a vertical, water-tight cylinder that regulated the flow of water through vanes within the turbine that sent its shaft spinning. Transmission of gears carried the power generated by the spinning shaft to the pump.

When the city was consolidated in 1854, it acquired a number of steam-powered pumping stations from various districts. But, thanks to the greater economy of water power, the waterworks at Fairmount continued to benefit the city financially. The challenge of ever-increasing demand for water was met by the shift to turbines and by continuing to expand the distribution system.

The last great effort to keep up with this demand came in the years 1868 to 1872, when the old mill house was altered to make room for an additional set of three turbines. Graff Jr., who had resigned as superintendent in 1856, was again in charge, this time as chief engineer for the city's Water Department and a member of the newly created Fairmount Park Commission.[5]

Today, the Philadelphia Museum of Art rises above the waterworks where the reservoirs once stood on Fairmount's summit. Graff's engine house is to the right.

Once more, it was he who created the alterations. He utilized a design his father had made in 1820, when the move from steam to water power was under way. The elder Graff had included a proposed central-columned pavilion, larger but in the same style as the two pavilions at either end of the mill house roof. His son now implemented that plan, while extending the river wall by eight feet in places into the stream to accommodate the new equipment. On each side of the central pavilion, entrance houses gave access to the room below. Rush's two carved figures depicting the Schuylkill were reinstalled above the doors.[6] Once completed, the waterworks took on the appearance familiar to visitors today.

By the time this work on updating the waterworks was finished, the era of significantly increasing the size of Fairmount Park was well under way. That process is considered fully in Chapter 3, where it is presented in part as a long effort to create a world-class city park. But the park's expansion was at least as much a response to the purpose of the waterworks, which was to provide potable water to a burgeoning city. Frederic Graff Jr. put it clearly in the Fairmount Park Commission report of 1870, stating that the encroachment of industries on the water supply was the reason for the establishment of the park.[7] In the previous year, the commission's report had observed that "for more than twenty years after the foundation of the Fairmount Water Works, Philadelphia reposed in the belief of their unsurpassable excellence and their perpetuity, and indeed did not become fully awake from this pleasant dream for about thirty years."[8]

Yet, in spite of years of antipollution laws, the Schuylkill continued to be fouled by its industrial users. As was true throughout the nineteenth century, large-scale industrialization was taking place almost everywhere, and the accompanying degradation of the environment created costs that were mostly ignored or at best postponed. Industrial growth in and around Philadelphia continued relentlessly, giving the city its sobriquet, the "Workshop of the World." But along with that claim, the poisoning of the Schuylkill's waters proceeded inexorably. In 1890, Philadelphia suffered one of the worst epidemics of typhoid and cholera in the nation. The city evidently was falling back into the kind of clean water emergency that had prompted the creation of the

Philadelphia's Top Attractions in the Mid-Nineteenth Century

In the days before Philadelphia's Independence Hall drew tourists, the Fairmount neighborhood held three sites that were on every visitor's must-see list. The Fairmount Water Works were a leisure-time destination from the time the Schuylkill Dam was completed in the 1820s and the South Garden and Cliffside Walks turned the grounds along the riverbank into a park.

From 1829 to 1836, Eastern State Penitentiary rose nearby on Fairmount Avenue to house prisoners "in confinement in solitude with labor." The noted architect, John Haviland, designed this first "penitentiary" in keeping with the novel idea that keeping inmates apart from each other would encourage their penitence. The prison's wheel-shaped design, with cell blocks radiating out from

a central watch tower, became the model for hundreds of other prisons worldwide. While under construction, it drew visits from both the Marquis de Lafayette and Alexis de Tocqueville. Charles Dickens came in 1841, later writing that he believed the effects of solitary confinement were "cruel and wrong." The practice of solitary confinement was abandoned in 1913. Eastern State closed as a prison in 1971. In 1996, it was listed by the World Monument Fund as one of the hundred most endangered properties in the world. In 1998, the Eastern State Penitentiary Historic Site was formed to preserve the prison and open it for public tours (www.easternstate.org).

When the fabulously wealthy Stephen Girard died in 1831, he left a substantial bequest to

create Girard College as a school for orphans.* He also precisely specified the layout and dimensions of the grand building he wanted to house it. In the first truly nationwide architectural competition, the award went to Thomas U. Walter, who would later design the new dome for the U.S. Capitol in Washington. The resulting Founders Hall was one of the grandest buildings in America when the school opened in 1848, and remains a leading example of Greek Revival architecture (www.girardcollege.edu).

*Girard's will specified "poor, white, male orphans," which from the beginning was interpreted to mean fatherless boys. The school was desegregated in 1969 and made coeducational in 1984. Today, its enrollment is about evenly divided between male and female students and is about 80 percent African American.

first waterworks at Centre Square nearly a hundred years earlier. But while the Schuylkill's pure water then had been the solution, now it was so poisoned as to doom the Fairmount operation.

Filtration systems at steam-powered pumping stations were being built in other places to treat contaminated water. But no additional space on Fairmount's summit was available to construct a large slow sand filtration system to leach out impurities in the water held in its five reservoirs. Gradually, meanwhile, other pumping stations around the city with active filtration systems were taking over the enterprise of the waterworks.

The death knell came in a report released in 1899 that indicated the serious level of pollution in the river. Ten years later, plans were made to decommission the Fairmount plant. The waterworks had fulfilled their essential purpose for nearly a century. Two years after the report, in 1911, a city ordinance was passed giving the Fairmount buildings along the river to the mayor for use as a public aquarium. A second ordinance provided for the Fairmount Park commissioners to receive ownership of the obsolete reservoirs at the top of the hill as the site for a new public art museum.[9] Due to a change in the city administration, the waterworks buildings were placed in the charge of the Fairmount Park Commission the following spring.

What had been the novel concept of aquariums became familiar to Americans as the result of world's fairs at Chicago (1893) and St. Louis (1904), both of which had fisheries exhibits. On Thanksgiving Day in 1911, Philadelphia's aquarium opened to the public in the old engine house, which had been stocked with nineteen small tanks brought from the Chicago and St. Louis expositions. A series of lectures on marine life also was inaugurated. In 1912, the two mill houses were emptied of their machinery to become the main exhibition halls. The sheets of glass in the tanks were large and strong, thanks to recent technological innovations, giving visitors the remarkable ability to watch fish swimming at eye level. Freshwater fish were exhibited in the larger old mill house, which measured two hundred feet by fifty feet, and saltwater marine life in the newer structure (one hundred feet by fifty feet). The flat roofs of the former plaza above were pierced with skylights. The aquarium was an immediate success; 290,000 visitors came during its first year of operation.[10]

For a time, seals and sea lions were allowed to frolic in the forebay, where visitors could gape at them from the bank or the rooftop promenades. But that experiment was ended after the animals repeatedly escaped. Worse, like many of the fish in the indoor tanks, they were sickened by the polluted Schuylkill water, which initially was supplied for them by the remaining small Jonval turbine and pumps in the engine house. Before long, it became clear that the animals held there—like the citizens of Philadelphia—must have filtered water for their health. In spite of these difficulties and the intervention of World War I, which slowed the conversion, by the 1920s, the Philadelphia Aquarium was state of the art and the fourth largest of its kind in the world.[11]

In 1923, more than a century after the forebay was dug out of the rock at the foot of Fairmount, it was filled in again. What was originally called Aquarium Drive—renamed Water Works Drive in 2003—was laid out over much of the new landfill. A stone pedestrian bridge that had provided access across the channel to the old mill house deck was buried intact. What had been the boat basin and entrance to the forebay behind the new mill house on the dam was replaced with a grassy lawn (the slight indentation of the terrain there lets today's visitors imagine how the river water once was channeled behind the Greek temples and the mill houses).

From the beginning, the aquarium was plagued by funding problems. Through most of the decades when the waterworks had supplied Philadelphia with potable water, it was a moneymaker for the city. Once that function ceased and its buildings were turned into merely a public "amusement," it had to compete with many other priorities. Fairmount Park was one of the largest in the world by the time the waterworks were decommissioned, and the Fairmount Park Commission was responsible for maintaining all of it.

The aquarium survived without too much difficulty into World War II, maintaining its popularity and receiving at least barely adequate financial support from the city. It continued to draw a million visitors annually. But then it gradually fell into disrepair in the postwar period, when inadequate funding and political maneuvering mirrored Philadelphia's larger losses: population decline accompanying rapid suburbanization, and the ceding of its place as the world's workshop in the emerging postindustrial age. Aquarium attendance fell off while exhibits shrank and diminished in variety and appeal amid the deteriorating condition of the waterworks facilities. Financial decline fed physical decline in a vicious cycle. The aquarium eventually looked so threadbare that its attendance fell off precipitously. Annually, huge numbers of fish failed to survive in Philadelphia's tap water. The Fairmount Park Commission recommended building a new aquarium elsewhere in the park, presumably as a more economical alternative to restoring the waterworks.[12] Nonetheless, city officials refused to act.

Meanwhile, a group of frustrated citizens raised $3 million in private funds to build a new facility far from Fairmount and the city's park system, on a ten-acre site at Broad and Hartranft Streets in South Philadelphia. In 1962, the year that new building was constructed, the Philadelphia Aquarium at the Fairmount Water Works ceased operations and closed its doors. This new "Aquarama," which billed itself as the "Theater of the Sea," was to have a much briefer life than the old aquarium. Opened in 1962, in a spiffy modernist building constructed for it, its aquatic acts were briefly popular but costly in overhead. Crowds came at first and then fell off. The Aquarama closed after barely seven years, and the building was demolished. Today the area is the site of Philadelphia's main sports complex.

The family of Olympic rower John B. Kelly, meanwhile, provided funds to create a public indoor swimming pool in one of the aquarium's former chambers. That pool was built in the new mill house in place of the tanks that had held saltwater fish. It lasted only a decade, however, and never reopened after flooding caused by Hurricane Agnes in 1972. It was closed in 1973. For the first time since the engine house was completed in 1815, the waterworks complex at Fairmount was silent, a forlorn tribute to an earlier era, a ghost of what it once had been.

But the approach of the bicentennial of the United States in 1976 began to stir acknowledgment from various groups of the historical importance of the waterworks. In 1975, the American Society of Civil Engineers declared the Fairmount Water Works a National Historic Civil Engineering Landmark. In 1976, the U.S. secretary of the interior designated it a National Historic Landmark, and in 1977, the American Society of Mechanical Engineers named it a National Historic Mechanical Engineering Landmark.

Each of these actions helped to spur the effort to preserve and renovate the complex of buildings, gardens, and walkways below Fairmount. A campaign combining the work of public and private agencies got under way to achieve that goal. It began with the work of the Junior League of Philadelphia in 1974, which, in conjunction with the Philadelphia Water Department and the Fairmount Park Commission, began a fund-raising drive. In the 1990s, Ernesta Drinker Ballard, a Fairmount Park commissioner, took up the cause, creating the Fund for the Water Works (FFWW) as the umbrella organization in charge of restoration. After Mrs. Ballard's death in 2005, that work was continued by a committee of the Fairmount Park Conservancy, Women for the Water Works. Eventually, these efforts raised $23 million in funds.[13]

As a result, from 1988 to 2008, a careful restoration of the waterworks buildings took place. The principal chambers of the old mill house and adjoining machine level of the engine house became the Fairmount Water

Works Interpretive Center (FWWIC), which opened in October 2003. The engine house and adjoining caretaker's house opened in July 2006, as the Water Works Restaurant and Lounge. Although the building's use as an eating place goes back to 1835, when the early steam engines were taken out of use, it is surely the case that today's restaurant is the most substantial and elegant in all its history. Twice during the years when the waterworks were being restored, the engine house was struck by fire—first, in 1981, when the café operating there at the time was forced to close, and second, on January 1, 2002, delaying the opening of the current restaurant.

Since 2003, the Fairmount Water Works Interpretive Center has told the story of these structures and the river in Philadelphia's water history. A narrative film provides part of that history, along with other explanatory material. The FWWIC contains a model of the plant in operation and allows visitors to inspect the remaining turbine and pump. There are graphic portrayals of the Schuylkill watershed, including its pollution and regeneration during the past half century.

Early in the twenty-first century, the fish ladder was rebuilt beside the Schuylkill dam to provide better access upstream to migratory species.

A Park Grows from Fairmount

School children visit the Water Works Interpretive Center in the newly restored complex at Fairmount.

On the western side of the Fairmount Dam across from the waterworks, the canal and lock that for more than a century had allowed barges to move up- and downstream past the dam were removed in the 1950s when the Schuylkill Expressway was constructed. But with the long effort to clean up the river beginning in the next decade, a fishway ladder was opened along that bank in 1979. That again allowed shad, herring, striped bass, and other migratory species to continue their journeys from the ocean to their freshwater birthplaces to spawn.

Thirty years later in spring 2009, renovations were completed to the fishway that increased water flow to direct some forty-five varieties of fish through the ladder. Those improvements also created an outdoor classroom with amphitheater-style seating beside the ladder, as well as a live video feed into the FWWIC and the Philadelphia Zoo. Water levels rise slightly from the first chamber to the last, allowing fish to swim upstream gradually and bypass the dam. The project was a joint effort of the Philadelphia Water

Department, the U.S. Army Corps of Engineers, and the Pennsylvania Fish and Boat Commission.

The latest piece of the campaign to restore the area around the waterworks came from 2006 to 2008, when the Women for the Water Works succeeded in raising an additional $5 million to restore those grounds. Since that work was completed late in 2008, the South Garden has looked very much as it did in its heyday between the 1820s and 1840s. Its formal and geometrical pathways, hedges, and lawns extend south from the engine house to where the Spring Garden ramps that lead to the Schuylkill Expressway rise over the neck of land along the riverbank leading into the new Schuylkill Banks Park.

In the midst of the garden are the 1830 marble fountain, restored to use after more than a century when it was inoperative, and the memorial to Frederick Graff Sr., cleaned and refurbished, its marble again as white as it must have appeared when it was installed in 1848. Visitors can descend a flight of steps from there to the riverbank esplanade, now restored with benches and plaques recounting the history of settlement along the river and the work done to restore it in the last decades of the twentieth century. A fisherman of metal alloy now looks out over the water.[14]

The nineteenth-century Rustic Pavilion, beside the ramp that leads from the waterworks to Fairmount's summit, was re-created in steel early in the twenty-first century.

The Cliffside Paths along the riverside granite face of Fairmount had long been hazardous where they were not unusable, having deteriorated throughout much of the twentieth century. Now they are restored as they were in the nineteenth century, with two paved ramps, one to the north and the other to the south side of the cliff, leading up to two lookout structures. The Rustic Pavilion near the summit beside the south ramp is a 2007 re-creation in steel of the original timber pavilion, long since vanished, which dated from the 1860s. At the summit, the earlier Mercury Pavilion has been re-created, albeit without Rush's figure of Mercury at the top.[15]

The entire area is now restored to its condition as a delightful pleasure garden, looking much as it did nearly 150 years ago, when the waterworks underwent their last transformation. The funding campaign that led to the completion of all these renovations to the Fairmount Water Works and surroundings also established a fund for their continued maintenance. As a result, it now seems more likely than it has throughout most of the last century that Philadelphia and its visitors will be able to celebrate this uniquely romantic complex of natural and civic marvels for centuries to come.

A Park Grows from Fairmount

Fairmount: From the Head Arches of the Forebay (Childs and Hobson, 1829). The Mercury Pavilion rises near Fairmount's summit; beside the forebay, visitors stroll across the terrace roof of the mill house. (Courtesy of Historical Society of Pennsylvania)

The Nineteenth-Century Park
in a Booming Industrial City

3

Fairmount Park surely would not have developed as it did had it not been for Philadelphia's rapid growth throughout the nineteenth century. From 1800 to 1850, the city's population increased by an average of more than 27.5 percent in each decade. Then in 1854, the momentous Act of Consolidation made the city limits coterminous with the adjacent Philadelphia County. That increased the city's area from 2 to 129 square miles. It also meant that in the decade bracketing the year consolidation took place, Philadelphia's population nearly quintupled, growing from a confined city of 121,276 in 1850 to a sprawling one of 565,529 by 1860. From then until 1900, the rate of growth returned to something closer to that in the first half of the century, which was still dizzyingly rapid. Over the course of the period when the Fairmount Water Works and Fairmount Park were being developed—roughly 1810 to 1890—Philadelphia grew from a small city of some 54,000 to a metropolis of 1,046,964.[1]

Fairmount Park owed its birth and growth primarily to Philadelphia's need to protect the watershed above its waterworks on the Schuylkill. Few could have imagined in the early years of the century that the city's burgeoning population and industrial development along the river to the north would continually challenge that effort, forcing city officials to look ever farther upriver for the tools to maintain the water's purity. That was the utilitarian necessity that drove land acquisition.

But a different stimulus also favored expansion. Private groups of citizens often pushed for more acreage out of a desire for recreational escapes from the crowded living conditions in the city. When the decision was made to move the waterworks to Fairmount from Centre Square, it had been widely assumed

A view of Laurel Hill Cemetery.

that the area was too far from the city to have appeal as a public park. In the words of the Fairmount Park Commission's first annual report in 1869: "Fairmount was then [in 1812] outside of the City limits and much too far away to be thought of as a resort for public recreation; the most remote spot reached by the pedestrian of that day was the water basin on the Schuylkill at the head of Chestnut Street."[2]

Yet, from the time the engine house opened in 1815, that charming building became an aesthetic and engineering attraction, perched as it was on the river's edge, an ornament in a natural pleasure garden. Starting in 1822, when water first poured over the newly built dam onto giant waterwheels, the waterworks became Philadelphia's principal leisure time destination and the chief attraction for visitors to the city. The city, meanwhile, was pushing ever nearer to Fairmount.

The utilitarian and the recreational impulses behind park expansion were often, but far from always, in harmony.[3] The truly remarkable rate of growth of Philadelphia's population throughout the century, combined with its rapid development as an industrial powerhouse, account for the decades-long expansion of parkland along the Schuylkill. These same factors also created perpetual tension in the community over priorities for the park and a contest over how it should be developed. It was imperative for the city to respond to the ever-greater demand for pure water. For park advocates, it also was critical—in an era when the transcendentalist ideas of Ralph Waldo Emerson were affecting popular thinking—for Philadelphians to have access to the "purifying" environment of unspoiled nature for their health and rejuvenation.[4]

That latter goal led first to a curious historical twist. The 1830s gave rise not to an expanded municipal park, but to a privately developed rural garden for the dead, Laurel Hill Cemetery. Established in 1836 on the east bank of the Schuylkill River several miles north of the waterworks, Laurel Hill was the second rural cemetery in America conceived as a romantic garden landscape. Its founding—along with that of its predecessor, Mount Auburn in Cambridge, Massachusetts—quickly became a model for similar developments in cities throughout America. They marked the rise in the Victorian age of a new obligation to honor the departed in lovingly tended gardens, where meditation and contemplation of refined nature might contribute to the visitor's well-being and moral purpose. They were meant to be enlightened alternatives to the often cramped—and frequently disturbed—traditional burial grounds in dense cities.

The design of Laurel Hill was awarded to John Notman, who also designed the principal structures for administration of the cemetery. He created, in the words of a twentieth-century observer, "a curious fusion of the formal, geometric garden with areas which retain an informal, even natural, appearance."[5] His design would very much influence that of an enlarged Fairmount Park, starting a decade and more later.

Laurel Hill and its counterparts in other cities quickly became immensely popular, not simply as burial grounds, but as places of retreat from urban life. Andrew Jackson Downing, the first landscape architect in America, reported that in 1848, nearly thirty thousand persons had visited Laurel Hill between the months of April and December. It became so popular as a destination for strollers that the owners had to issue tickets of admission to control the size of the crowds.[6] That same year, Downing drew the obvious conclusion. The popularity of this and other rural cemeteries was sufficient evidence of "how much our citizens, of all classes, would enjoy public parks on a similar scale."[7] Without question, the attraction of Laurel Hill as a pleasure ground not far upriver from Fairmount gave weight to the views of Philadelphians interested in creating a larger urban park.

The push and pull of the utilitarian and recreational strains made park expansion proceed in fits and starts in the first half of the nineteenth century. Certainly, no very clear plan was then evident for growth beyond the waterworks. Lemon Hill was purchased in 1844 only when the price was right, thanks to an absentee landlord who had let the property deteriorate in an era when this one-time neighborhood of the gentry was in decline. Sedgley was added three years later through the initiative of private citizens who had first raised half the purchase price. Although proposals then emerged to unite the new parkland with the waterworks at Fairmount, these initially went nowhere.[8]

The 1854 Act of Consolidation required the city to acquire significant open spaces "for the health and enjoyment of the people forever." Even though Fairmount Park was officially created the next year, it existed at first in name only. Determined advocates for a functioning, integrated park visited

Lemon Hill in 1856—twelve years after the estate ostensibly became public land—where they found the entrance barred and boarded up, with a "no trespassing" sign attached, and tenants still engaged in farming. Not until after they published their unflattering findings did the city finally eject the tenants.[9] This was the year in which Frederic Graff Jr. resigned his post as waterworks superintendent, perhaps in frustration at the lack of serious action by city officials on behalf of the waterway and the park. Two years later, Philadelphia's city councils did pass resolutions that invited plans "for laying out the ground of Fairmount Park." Yet, even though the councils eventually accepted a plan, little of it was executed.[10] If the Act of Consolidation was meant to rationalize the city's governmental authority, little of the vision underlying it had yet penetrated as far as the park.

A visitor shortly after the Civil War broke out in 1861 wrote that "not much work appears to have been done at the park, except to make some winding drives. A few clumps of trees most of them evergreens have been planted, but seem neglected. No work is going on there now, the city finances not being very flourishing during the war."[11] Finally, however, in the year after that somewhat mournful comment, the city finally bought (for the sum of $55,000) a narrow neck of land west of Landing Avenue to connect the waterworks to Lemon Hill.

Meanwhile, concerned citizens had begun to lobby for expanding the park on the west bank of the Schuylkill. On September 15, 1859, a petition to that effect signed by 225 citizens was presented to city officials. At about the same time, a detailed design for a Fairmount Park that would span the river was prepared by Andrew Palles, a Philadelphia-based engineer, who further developed the proposal put forward by the firm of Sidney and Adams in the previous year.[12] The Palles proposal, like the earlier one it was based on, was met with inaction. Yet it must have lived on as a dream in the minds of some that something like it might become reality. In fact, the days of little action on behalf of Fairmount Park were drawing to a close.

In the aftermath of the Civil War, Philadelphia was booming, with much of its industrial might spreading rapidly along the banks of the Schuylkill and up its tributary, Wissahickon Creek. Protection of the water supply took on new urgency. A number of Philadelphia's leading citizens were pressing the case for a far more robust effort to acquire land along the river basin. As a result, the park soon underwent major institutional change and expansion. A crucial advance—actually, *the* crucial advance—was the creation of the Fairmount Park Commission (FPC) on March 26, 1867, by an act of Pennsylvania's legislature.

Public Law 547 authorized the city to purchase land for Fairmount Park to preserve the purity of the city's water supply and provide a place of public enjoyment for the people of Philadelphia. The Board of Commissioners would be composed of the mayor, presidents of select and common councils, two city engineers ex officio, and ten unpaid citizens. That latter group was to be appointed for five-year terms by the Board of Judges of the Court of Common Pleas of Philadelphia.[13] One consequence of this legislation was that Frederic Graff Jr. would soon return to service as chief engineer of the Water Department and an ex officio member of the Fairmount Park Commission. The real leadership roles, however, would be assumed by several new commissioners, notably the mayor and commission president, Morton Mc-Michael; the Civil War hero, Major-General George G. Meade; and the attorney, Eli K. Price.

An early indication that the new commission would be aggressive in enlarging the park came in 1869, when it authorized the purchase of the triangular "Flat Iron" district that lay between Fairmount and Lemon Hill, adjacent to the narrow link along the river that had been obtained several years before. That provided a wider band and more open flow between the park's major holdings on the Schuylkill's east bank, and prevented further industrialization there to threaten the water supply. But it also required the removal of a number of houses and businesses on what at the time were city streets, turning back to nature what had become a rather dismal strip of urban development. During the next several years, once the buildings were demolished, workers hauled wheelbarrows of silt from the river and slowly buried the rubble so that the area could be landscaped.[14]

The commission had asserted itself in the same area within months after its creation in 1867. From the time in the 1820s when the dam was completed

From Flat Iron to Azalea Garden

Lying between Kelly Drive and the waterworks, and between the Philadelphia Museum of Art and Boat House Row, the Azalea Garden is on a portion of the site of the early nineteenth-century commercial district known as the Flat Iron. It lay in an area of irregular cliffs and flatlands. After this land was purchased for Fairmount Park in 1869, its buildings were razed, and huge amounts of earth were moved in to fill the pits of former foundations and then to raise and level the terrain above flood stage. Roads were added to connect the waterworks and Fairmount to Lemon Hill.

Just more than four acres of the site was converted to an azalea garden in 1952. It is designed in the English Romantic style with curved walkways and large specimen trees for shade. The garden holds several pieces of sculpture. It remains a popular spot for lounging and taking wedding photographs (www.fairmount park.org/gardens.asp).

across the Schuylkill above Fairmount, the placid pond created above it became a fine site for boating, including competitive races between professional rowers. The first full-scale regatta had been held there in 1835. But even with the purchase of Lemon Hill in 1844, the city had asserted no real oversight of the adjacent riverbank. Equipment for races was stowed in simple brick structures along Landing Avenue and at the foot of Lemon Hill. Then boathouses gradually were built along the shore. In 1858, a grassroots organization grandly named the Schuylkill Navy came into being as an association of rowing clubs meant to regulate competitions on the river. As such, it was the first amateur athletic governing body in the United States. Finally, in October 1867, the Fairmount Park Commission ordered that club buildings constructed "without regard to architectural adornment" should be replaced by June 1, 1868, with structures deemed acceptable to the commission.[15] From that point, it was clear that Boathouse Row would become an attractive feature of Fairmount Park and that the commission would oversee it.

The Azalea Garden was created in 1952 on land that had been part of the commercial district known as the Flat Iron before its buildings were razed and it was added to Fairmount Park in 1869.

In 1866, the year before Public Law 547 created the commission, an opportunity arose to add parklands on the west side of the Schuylkill. Four citizens learned that the Lansdowne tract, which was held by a family residing in England, was about to be sold, and that "the owners were disposed to accept a price much below the actual value of the ground."[16] In the following year, with major organizational changes under way for Fairmount Park, the land was purchased by the city at cost. That set the stage for the further stipulation of Public Law 547, setting out the new and expanded park boundaries. Included within its limits on the west side of the Schuylkill were the "West Philadelphia Water-Works, which were opposite Lemon Hill, and the noted country-seats of Solitude, Egglesfield, Sweet Brier, and Lansdowne, with a gore of ground north of the latter, between the regular line of Lansdowne and Montgomery Avenue."

Here was proof of the ascendancy of the advocates of park expansion, in Harrisburg as well as Philadelphia, for a substantial amount of this land now designated as lying within the boundaries of Fairmount Park remained in private hands. But that was the larger reason for Public Law 547, whose potency would now be proved. It provided Philadelphia, and specifically its Fairmount Park Commission, with the authority needed to acquire that land, whether by outright purchase, donation, or condemnation through eminent domain. Very soon, a leading park commissioner not only would exercise that authority fully but also push it well beyond those anticipated limits in the name of protecting the city's water supply.

Eli Kirk Price, a real estate attorney, came to the commission as an appointed citizen. Fourteen years earlier, in 1853, he had been elected to the Pennsylvania State Senate as an independent, specifically to bring about the consolidation of the city and county of Philadelphia. Before quitting his office at the end of a single term, Price was also instrumental in securing the land for Fairmount Park. With the creation of the Fairmount Park Commission in 1867, he was named chairman of its Committee of Land Purchases and Damages. He soon argued forcefully for very different and more expansive park boundaries than those set out in Public Law 547. His committee agreed with him in its report later that year:

> Now, if ever, while it is yet possible to be done at a cost which is moderate when compared with its advantages, we must possess the ground which surrounds our water supply so closely that the impurities which are drained from its surface must necessarily be drawn into the reservoirs, and, by preventing the erection of dwellings and manufactories

James Peale's romantic *View on the Wissahickon Creek* was painted in 1830.

James Hamilton's *On the Wissahickon* dates from 1843. Both Hamilton and James Peale were Philadelphia artists. (Courtesy of Philadelphia Museum of Art)

on the shores of the basin and of the waters closely adjacent, provide against the pollution of the water which is the sole supply for domestic uses of the present and of the future population of this vast and rapidly-growing city.[17]

The era of Fairmount Park's remarkable growth was on. In a further sweeping enlargement of parklands, an Act of Assembly of March 4, 1868, authorized the commission to appropriate the Wissahickon Valley, including the existing road that ran beside the creek.[18] This drew under protection almost all of the most important tributaries of the Schuylkill in Philadelphia, and extended the reach of Fairmount Park more than eight miles to the city's northern boundary. Industrial mills had come to the fast-flowing Wissahickon from the start of the eighteenth century—there were reportedly twenty-four mills along its banks by 1793, and more than sixty by the time the land was acquired for Fairmount Park.[19]

In 1856, a road had been completed beside the creek by the Wissahickon Turnpike Company, thus providing that the goods produced in the valley should have easier access to Philadelphia and points west of the city. Once the road was incorporated into Fairmount Park, the commission in 1870 ordered the removal of all toll gates along the turnpike, and then determined that the

The Wissahickon Valley: Sublime to Industrial, and Back Again

By the mid-nineteenth century, the natural scene could appear sublime to Romantic artists and writers where it was ruggedly picturesque. That was so for the Wissahickon Valley for a number of artists in the Philadelphia region, who had only to venture as far as its dramatic gorge for inspiration. The celebrated painter James Peale was among the first to depict the rugged beauty of the creek and valley in the 1820s. Over the next decades, William Trost Richards, James Hamilton, Carl Weber, and Thomas Moran all painted their own tributes to this wild landscape. While living in Philadelphia, Edgar Allen Poe also walked through the Wissahickon's forest. He published his closely observed sketch of the experience, "Morning on the Wissahiccon (sic)," in 1844.

Today the Wissahickon Valley in Fairmount Park is again mostly an unspoiled wilderness of forests, boulders, and rushing streams. But the area only returned to its natural state after 1868, when this land was acquired by the city. For the previous 180 years, even while much of its landscape remained pristine, it had been one of the busiest early industrial sites in the region. The attraction was abundant water power, which included two waterfalls near the Wissahickon Creek's mouth at the Schuylkill. The first gristmill and sawmill were built there in 1688. A small industrial village grew up at Rittenhouse Town, and mills and mill complexes dotted the banks of Cresheim Creek. Robeson's Mills thrived near the Wissahickon on the east bank of the Schuylkill (sections of the road from Philadelphia to the site were later incorporated into East River—today's Kelly—Drive). The Robeson mansion on Ridge Avenue was reincarnated as a restaurant after the area was added to Fairmount Park. It survived until the 1950s, when it was demolished to construct ramps for the new Schuylkill Expressway.

mills along the creek should be demolished. That was a sweeping power to put any number of industries—large and small—out of business, albeit after negotiations over adequate compensation. A number of the taverns and inns along the waterway remained, but under the jurisdiction of the Fairmount Park Commission, which forbade the sale of alcohol on their premises.[20]

Further expansion came quickly. Eli Price prepared most of the Park Act of April 14, 1868, which enlarged the park's boundaries by 461 acres on the east bank and 600 acres on the west. In that same year came a windfall for the park in the form of a gift from Jesse George and his sister, Rebecca, who were elderly. The Georges owned 83 acres of farmland west of the Schuylkill that culminated in a hill from which there were fine views down to the river. After years in which they had refused to sell their land to real estate speculators, they agreed to deed their farm to the Fairmount Park Commission, with the proviso that they should receive $4,000 annually during their lifetimes. In 1873, when both the Georges had died and the city acquired the land, the commission resolved to name the property Georges Hill in their honor.[21]

Morton McMichael monument.

From 1867 to 1876, Price was unrelenting in his pursuit of an expanded Fairmount Park. By the latter year, he could write to his grandson:

> I this day passed title for the last property of importance acquired for Fairmount Park; that of William Simpson's seventeen and a half acres, on the west side of the Schuylkill, at the Falls, after several years' negotiation, at a price of three hundred thousand dollars. Thus my great work . . . of acquiring nearly three thousand acres of land, some of it divided into many lots of five villages, as Chairman of the Land Purchasing Committee, and the passing of the titles to all real estate purchased has been brought to a close.[22]

Price's "great work" had extended the park's boundaries virtually to those that exist today for what Philadelphians still generally think of as Fairmount Park, that is, the largest open space along the Schuylkill basin and its tributary, the Wissahickon, within today's larger park system.[23]

General George Gordon Meade
monument.

Eli K. Price. McMichael, Meade,
and Price were three original
members of the Fairmount
Park Commission who led
in shaping the park's great
expansion from 1867 through
1876. (Photo courtesy of
Fairmount Park Historic
Resource Archive)

The rapid growth of parkland required planning for roads and landscaping. The Fairmount Park Commission's annual report for 1871 provides a glimpse of what was under way in the west park, where temporary roads were widened, paved, and made permanent:

> A road leading from Elm Avenue to George's [sic] Hill summit was constructed giving access to a new pavilion and landscaped area with walks, flower beds, shrubs and lawns. A road was installed leading from Belmont Mansion to Belmont Glen with a rustic pedestrian bridge running over the Columbia Railroad track to "a commodious building for women and children." In addition, a bridal path was created running from the western end of Girard Avenue through the Sweet Briar, Lansdowne, Belmont and Ridgeland estates culminating near Chamounix Mansion.[24]

While this kind of work was impressive, it was proceeding in the absence of a genuine master plan for the park. To that purpose, the commission solicited advice from the firms of two noted landscape architects for their visions of the park's future. Robert Morris Copeland of Boston, and Frederick Law Olmsted and Calvert Vaux of New York presented preliminary proposals in December 1867. It is not clear that Copeland even visited Philadelphia before his part in the planning came to an end. He may have sealed his fate with the commissioners when he wrote: "If this is to be a penurious affair or if I am to be subject to the control in matters of taste of those whom I did not think my equals in such matters I should not undertake it."[25] In any case, he was paid a $500 fee and had no further role in Fairmount Park.

That left Olmsted and Vaux. Ten years after they were named the design team for New York's Central Park, they were the leading landscape architects in America, with an array of park projects to their credit. Yet, when they submitted a detailed plan for designing all of Fairmount Park in 1868, the commission declined to accept it. The FPC's Committee on Plans and Improvements were politic in complimenting them as well as Copeland, noting that their "large experience in such works, excellent judgment and refined and cultivated taste, has greatly assisted us."[26] The commission then dismissed them.

Olmstead and Vaux were again asked for their ideas for improving the "old" (east) park in 1871, and once more their proposal was rejected. How, then, can it still be argued that, in the words of a twentieth-century account, "their influence on Fairmount Park was profound"?[27]

If so, it is only because the ideas of this design team were too influential not to have an impact, even indirectly, on the park's development in this period. Olmsted and Vaux were creating a powerful new paradigm for landscaping public spaces in America. They had shown how to apply the principles of creating romantic landscapes—hitherto restricted largely to the private gardens of the privileged—in huge urban spaces. They saw that nature could be enhanced on a grand scale in accordance with egalitarian principles that allowed access and enjoyment for all. In Central Park, they had carried out this novel vision in the use of curving paths and walkways, asymmetrical compositions, and existing landforms enhanced by focal points in fountains, classic urns, and rustic bridges.

When they turned their attention to the east park, they admired the earlier development of the waterworks and gardens below Fairmount as a precedent for their views. But their main concern in 1871 was that the expanded area had become too cramped, trying to perform too many functions at once. They always had insisted that parks should provide tranquil open space above all. Moreover, their plan for the east park had to cope with something not present earlier in undeveloped upper Manhattan: the presence of a number of distinguished villas, many complete with their own garden plots and other landscape elements. Olmsted and Vaux viewed these as a challenge, lamenting to the commission that it forced complications in the scale of what they proposed.

They nonetheless succeeded in integrating the villas sensitively into their overall scheme. As can be seen today, their basic intention of preserving these structures by enhancing their surroundings has been followed.[28] But just a few years earlier, the Park Commission clearly had not made preservation of the villas a priority, and may even have been tempted to level them. Commission minutes of June 20, 1868, note that it is important "to retain and preserve the ancient names of important Estates which have been absorbed in the Park," which should be permanently marked "either by groves of Trees to bear the name of the Estate, or other permanent memorial."[29] It may well be that the villas were only spared once their utility as lodgings for park employees came to be appreciated.

From the time Fairmount Park was born, many who have an affectionate regard for it also have noted that its natural beauty ultimately inhibited developing it as a designed landscape like Central Park. That theme is echoed in some of what Frederick Law Olmsted said about the park. But in the final analysis, Olmsted and Vaux balked at committing themselves fully to anything less than a comprehensive plan for the entire park, and that was never to be. The land was still being acquired in parcels and turned into recreational space over time. As one recent commentator has noted, "at first glance, Fairmount Park seems to be designed according to romantic gardening principles implemented in an eclectic and relatively unstructured manner. In reality, Fairmount Park is a patchwork of thought contributed for over two hundred years by wealthy merchants, politicians, lawyers, designers, and common citizens."[30]

One of the most important of those individuals in his day, Eli Kirk Price also was influential in bringing to bear the landscape of the private garden cemetery on that of Fairmount Park when he took the helm of land acquisition for the commission in the 1860s. Twenty years earlier, Price had been instrumental in creating Woodlands Cemetery, a West Philadelphia counterpart to Laurel Hill. Formed from the remnant of the estate of the noted eighteenth-century Philadelphia lawyer Andrew Hamilton, the property

The Glendinning Rock Garden was created in the 1930s on the site of the former Spring Garden Water Works. (Photograph by Mark Garvin)

The Glendinning Rock Garden

About a mile north of Fairmount, the Spring Garden Water Works was one of a number of pumping stations that supplied water from the Schuylkill to area residents early in the nineteenth century. Long after that site had been absorbed into East Fairmount Park, a gift from Robert and Elizabeth R. G. Glendinning led to the creation of a rock garden there, starting in 1936. It is entered from Kelly Drive just to the north of the Girard Avenue overpass, marked by a boulder at the entrance. In addition to impressive rock walls and a grassy lawn, a meandering pond leads to a waterfall and stone steps into the woods.

was crowned by a handsome Federal mansion and gardens overlooking the Schuylkill. Though himself a lawyer, Price's intimate involvement in creating a new cemetery on the grounds of the former estate led him to study and admire its landscaping. He wrote that it "had been designed to enhance rather than to overpower nature," and was in keeping with his own preference for a rather practical view of landscape design, in which nature was enhanced more than made artificially picturesque.[31]

Whether or not Price expressed such a view in opposition to the design proposals of Olmsted and Vaux remains unknown. But it certainly is in harmony with the direction of the park's design during the next decades. By the time Price had led the commission in assembling the pieces for one of the largest urban parks in the world, he had no doubt left his imprint, along with that of like-minded others, on its landscape as well. The creation of Laurel Hill and Woodlands had clarified the need for an expanded public retreat from the crowded city. The design of these cemeteries produced great inspiration for how the landscape of Fairmount Park would be conceived and how it would grow.

Horse Car Terminal, Centennial. This 1876 magazine illustration conveys a sense of the huge crowds that thronged the exposition grounds. (Courtesy of Steve Lynch; from Frank Leslie, *Illustrated Historical Register of the Centennial Exposition* [Philadelphia, PA: Frank Leslie's Publishing House, 1876])

The Post–Civil War Period and the Centennial Exposition

In the first decade after the Civil War, Fairmount Park was emerging as a distinctive urban park among those being created in America then. It also was about to enter the national spotlight as the site for an event with global reach. The 1876 Centennial Exposition would leave a lasting imprint on the park and mark the rise of Hermann Schwarzmann as the chief influence on the structures built there at the time.

By 1869, the Fairmount Park Commission had joined the Franklin Institute and the Pennsylvania Academy of Fine Arts in initiating plans to make Philadelphia the site of an international celebration of the hundredth anniversary of American independence. (As an idea for how the park should be used, this would have been anathema to Olmsted and Vaux, whose ideal park was an oasis of tranquility amid urban clamor.) After those Philadelphia institutions appealed to the House Committee on Manufactures and its Committee on Foreign Relations, the United States Congress established the Centennial Commission on March 3, 1871, and declared that the nation's birthday party would be held in Philadelphia. On July 4, 1873, the Fairmount Park Commission formally transferred 236 acres of parkland west of the Schuylkill to the Centennial Commission. Ground was broken for the first building exactly one year later.

The centennial itself, and preparations for it, were unprecedented for Philadelphia and, indeed, the nation. The first official world's fair to be held in the United States, the exhibition opened on May 10, 1876, and ran through November 10 of that year. More than two hundred buildings, most of them intended to be temporary, had been constructed on the grounds in somewhat less than two years.[1] The centennial's official name was the International

Exhibition of Arts, Manufacture and Products of the Soil and Mine, which was a precise description of the kinds of products on display.

The opening ceremonies began when the mounted and smartly dressed First Troop Philadelphia City Cavalry escorted President and Mrs. Ulysses S. Grant to their places in the grandstand. There, they were joined by Emperor Dom Pedro II and Empress Teresa of Brazil, the first reigning monarchs to visit the United States. An orchestra played the anthems of more than a dozen nations, closing with "Hail Columbia." This was followed by Richard Wagner's commissioned "Centennial Inauguration March," a prayer, the reading of a poem by John Greenleaf Whittier, remarks from notables, and a brief address by President Grant. The president and the emperor then led a procession to Machinery Hall where they grasped the master levers that started the Corliss Duplex Engine, the largest steam engine in the world, setting in motion hundreds of machines throughout the hall.[2]

Most of the exhibits were housed in the five largest structures. The enormous Main Building—constructed of wood, iron, and glass—was the largest building in the world by area, enclosing 21.5 acres. Machinery Hall was located to its west; the Gothic Agricultural Hall to the north; and both the Moorish-inspired Horticultural Hall and the classical Memorial Hall were meant to be permanent.

In addition, seventeen states constructed buildings to exhibit their products, as did nine foreign governments. There also were smaller buildings such as the Women's Pavilion, the Bible Pavilion, and the Nevada Quartz Mill, as well as beer gardens, restaurants, and assorted other attractions. Unofficial stalls, booths, and cafés drew crowds just outside the fairgrounds. By the time the centennial drew to a close, nearly ten million visitors, or roughly one-fifth of the total population of the United States, had been visitors. That made this

Centennial Arboretum

The beginnings of this grove on ground near the Horticultural Center in West Fairmount Park predate the 1876 Centennial Exposition. What is now designated as Michaux Walk was established in 1870–1871 as a memorial to two French botanists of the eighteenth and early nineteenth centuries with important ties to Philadelphia. François André Michaux selected the trees initially planted in Washington Square. His son of the same name came to Philadelphia some years later and saw to the replanting of trees in that park. A member of the American Philosophical Society, the younger Michaux left that organization a bequest at his death in 1855. That resulted in the agreement to plant some forty-four species of oak at this site in honor of father and son. The grove was enlarged as the botanical garden for the Centennial Exhibition in 1876. Some notable specimens remain from that time (www.fairmount park.org/hortcenter.asp).

international exposition larger than any that had been held previously in European capitals.[3]

When preparations for the centennial began, a Fairmount Park commissioner and president of the Board of Trade, John Welsh, was named president of the Centennial Board of Finance. He had led preparations for the Great Central Sanitary Fair of 1864 in Logan Square, to which a number of Philadelphia women had contributed greatly. He eagerly enlisted them again to help organize grassroots support for the centennial. Mrs. Elizabeth Duane Gillespie, a descendant of Benjamin Franklin, became president of the Women's Centennial Executive Committee, which organized women representing all the wards in the city to go house to house to solicit funds. They quickly raised more than $40,000 and collected 82,000 signatures in two days on an appeal to city councils and the Pennsylvania Assembly to appropriate money for buildings that would be suitable for foreign exhibits.

When the women were denied permission to present their own exhibits in the exhibition's main building, they raised more money under Mrs. Gillespie's leadership to construct their own exhibit space. The resulting Women's Pavilion demonstrated all manner of things produced by women. These included the obvious—needlework, household items, corsets—and the unexpected, such as a patented land pulverizer, emergency flares, and interlocking bricks. Only the building itself had been designed by a man, the indefatigable Hermann Schwarzmann, but only because a female architect from Boston had applied too late for consideration.

A formally dressed lady tended a steam engine that powered other machines in the pavilion, including a printing press that produced the official newspaper of the Women's Centennial Committee, the *New Century for Women*. Mrs. Gillespie and her committee were careful not to associate themselves too closely with the women's suffrage movement, which many regarded as too radical, and stayed away when Susan B. Anthony led a demonstration at Independence Hall on July 4. But they then had to endure the indignity of having Women's Day at the centennial celebrated on November 7, which was Election Day, and it was said that men would happily go to the polls rather than participate.

The individual who was most responsible for the design of the centennial also had the greatest impact on Fairmount Park more generally through the years in which that great event was being planned and executed. Hermann J. Schwarzmann was born in Bavaria, learned engineering while a student in a military academy in

Hermann J. Schwarzmann was the architectural genius behind the Centennial. By the age of twenty-seven, this young emigrant from Bavaria became the leading planner for the centennial and the chief engineer for Fairmount Park. (Courtesy of Steve Lynch; from Frank Leslie, *Illustrated Historical Register of the Centennial Exposition* [Philadelphia, PA: Frank Leslie's Publishing House, 1876])

Munich, and may have attended architecture school there. He immigrated to Philadelphia at the age of twenty-three in 1868. By April 1869, he was working for the Fairmount Park Commission as junior assistant engineer. Within a year, he was given significant responsibility, directing plane table surveys used to assess park holdings and designing temporary roads in the east and west parks. Promoted to senior assistant engineer in January 1870, he soon was designing buildings for the Park Commission, including a dining saloon at Belmont Mansion.

In January 1872, the commissioners voted to reject Olmsted and Vaux's proposal for the east park and to adopt that "volunteered by Senior Assistant Engineer Schwarzmann" for improving that section. In addition to having "volunteered" his proposal—perhaps as part of his park duties, without an added fee—Schwarzmann's plan made use of existing roads, which no doubt appealed to the commission as a matter of economy. After further praising Schwarzmann's "general plan for the improvement of the Old Park," the commissioners made what is surely a veiled reference to their rejection of the Olmsted and Vaux proposal: "In these respects, [Schwarzmann's] plan possesses important advantages, which make it preferable to a very beautiful design for study, prepared by professional landscape artists, of well known skill and large experience."[4]

Months earlier, the Park Commission's chief engineer had pointed to another of Schwarzmann's skills, as well as his devotion to duty. He noted that "the laying out of the planting had been under the immediate supervision of . . . H. Schwarzmann, who gave much of his leisure time outside office hours to the assiduous study of the subject as presented in many standard works, especially those in French and German, for which his familiarity with European languages gave him peculiar advantages."[5]

With plans both for the creation of a zoo in the park and for the Centennial Exhibition then under way, Schwarzmann was brought front and center for those enterprises as well. The commission made him engineer of the exhibition and sent him to Europe with the double assignment of accumulating ideas for the Centennial Exhibition and of studying zoological garden designs.[6] By the time he returned at age twenty-seven, Schwarzmann effectively had become the superintendent and chief architect of Fairmount Park. In addition to his designs for Horticultural Hall and Memorial Hall, he created the plans for some dozen smaller exhibition buildings, including the Carriage Building, Judges Hall, Pennsylvania State Building, and Women's Pavilion.[7]

In 1873, the Centennial Commission sponsored a competition for the design of the main building, or buildings, for the exhibition. When the first

Centennial District

Signs now designate the land in West Fairmount Park where the Centennial Exhibition was held in 1876. From the south, the grounds today can be entered from Lansdowne Drive through the Smith Memorial Arch, a postcentennial monument. The park's boundary here is Parkside Avenue. Beside it run the parallel Avenue of the Republic and South Concourse, the main avenues of the 1876 fair, which continue through the district past Memorial Hall to the right and the Carousel House between the two streets. Beyond Belmont Avenue, which intersects both parallel streets, lie the Centennial and Concourse Lakes. At the approach to Georges Hill is the Catholic Total Abstinence Union Fountain and, beyond it, the Mann Center for the Performing Arts. Also in the district are the Ohio House, which remains from 1876 and now houses the Centennial Café; Shofuso, the Japanese House and Garden; and the nearby Horticultural Center on the site of the 1876 Horticultural Hall. The area also contains a number of pieces of sculpture.

round of the competition closed, on July 15, forty-three designs had been received. Of these, ten were selected and their creators were asked to submit designs for the final competition. Again, winners were chosen and prizes awarded. Yet the proposals were for very expensive structures, which evidently figured in the decision by the commission to dispense with the services of the winners—they had their cash prizes—and to rely instead on those nearer at hand.

On June 2, 1874, they approved a design volunteered by Schwarzmann for the most coveted award. It was for a building, unlike most of the others, to remain as a permanent adornment of Fairmount Park. Memorial Hall—or as it was first named, the Art Building—was to display both American and foreign works of art. Even though he had not participated in the architects' competition and had only limited experience in designing buildings, Schwarzmann had quickly gained the trust of his elders, who no doubt recognized his great talent and ability to achieve much on a limited budget.[8] His energy and efficiency were made clear in the fact that it took only twenty days from the approval of his design for Memorial Hall for him to produce drawings and detailed specifications, obtain bids, and award the building contract.[9]

Schwarzmann's design for Memorial Hall, named to honor the soldiers in the Revolutionary War, was based on one by Nicholas Felix Escalier published in *Croquis d'Architecture* in 1867–1869.[10] It consisted of a central domed area surrounded by four pavilions on the corners. Open arcades flanked the façade on each side of the main entrance, which was marked by three tall arches at the top of thirteen steps, one for each of the original states. Huge though the building was, the amount of art received was so great that an art gallery extension had to be built behind the main building to accommodate it all.[11] On May 10, 1877, and exactly one year after it opened for the centennial, Memorial Hall became Philadelphia's Museum of Art and Industry. There it remained until 1928, when it moved to its newly completed neoclassical temple on the summit of Fairmount.

Memorial Hall continued to house some of the holdings of the Art Museum until 1954, when it ceased to serve as a museum. Three years later, an architectural firm was hired to restore and adapt the building for other uses.[12] That led to a period in which the former museum housed administrative offices for park officials, and served as a kind of community center with the installation of an indoor swimming pool in the east wing and a basketball court in the west wing. The great hall continued to be used occasionally for public and civic events.

Horticultural Hall, also designed by Schwarzmann, was intended to remain as a permanent structure in West Fairmount Park. The smallest of the exhibition's five principal buildings, but the largest botanical conservatory in existence at the time, it was essentially a gigantic greenhouse. One of its features, an outdoor sunken garden whose flowers were arranged in complex patterns, was set below a viewing walkway and proved a particular favorite, even sparking a craze for elaborate carpet bedding. The garden was preserved into the twentieth century and became the model for the Victorian garden at

Memorial Hall

Built for the 1876 Centennial Exposition from a design by Hermann J. Schwarzmann, Memorial Hall was the main art gallery for the exhibition. Six months after the close of the centennial, the hall reopened as the Pennsylvania Museum of Art and Industry, the forerunner of today's Philadelphia Museum of Art (PMA). In the 1890s, its officials concluded that the building was both too far from center city and too small to serve as a first-class gallery. Early in the twentieth century, it was decided to build a new art museum at Fairmount. Once that was completed in 1928, Memorial Hall remained as a kind of annex to the new facility. Starting in the 1950s, when the building no longer served the PMA, it housed administrative offices for park officials and also became a recreation facility and an occasional venue for public events. The Philadelphia Orchestra even made recordings there.

In 2005, the Fairmount Park Commission signed an eighty-year lease with the Please Touch Museum, which had outgrown several other sites in center city during its thirty years of serving the play and educational needs of children under the age of seven. After a three-year restoration of Memorial Hall, the interior was returned to much the way it had appeared in 1876, albeit with a carousel installed in the east wing. Please Touch Museum moved into its new quarters on October 18, 2008. Placed in a central location in the great hall was a forty-foot interpretation of the Statue of Liberty's arm and torch, made entirely of children's toys. To those familiar with the history of the centennial, the display was a sly reminder that, prior to the installation of that icon in New York Harbor, Bartholdi's original arm and torch had risen on the grounds of the 1876 exhibition in Fairmount Park (www.pleasetouchmuseum.org).

Memorial Hall, designed by
Hermann Schwarzmann to
house the international art
exhibit for the centennial, is the
principal building remaining
from that 1876 exposition.
(Inset photograph courtesy of
Steve Lynch) It is now home to
the Please Touch Museum.
(Contemporary photograph
by Mark Garvin)

the Smithsonian's Art and Industry Building in Washington.[13] In 1911, the Fairmount Park Commission determined that deferred maintenance of Horticultural Hall had rendered it a hazard. Still, it survived for almost another half century. On October 15, 1954, Hurricane Hazel damaged the building so extensively that park officials ordered its demolition. In 1976, a new Horticulture Center was built on the footprint of the original building to mark the nation's bicentennial.[14]

A number of roads and buildings in the west park remain today from the centennial. The Avenue of the Republic has had its original name restored after having been known as the North Concourse throughout the twentieth century. It ran the length of Machinery Hall and the Main Building, and today connects Memorial Hall with the Catholic Total Abstinence Fountain, another artifact of the Centennial Exhibition. Of the two dozen buildings representing various states in the Union, only the Ohio House remains today, located at the eastern end of State Avenue and immediately west of Belmont Avenue. Constructed of dressed stone quarried at twenty-one locations in Ohio, it was refurbished early in the twenty-first century and reopened as a café and ice cream parlor.[15]

As for Schwarzmann, his time at the center of all things Fairmount Park soon came to an end. For reasons unknown, he left Philadelphia not long after the close of the centennial and moved to New York. There, he practiced architecture in partnership with Albert Buchman until his death from syphilis in 1891. He was forty-six years old.[16]

Not only was the Centennial Exposition a huge success on its own terms, it also marked a shift in the aesthetic underlying the landscaping of Fairmount Park. From the time "rustic" pavilions began to be added to the gardens at Fairmount, Romanticism had been the dominant note. The terrain frequently had been left in its natural state, or, where development had already taken place, as in the Flat Iron and the Wissahickon Valley, returned to an approximation of its primordial appearance. Winding paths and asymmetrical drives emphasized the beauty of the unrefined landscape. But the Centennial Exhibition created a temporary fantasy city of sorts on a huge tract of Fairmount Park. While it included curving paths in the traditional mode, "the primary roads . . . were broad axial diagonals with formal focal points emphasized by statuary, architecture, and circular drives that foreshadowed the design principles of the World's Columbian Exhibition held in Chicago in 1893."[17]

That shift to a more formal model for landscaping reflected what soon would be known as the "City Beautiful" movement. Its principles would leave a lasting imprint on Philadelphia and Fairmount Park at the start of the twentieth century in the construction of the Benjamin Franklin Parkway.

Following the enormous effort of land acquisition and then by planning for the 1876 Centennial Exposition, Fairmount Park passed the last two decades of the nineteenth century more quietly. The work of the Fairmount Park Art Association, a volunteer body incorporated in 1872, began to bear fruit in this period.[18] As early as 1871, city councils had adopted a resolution calling for an art gallery in the park "to keep pace with the civilization and refinement of the older states of the Christian world," and recommended Lemon Hill as the site.[19] A small gallery was built there the next year. Then came the centennial, and the much larger Memorial Hall was constructed with the purpose of being turned into such an art museum following the exposition. Even when that was done, it did not end the debate in the 1880s and 1890s over alternative locations nearer center city, with the Lemon Hill site the favorite of many. The controversy would continue into the first years of the twentieth century and would not be resolved until the decision was made in 1911 to declare the Fairmount Water Works obsolete and to allocate its reservoir as the site for a new art museum.

In 2005, the Fairmount Park Commission, Fairmount Park Conservancy, Please Touch Museum, Philadelphia Zoo, and Mann Center joined to create a master plan for the "Centennial District." Its purpose was to revive this area of Fairmount Park as a distinctive historical and cultural attraction. The year 2026, the 250th anniversary of American independence, was set as the target date for completing the goals of the plan.[20]

Although the origins of this house date from the 1750s, the name Strawberry Mansion was attached to it only after it was acquired by Fairmount Park in 1871 and became a popular restaurant where chicken dinners, ice cream, and strawberries were served. (Photograph by Mark Garvin)

The Country Houses of Fairmount Park

In the 1970s, a noted English architectural critic wrote: "It is one of those odd accidents of history that the best illustration of villa life as it was understood in England and developed along the banks of the Thames in the eighteenth century should exist in Pennsylvania along the banks of the Schuylkill River a few miles from the centre of Philadelphia."[1] The villas he referred to are almost all situated within Fairmount Park, where they continue to form one of the park's most distinctive features. Their continued presence as elegant reminders of a distant era has long made Fairmount unique among urban parks in America. If these villas have been acknowledged for most of the past century as jewels in the crown of the Philadelphia park system, that was not always so. Their history says much about the perceived relevance of these houses to the creation of an important urban park, as well as to Americans' shifting attitudes toward their nation's past.

From the time the park first began to expand to the north of Fairmount itself, the villas of Philadelphia's early gentry were in its path. Other structures also came under the authority of the Fairmount Park Commission as the park's acreage grew rapidly after the Civil War. But the eighteenth-century villas usually come to mind first when one thinks of the Fairmount Park houses.

Pennsylvania's founder, William Penn, set the stage for the development of an idyllic suburbia along the Schuylkill when he and his surveyor, Thomas Holme, laid out the city of Philadelphia in 1682. Penn offered some of the best building lots to the "first purchasers" of land in Pennsylvania with an added incentive: each buyer of five thousand acres in the surrounding counties was entitled to a bonus of eighty acres in the so-called "Liberty Lands," areas just north and west of the city proper.[2] With the Act of Consolidation of 1854, these Liberty Lands became part of a much-expanded Philadelphia. They include the 4,700 contiguous acres that constitute Fairmount Park on both sides of the Schuylkill up to its feeder creek, the Wissahickon.

Within a century after its founding, Philadelphia was the largest and most affluent city in the British colonies, and had begun to produce an elite class of merchants and professionals who increasingly patterned their way of life after that of the English gentry. Penn himself also served as a model, for he had built his country estate, Pennsbury Manor, on the Delaware north of the city, commuting down the river from there to his townhouse in Philadelphia on his own private barge. Pennsbury Manor was completed by about 1686 as a working plantation. Although it remained under the

The Penn Family in Philadelphia

The remarkable political and social legacy of William Penn (1644–1718)—which included religious toleration, limited government, an amendable constitution, and minority rights—eventually extended clear across America. Yet Penn spent only about four of his seventy-four years in the province that made him the largest nonroyal landowner in the world. He came to establish the city of Philadelphia between 1682 and 1684, and then returned to England. He did not set foot in Pennsylvania again until 1699, this time with his second wife and daughter and James Logan, who eventually would become Penn's near stand-in as the effective governor of the colony. Penn left Pennsylvania for the last time in 1701 for his native England.

His grandson, John Penn (1729–1795), first came to Philadelphia in 1752—a year after Logan's death—to learn to govern the province, although much of the real political power already had passed to elected officials. Summoned home three years later, he returned as governor in 1763, staying for eight years before another sojourn in England. Back in Philadelphia in 1773, he built a magnificent house, Lansdowne, outside the city on the west bank of the Schuylkill. There, he and his wife entertained the political and social elite. But within a few years, the American colonies were in rebellion, and the governor looked on anxiously as the Penn family's proprietorship grew increasingly precarious. He was effectively exiled to New Jersey while British forces occupied Philadelphia, and only returned to the city in July 1778. Penn took an oath of loyalty to the new Commonwealth to avoid confiscation of his private lands and estates, but in 1779, the assembly took title to some twenty-four million acres of unsold land across Pennsylvania.

Once America's independence was certain, Governor Penn's young cousin, also named John Penn (1760–1834), arrived in Philadelphia to try to claim his portion of the family inheritance. In 1784, he bought land and built The Solitude near his cousin's estate, residing there while he sought compensation for the vast stretches of Pennsylvania that had been wrested from his family. Eventually, the Penns were paid 130,000 pounds as a final settlement for the lands they had lost. Young John Penn sailed back to England and never returned to Philadelphia. The Solitude remains on the grounds of the Philadelphia Zoo as the only Penn family residence still standing in Pennsylvania.

Only three houses survive that belonged to men associated with the founder: Bellaire, the home of Samuel Preston, the provincial treasurer and trustee of Penn's estate; James Logan's Stenton, in Philadelphia's Logan neighborhood; and Belmont, the mansion built for William Peters, the Penns' land manager (Chapter 6).

ownership of Penn's heirs after his final departure for England in 1701, it gradually fell into complete ruin. The manor house was re-created in the 1930s and is open to the public.[3]

Beginning several decades after Penn's final departure for England in 1701, villas began to rise along the banks of the Schuylkill. Although Pennsbury had been a working plantation where livestock was raised and food and clothing produced, the owners of the new Schuylkill villas often maintained their primary residences in the city. These "country seats" were not working farms, but instead second homes to which the owners could escape during Philadelphia's steamy summers and enjoy a social life with neighbors of their own elite standing. Many had ornamental gardens, gazebos, and the like, with vistas out over grassy lawns to the river below.

The way of life they represented thrived for decades both before and after the Revolution. Then the completion of the Schuylkill dam above the waterworks in 1821 marked the first step in the area's decline as an elegant neighborhood. That alteration in the river produced a quiet pool above the dam as far as the falls of Schuylkill, some four miles upstream. While that created an ideal stretch for rowing, it also erased some of the waterfront acreage of the Schuylkill mansions and, worse, allowed mosquito-breeding marshes to expand along the banks. The rapid industrial development of much of the Schuylkill followed, both to the north and south, and with it the transformation of the river into a commercial highway. When a financial crisis hit the nation in 1837, land values there, as elsewhere, plummeted. All these factors combined to make it feasible for the City of Philadelphia to begin to acquire a number of these properties at just the time it became urgent to do so in the effort to protect the city's water supply.

The first of these properties to come on the market in 1844 was the forty-five-acre estate a short distance north of the waterworks. The mansion on the site today, Lemon Hill, was completed in 1800 and is, in fact, at least the third villa on the property (Chapter 1).[4] In 1799, Henry Pratt (1761–1838) purchased a forty-five-acre parcel of the Morris estate, and proceeded to plan and design his own house for the site, today's Lemon Hill. The house, in the Federal style, is notable for its sophisticated design, including three large oval rooms and spectacular views from their windows overlooking the city.

Pratt lived at Lemon Hill until 1836, while also maintaining a city house. In his day, it was the estate's greenhouses that were a public attraction, giving the property its name. There he raised citrus and coffee trees, sugarcane, pepper trees, and bananas. Foreshadowing the property's metamorphosis into parkland, Pratt opened his garden to the public free of charge. A visitor in

Lemon Hill, on land first developed by the financier of the Revolutionary War, Robert Morris, was acquired by the city of Philadelphia in 1844. An 1855 ordinance declared that it be joined to the adjacent lands surrounding the Fairmount Water Works, "to be known by the name of Fairmount Park."

1819 wrote that one could admire the cultivated landscape with its "pretty bowers, grottoes, summer houses and fish ponds."[5]

Two years before his death, Pratt sold Lemon Hill to a New York speculator. The ensuing financial crisis immediately caused the property's value to plummet. After nearly nine years in which the new owner let it deteriorate, Philadelphia officials finally were persuaded to buy the property in 1844. But instead of restoring the gardens and reopening them to the public, the city leased the site to a brewer. Not until twelve years later, following the Act of Consolidation and a growing public demand for action, were the tenants evicted and the Lemon Hill estate combined with Fairmount and the waterworks to create the recently named Fairmount Park. But by that date, the wonderful greenhouses that had been landmarks since the time of Robert Morris had been destroyed by fire. For the next seventy years, what had been one of the most exquisite houses in the region was used mostly as a public sa-

The Country Houses of Fairmount Park

loon and beer garden. New porches were wrapped around the façades, awnings added, and a bandstand for summer concerts built on the grounds.

Meanwhile, Fairmount Park had begun to grow. In 1856, citizen action led to the purchase of the Sedgley estate. Adjacent to Lemon Hill and originally also a part of Robert Morris's lands, it too had been sold at sheriff's sale in 1799. The buyer was William Cramond, a wealthy merchant, who hired Benjamin Henry Latrobe as the architect for his new house. Latrobe, who at about the same time was designing the pump house at Centre Square, was already making his mark as the father of American architecture. At Sedgley, he designed one of the first Gothic Revival houses in America. But Cramond, like Morris, was soon deeply in debt, and his property then passed to three additional owners during the next dozen years. The last of these used the villa as his summer residence for a time. But while the neighborhood began its slow decline, the house was leased or left vacant. Sedgley was bought by a speculator in 1836, the same year when Lemon Hill was similarly sold. The new owner subdivided the house and then let it deteriorate. By the time it was acquired to add to the park's acreage, it was deemed to be beyond repair and was soon demolished. Since then, only the name of Sedgley remains to memorialize that section of Fairmount Park. Today it is the site of a disc golf course.

However regrettable the destruction of the villa, a small dependency of Sedgley has escaped the wrecking ball. The porter's house was for many years a headquarters for the Fairmount Park guard, who also used it as a jail. Finally, in the 1990s, nearly two hundred years after it was built, the Fairmount Park Historic Preservation Trust rescued and restored the porter's house, adaptively reusing it as office space. This modest structure, which now houses the local offices of Outward Bound, is the only remaining example of Latrobe's work left standing in Philadelphia.[6]

This brief sketch of the history of two of the houses acquired by the Fairmount Park Commission suggests something of the evolving attitudes toward historic preservation in Philadelphia. When these properties were added to the park, the area had been in decline for years. Once elegant villas had grown shabby or dilapidated, as in the case of Latrobe's Sedgley, where few evidently questioned the decision of park officials to demolish it in the 1850s. Also destroyed was a house on the Schuylkill's west bank known as Eaglesfield, when park officials deemed as impractical any effort to restore and maintain it, even though it had been much admired half a century earlier.[7] With the addition of more estates to the park, the Fairmount Park Commission was also quick to demolish the many outbuildings that accompanied their newly acquired houses.

A truism is at work in this account of the action officials took soon after these properties were acquired by the city: generational change brings changing attitudes about what should be preserved—certainly in Philadelphia, but no doubt much more widely. Each new generation tends to denigrate the stylistic choices in the built environment of its parents' generation, which look old-fashioned and quaint. When that era's buildings deteriorate, they may well be viewed as not deserving preservation.

Lemon Hill's fate provides another example of that attitude at the time, but one with a happier ending. Once they were pressured into evicting its tenants, park officials did not restore the mansion to its original splendor. But they did appreciate its utility as a park asset, and proceeded to transform it into a public house. The happy ending, as for the other Schuylkill villas that have survived to this day, is that the utilitarian uses to which they were put by the Fairmount Park Commission saved them from demolition. Then, when later generations began to appreciate their historic worth, it would prove relatively simple to restore them.

Here, then, is the rest of that truism about changing attitudes toward historic preservation: while overlooking the work of their parents, each succeeding generation tends to appreciate the architectural tastes of those two, or better yet, three generations removed, which of course are those found out of date by the generations that lie between.[8] When Fairmount Park grew to encompass a number of the Schuylkill estates, the Fairmount Park Commission did acknowledge that many of their original owners had been important to the "social and civil progress of Philadelphia." It promised somewhat vaguely to honor them in the park by "clustering around its most attractive portions inspiring memories of the deeds and the men of times long since passed away."[9] There is no reference here to an effort to preserve and restore the houses of those men. Yet, most of them were preserved. Those that did not directly serve the public during the next half century typically became residences or offices for park employees.

Not until the 1920s did the country houses of Fairmount Park come to be viewed in a new, more reverential light. That transformed outlook was due largely to the efforts of Fiske Kimball (1888–1955), the first director of what today is the Philadelphia Museum of Art. With his leadership, the villas came to be acknowledged as important contributions to the art and architectural history of the nation, deserving to be treated as museums rather than simply as useful structures for the administration of the park.

Kimball arrived in Philadelphia shortly before the new Art Museum opened at the site of the old reservoirs atop Fairmount. He immediately made clear the importance of the remaining Schuylkill villas as objects of great architectural, cultural, and artistic interest to the city. He noted that Philadelphia had

> a series of whole houses, mostly in their original setting. . . . [including] a dozen in Fairmount park, conveniently located a few hundred yards apart, near its Museum. These by themselves are sufficient to illustrate the evolution of American art from the time of William Penn until the nineteenth century. In several cases these houses are the very finest of their respective period and types.[10]

Kimball's attention to the villas coincided with the nation's sesquicentennial celebrations in 1926, which were held in South Philadelphia, and the new interest it helped stir in Colonial Revival architecture and decoration. He largely succeeded in focusing Philadelphia's attention on the latent treasures that dotted Fairmount Park. Even so, in nearly a century since then, some of the villas have been lost thanks to financial exigencies and the ravages of time. We begin with a look at those now furnished and regularly open for visitors, starting with four in the east park, followed by two west of the river.

Mount Pleasant came into being several decades before Lemon Hill and Sedgley were built, as the estate of a successful Scottish privateer. Captain John Macpherson had captured several rich prize ships for the British during the French and Indian War. Settling in Philadelphia as a rich man, he bought some one hundred fifty acres of land several miles north of the city, and built a grand villa on the property between 1762 and 1765. His master builder constructed a mansion house that remains a prime example of the Middle Georgian architectural style, characterized by Palladian design principles and precise adherence to symmetry and proportion.[11] In 1775, after John Adams was invited to dinner at Mount Pleasant, he described it in a letter to Abigail as "the most elegant seat in Pennsylvania."[12]

The wealthy captain Macpherson found himself overextended financially by the late 1770s, so he rented out his mansion to the Spanish minister to the American cause during the Revolutionary War, Don Juan de Miralles. In 1779, the property was sold to General Benedict Arnold in trust for his bride to be, Peggy Shippen, who came from a prominent Philadelphia family. But before the Miralles lease was ended, Arnold's intended betrayal of the American cause was discovered. Because of his arrest, the Arnolds never took possession of the villa. Mount Pleasant changed ownership several times during the 1780s, and in 1792, it became the property of Colonel Jonathan Williams,

Mount Pleasant has been among the grandest of the Schuylkill villas since the time of its construction in the 1760s. A century later, its then owner, a descendent in the family of Benjamin Franklin, sold the property to the city to be added to Fairmount Park.

a great-nephew of Benjamin Franklin, who later would become the first superintendent of the U.S. Military Academy at West Point.

Williams's son and heir began selling off portions of the estate in the 1840s to new industries in the area. The Knickerbocker Ice Company bought or leased parcels in order to harvest ice from the Schuylkill. German brewers also had leases. Philadelphia's growing German population used the property as a recreation center known as "Washington's Retreat."[13] In 1868, the Williams family sold the house and its remaining acreage to the city to be added to Fairmount Park. The park keeper soon was authorized to move into one of the buildings.[14] Throughout the 1870s, the commission received numerous petitions from local entrepreneurs to establish various commercial enterprises at the site. In 1878, George Dallas Dixon was granted a license to create a "dairy" on the premises. From there, milk and ice cream were sold to park visitors until the early years of the twentieth century. In 1906, the mansion became the headquarters of a ladies' automobile club.[15]

Remarkably, throughout this history, Mount Pleasant itself remained largely unchanged. The ornately carved cornices and moldings, grand Palladian windows, and distinctive chimneys, as well as the symmetrical pavilions with their bell curve roofs that frame the great house all came down to us intact. Once it underwent its first restoration in the 1920s, it reemerged as one of the architectural and artistic masterpieces of its time. Today, under the management of the Philadelphia Museum of Art, and several restorations later, it remains one of the greatest American houses of its type. The dwelling, like most of the others described in this chapter and the next, is now listed on the National Register of Historic Places, as is Fairmount Park itself.

Laurel Hill, a short distance upstream from Mount Pleasant, began as a more modest summer retreat than its neighbor, whose Georgian style it nonetheless echoed. The land had been left to a young widow, Rebecca Rawle,

Distinguished Residents and Visitors

Because the country villas near Philadelphia were built by people of means, their residents and guests often were among the movers and shakers of the period. Patriots of the Revolution, including Washington, Adams, and Jefferson, were hosted at Belmont by William Peters and his son Richard Jr., who served in the Continental Congress, the Pennsylvania legislature, and the U.S. District Court. Benjamin Franklin's daughter, Sally Bache, came repeatedly to The Cliffs during the Revolution to sew bandages and clothes for American soldiers. Years later, the exiled Joseph Bonaparte would lease John Penn's Lansdowne as a summer retreat.

Strawberry Mansion's early owner, William Lewis, was responsible for Pennsylvania's Act for the Abolition of Slavery in 1780, the first such law in the nation. The mansion's next owner, Joseph Hemphill, was a longtime member of the U.S. Congress. Among those he entertained at his home were John C. Calhoun, Daniel Webster, and the Marquis de Lafayette.

Invitations to Mount Pleasant were prized by wealthy Philadelphians and members of the Continental Congress throughout the 1760s and 1770s. During the Revolution, the mansion was leased to the Spanish minister to the new nation, Don Juan de Miralles. In 1792, the property was bought by Benjamin Franklin's great-nephew, Jonathan Williams, who would become the first superintendent of the West Point Military Academy.

Sweetbriar's Samuel Breck had a long career in the Pennsylvania legislature. Having grown up in France, Breck hosted a number of leading French exiles during the French Revolution, including Talleyrand, the great French diplomat; the future king Louis Philippe and his brothers; and Lafayette.

For years early in the nineteenth century, Laurel Hill was the summer residence of a leading American physician, Philip Syng Physick, who famously removed the gall bladder of Chief Justice John Marshall, and ministered to John Adams's daughter, to Dolley Madison, and to his fellow surgeon, Benjamin Rush. Earlier, the house had been the summer retreat of France's minister to the new republic, the Chevalier de la Luzerne.

Like several other Schuylkill villas, in the 1760s, Laurel Hill was constructed as a modest summer retreat. The octagonal wing was added in the mid-nineteenth century. The property was added to Fairmount Park in 1869. (Photograph by Mark Garvin)

when her husband was killed in a shooting accident. The original center section of the house was built in about 1767, at the time of Mrs. Rawle's remarriage to a prominent Philadelphia civic leader, Samuel Shoemaker, who would become the city's mayor two years later.

The Shoemakers used the little house as their summer retreat for much of the next decade. But when the British army occupied Philadelphia during the winter of 1777–1778, Shoemaker collaborated with the occupiers as a Loyalist. In 1778, the Pennsylvania Assembly declared him guilty of treason and confiscated his property, including his life rights to his wife's property at Laurel Hill. He fled to England, taking his and Rebecca's young son Edward with him, but left his wife in Philadelphia with her children from her first marriage. She spent several years trying to regain her house. But Laurel Hill's tenant at the time, the French minister, the Chevalier de la Luzerne, balked at giving up his summer retreat without being compensated. Finally, in 1784, Rebecca succeeded in reclaiming the house. Some ten years after he fled, Samuel returned from England with their son, and by 1791 the Shoemakers were again summering at Laurel Hill.[16]

After Samuel's death in 1800, his son Edward took possession of the house. It is likely that the small, one-story wing at the building's south end was added at that time, destroying the cottage's symmetry, but adding essential space for Edward's family with its nine children. Edward's prosperity as a merchant was short-lived, Congress's Embargo Act of 1807 having severely damaged his business in international trade. Dr. Philip Syng Physick, known as the father of American surgery, was among those who loaned him money. By 1813, Edward had moved to a Bucks County farm, and Dr. Physick and his family leased Laurel Hill as their summer getaway. Although another of Rebecca's sons, William Rawle, inherited the property after his mother's death in 1819, he sold the house to Dr. Physick in 1828.[17] At some point after Philip Syng Physick's death in 1837, his daughter and her surgeon

Loyalists and Traitors

The American Revolution caused a sharp line to be drawn between those fighting for independence and those who remained loyal to the crown. Perhaps in part because of their wealth and social standing, a number of those with connections to the Schuylkill villas were Tories. The widowed owner of Laurel Hill married Samuel Shoemaker in 1767, and he became Philadelphia's mayor two years later. But when the British occupied the city in 1777, Shoemaker collaborated with the enemy and was declared guilty of treason. He fled to England, leaving his wife who finally succeeded in regaining possession of their property in 1784, when the Shoemaker family was reunited in Philadelphia.

David Franks had bought Woodford in 1771 and greatly expanded it. But in 1778, he was arrested as a Loyalist and fled Philadelphia. He never regained his confiscated property.

Nearby Ormiston (Chapter 6) was built after the Revolution on land previously owned by Joseph Galloway, a notorious Tory. Galloway served the British as provost marshal during their occupation of Philadelphia, which put him in charge of imprisoned Continental soldiers captured by the redcoats. Francis Hopkinson wrote Galloway an open letter accusing him of making no effort to feed the starving prisoners who "have plucked the weeds of the earth for food, and expired with the unchewed grass in their mouths."

The Woodlands mansion was built by the young William Hamilton, scion of a prominent Philadelphia family, whose grandfather Andrew had been the Philadelphia lawyer lionized for his defense of freedom of the press. William was a Tory and only narrowly escaped conviction for treason. After retreating for a time to London, however, he returned to Philadelphia after the war, greatly expanded Woodlands, and became an active and respected botanist.

Benedict Arnold had recently become the owner of Mount Pleasant when evidence was found of his intention to hand over to the enemy the American fort at West Point, which Arnold commanded. He narrowly escaped capture by Washington before he defected to the British army, where he was made a brigadier general.

In the 1780s, William Lewis re-created the existing farmhouse at what today are Thirty-Third and Dauphin Streets, which now comprises the central core of Strawberry Mansion. The neoclassic wings were added by the new owner, Joseph Hemphill, after 1821. It was acquired by Fairmount Park in 1871. (Photograph by Mark Garvin)

husband, Jacob Randolph, added the two-story octagonal wing on the north end of the house. Although it is jarringly out of place with the older structure, it created a large and handsome music room on the first floor.

Mrs. Randolph sold the property, then generally known as the Randolph House, to the City of Philadelphia in 1869. For the next thirty years, it was used to house Fairmount Park employees. In 1900, Laurel Hill was leased to the Colonial Dames of America Chapter II. By the next year, that organization had restored the house and opened it for visits from the public. That made it likely the first effort at creating a house museum in Fairmount Park.[18]

Strawberry Mansion takes its name from the years after it was acquired for Fairmount Park when it became a restaurant serving chicken dinners, ice cream, and strawberries to crowds of visitors from the city below. It had begun its life very differently. In 1783, the thirteen-acre property on which the house stands had been bought by a leading Philadelphia attorney, William Lewis (1751–1819). Although an ardent proponent of American independence, Lewis had made a name for himself defending Quakers for their refusal to pledge allegiance to the revolutionary government. He became the principal author of the "Act for the Abolition of Slavery," which was adopted by the legislature on March 1, 1780, making Pennsylvania the first state in the Union to pass an antislavery law.

Soon after he bought the property, Lewis reconstructed the farmhouse that had been built on the site in the 1750s, creating the central section of the house as it exists today, and named his property Summerville. The plain exterior belies more delicate neoclassic touches within, including fanlight transoms, arched niches, and a plaster medallion in the hall ceiling. In 1821, the property was sold in a sheriff's sale following Lewis's death—he too had been in debt at the end of his life—to U.S. representative Joseph Hemphill (1770–1842). In the course of his career as a political figure, and to support his lavish style of entertaining, Hemphill added the two enormous, neoclassic wings to the central house, nearly tripling its size. The ballroom in the south wing contains scrolled pediments above the windows and a Grecian plaster carved medallion on the ceiling. Like so many others, Hemphill's fortune began to decline in the 1830s, and his sister acquired the house at his death. Four years later, in 1846, she sold the property to George Crock, who maintained it as a dairy farm until 1871, when he sold it to the city to be added to Fairmount Park. That began the mansion's incarnation as one of the most popular "resorts" for daytime excursions in the park. A music pavilion was built on the grounds in 1906.[19]

America always has been a land of dizzying financial success and failure. Not surprisingly, several owners of the Schuylkill villas experienced such boom and bust. The most famous of these was Robert Morris, the original owner of Lemon Hill. One of the richest men in the colonies, Morris financed the Revolutionary War and then lost his fortune, landing in debtors' prison while his country property was sold at a sheriff's sale. A piece of that land adjoining Morris's mansion was bought by William Cramond, who built Sedgley there. Then Cramond himself fell into debt and lost his property. John Macpherson, the builder of Mount Pleasant, had made a not-very-respectable fortune as a privateer by seizing French ships during the Seven Years' War. He seldom lived in his grand house following the death of his estranged wife and then his son, an officer in the Continental army who died at Quebec. Macpherson lost his fortune in bad investments and died impoverished in 1792.

The two principal owners of Strawberry Mansion from 1783 to the 1830s, William Lewis and Joseph Hemphill, also ended deeply in debt. The property went to Hemphill in 1821 through a sheriff's sale. But in the 1830s, his fortunes declined, and in 1838 he was forced to take out a mortgage on the house from his sister-in-law. The builder of Chamounix in 1802, George Plumstead, was a successful Quaker merchant at the time, the son and grandson of Philadelphia mayors. But three years later, Plumstead also died deeply in debt.

A highlight of Philadelphia's Sesquicentennial Fair of 1926 was its exhibit of re-created eighteenth-century buildings. As a result, in 1930, a women's group formed the Committee of 1926 with the goal of transforming Strawberry Mansion into a house museum. Fiske Kimball supervised the restoration, which was made possible by a gift from the founder of the Horn and Hardart chain of restaurants. The house was appropriately refurnished and has remained under the supervision of the Committee of 1926 ever since.

Woodford is Strawberry Mansion's near neighbor in the east park. In 1756, Judge William Coleman (1704–1769) purchased twelve acres carved out of an original Penn grant. Coleman was a successful merchant, civic leader, and later a justice on Pennsylvania's Supreme Court. His friend Benjamin Franklin said of Coleman after his death: "He had the coolest, clearest head, the best heart, and the exactest morals of almost any man I ever met with." Coleman built a one-story summer retreat on his property; it changed hands twice in just three years after his death. Starting in 1771, the new owners,

The Sesquicentennial and the Colonial Revival

The Sesquicentennial International Exposition of 1926 was a world's fair held in Philadelphia from May 3 through November. The site created for it, now Franklin Delano Roosevelt (FDR) Park, was then known as League Island Park. Today, the park and Marconi Plaza share the area with the city's sports complex in South Philadelphia. President Coolidge initiated the festivities in a downpour. The fair's duration, in fact, coincided with an unusually rainy period. Twenty-five million visitors had been hoped for, but only about one-third of that number actually came. The exposition ended as a financial loss. Yet the first bridge spanning the Delaware River from Philadelphia to Camden—the Benjamin Franklin Bridge, as it would be named—was completed for the occasion.

The sesquicentennial gave a large boost to the Colonial Revival style across America. The exposition was avidly promoted as a commemoration of America's past. It featured a "High Street" of twenty homes along a colonial Philadelphia street; guides were appropriately costumed and traditional foods were sold. That display proved so popular that it soon would lead to the establishment of several reconstructed village museums across America, such as Colonial Williamsburg. In Philadelphia, the Colonial Revival enthusiasm also boosted appreciation and conservation of many of its historic houses, including those in Fairmount Park.

David Franks and his wife, greatly expanded the house, adding a second floor with a Palladian window above the front door and a long wing extending from the back of the house. That created a grand new stair hall leading upstairs to a ballroom and new bedrooms, with a kitchen below. The original ground floor was left largely intact, and its Georgian drawing room survives unchanged from Coleman's day.

David Franks, like Samuel Shoemaker, was a Loyalist who was forced to flee Philadelphia after his arrest in 1778. He forfeited Woodford, and the new owner sold it to Isaac Wharton in 1793. The Whartons created a second large parlor in the original part of the house by removing the wall between the Coleman-era bedrooms on the ground floor. The property was acquired by the city from Wharton's descendents in 1869. For some years, Woodford then served as the residence of Fairmount Park's chief engineer and supervisor. In 1912, it became the park guard headquarters and traffic court. Fines were paid in Woodford's parlor. Then in 1926, as one of the first initiatives to

Originally a one-story summer retreat, Woodford was built in the late 1750s, but was greatly expanded by new owners in the 1770s. The original Georgian drawing room remains unchanged today, even though it served for years in the twentieth century as the park guard headquarters and traffic court. (Photograph by Mark Garvin)

by the Junior League in 1932; in 1939, its maintenance was given ove[r]
Modern Club of Philadelphia, whose supervision continues today
operation with the Fairmount Park Commission. The house was l[a]
restored by the city in time for the bicentennial celebration of 1976.

Cedar Grove is unusual among these park houses in that it w[as]
moved to its location on the Schuylkill's west bank starting in 1926, i[ts]
struction completed there in 1928.[23] For 180 years previously, it ha[d]
about four miles northeast of Philadelphia's original boundaries in [Frank]gate, today's Frankford section of the city. There, a Quaker widow, E[lizabeth]
Coates Paschall, had built a modest farmhouse in 1748 as a summer re[treat for]
herself and her three children. Two generations later, at the end of t[he eigh]teenth century, Elizabeth's great-niece and her husband more than

restore some of the Park villas as house muse
mission agreed to lease the house to the Nac
had directed that $50,000 from her estate be u
priate to display her collection of eighteenth-
items. That sum was then used to restore W
the Naomi Wood collection ever since.[20]

On July 11, 2003, a painter using a heat gu
of the roof. Fortunately, it was discovered in
collection, although severe water and smoke
years of work before the restored house could

Sweetbriar, on the west bank of the Sch
year-round residence. Its owner, Samuel Bre
born son of a fiscal agent for the French for
the Revolutionary War. Young Samuel was
family moved to Philadelphia in 1792. Settin
the Walnut Street wharf, he soon met and m
had amassed a fortune in the East India trac
the newlyweds the twenty-four-acre parce
Sweetbriar in the next year. The result was a
tecture, complete with floor-to-ceiling wind
as "a beautiful sloping lawn, terminating at
house, etc."[21] Samuel Breck proceeded to dev
service, supporting a number of local instit
in the Pennsylvania legislature, years after
Congress, he introduced a bill that would cre
Pennsylvania.

The Brecks may have been motivated to li
congested city because of the constant threa
Once the Fairmount dam was completed in
teen acres of meadowland, and some of the
nant water. Perhaps as a result, his only child,
Still, the Brecks remained at Sweetbriar unti
into town. They sold their country property in
new owner may have used the house as a tav
mount Park in 1867. Thereafter, it became a re
banned from the park by the commission), an
across the front and back. Following the cente
into a day camp for children. Sweetbriar was re

Cedar Grove began as a modest farmhouse built in Philadelphia's
Frankford neighborhood in 1748. Moved to Fairmount Park in the 1920s,
the much-enlarged house displays furniture and other objects acquired
by five generations of a single family. (Photograph by Mark Garvin)

the size of the house, adding a gambrel roof and a large lunette window in
the new gable. By about 1848, the next generation of the family had added the
piazza, wrapping it around two sides of the stone house. All the downstairs
rooms give access to it. The house continued in the family until 1888, when
newly constructed railroad tracks ran nearby, forever spoiling the peace and

quiet. Miss Lydia Thompson Morris and her brother John closed Cedar Grove and moved to a new country house in Chestnut Hill.

Following John's death, Lydia Morris offered the house to the City of Philadelphia, and paid for its dismantling and reconstruction in Fairmount Park. She also refurnished the house with numerous original family objects. As a result, it is one of the few houses in the region whose furnishings are entirely in context. The simplicity of Cedar Grove's architecture reflects the family's Quaker origins, while its long occupancy by five generations of the Coates, Paschall, and Morris families is visible in the changing styles of its furnishings. From the time it was moved to Fairmount Park, Cedar Grove has been administered by the Philadelphia Museum of Art.[24]

Before leaving the seven principal houses now generally open to visitors, a final comment on Lemon Hill is in order. Even though the Fairmount Park Commission initially treated the property as a place for public refreshment, this was seen at the time as responsible usage. The commission pointed with pride to how its intervention after 1867 had saved Lemon Hill from its unsavory history of the previous two-plus decades, including more than a decade while under the city's ownership: "The triumph of right was, for a time, only on the statute book, the vandal spirit that held its orgies on these fair terraces defied law, and persisted in its work of ruin some years longer."[25] At least the house was then maintained sufficiently, so that by the 1920s, it could be restored to its original condition by Fiske Kimball, who lived there with his wife throughout the years when he was director of the Philadelphia Museum of Art, 1925–1955.

Long before Belmont Mansion was added to Fairmount Park and became a restaurant with porches constructed for warm-weather dining, it was the heart of a country estate where leading Americans of the eighteenth century, including Washington, Adams, Jefferson, and Madison, were guests. (Courtesy of Steve Lynch)

Belmont Mansion, Fairmount Park   *Just received your letter. That time will suit, since it cannot be sooner. Kind regards to all — M. H. Young.*

Historic Structures
in Philadelphia's Parks

Chapter 5 considered the principal country houses in Fairmount Park that are now generally open to the public as house museums. As the park system has grown, it has acquired additional structures that are of historical interest for a variety of reasons. Still other such buildings, while not officially a part of Fairmount Park, have been left to the City of Philadelphia and assigned to non-profit groups as their custodians. Here we discuss those relevant to the city's parks. Some were the property of important historical figures; others were left to the city as benefactions for the public to enjoy.[1]

In addition to the house museums in Fairmount Park, a number of other important residences are scattered about the park's core grounds on the Schuylkill. Of these, two that remain and the ghost of a third resonate strongly with Philadelphia's history generally and the Penn family specifically.

The ghostly property is the vanished mansion Lansdowne, one of the grandest houses in North America in the late eighteenth century. It was lost when boys playing with fireworks on July 4, 1854, set fire to the building, leaving it a shell. It had been constructed in 1773 by Governor John Penn (1729–1795), the grandson of William Penn by his younger son, Richard. That was the year in which John Penn had returned to Pennsylvania from England to serve as governor for the second time.

For Penn's first years at Lansdowne, the house was the center of social life for Philadelphia's elite. But with the coming of the American Revolution in 1776, Penn could only watch while political power was taken from him. For a time, while British forces under General Howe occupied Philadelphia, Penn was exiled by Patriot leaders to New Jersey. When he and his wife returned after the departure of the British in 1778, he was made to take a loyalty oath to the new government, as were all Pennsylvanians.

As a result of the Divestment Act passed by the Pennsylvania Assembly in 1779, some twenty-four million acres of unsold proprietary lands throughout the Commonwealth were confiscated. Although Governor Penn and his younger cousin, also named John, were eventually awarded 130,000 pounds by the legislature as compensation for what had been the family's private holdings, that award ended their proprietary claim to all of Pennsylvania. Once the Penn cousins finally acknowledged that their lobbying of the legislature could avail them nothing further, they sailed for England in 1789 to press for additional compensation from Parliament.

Eventually, the former governor Penn returned to Philadelphia and quietly lived out the rest of his life at Lansdowne. At his death, he was interred at Philadelphia's Christ Church, the only proprietor buried in Pennsylvania.[2] In the decades after his death, Lansdowne was occupied as a summer retreat first by Joseph Bonaparte, Napoleon's older brother, and then by William Bingham, one of America's richest men. But the estate had been sold by Penn's widow after her husband's death, and eventually began to decline. In 1858, four years after the house burned down, the property was purchased for Fairmount Park and its ruined shell of a mansion demolished by the city.

When John Penn had first come to Pennsylvania in 1752 he was in his early twenties, and lived so extravagantly that he alarmed his uncle, Thomas Penn, who ordered him back to London. But eleven years later, John was sufficiently trusted by the family to return to Pennsylvania as its governor, serving his first term from 1763 to 1771. Yet his taste for the lavish remained evident when, after another sojourn in London, he returned to Philadelphia in 1773, began his second term as governor, and built his mansion. Lansdowne was the largest Middle Georgian house in prerevolutionary America. Had it survived a few years longer and become a part of Fairmount Park, it surely would be viewed as the crown jewel among park houses today.[3] The park's Lansdowne Drive now commemorates the grounds of the estate.

The Solitude is the park's most tangible remaining connection to the family of William Penn. The other, much younger John Penn (1760–1834) was also the grandson of Pennsylvania's founder. He only arrived in Philadelphia from London after America's independence was achieved to contest, with his cousin the governor, their proprietary interests. Then twenty-three, he controlled three-fourths of the proprietorship through inheritance from his father, Thomas, William Penn's oldest son.

(Facing page)

John Penn, the grandson of Pennsylvania's founder, built The Solitude as an elegant bachelor retreat in the 1780s. After the property was acquired for Fairmount Park, the house and thirty-three acres became the site for the Philadelphia Zoo in 1873.

Historic Structures in Philadelphia's Parks

In 1784, months after he arrived, he paid six hundred pounds for fifteen acres on the Schuylkill's west bank, and proceeded to design his retreat. Because of his close tie to Governor Penn, he had comfortable access to his cousin's Lansdowne nearby. The younger Penn's little villa was therefore intended as the small retreat of a stylish single gentleman. The result is a severe classical cube (29' x 29' x 29') containing a parlor and stair hall on the ground floor and a library and two small bedrooms above. Delicate plaster medallions decorate the parlor and library ceilings. Penn's own sketches for the house have survived, as has the surveyor's plan for the garden and an inventory of the house's contents from shortly after Penn occupied it.[4]

Penn stayed only five years in Pennsylvania. Finally recognizing that he would receive no further compensation from Pennsylvania for the lost family lands, he returned to England, where he would remain for the rest of his life. There, he became a man of affairs and sometime poet, eventually serving as a member of Parliament.

After Penn's departure, The Solitude's contents were sold at public auction. The villa evidently was leased to tenants through the rest of its owner's lifetime. After its ownership passed, first to John's brother, Granville, and then to a nephew, the Reverend Thomas Gordon Penn—the last direct descendant of William Penn and the last private owner—the property was acquired for Fairmount Park in 1867.

In 1873, thirty-three acres that included the Penn property were designated as the site for the Philadelphia Zoological Garden. For many years after the zoo opened the following year, The Solitude served as the reptile house. More recently, it has housed the zoo's administrative offices. The Friends of The Solitude were formed in 1991 to assist in restoration of the house, which is now complete. It has been refurnished as in Penn's time there and is now available to rent for private occasions and for group tours. The gardens also are being returned to approximate their appearance when Penn was in residence.

This early twentieth-century postcard of Belmont Mansion shows the porches that were added in the nineteenth century when the building housed a Fairmount Park restaurant. (Courtesy of Steve Lynch)

Historic Structures in Philadelphia's Parks

Belmont Mansion, dating from the 1740s, also has Penn family connections. Its builder, William Peters (1702–1786) was an English-born land manager for the Penns. His son, Richard Jr. (1744–1828), was a member of the Continental Congress, a member of Pennsylvania's legislature, and a judge of the U.S. District Court after the Revolution. As a member of the Pennsylvania Society for the Abolition of Slavery, he opposed the Fugitive Slave Act of 1793. Leading figures of the period—Washington, Adams, Jefferson, and Madison, among others—were guests at the expansive estate.

Hannah Callender, a visitor in 1762, provided a description of the estate's riches, noting that its large hall was "well furnished, the top adorned with

Today, Belmont Mansion commemorates the Underground Railroad that helped slaves escape to freedom before the Civil War.

Historic Structures in Philadelphia's Parks

instruments of music, coats of arms, crests and other ornaments in stucco, its sides by paintings and statues in bronze. From the front of this hall you have a prospect bounded by the Jerseys like a blue ridge." Her description followed of the large garden with its statuary, hedges, and summer house.[5]

After the property was acquired for Fairmount Park in 1869, a large dining pavilion was built on the lawn in anticipation of the centennial, whose grounds soon would be prepared for the exhibition nearby. Belmont remained a dining facility for many decades thereafter, and has been much altered over the years. In 1986, the American Women's Heritage Society was created by African American women to restore and maintain Belmont. It is the first organization to operate Belmont as a historic site. Following the first extensive restoration undertaken by the Fairmount Park Trust for Historic Preservation starting in 1994, it has been designated since 2007 to commemorate the Underground Railroad of the pre–Civil War period. The mansion is open for group tours and is available for special events.[6]

Back in the east park, two important villas stand between Mount Pleasant and Laurel Hill. The Federal-style houses have been restored, and both are now occupied by nonprofit organizations. Ormiston (1798) was originally held by a noted Tory, Joseph Galloway, who was provost marshal during the British occupation of Philadelphia in 1777. The villa built on this site after the Revolution was a summer retreat for Edward Burd. Appropriately enough, Ormiston now houses the Royal Heritage Society of the Delaware Valley.[7]

Rockland (circa 1810) recently has been restored with help from the Fairmount Park Preservation Trust and is home to the Psychoanalytic Center of Philadelphia. This two-and-a-half-story, stucco-over-stone structure overlooks the Schuylkill from a broad porch at the rear. The delicacy of its front

The Letitia Street House

This unprepossessing little brick townhouse, now at 3400 W. Girard Avenue, reflects Philadelphia's growing interest in historic preservation following the Centennial Exhibition of 1876. It was built in about 1713 for Thomas Chaulkley, a Philadelphia merchant and Quaker preacher, near Second and Chestnut Streets on land originally owned by William Penn's daughter, Letitia. Some interested citizens surmised that it had been built as her residence, basing their conjecture on tales passed down to them rather than any hard evidence. In 1883, the presumed Penn connection to the house persuaded the city to buy it and relocate it to Fairmount Park to be refurbished as a museum. By the mid-twentieth century, experts concluded that the Penn connection was spurious. It eventually became office space for the Philadelphia Zoo, but has long been vacant. It is among a number of properties in the park awaiting renovation and adaptive reuse.

Rockland, a Federal house dating from circa 1810, has been restored with the assistance of the Fairmount Park Preservation Trust and is maintained by its tenant, the Psychoanalytic Center of Philadelphia.

façade, which includes a half-round, columned portico, led one commentator to note in the 1990s: "Nothing else from the Federal period in Philadelphia even approaches the sophistication of this composition."[8]

Also in the east park is the Greek Revival Hatfield House, which began life as a farmhouse in 1750 in today's Nicetown section of Philadelphia. For two decades in the early nineteenth century, it was home to Catherine Mallon's Boarding School for girls. In 1831, a new owner glamorized and updated the house by adding the portico and Greek Revival columns. In 1929, it was donated to Fairmount Park and moved to its current location the following year. For a brief period at the time of the nation's bicentennial in 1976, the house was renovated, furnished, and opened as a house museum. But after a break-in, its caretakers, the Philadelphia Museum of Art and Fairmount Park Association, determined it could not be securely maintained. The house is now leased as office space by the Father's Day Fund.[9]

On the west bank of the river, deep in the park, is Ridgeland Mansion, which probably was built between 1752 and 1762. By early in the nineteenth

Historic Structures in Philadelphia's Parks

century, a new owner used it mainly as a summer residence, adding the porch that overlooks the Schuylkill. For much of the next century after the city acquired the property in 1869, Ridgeland housed city officials and park offices. Today, it is occupied by the Suzanne Morgan Center at Ridgeland, which serves cancer patients and their families.[10]

At the northern edge of the west park, Chamounix has served as a youth hostel since 1964, and now proclaims itself the oldest urban hostel in America. It is also available for workshops and retreats. Chamounix began life as a summer house for George Plumstead in 1802. Built on a bluff overlooking the Schuylkill, it was enlarged to its current form by a successive owner in the 1850s, the first to use it as a full-time home. It contains two rooms and a center hall on the first floor, four rooms above.

Until the mid-twentieth century, the house served variously as a restaurant and boardinghouse, and in 1901 gave its name to the adjoining racetrack for light, horse-drawn vehicles (Chapter 7). The house fell into such disrepair in the 1950s that the commission considered demolishing it. But after the empty house caught fire in 1962, the commission repaired and restored it to become the youth hostel that it remains today. The Fairmount Park Historic Preservation Trust obtained grant money in 1996 to begin extensive restoration of the mansion. In keeping with its appeal to travelers seeking inexpensive lodging, the house is partially furnished with period reproductions. Sleeping accommodations are communal. The handicapped-accessible carriage house is available to groups.[11]

When the Pennsylvania legislature enacted Public Law 547 in 1867, it created the Fairmount Park Commission and authorized it to purchase land for the park. Apart from gifts of land, the commission either purchased additional property or condemned it through the power of eminent domain (Chapter 3).

However, the recent heir of Chamounix first appealed for the right to maintain ownership of the house while ceding most of the surrounding land to the park. He pledged to sign a covenant "that the place shall be forever occupied only as a private residence and the grounds &c. kept in such good order that it will be no detriment to the beauty of the Park." He cited London's Regent's Park as a precedent, noting that several private enclosures existed within its boundaries without much impinging on the public space.[12] But the commission refused his request and the owners of Chamounix were forced soon thereafter to sell the entire property for the park.

Had the alternative been accepted, this house and other properties now at least theoretically available to the public no doubt would remain today as

private enclaves. But that alternative quite likely would have kept those residences from succumbing to neglect when public funds were unavailable for their upkeep, and would have done so at the expense of their owners.

South of Chamounix and next to Lansdowne Avenue on the centennial grounds is a very different example of domestic architecture from halfway around the world. Shofuso, the Japanese House and Garden, was donated to Philadelphia in 1958 by the America-Japan Society. The gift was partly to acknowledge that Fairmount Park at the time of the 1876 centennial had been the site of the first Japanese garden created in America. Shofuso was constructed in Japan in 1953 using the traditional materials and techniques of the seventeenth-century shoin architectural style, and was first exhibited in the courtyard of the Museum of Modern Art in New York. It consists of a small complex including a guesthouse, kitchen, bath, and teahouse, and is surrounded by a pond, a creek, a waterfall and boulders, and a stone bridge and pagoda, as well as three gardens.

The Japanese House and Garden, Shofuso, was a gift to the City of Philadelphia in 1958, and is regarded as one of the finest examples of traditional Japanese architecture outside Japan. (Photograph by Mark Garvin)

Historic Structures in Philadelphia's Parks

This David Rittenhouse birthplace and bake house from the 1690s are the oldest structures remaining at Rittenhouse Town, an early paper mill complex whose land was incorporated into Fairmount Park in the 1870s.

In 2012, a professor of Asian art history asserted that "the house, arguably, is the best Japanese structure in North America, if not outside of Japan."[13] In 2012, two comfort stations that had served Horticultural Hall during the centennial were restored. Renamed the Sakura Pavilion together with a connecting bluestone terrace, the buildings now provide Shofuso with storage and program space. A nonprofit group, the Friends of the Japanese House and Garden, maintains the property.[14]

Boelson Cottage is an unprepossessing little stone house built by Swedish settlers in about 1660, making it probably the oldest recognized building still standing in Philadelphia. From the time it came under the jurisdiction of Fairmount Park, its utilitarian use has been continued. Today, it houses park employees and is not open to the public[15]

In Fairmount Park's Wissahickon Valley, Rittenhouse Town is unique as a remnant of a self-contained industrial village whose origins date from the earliest European settlements in the area. William Rittenhouse and his son, Nicholas, leased twenty acres there in 1690, on which they built a paper mill. Before long, other cottage industries followed. For the next two hundred years, eight generations of the Rittenhouse family continued to live and work there along the Monoshone and Wissahickon Creeks. Among them was David Rittenhouse, one of the greatest American mathematicians and astronomers of the eighteenth century and the first director of the United States Mint.

After Fairmount Park acquired forty-five acres of Rittenhouse land in 1872–1873, the commission demolished the mill and other industrial buildings, but in response to a petition from the Rittenhouse family, left most of the domestic structures.[16] Seven of the early buildings survive. Since 1984, the Friends of Historic Rittenhouse Town have been in charge of maintenance and restoration of the site.[17]

Several additional examples of notable domestic architecture lie outside Fairmount Park's main component along the Schuylkill. The first of these, Bartram's House and Gardens, was built in about 1730 on the west

The Bartram house was built by John Bartram, America's first important botanist, in about 1730. On the Schuylkill's west bank several miles south of the waterworks, the property was opened to the public in 1893, making it one of the first house museums in America.

bank of the Schuylkill, but several miles south of the waterworks and villas later absorbed into Fairmount Park. John Bartram (1699–1777) became the first important botanist in America, whose accomplishments led to his appointment by King George III in 1765 as royal botanist for America. He is credited with having introduced more than two hundred native plant species. Linnaeus described him as "the greatest natural botanist in the world."[18]

Incorporating an earlier structure, Bartram built his house himself from stone he quarried, carving some of the schist to resemble Ionic Georgian columns and brackets. His scientific work was carried on by his son William (1739–1823), who established the first botanical garden in America on the property, selling live plants from the catalogs he and his brother produced. The property was purchased by the city in 1891 and has been operated by the John Bartram Association in cooperation with the Fairmount Park Commission since 1893, making it one of the first house museums in America.[19] A number of Bartram family possessions are on display in the house. The garden is open to visitors year-round. Guided tours of the house and garden are available from April through October.[20]

Bellaire has stood since circa 1720 near the mouth of the Schuylkill where it empties into the Delaware River. In the eighteenth century, it was one of many farms and country seats that lay below Philadelphia near the banks of

The Botanists: John and William Bartram

Like his friend Benjamin Franklin, the native Pennsylvanian John Bartram was almost entirely self-educated, immersing himself in learning about the natural world from an early age. After creating an extensive garden on the property where he built his house, he traveled widely to explore plant life and gather and classify specimens. After his visit to Lake Ontario and Canada in 1743, he wrote on the plant and animal life he found there. Two decades later, he explored the Florida habitat. His findings from both trips were published in London, where he had developed a clientele of wealthy buyers for the seeds and plants he shipped from his nursery. He was one of the first Linnaean botanists in North America. With Franklin, he cofounded the American Philosophical Society in 1743, and it was Franklin who promoted his case to be made a royal botanist to King George III. He introduced new species of kalmia, rhododendron, and magnolia to the public.

William Bartram (1739–1823), John's third son, succeeded his father as the leading botanist of his generation. Also an artist of natural history and an ornithologist, he continued his father's botanical explorations in the Carolinas, Georgia, and Florida, and published his findings. He operated the family garden and nursery with the help of a brother. They added greenhouses and increased the sale of live plants to clients throughout America and Europe. William named a species of tree discovered by his father in southeast Georgia to honor Benjamin Franklin, *Franklinia alatamaha*.

both rivers. What was originally much of the farm surrounding the house is now a municipal golf course in South Philadelphia's F. D. Roosevelt Park. It was originally the home of Samuel Preston (1665–1743), who served as provincial treasurer and as a trustee of William Penn's estate.[21] The rather simple two-and-a-half-story house is of brick and features a small second-story balcony with a projecting hood above it. Dormers rise from a steeply peaked roof. The house's central passage and large reception room retain their original fine wood paneling. It is open by appointment.[22]

Glen Foerd takes its name from the Foerderer family, who acquired this mid-nineteenth-century estate on the Delaware in 1893, then enlarged it in Georgian Revival style at the start of the twentieth century. It had begun a half century earlier as the home of the banker and philanthropist Charles Macalester, when it was an Italianate villa. The second owner, Robert Foerderer, was a wealthy manufacturer who also served in Congress and gave the name Torresdale to his estate's neighborhood at the northeastern edge of Philadelphia.

In the center of the house, Foerderer's architect carved out a dramatic space for a new two-story art gallery to house the paintings and other art objects the owner had acquired. The hall also holds a pipe organ and is capped by a domed skylight forty feet above the ground floor. Administered by the Glen Foerd Conservation Corporation, the estate is held in trust by Philadelphia Parks and Recreation. The property is now mostly used as a rental facility for weddings and other social events.[23]

Burholme, also known as the Ryerss Mansion and Library, in the Fox Chase section of Philadelphia, was constructed in about 1859 in an Italianate style. It was built on an eighty-five-acre estate as the summer retreat of Joseph Waln Ryerss, a wealthy trader and railroad baron, and the descendant of prominent early settlers in Pennsylvania. At his death a decade later, the property passed to his son, Robert, who expanded his father's collection of fine and decorative arts through his travels. At his death in 1894, Robert left a comfortable annuity to his recent bride (and longtime housekeeper), and provided that "my country seat . . . be used as a Public Park, the . . . house to be fitted up as a Public Library," calling for his art and antiquities to be displayed there as a museum.[24]

The property went to the city in 1905, and it was opened in 1910 as a museum and library. Today, the extensive art collection, containing many works from Asia, is housed in a wing added by the Fairmount Park Commission in about 1920.[25]

Burholme Mansion was built in about 1859, as the summer home of a wealthy trader, Joseph W. Ryerss. His son left the house and adjacent acreage to the city in 1894, as a library, museum, and public park. (Courtesy of Fairmount Park Historic Resource Archive)

James Logan, who served as William Penn's near surrogate after the founder returned to England, had Stenton built in the 1720s. It remained his home and that of five succeeding generations of his family until it was given to the city in 1908.

Stenton was built between 1723 and 1730 as the home for James Logan (1674–1751), one of Philadelphia's most important citizens in the first half of the eighteenth century. Logan first came to America as the twenty-five-year-old secretary to William Penn, eventually becoming the virtual surrogate of the founder. By the time he moved into Stenton, naming it for the village where his father had been born in England, Logan had served in every important capacity in the provincial government: mayor of Philadelphia, chief justice of the provincial Supreme Court, and then acting governor.

Logan acquired 511 acres four miles north of the city some nine years before he began building his house. The early Georgian residence is laid in Flemish bond brick with a steeply hipped roof pierced by dormers. Inside, a fully paneled parlor and other paneled rooms hold a number of pieces of furniture and other objects owned by the Logan family. While he was a resident there, Logan continued to add to his library which, at his death, was one of the finest on the continent. That library, bequeathed to the Library Company of Philadelphia, is preserved at its Locust Street headquarters to this day. Six generations of Logans occupied Stenton, which was

In the century following James Logan's death, much of his original estate of more than five hundred acres was sold off. In 1810, some forty-five acres half a mile to the southeast of the mansion was laid out as a racetrack, where it became the nation's first trotting course. When, in 1854, the Pennsylvania Assembly outlawed betting on horses in the Commonwealth, a group of citizens acted to preserve the track as a pleasure ground. In 1871, what by then was known as Hunting Park came under the jurisdiction of the Fairmount Park Commission as the first noncontiguous park under its authority. Hunting Park Avenue was constructed to connect this land to East Fairmount Park. Today, the park has grown to eighty-seven acres, where it serves as a neighborhood recreational center.

carefully protected from substantial change until it was deeded to the City of Philadelphia in 1908.[26]

Stenton is open for tours several days a week from April to December, and by appointment from January through March. It is operated by the National Society of Colonial Dames.[27]

This inventory of notable houses with connections to Fairmount Park only scratches the surface of historic residences in Philadelphia and its surrounding countryside. The dozens of others include the sumptuous former mansions of the rich and powerful, as well as the charmingly mundane and modest homes of farmers and laborers. Those that are most accessible to the public are generally those in best repair. Each has something to teach about the life of the nation.

Over time, the Fairmount Park Commission has come to have responsibility for so many buildings, from the grand to the very modest, that its ability to maintain them all has been a daunting—sometimes a losing—proposition, as in the destruction by fire of the Cliffs. In addition to the houses, there are buildings intended for public use that also must be maintained. The commission now points to the progress it has made recently in improving the management and conservation of its historic buildings, particularly since the creation in 1993 of the Fairmount Park Historic Preservation Trust, which has been responsible for restoring some of the properties described previously.

The trust is a public/private venture intended to be innovative in accomplishing historic preservation for the park system and other public buildings in Philadelphia. When created, it was authorized by City Council to attract and secure long-term leases for historic properties and oversee the restoration of historic buildings. According to Fairmount Park's website, "the Trust has flourished by returning over fifteen buildings to active use, improving stewardship at other sites, and raising interest in historic preservation in the Park."[28]

Life and Death of the Cliffs

The Cliffs was built as a summer retreat by the Quaker merchant Joshua Fisher (1707–1783) in 1753. It served the family into the 1830s. Benjamin Franklin's daughter, Sarah (Sally) Bache, frequented the Cliffs during the Revolution to help sew bandages and clothing for Continental soldiers. The property was bought for Fairmount Park in 1868, and housed park employees into the 1960s. It was unoccupied after 1970, when it was repeatedly vandalized. On the night of February 22, 1986, the house was destroyed by fire, probably arson. The shell remains near Thirty-Third and Oxford Streets. The loss of this house helped stimulate action toward the creation of the Fairmount Park Historic Preservation Trust, in 1993.

It is no doubt a romantic view of Fairmount Park's history to suppose that there was ever a time when it was an easy matter to pay for its work of preserving the public legacy as found in its historic structures. Even a cursory review of the commission's annual reports during its first decades is a reminder that finding the money for reasonable maintenance always has been a problem. Now, after a long era when Philadelphia's tax base has been in decline, and at a time when public goods are no longer viewed as the sole financial responsibility of taxpayer dollars, the work of the relatively new Historic Preservation Trust has become essential—and urgent.

It remains the case that Philadelphia's park system contains an unrivaled number of significant historic buildings, mostly domestic in origin. They are now, as they have been since Fairmount Park was created, both a unique blessing for the city and the greatest challenge for park officials.

Regattas on the Schuylkill
have been a popular activity
in Fairmount Park since the
mid-nineteenth century.
(Courtesy of Michael Murphy,
https://flickr.com/photos
/michaelwm25)

Boating and Playing in the Park

By 1821, Philadelphians were introduced to a new recreational feature above Fairmount. With the completion of the spillway dam on the Schuylkill, a long and placid pool of water was formed above it where there had been rushing currents. That created a nearly four-mile stretch of water that was ideal for rowing in summer and ice skating in winter. Both pastimes grew in popularity as the century progressed.

In 1836, ownership of the waterfront and the Lemon Hill estate on the eastern side passed to an absentee New York owner who ignored the property. With increased boating, many rowers formed clubs and began to build shacks along the estate's riverbank in which they could store their boats while giving them easy access to the water. Even after the city bought Lemon Hill in 1844, officials did nothing to regulate recreational activities on or beside the river. The city leased the property for the next dozen years to a brewer.[1] Although Lemon Hill became part of Fairmount Park in 1855 and was designated as public land, the city did not evict the mansion's tenants until after an outcry from concerned citizens the following year.

Meanwhile, regattas and rowing contests increasingly were held on the river. The first such event took place on April 14, 1835, between the Blue Devils and the Imps Barge clubs. The race reportedly "attracted several thousand persons to the banks of the river, some coming in carriages and some on foot, and they occupied every available place of lookout."[2] Many other races followed. With no oversight of these activities, they were often accompanied by heavy betting and race fixing. In response to growing concern and complaints from boaters and others, the rowing clubs themselves finally took on the task of self-regulation. In 1858, nine boat clubs formed

the Schuylkill Navy, "to promote amateurism on the Schuylkill River."[3] Thus was formed the first amateur governing body for an athletic association in America.

Soon after the Schuylkill Navy was formed, city officials finally took notice of the fact that boating clubs had built their facilities on land that was indisputably public. They first called for these structures to be dismantled. By then, however, many boaters had grown accustomed to the use of what they saw as their property on the shore, and the order was resisted. As a result, in 1860, the city eventually allowed the construction of three permanent boathouses and a skating club on the site.[4] The only structure built at the time that survives largely unchanged is No. 14, originally home to the Skating Club, now the Philadelphia Girls' Rowing Club, to the design of James C. Sidney in an Italianate style.[5]

With the creation of the Fairmount Park Commission in 1867, the park at last had vigorous proponents in the deliberations of city officials. But even though the commissioners were aggressive in acquiring new land for the park and establishing regulations for its use, they could not ignore the fact that after nearly half a century, Boathouse Row was a fact of life and a popular feature of the new park. In light of that, the commissioners created a subcommittee comprised of Frederic Graff Jr. and Strickland Kneass, chief engineer for the city of Philadelphia, for recommendations. These men proposed granting permission to the clubs "to erect larger and better houses than they had yet possessed," requiring them to be "architecturally neat and attractive." As a result, all the structures with the exception of those approved for construction several years earlier were razed and replaced, largely with stone structures in the Victorian Gothic style.[6] To this day, the houses remain private property on public land.

From the time of its founding to the present, the Schuylkill Navy has played an indispensable role in making the Schuylkill one of the centers of the rowing community in the United States. Today, rowers compete at all levels, from local clubs to high schools, colleges, and international competitions.

The Bachelor (shown) and Malta clubhouses are home to two of the long-established rowing teams in Philadelphia. (Photograph by Mark Garvin)

(Facing page)
A stretch of Boathouse
Row is seen from the
banks of the Schuylkill
behind Lloyd Hall.
(Courtesy of Ian Hartsoe)

The Malta clubhouse.
(Photograph by Mark
Garvin)

Major rowing events now include the Aberdeen Dad Vail, Stotesbury Cup, the Navy Day, the Independence Day, and the Head of the Schuylkill regattas.

In 1979, lights were installed on each of the boathouses to outline them at night. That installation, upgraded to computerized LED lights in 2005, brought their architecture to the attention of passersby, especially to those driving on Martin Luther King Drive and the Schuylkill Expressway. The enchanting effect immediately dispelled rumors that the city might want to destroy these aging landmarks. Boathouse Row was added to the National Register of Historic Places as a U.S. National Landmark in 1987. In the

Boating and Playing in the Park

Boathouse Row

Fairmount Park's Boathouse Row is a stretch of privately owned houses for boating clubs on the river, some of which date from the 1860s and 1870s. Beginning at the lower end of the park, today's Boathouse No. 1 is also the newest, Lloyd Hall (1998), the only public facility and community recreation center in the group; No. 2-3 houses the Fairmount Rowing Association (1904); No. 4, Pennsylvania Barge Club (1892); No. 5, Crescent Boat Club (1871); No. 6, Bachelors (1894); Nos. 7 and 8, University Barge Club (1871); No. 9, Malta Boat Club (1873); No. 10, Vesper Boat Club (1873); No. 11, College Boat Club (1874); No. 12, Penn AC Rowing Association (1878); No. 13, Undine Barge Club (1883); No. 14, Philadelphia Girls' Club (1860); and No. 15, Sedgley Club (1902), is built around the 1887 lighthouse Turtle Rock, operated by the club.

More recently, an additional boathouse was built well to the north of Boathouse Row proper. In 2002, St. Joseph's University and St. Joseph's Prep completed the first modern facility a short distance south of the Strawberry Mansion Bridge. In 2014, Temple University planned to renovate the nearby East Park Canoe House for its rowing teams.

The Schuylkill Navy

This first amateur athletic association in the United States was created in 1858 by nine boat clubs that had been formed over the previous twenty years to engage in rowing contests and regattas on the river. The Schuylkill Navy's purpose was to regulate those activities by restricting betting and preventing race fixing.

Many of America's premier oarsmen have emerged from the Schuylkill Navy. Since 1900, when a Vesper Boat Club eight won the gold medal at the Olympics, the Navy has produced many other Olympic oarsmen. Today, the navy oversees the rowing activities of all the amateur teams with boathouses on the Schuylkill in Fairmount Park (www.boathouse row.org and www.schuylkillnavy regatta.com).

In 1920, John B. Kelly was ruled ineligible to compete for the Diamond Sculls in Britain's Henley Regatta because he had "worked with his hands" as a former brick-layer. But later that same year, he was twice a gold medalist as an oarsman at the Olympics. After he became a highly successful businessman, he served both as president of the Fairmount Park Commission and as commodore of the Schuylkill Navy. His son, John B. Kelly Jr. also was a member of the Fairmount Park Commission and an at-large member of Philadelphia's City Council. He was elected president of the U.S. Olympic Committee in 1985, shortly before his death. His sister, Grace, achieved fame as an actress before her 1956 marriage to Prince Rainier of Monaco.

A statue of the elder John B. Kelly as a rower stands on the east bank of the Schuylkill near the finish line for races, where it is easily visible from Kelly Drive, which was renamed for John Kelly Jr. following his death in 1985. The younger Kellys grew up in the family home in the East Falls neighborhood of Philadelphia, close to East Fairmount Park and the regatta stand.

same decade, the address of Boathouse Row was changed from East River Drive to Kelly Drive, in honor of the late John B. Kelly Jr. (1927–1985), who, like his father, John B. Kelly Sr. (1889–1960), was one of Philadelphia's greatest oarsmen. The father won two gold medals at the 1920 Olympics. His son represented the United States in the Summer Olympics of 1948, 1952, 1956, and 1960.

Toward the end of the twentieth century, dragon boat racing also came to the Schuylkill course in Fairmount Park. This two thousand-year-old sport stems from a Chinese legend that tells of a man, Qu Yuan, who threw himself into a river on being sentenced to exile. Local fishermen attempted to save him by beating their drums wildly and splashing the water with their paddles to prevent water dragons and fish from eating him. Today's sport is said to be second in popularity only to soccer worldwide. The standard crew consists of twenty paddlers rowing in pairs, one drummer or caller at the bow facing the paddlers, and one steersman at the boat's aft.

Among the teams that call Philadelphia home are the Manayunk and Philadelphia Dragon Boat Racing Teams, the Schuylkill Dragons, the Philadelphia Flying Phoenix, and the Tsunami Dragons. The Philadelphia Dragon Boat Festival, held on the Schuylkill in early autumn, bills itself as the largest of its kind in the United States. Since 2007, the river also has been the site of a late spring Dragon Boat Regatta.[7]

Ice skating was a novelty in the United States when it first became possible, starting in the 1820s, to enjoy the sport during the brief wintertime period when the Schuylkill froze solidly above the dam. The Skater's Club of the City and County of Philadelphia was founded in 1849, as the first skating club in America. In its new clubhouse on Boathouse Row, it became the Philadelphia Skating Club and Humane Society in 1861 when the latter group—founded in 1770 to rescue people from drowning—ceased to function as an independent body. The club was an all-male preserve when ice skating was largely a male pastime. But by the 1860s, women were beginning to try the sport. It quickly became so much the rage for both sexes that meadows and other empty lots were flooded to create skating rinks outside Fairmount Park.[8] These facilities produced more-dependable ice than was possible by relying on nature to freeze the Schuylkill. As a result, they largely displaced skating on either of Philadelphia's rivers after the Civil War, although a postcard from about 1900 shows skaters still enjoying the ice on the Schuylkill.[9]

In the first half of the nineteenth century, urban parks in America were not generally viewed as places for active recreation. They were meant to allow for edifying and uplifting escapes from the crowded conditions of the city, where citizens might come to contemplate nature, either on foot, horseback, or in a carriage.[10] It was this kind of pleasure that visitors to the Fairmount Water Works sought in the first decades of its operation. But by midcentury, parks were becoming more active places of recreation. Vigorous sports such as rowing, cricket, and baseball—engaged in only by males—became part of the park experience. Park activities went from the passive to the unstructured, to use the terminology of a late twentieth-century commentator, since almost all of this activity was meant to be organized by family and church groups, without official supervision:

> Children were expected to romp, adults to row, ride horseback, and walk, men and boys to play vigorously at sport. The spectators at these picturesque events were expected to be mentally alert in their appreciation of them. Their pleasures were of a different order from those of, say, the modern stadium spectator.[11]

Here is the way in which the Fairmount Park commissioners proposed to attend to the recreational needs of Philadelphians in 1870:

> As soon as favorable weather will permit, a playground for children and a parade-ground for the military will be provided. . . . In the former the inducements for healthful exercise and harmless pastime will blend amusement with profit for the young; . . . suitable places for

cricket and base-ball, and other athletic exercise will be set apart, and croquet grounds will not be overlooked. Bridle paths for horsemen will soon be opened, and, in connection with these, turfy enclosures will be appropriated for equestrian exercises.[12]

All of this came to pass in Fairmount Park during the last decades of the nineteenth century. All but perhaps the croquet and parade grounds for the military remain today, while many more kinds of recreational facilities have joined them.

Both healthful exercise and harmless pastime for the young were combined in one popular activity in the 1870s. On "Nutting Day" each autumn, children were invited into the park to collect walnuts and hazelnuts. The event typically combined work with play in an era when children were expected to contribute to the economic life of the family, even while they were being entertained. As the commissioners reported with satisfaction in 1871, "besides the innumerable throngs which came and went at all hours, not less than thirty thousand persons spent the entire day in wandering through its [the park's] spacious confines."[13]

For a half century starting at the end of the Civil War, carousels drew families with children into the park. When these merry-go-rounds were at the height of their appeal, visitors could choose among five locations: Strawberry Mansion, Parkside, Lemon Hill, and Boathouse Row, in addition to one in Hunting Park. All were built by the Dentzel Company, established in Philadelphia in 1860, the first carousel factory in the United States. A German immigrant, Gustav Dentzel (1844–1909) also created a carousel for the 1876 Centennial Exposition. After decades of popular use, visits to those in the park gradually declined. Over time, all the Fairmount Park carousels were removed from service, with none remaining by 1920.

But one of Dentzel's finest, the carousel that had entertained children at Woodside Park for decades, was returned to Fairmount Park in the first decade of the twenty-first century. To house it, a nine thousand-square-foot glass pavilion was added to the east side of Memorial Hall when the Please Touch Museum opened its doors there in 2008. After forty years in storage, it is now a highlight of the children's museum.

Even though Nutting Day has ceased to be, and the number of carousels is now reduced, play facilities for children have long been a mainstay of the park. In 1870, an additional piazza was built on the west front of Sweetbriar, and some of its rooms became a restaurant for children. Grounds in the rear were enclosed as a playground, and the whole property was leased to one

Henry Eggeling, "by whom swings, carrousels and other appliances for children's sports were provided."[14]

From 1899, when it first opened in East Fairmount Park, the Smith Memorial Playground and Playhouse has been the most prominent children's facility. Funded by a trust from Richard and Sarah Smith in memory of their son, the impressive building with its neoclassic portico—no doubt designed to harmonize with nearby park villas—was a product of the period's American Playground Movement. Its proponents were largely social workers and other reformers who urged local governments to construct playgrounds for the safe, supervised play of young children as a way of furthering their mental, moral, and physical development.[15] The Smith Playground is open free of charge and serves children twelve years old and younger.

For a century, one favorite attraction has been the giant enclosed wooden slide. Today, preschool children are entertained in "Smithville," a street with pedal push cars and tricycles, along with game rooms and outdoor activities. In 2004, after more than a century when the facility was maintained entirely

The carousel that was long a popular feature at Woodside Park was given a new home in a pavilion added to Memorial Hall when that became the home of the Please Touch Museum in 2008.

Boating and Playing in the Park

with funds from the beneficiaries' trust, a nonprofit corporation was formed to permit restoration, maintenance, and expansion of the playground and playhouse. After a successful capital campaign, the main building was fully renovated by 2009.

Baseball became America's national pastime starting in the mid-nineteenth century. Sandlot games have been a feature of Fairmount Park ever since. Today, its premier baseball facility is in Franklin Delano Roosevelt Park in South Philadelphia. Named for the champion Phillies outfielder Richie Ashburn (1927–1997), the first of Ashburn Fields' two diamonds is regarded as one of the finest in the city; regulation size, it is designed for collegiate play and championship games. Its smaller twin is reserved for Little League contests. Players can apply for one-time, seasonal, or tournament use in these and all other athletic fields within the park system.

Although cricket does not play as important a role as it once did in the recreational lives of especially upper-class Philadelphians, it lives on in Fairmount Park among a host of other locations for organized sports, including rugby, soccer, polo, and T-ball fields. Lloyd Hall on Boathouse Row is the site for local basketball leagues in its indoor court. Pennypack Park in the northeast section of the city contains eight soccer and four softball fields within its 150 acres. Belmont Grove in the west park is a gated recreational area with a softball field, a volleyball court, and two horseshoe pits, along with two picnic pavilions—both with water and electrical hookups—and eight picnic tables. Sports equipment is available there for rent. Mander Recreation Center at Diamond Street at the east park boundary, and the Parkside/Evans Recreation Center on the park's western edge near Fifty-Second Street include a variety of sports and play facilities, as well as meeting rooms for community groups. The public has access to swimming pools at Mander and next to Memorial Hall.

There are tennis courts at a number of sites throughout the park system. The crown jewel of its golf courses is the "Olde Course" at Cobbs Creek. Opened in 1916, it is adjacent to the newer Karakung links. The FDR Golf Course in Roosevelt Park was established in 1940 on what had been the farmland of the eighteenth-century Bellaire Mansion, now maintained by Fairmount Park. Three additional park-based golf clubs are Juniata in Tacony Creek Park, John F. Byrne

A postcard depicts the pergola in League Island Park—Franklin D. Roosevelt Park today—when this South Philadelphia site was home to the nation's sesquicentennial celebration in 1926. (Courtesy of Steve Lynch)

Franklin Delano Roosevelt Park

This park near the southern boundary of Philadelphia was created in 1914 as League Island Park on land that had been crisscrossed by swamps and other channels near the mouth of the Schuylkill. Its ponds and lagoons are remnants of the area's tidal marsh and channel system. The park's original design by the Olmsted Brothers firm is still visible in the 348-acre site to the west of Broad Street. The city's sports complex lies just across that street to the east. To the south beyond the ship basin is the Navy Yard. The park was renamed in honor of the 32nd president after his death in 1945.

In addition to the Richie Ashburn Fields on the south side, more baseball and softball facilities, as well as tennis courts, are on the north. A perimeter roadway encircles the park for bicycling. The FDR Golf Course was created as a public works project in 1940. The American Swedish Historical Museum, created for the sesquicentennial of 1926, presents the contributions of Swedish settlers to North America. In the lower Delaware Valley, the Swedish presence predates the arrival of William Penn by some three decades.

in the Torresdale section of the city, and Walnut Lane in the Wissahickon Valley. On the site of the long-destroyed Sedgley Mansion north of Lemon Hill is a disc golf course, the first on the east coast. Boccie courts are available both at Marconi Plaza in South Philadelphia and at Vine and Daggett Streets at Cobbs Creek Park. Philadelphia's Parks and Recreation Department now claims to provide 368 athletic fields and outdoor courts scattered throughout its system of parks.[16]

In addition to bridle paths, "turfy enclosures" for the exercise of horses have been a feature of Fairmount Park throughout most of its history. On Martin Luther King Drive, Belmont Stable was constructed by the Works Progress Administration in 1936, as headquarters for the Park Guard. After the Guard was merged with the Philadelphia Police Department in 1971, Belmont became a riding and teaching stable open to the public. The Chamounix Equestrian Center rents horses to the public and also sponsors the acclaimed Work to Ride program for low-income, inner-city children.

In the Wissahickon, the Northwestern Stables at the northern end of Forbidden Drive is a boarding and teaching facility. Nearby, on the five-and-a-half-acre Monastery complex, the Boarders and Stewards of the Monastery (BSM), a nonprofit group, now leases the property with the aim of restoring it, "and to preserve the long tradition of horseback riding in the Wissahickon Valley."[17] In addition to the property's 1747 mansion are a twenty-six-horse stable, caretaker's cottage, and separate four-horse stable. Courtesy Stables offer riding lessons and boarding at the edge of the Wissahickon. At Pennypack Park are the Solly Stables and Pegasus Riding Academy, which offers a therapeutic riding program for people with disabilities.

An 1899 report from the captain of the Park Guard brought the first report on the impact of a new invention on the peace of the park:

> The automobile has not yet entered the Park in sufficient numbers to warrant an expression of opinion as to their safety to the public. In only one instance do I find the machine was not stopped when it frightened horses. In this case the occupants went rapidly away, before the Guard reached the place. It seems to me a man versed in mechanics will have to be stationed in each District of the Park to afford relief when the machine breaks down. The standing of these machines on the drives is more calculated to frighten horses than when they are moving.[18]

By the next year, the Chamounix Speedway was proposed—for horses, not automobiles. Approved by the commission in June 1901, the track was created for "a large number of driving people [who] are anxious to speed their horses in the Park at a greater speed than seven miles an hour."[19] The facility included a racing area, return drive, and observation area diagonally across Belmont Plateau along what is now Chamounix Drive. But with the advance of the new motorized technology, the Chamounix Speedway was soon adapted for cars, and in 1908, the Quaker City Motor Club held its first annual race there. In 1909, the club looked forward to a second contest "of about 20 of the highest grade automobiles, and nearly all of the same power and speed which assures us a great race and [one that] should be viewed by nearly a million people."[20]

Yet, within another few years, the increased number and speed of automobiles challenged the tranquility of the park even while their availability to the masses provided greater access than ever before. Eventually, speedways were ended as recreational outlets in the park. Those that remained did so as fast-moving public roadways and, after 1952 in the case of the Schuylkill Expressway, by obliterating any experience of the park for millions of drivers while they speed through it (Chapter 13).

By the twenty-first century, Philadelphia's parks offered many additional opportunities that, broadly speaking, fell under the heading of recreation. Among them were weekly juggling events, as well as folk dancing in summer near the Philadelphia Museum of Art. Yoga, gymnastics, volleyball, and the less strenuous activity of watercolor painting also were available at a number of sites in the park.

129:—East River Drive, Fairmount Park, Philadelphia, Pa.

This early twentieth-century postcard depicts a lone automobile passing through Promontory Rock's tunnel while pedestrians stroll beneath an arch of the Girard Avenue Bridge. (Courtesy of Steve Lynch)

Boating and Playing in the Park

In recent decades, young people here and abroad have embraced the vigorous sport of skateboarding. For a time, that activity grew controversial in Philadelphia after LOVE Park—formally, the John F. Kennedy Plaza—at the eastern end of the Benjamin Franklin Parkway became its hugely popular site. Praised by many skaters as perhaps the world's greatest such venue thanks to its combination of hard surfaces and changes in levels, city officials eventually responded to complaints from more passive users of the park and, citing damage to the park's hard surfaces, banned skating activity there. It seemed a classic example of a generational conflict, in which skateboarding aficionados were viewed by their elders as an undesirable element on public property.

But in 2003, Mayor John L. Street offered to set aside a two-and-a-half-acre site near the Philadelphia Museum of Art for a new skateboard park. The catch in the offer was that supporters had to raise the funds, $4.5 million, for the park to become reality. Remarkably, they did so. An architect was hired and produced a new park that received enthusiastic plaudits when it opened in May 2013. Praised both for its aesthetic appeal and the way it accommodated diverse users of the new space, it carefully replicated all the features that had made skateboarders and their fans love LOVE Park. In the words of the architecture critic of the *Philadelphia Inquirer*: "It is a measure of how far our ideas about urban space have evolved that the deluxe skate park . . . has been designed in an ecumenical spirit that welcomes skateboarders and passive users alike."[21]

The acceptance of skateboarding as a legitimate, even desirable activity for Fairmount Park is simply the latest indication of how generational changes in recreational interests and lifestyles come to be reflected in the life of the city's parks. Such changes have been evident throughout this survey of recreational activities since Fairmount Park was created. But generational shifts are by no means the only cause of the rise and fall in popularity of various recreational activities. Underlying those transformations is increased democratization of American society during the past two centuries, combined with demographic change. Together, those forces determine how Philadelphia's parks are perceived and used from one era to another.

When Fairmount Park was coming into being in the 1850s, white working-class Philadelphians sometimes voiced skepticism—nonwhites scarcely had a voice at all—that the park was meant for them. They saw that the members of the Fairmount Park Commission were drawn from the city's business and professional elite, and had been given sweeping power to create a pleasure garden where presumably they and those of their own class might

stroll and ride. Some of the land they took had held small farms and manu-factures, along with taverns popular with workers that the commission pro-ceeded to abolish (Chapter 8).

Yet leading advocates of urban parks, men such as Andrew Jackson Dowling and Frederick Law Olmsted, preached that parks could "civilize" the lower orders of society.[22] Philadelphia's leaders no doubt discerned that as an argument for the kind of social engineering they approved; they de-fended themselves from charges of elitism by insisting from the beginning that the park they were creating welcomed all (well-behaved) comers. The commissioners' self-congratulatory insistence on that point is clear in their second annual report:

While imposing restraints designed only to prevent unwarranted li-cense, the Commissioners have assiduously sought to furnish to the

In 2013, Paine's Park was opened behind a berm beside the Benjamin Franklin Parkway to provide a skateboarding facility authorized by the city.

Boating and Playing in the Park

masses of the people every facility of access to, and recreation within, the splendid domain which owes its existence to their liberality, and which is sacredly set apart that they, and the masses of the people who are to succeed them, may find in it a blessing and a solace forever.[23]

The report then lists the arrangements the commission has made for the general public to travel into and about the park, by steamboat, rowboat, carriages, and railroads.

Once the public grew to expect that parks might serve as places for more active recreation than the appreciation of nature, the authorities encouraged a variety of sports. The upper classes might prefer sculling, riding, and cricket, while other park goers would choose to spend a few hours at horseshoes, baseball, or paddling a rented rowboat. The kind of rowing that began on the Schuylkill in the 1830s was in general a rich man's sport. That may help account for the somewhat laissez-faire attitude the early park commissioners took toward the construction of rowers' clubs on parkland, and, conversely, on those clubs' resistance to submitting to the commission. But greater democratization of rowing has clearly taken place during the past century, which includes opening it to women and minorities.

By the early twentieth century, reform movements in America emphasized the need for more structured recreation, which continued the playground movement for children and encouraged recreation centers for all. Yet these public facilities especially served the general public and not the elite, who increasingly had access to private recreational venues.[24]

Meanwhile, during the second half of the twentieth century, in Philadelphia as in many other American cities, the neighborhoods surrounding its most prominent parks—much of Fairmount along the Schuylkill, Cobbs Creek, and Hunting Park, in particular—were being abandoned by the middle classes and given over to some of the city's poorest citizens, especially African Americans. White flight from the city also meant a decline in the city's tax base and, therefore, in the tax revenues needed to support the parks. Increasingly, the parks were left as somewhat forlorn and bedraggled open spaces where those without alternatives were left to whatever forms of recreation they could muster.

Now came a shift in the public's view of city parks that directly opposed the charge of elitism made more than a century before. To many middle-class citizens, large swaths of the parks had become dangerous urban jungles to be avoided. Only Boathouse Row and a few other safe and attractive islands, such as the Philadelphia Zoo and Robin Hood Dell, still drew citizens from the wider population into portions of Fairmount Park. Some smaller public spaces, such as Hunting Park, at times seemed to be largely given over to a semicriminal underclass. In this context, the badly underfunded Recreation Department and Fairmount Park Commission were hard pressed to provide minimal services and upkeep.

We explore these issues and efforts to address them in Chapters 17 and 18. First, however, there are further pieces in the history of rest and recreation in Philadelphia's parks to be considered.

Forbidden Drive is a gravel route that runs for several miles along the west bank of the Wissahickon Creek through Fairmount Park. Closed to automotive traffic, it is the only trail through the valley open to pedestrians and bicyclists without permits. (Photograph by Mark Garvin)

Rest and Recreation
Eat, Walk, Hike, Run, and Cycle

From the time the waterworks were built at the foot of Fairmount, their beautiful grounds were viewed by the public as a wonderful place for strolling, which was the standard recreational pastime in that era. For decades, from about 1815 when the great pumps first went into operation until at least the time of the Civil War, crowds of visitors came, especially on Sundays, to marvel at the machinery and the constant splash of waters, to wander through the South Garden, and then to climb the steep paths that led up to the reservoirs at the top. Some would have crossed to the site from the Schuylkill's west bank across the Upper Ferry Bridge, the longest single-span wooden bridge yet built in the United States, whose eastern foot was just below the waterworks. Others might have come up from center city by stage or steamboat.

Since 1868, when the Wissahickon Valley was acquired for Fairmount Park, that narrow ravine has been a more rugged favorite of walkers and hikers who sought release from the city. Today, the dramatic stretch of Wissahickon Creek in Fairmount Park reaches from the border of Montgomery County nearly seven miles south to its mouth at the Schuylkill, its gorge encompassing fourteen hundred acres of parkland. It is said to be the first piece of publicly owned land in the United States to be preserved mainly because of its scenic attributes. Yet, the pristine views that confront the visitor today are never of a primeval landscape; if they seem to be, it is largely because of work undertaken by the Fairmount Park Commission late in the nineteenth century.[1]

From the beginning, because of its obligation to protect the city's water supply, the commission was determined to eliminate the industrial life of

The Wissahickon Valley of Fairmount Park is attractive in all seasons.

the Wissahickon. But while that effort also would help re-create a bucolic wilderness, the question of what kind of recreation should be allowed there was a controversial matter. The first issue was what to do about the many inns that already existed throughout the valley. Virtually all of them served catfish and waffles, and alcohol was plentiful. Some, like the Maple Spring Hotel, drew genteel customers. Wissahickon Hall at the base of Gypsy Lane also attracted well-to-do residents from the time it opened in about 1849.[2]

But the working-class nature of the industrial valley meant that other establishments catered to a rougher clientele. Where carousing sometimes turned to brawling, a number of inns had long been notorious for their patrons' drunken and disorderly conduct. That with the worst reputation, Old Log Cabin, had been established by a member of the Rittenhouse family in about 1840 as a meeting place for local Whigs. During the presidential campaign that year, rival Democrats attacked the building, drove out the supporters of William Henry Harrison, and destroyed the interior. But the Whigs regrouped at a Germantown tavern, counterattacked, and reoccupied their building. Soon after, they enlarged it, and the cabin continued to attract boisterous patrons.[3] Its popularity was such that the New Log Cabin was built across the stream from the original.

Almost the first order of business for the commission, once the Wissahickon was added to Fairmount Park, was to ban the consumption of alcohol throughout the park. That may have prompted the construction in 1869, the year following that ban, of the New Indian Rock Hotel just outside the commission's jurisdiction, and not far from the earlier Old Indian Rock Hotel, which was the northernmost tavern inside the park. The commission's ban on alcohol on park grounds was a serious blow to virtually all the inns along the creek. Some succumbed and were eventually demolished in large part because of this restriction.

Only one of the public houses that once lined the waterway remains as such in the Wissahickon. Valley Green Inn has been serving food and drink to guests since the 1850s. It opened to the public at the same time the Wissahickon Turnpike (today's Lincoln Drive) was being completed beside the creek, allowing recreational visitors to explore the valley for the first time. Once the turnpike, creek, and valley were acquired by Fairmount Park, the commissioners purchased Valley Green Inn (then called the Valley Green Hotel) in 1873.[4]

But unlike the others, Valley Green was saved from demolition early in the twentieth century by the support of private groups, who funded its

Wissahickon Hall faces its namesake waterway on Lincoln Drive. It is one of only two nineteenth-century taverns that survive in Fairmount Park.

Valley Green Inn continues to serve as a restaurant for visitors to the Wissahickon Valley, as it has since the 1850s. It is accessible by motor vehicles at about the midpoint of Forbidden Drive.

"restoration," which in fact amounted to recasting this mid-Victorian road-house in the Colonial Revival style. The makeover was so deceptive that the inn's menu in the 1960s claimed that Washington and Lafayette had dined there at the time of the American Revolution—some three-quarters of a century before the inn was built.[5] The business itself has long been privately operated, which permits the serving of alcohol again.

The commissioners' ban on alcohol was in keeping with the strict Protestant traditions of the nation's establishment, and fully in harmony with the Victorian-era view that public parks should be places of moral uplift. Thus the ban generally appealed to the wealthy residents of Northwest Philadelphia, the neighbors of the Wissahickon. Like the commission's determination to demolish the mills along the creek, this policy supported their inclination to regard this valley as their own preserve. In this way, nature would be returned to the city for their genteel amusements, which were mainly riding, walking, and picnicking.

That this goal largely triumphed may at first have been seen as a victory for Philadelphia's upper classes. But it had the serendipitous effect of preserving a wild and pristine stretch of the landscape for what at the time would have been the "unimagined recreational activities" of the more democratized public of today.[6] If these activities are no longer refined in the Victorian sense, they are made at least to respect the natural landscape. Most remarkably, this place that has been restored to approximate its primeval wilderness also lies within the limits of one of the continent's great cities.

Valley Green Inn remains, as it has long been, a place of refreshment for walkers, riders, and cyclists on Forbidden Drive, a name that derives from the 1920s when automobiles were first banned from the road (travelers may come to the inn by car, which must be parked there). It is a gravel route along the creek's west bank, and the only trail in the valley that is open to bicyclists and equestrians without a permit. A favorite of walkers and joggers, the road is accessible at each end of the park as well as at Valley Green, which sits at approximately the halfway point.

A ruder footpath also follows the creek along its east bank. From there, as well as from Forbidden Drive, several trails climb up the valley's slopes to others that run along the crests. Many are marked with blazes to indicate whether they are approved for hiking only, or also for mountain bikers (with permits). Along the seven-mile stretch of the Wissahickon that lies within Fairmount Park, explorers may find some twenty or more landmarks, from the Andorra Natural Area at the northern border to the hundred steps that lead to Roxborough near the mouth of the creek on the south.

A bridge spans
Wissahickon Creek
at Valley Green.

Forbidden Drive's name dates from the 1920s, when autos were first banned from this road beside Wissahickon Creek. (Photograph by Mark Garvin)

(*Facing page*)
Devil's Pool is a popular, if unsafe, swimming hole where Cresheim Creek flows into the Wissahickon. (Photograph by Mark Garvin)

The Andorra Natural Area at Northwestern Avenue is an interpretive facility providing year-round programs on the social and natural history of the Wissahickon Valley. Next door, the Wissahickon Environmental Center presents exhibits, native animals, and self-guiding materials that include detailed maps of its five miles of trails, where no bicycles are permitted.

In the northern stretch of the park, Indian Rock is a destination for hikers along the east bank of the creek near the Rex Avenue Bridge. The fifteen-foot marble sculpture of a native Lenape warrior, *Tedyuscung*, is a tribute to the Indians who roamed the Wissahickon before the arrival of Europeans. Nearly half a mile further up the creek is a covered bridge, which Fairmount Park advertises as the only one of its kind in a major American city.

More than a mile to the south is Devil's Pool, one of the most beloved features of the Wissahickon. It is reached by crossing the waterway at Valley Green, then following the footpath downstream to the mouth of Cresheim Creek. There, a basin is surrounded by rocky outcroppings just before the waters flow into the Wissahickon. Devil's Pool has long been a popular swimming hole in spite of its unsafe levels of pollutants.

Rest and Recreation: Eat, Walk, Hike, Run, and Cycle

Cobbs Creek Park

The creek from which this park takes its name runs along much of the western and southwestern boundary of Philadelphia. The park was created early in the twentieth century to restore and protect the waterway on its five-mile course through the city, while adding land along its banks to the Fairmount Park system. Cobbs Creek is the site of the first water mill in North America, which was built in 1645 on land that was then part of the colony of New Sweden. With the growth of the Philadelphia region in the nineteenth century, a number of tributary streams here, as elsewhere, were drained or converted to sewers.

An extension of the park north of Lansdowne Avenue, Morris Park, encompasses a Cobbs Creek tributary, Indian Creek. Two golf courses are among the many recreational facilities available today. Early in the twenty-first century, a number of play areas were renovated, and hard-surfaced courts were replaced with permeable surfaces to facilitate groundwater runoff.

Starting in 1991, the Fairmount Park Commission invited the surrounding community to direct what to do with an abandoned stable at Sixty-Third and Catharine Streets. The result was the creation of the Cobbs Creek Environmental Education Center, which now educates people with diverse backgrounds from the neighborhood and beyond to understand and appreciate environmental issues.

Pennypack Park

This nearly 1,600-acre park cuts through Philadelphia's northeast section from its Montgomery County border, following Pennypack Creek on its course to the Delaware River. Its varied landscape of woodlands, meadows, and wetlands is home to a scattered herd of deer. The oldest stone bridge still in use in the United States, dating from 1697, crosses the stream at Frankford Avenue. The Verree House near the park's northwestern limit was the site of a raid by British forces during the Revolutionary War.

In addition to a number of playgrounds, bridle paths, and hiking and bicycle trails, the park is home to a dedicated bird sanctuary. John James Audubon and Alexander Wilson, recognized as the fathers of American ornithology, both worked along the creek. Their contributions are noted in exhibits at the Pennypack Environmental Center, which also contains a reference library, an outdoor amphitheater, and campfire and picnic areas.

Tacony Creek Park

Tacony Creek Park follows its namesake waterway from the city limits at Cheltenham Avenue along the southern edge of Philadelphia's northeast section. The creek's name changes to Frankford Creek where it meanders across the Juniata Park Golf Course, then leaves the park and continues to the Delaware at Bridesburg.

The creek has long been badly polluted. The goal of a watershed partnership launched by Philadelphia's Water Department in 2000 was to improve the water quality to the point that it would again be safe for fishing and swimming. In spring 2013, the Recreation Department opened a newly paved Tacony Creek Trail, which runs a little more than a mile from Roosevelt Boulevard, meandering through forest and meadows, with access to it from four neighborhood gateways. Open to cyclists and runners, a tunnel was planned under Roosevelt Boulevard to connect north and south sections of the trail and park.

Fingerspan is a finger-shaped pedestrian bridge spanning a crevice overlooking the Wissahickon. (Photograph by Mark Garvin)

A quarter mile downstream from there, a 1987 bridge across a crevice in the rock is also a piece of sculpture. *Fingerspan*, like its sculptural partners to the north and south, is only accessible on foot by avid hikers. The work is an 18,000-pound steel construction in the shape of a slightly curved human finger, through which the walker passes to go from one outcropping to the other. The artist, Jody Pinto, designed the work so that visitors may view the spectacular ravine of the Wissahickon through its wire-meshed side while they pass beneath the solid form of the "finger" joints themselves.[7]

Nearly a mile downstream, past the Monastery House and Stables, is another favorite outlook. Mom Rinker's Rock is named for the mythical spy of the revolutionary era, Molly Rinker. It rises just to the north of the Walnut Lane Bridge on the eastern side of the park, close to the *Toleration* statue. That single word is carved into the base of the marble statue of a Quaker, clearly the founder, William Penn, which was erected here in 1883. It had been bought by John Welsh—one of the first Fairmount Park commissioners and, later, a U.S. minister to the Court of St. James—at the close of the Centennial Exposition, where it had been exhibited.[8] Continuing downstream past Rittenhouse Town, Lover's Leap is predictably a site on a precipice overlooking the gorge of the Wissahickon. Hikers can reach it from the Ridge Avenue entrance to the main path, and then by following the west bank to Hermit's Lane Bridge.

The generations of Philadelphians who first came to stroll in the garden below the Fairmount Water Works would no doubt be astonished at the far more vigorous pedestrian exercise of our generation. Instead of parasols and walking sticks, spandex and Bluetooth headsets adorn the bodies of many of those on foot in the park today. Joggers and runners have long made use of the footpaths along Forbidden, Kelly, and Martin Luther King Drives, as well as other thoroughfares in the park. Today, there are even more expansive opportunities for the energetic. New trails and footpaths are growing in all directions about the city.

Starting in the year 2000, a new strip of parkland was instantly popular with walkers and runners. The Schuylkill Banks Park, reserved for pedestrians and cyclists only, extends the park along the east bank of the Schuylkill from the foot of Fairmount below the waterworks and south into center city as far as South Street, the original southern boundary of Philadelphia as it was laid out in the 1680s. What had been a rather bleak riverbank in the heart of the city was landscaped and planted on each side of an asphalt path, with periodic access onto city streets both at ground level and via staircases up to the Market, Chestnut, and South Street Bridges. In 2012, a pedestrian bridge was completed at Spruce and Twenty-Fifth Streets to allow safe access from park to riverbank over the railroad tracks that lay between. Two years later came the Schuylkill Banks Boardwalk. Supported by caissons drilled into the riverbed between Locust and South Streets, it forms a curvaceous "walkway on the water," extending for two thousand feet, far enough away from the Schuylkill's east bank and close enough to the water to afford pedestrians and bicyclists unrivaled views of the center city skyline.[9]

The completed trail is the first step in a more ambitious plan, the next stage of which is to make this pedestrian-friendly extension of the park stretch across the river and downstream to Bartram's Garden, some four miles south of Fairmount. Work is proceeding in detached segments. In 2012, a new half-mile strip, the Gray's Ferry Crescent Park, was completed on the east side of the river. This eleven-acre tract was made inviting to walkers, bicyclers, fishermen, and wildlife enthusiasts at a cost of $2.85 million, funded by city and state agencies as well as private donors.[10] Next came a new boardwalk linking Locust Street to South Street, with a connector to the South Street Bridge, allowing pedestrians and cyclists to cross to the west bank. Those continuing downriver to the Thirty-Fourth Street Bridge could then cross back to the east bank and connect to Gray's Ferry Crescent. In 2015, work began on "Bartram's Mile on the west bank, which will start at Bartram's Garden and meander north to about Forty-Eights Street.[11]

(*Facing page*) Schuylkill Banks Park provided a walking trail and greenway along the east bank of the river through center city in 2000. For part of the distance, a boardwalk extends over the water. (Photograph by Mark Garvin)

Rest and Recreation: Eat, Walk, Hike, Run, and Cycle

The Schuylkill River Development Corporation, working in cooperation with public and private partners, is the main force behind this plan to link the Centennial District in Fairmount Park with the East Coast Greenway, Schuylkill Banks, and Bartram's Garden. The long-range goal is to create a greensward of parkland along both sides of the Schuylkill all the way from Fairmount Park to Fort Mifflin and the river's mouth at the Delaware. That is an additional five miles from Bartram's Garden, and some ten miles below the centennial grounds at Fairmount. The hope of city planners is that the creation of more parkland along the lower Schuylkill will draw new businesses to a region in Philadelphia that, once part of its industrial heart, is now desperately in need of revitalization.[12]

A promising start was reported in mid-2012. Children's Hospital of Philadelphia was completing an ambitious master plan to expand its campus on

The Delaware riverbank beside the monument to Christopher Columbus was made into a family park in the summer of 2014.

Rest and Recreation: Eat, Walk, Hike, Run, and Cycle

the west side of the Schuylkill across to the river's east bank to acreage below South Street. When realized, it would bring a dense cluster of medical research buildings, green parks, and walkways, as well as retail and service amenities to a neglected neighborhood. The hospital would deed to the city a sixty-foot-wide strip of river frontage running for seven hundred feet along the length of the property.[13] That would permit a bike path to connect to the Schuylkill River Trail, a recreational facility that extends far beyond Philadelphia and its parks. Once completed, the trail will run for nearly 130 miles along the river's course to a point close to its source near Pottsville, Pennsylvania. Sections of this hiking/walking trail are now open to the public; others await completion.

Other projects are connected to the East Coast Greenway, the largest of all of the green trail efforts on the Eastern Seaboard. It is intended to connect nearly three thousand miles of walkable green space from Canada to Key West, Florida. One piece of that connection through Philadelphia was well under way by 2014, the Fifty-Eighth Street Greenway. The Pennsylvania Environmental Council spearheaded the design of segments that will continue the East Coast Greenway through the city. It will connect the Cobbs Creek Park trail beside the Cobbs Creek Parkway starting at Fifty-Ninth Street in Southwest Philadelphia before turning north on Chester Avenue to Fifty-Eighth Street. It will proceed along that street to the southeast to Elmwood Avenue, from which it will connect to the trail at Bartram Garden and then to the Schuylkill.[14]

Meanwhile, the city was moving forward with its greenway plan for Spring Garden Street. When completed, it will also connect that important cross-town avenue to green trails on the Delaware, the Schuylkill, and thus the expanding network of the East Coast Greenway. A similar plan was advancing for Washington Avenue. Some viewed the latter as replacing South Street as the informal southern boundary of center city, just as Spring Garden was becoming the new northern edge of that district as it moved beyond Vine Street.

As proposed early in 2013, Eakins Oval at the base of the Benjamin Franklin Parkway also would be revitalized as the crucial link between the two sets of trails in the East Coast Greenway along both rivers.[15] For more on all these plans for additional and renovated parkland, see Chapter 17. For a comprehensive listing of all Philadelphia's parks, squares, and playgrounds, see the appendix.

The Deer House, one of the buildings of the Philadelphia Zoo that dates from its opening in 1874, was designed by a leading architect of the period, George Hewitt. In 1985, it was repurposed as the Widener Memorial Tree House by one of the most renowned architectural firms of that era, Venturi, Rauch, and Scott Brown. (Photograph by Mark Garvin)

The Philadelphia Zoo

In the 1840s, that decade when the City of Philadelphia acquired Lemon Hill but did nothing to turn it into a public park, one man had an idea for how those grounds might be used. Dr. Alfred Langdon Elwyn (1804–1884), a nonpracticing physician, author, and philanthropist, wrote to Dr. Samuel G. Morton, the president of the Academy of Natural Sciences and America's most renowned physical anthropologist, proposing that Lemon Hill become the site of a zoological garden, which would aid in "the oral and mental instruction of the citizens generally."[1] Neither Morton nor anyone else was persuaded, and Dr. Elwyn's myriad interests soon turned in other directions (he would help to create the Institution for the Blind and the Pennsylvania Agricultural Society; serve as president of the Society for the Prevention of Cruelty to Animals; and become the founder of a school for children with disabilities, later named Elwyn in his honor, which continues its work in several states today).

But a decade after Elwyn suggested it, the idea at last began to take hold that Philadelphia should have a zoo. By then, Fairmount Park had been named and was actually starting to become a park. This time, the cause was spearheaded by a well-to-do young gentleman scientist, William Camac (1829–1900), who was another nonpracticing medical doctor, thanks to his family's wealth.[2] Camac had been impressed by what he saw in the new zoological gardens he had visited in Europe. He was already a member of Philadelphia's Academy of Natural Sciences, the Franklin Institute, and the Historical Society of Pennsylvania. He appears to have had the kind of curiosity about the natural world that had long inspired other Philadelphians to make their city the leader in matters scientific in America.[3]

Among those who foreshadowed the idea of a scientific zoological collection was Charles Willson Peale (1741–1827), the great portraitist of revolutionary-era figures. In 1786, he created in Philadelphia the nation's first museum of natural history. For a time, his collection—its center-piece a display of mastodon bones pulled from a bog in New York State—was housed on the second floor of the State House, now Independence Hall. That display brought Peale into a long-standing debate between Thomas Jefferson and the Comte de Buffon. Buffon claimed Europe's biological superiority to America because of the size of its animals. Jefferson pointed to these "mammoths" as evidence of greater biodiversity in America.

In 1804, while in the White House, Jefferson sent Peale two prairie dogs that had been shipped back to Washington by Lewis and Clarke from their expedition to the Northwest, animals never before seen in the East. Four years later, the president sent Peale two young grizzly bears for his collection out of his desire to inspire Americans about the natural riches of the continent they were possessing. At first, these animals were tethered by chain outdoors in Independence Square. After they grew, Peale transferred them to an iron cage adjoining Philo-sophical Hall across Fifth Street.

Peale's museum was a combi-nation of live and stuffed animals, skeletons, and paintings. He was among the first to employ Linnaean taxonomy in exhibiting his specimens. His museum faded in popularity before his death, its scientific mission absorbed by the Academy of Natural Sciences, which was founded in 1812. See the iconic *The Artist in His Museum* (Philadelphia: Pennsylvania Academy of the Fine Arts) for Peale's self-portrait in 1822, welcoming visitors to his collection.

Camac, whose own scientific leanings were clear, had discovered that the latest zoological gardens in Europe were created to further the scientific study of animal life even while they entertained—and educated—the public. As time would tell, those diverse missions were not always easy to reconcile. Their educational and scientific goals often would take a backseat to the commercial aspect, which was, after all, to attract and amuse visitors with animal displays.[4] Even so, these new zoological parks, in such cities as London, Paris, and Dublin, were a considerable advance over the tradition of snatching exotic animals from the wild to display to the patrons of saloons or country fairs. They were also very different from the ancient practice of potentates who maintained menageries as a way of flaunting their power and wealth.

The London Zoological Society, which was founded in 1826 as the world's first zoo in the modern sense, seems to have been a particular inspiration for Camac. So, in 1859, he called together a number of like-minded citizens in his home to propose that they create a zoological institution for Philadelphia.

With this beginning, thirty-six individuals soon became the incorporators of the Philadelphia Zoological Society, whose charter was granted on March 21 of that year. The group included other men with a scientific bent, some of whom were also prominent industrialists. John Lawrence LeConte, MD, was

The Philadelphia Zoo

one of the nation's outstanding naturalists. John Cassin was perhaps the best-known ornithologist of his time, and also a writer on other aspects of natural history. Dr. Camac was made president of the society. The man chosen as vice president was James C. Hand, an iron merchant, supporter of the Pennsylvania Railroad, and member of the Academy of Natural Sciences. William Parker Foulke was an industrialist with a penchant for natural history. The year before, he had excavated the first complete dinosaur found in the United States—*Hadrosaurus foulkii*, as it was named in his honor—in Haddonfield, New Jersey. Others included George Biddle, the translator of scientific works from the Greek, and Dr. William Alexander Hammond, who would become surgeon general of the U.S. Army during the Civil War and do pioneering work in neurology. Morton McMichael, a future mayor and president of the Fairmount Park Commission, was also one of the incorporators, his presence marking the link between park and zoo from the beginning.

Yet, even the distinguished list of supporters and the grant of a charter were not enough to bring in the funds to create the zoo. When Camac looked back on this failure, he lamented: "There appeared to be great apathy shown to the project, and but few persons seemed to understand the objects of the society or could see the benefits to be derived."[5] The apathy seemed to mirror that which had overtaken the effort to make a genuine public ground out of the new Fairmount Park in this period, for this was not Philadelphia's finest moment for civic accomplishment.

This depiction in bronze of *Hadrosaurus foulkii*, the Haddonfield dinosaur, stands on the grounds of the Philadelphia Zoo. (Photograph by Mark Garvin)

The Haddonfield Dinosaur

After William Parker Foulke undertook the excavation of cretaceous-era bones from a marl pit in Haddonfield, New Jersey, he called on Joseph Leidy, the renowned paleontologist from Philadelphia's Academy of Natural Sciences (ANS), to assist him in making sense of his find. Leidy then described the first nearly complete fossil of a dinosaur ever uncovered, and named it *Hadro-saurus foulkii* in honor of his collaborator. In 1848, under Leidy's direction, it became the first dinosaur skeleton in the world to be mounted for display, standing some ten feet in height and twenty-three feet from nose to tail. It remains on display in the ANS collection today.

A small bronze replica has long stood outside the Reptile House at the Philadelphia Zoo in honor of Foulke, a charter member of the zoo. Early in the twenty-first century, a sculptural representation of *Hadrosaurus foulkii* by artist John Giannotti was installed in Haddonfield's commercial center. The nearby excavation site is now a National Historic Landmark.

It is also quite possible that, distinguished or not, the charter members—men mostly in their thirties and forties—were perceived by Philadelphia's establishment as still too green to be serious players in civic affairs. Two years after the society received its charter, its fund-raising effort was put in abeyance when shots were fired at Fort Sumter and the Civil War engulfed America.

But much changed once the war was over, and Philadelphia began a long period of vigorous growth. Creation of the Fairmount Park Commission in 1867 marked the decisive shift toward rapid development of a much-enlarged park, as well. Dr. Camac, who had served in the war, returned to Philadelphia and took up the cause of the zoo once more. He published an unsigned letter in a Philadelphia newspaper, the *North American and United States Gazette*—Morton McMichael was its editor—that again attempted to rouse the public to the zoo's cause. He noted that such facilities in European cities "have greater attention paid to them than any other places of recreation."[6]

Camac's dream got an undoubted boost from civic plans soon to follow. In February 1870, Philadelphia petitioned Congress to be made the site of a centennial celebration for the nation in 1876. Within a year, that plan had been approved and a Centennial Commission was appointed by Congress. It must have occurred to more than one of Philadelphia's leaders that this was an opportune moment to breathe life into the Zoological Society's charter. In any case, after returning from another trip to Europe in 1872, Camac tackled the zoo project with new determination. He invited the twenty-seven charter members still living to join him. Of that group, eight of the most committed men responded, forming an energized board that began to raise money. A committee was appointed to meet with the Fairmount Park commissioners to negotiate a site for the zoo.

A first proposal was for a five-acre strip running alongside the old Flat Iron district (comprising much of the site of today's Azalea Garden), just to the north of Fairmount. When that was deemed too small, the commissioners offered a second plot in the east park, above where the Girard Avenue Bridge was under construction. That site also was abandoned before the commissioners and the Zoological Society's representatives agreed on a thirty-three-acre site just south of the western terminus of the new bridge. This land contained The Solitude, the classic retreat built by John Penn in the 1780s.[7]

The society grew to 166 members within its first year, and financing began to succeed. The group's secretary, John Ridgeway, wrote an appeal to potential investors in October 1873: "The sum of $150,000 will enable the society to place the garden upon a solid and permanent basis and permit its being opened to the public in the spring of 1874, in a condition that will ensure its future prosperity and reflect credit upon the city."[8] That sum would be a loan in return for which shareholders would be paid interest as well as tickets to the zoo. By March 1874, the full amount had been raised. A devout Quaker, Alfred Cope, attached a condition to his $25,000-share of the loan, namely, that "all malt, vinous or spirituous liquors shall be forever excluded from the premises occupied by the Society."[9] So the public grounds of the zoo remain off-limits for alcohol to the present day, although that restriction no longer applies to private groups renting facilities there.

What no doubt helped this fund-raising effort immensely was knowing that the nation's Centennial Exhibition would be held in Philadelphia, and specifically in Fairmount Park, in 1876. The prospect of millions of visitors, many of whom could be expected to visit the zoo next to the fairgrounds, made the investment look like a sure thing. As Ridgeway put it, "The millions of visitors to the Centennial Exhibition . . . will scarcely fail to avail themselves of the privilege of seeing its curious collection of birds, beasts and reptiles."[10] Suddenly, time was of the essence for creating the zoo.

Enter Hermann J. Schwarzmann. This young German immigrant had risen quickly in the employ of the Fairmount Park Commission. By 1872, the commission charged him with traveling to Europe to visit zoological gardens for ideas, and for the Centennial Exhibition as well. In addition to laying out the grounds and designing dozens of other buildings for the nation's birthday, the indefatigable Schwarzmann was at the same time determining the plan of the zoo. He hired a number of Philadelphia's leading architects to design the original structures. Within two years, construction was completed on many of them, including Frank Furness's iconic gatehouses, which remain unchanged to the present day.[11]

Meanwhile, the Zoological Society was busy acquiring animals. Camac soon hired a renowned naturalist and explorer, Frank J. Thompson, to act as the zoo's superintendent. Then based in Australia, Thompson had traveled widely in Africa; dug diamonds in Kimberly, South Africa; and, most important, caught and transported live wild animals across continents. He accepted the society's offer of a $2,000 annual salary, and had a number of animals shipped to the zoo in time for its opening.[12]

One of the directors, Theodore L. Harrison, donated more than a hundred animals. In 1873, an army general, James S. Brisbin, was authorized to purchase animals from the western plains while he was stationed in Omaha, Nebraska. Within the year, he shipped back grizzly, black, cinnamon, and brown bears, as well as foxes, moose, elk, wildcats, wolverines, eagles, and deer. Brigham Young, the president of the Mormon Church and governor of Utah territory, sent two bears. Mrs. William Tecumseh Sherman presented "Atlanta," the cow that had followed her husband in his march through Georgia in 1864.[13] Months after the zoo's opening, the first pair of lions was acquired. The African American artist Henry Ossawa Tanner came to the zoo to paint the male lion, Pompeii, three times and to do sketches of other animals.

A twentieth-century author writing about the zoo's opening noted the complexity in transporting animals; even though railroad lines stretched across the nation, they did not reach everywhere:

> However, the railroads were interested in the new zoo and allowed animals from the West free transportation to Philadelphia. Animals coming from foreign countries were not exempt from a customs fee until Congress passed a bill allowing free entry for all animals consigned to the Philadelphia Zoo.[14]

The Philadelphia Zoological Garden opened its gates to the public on July 1, 1874, when more than three thousand visitors poured in to marvel at the hundreds of exotic creatures installed about the grounds. On Indepen-

This early postcard pictures Furness's entrance gates to the zoo, its sculpture, *The Dying Lioness*, and a long-distance view across the Schuylkill of center city Philadelphia. (Courtesy of Steve Lynch)

GIRARD AVE., ENTRANCE TO ZOOLOGICAL GARDENS, PHILADELPHIA, PA.

The Philadelphia Zoo

The Zoo's Architecture

The zoo largely remains what it has been since its beginning: an animal park within a garden. Both garden and zoo still retain much of the Victorian character present at the 1874 opening, when many of its buildings had been designed by some of the leading Philadelphia architects of the period. In addition to the gatehouses by Frank Furness, his then partner, George Hewitt—with whom he would collaborate on the design of the new Pennsylvania Academy of the Fine Arts—was the architect for the Deer House. He and Furness also collaborated on the design of the Elephant House. The Monkey House was the creation of Theophilus P. Chandler, who soon would found the Department of Architecture at the University of Pennsylvania. Edward Collins and Charles M. Autenreith partnered in designing the Lion and Tiger House (years later, they would create the cast-iron façade of the Lit Brothers Department Store in downtown Philadelphia). John Crump, architect of the Chestnut Street Theater and much else, created the Horse Sheds.

Of those structures that have not been demolished over the years, Hewitt's Deer House was transformed in 1985 into the George D. Widener Memorial Tree House by the architectural firm of Venturi, Rauch, and Scott Brown. It provides youngsters with colorful environments in which to imagine the lives of various animals. A twenty-four-foot artificial ficus tree grows through the roof of the building into an added cupola. The building remains one of Philadelphia's most popular indoor spaces for all kinds of events.

Paul Cret was named chief architect of the zoo in 1930. Ten years later, his Pachyderm House was built in the style of a huge Pennsylvania Dutch barn. After zoo officials decided, in 2006, to retire their elephants to larger pastures, the Pachyderm House was transformed into the new Hamilton Family Children's Zoo and Faris Family Education Center, emphasizing sustainability as well as animal husbandry. After this largest construction project in the zoo's history was completed, the KidZooU was opened in and around the Cret building in April 2013.

Source: Sandy Bauers, "A $33 Million 'Wildlife Academy,'" *Philadelphia Inquirer,* April 7, 2013, pp. A1, A18; Natalie Pompilio, "'Look! A mouse!'" *Philadelphia Inquirer,* April 12, 2013, pp. W18–20.

dence Day, three days later, the new Girard Avenue Bridge opened, and some 8,500 visitors came to see the zoo. A year and a day later, that number was surpassed when 11,245 visitors were counted—a remarkable figure since that July 5 fell on a Monday. The price of admission was twenty-five cents for adults and ten cents for children, fees that would hold for the next half century. Every fifteen minutes, steamboats landed at the zoo's own wharf just below the garden on the Schuylkill. Visitors also came on foot, by streetcar, and by horse and carriage. Zoo membership climbed throughout that first year to 770 who paid annual fees of ten dollars, and 179 life members, who made single payments of fifty dollars. More than four hundred shareholders had invested in the zoo, whose loan totaled more than $250,000.[15]

Zoo attendance in 1874 came to some 250,000; it rose to 475,000 in the next year, well exceeding the numbers for the London Zoo. Then came the centennial year, 1876, and zoo attendance met the highest expectations of its investors. By autumn, after a long, hot summer, swarms of visitors packed the zoo, as well as the Centennial Exhibition. The zoo had a single-day

Today's Widener Memorial Tree House was originally George Hewitt's Deer House. (Photograph by Mark Garvin)

attendance of 20,715 people on Sunday, October 29, a record that would not be broken for seventy-five years. During the centennial year, zoo attendance topped 657,000, a figure only reached again in 1951 with the opening of a new Carnivore House. President Ulysses S. Grant stopped by with his wife after he opened the Centennial Exhibition and had a look at the two Australian cassowaries he had presented to the zoo months earlier.[16]

But in the year after the Centennial Exhibition closed, attendance dropped alarmingly, to less than a third of the number of visitors in 1876.[17] That created a deficit in the zoo's operating budget for the first time. More than a thousand animals were resident by 1879, but attendance did not rise accordingly. By 1885, the number of dues-paying members had declined to only 350 from well over a thousand in the early days. The 1890s proved even worse, particularly after the Panic of 1893, which was brought on by the collapse of Jay Cooke's financial empire. Philadelphia's City Council was forced to rescue the zoo's operation with a $10,000 appropriation. Here was the first, but by no means the last, time when the city's coffers had to be opened to help the zoo survive. In 1898, a fire destroyed the zoo's restaurant.[18] To add to its woes, in the 1890s, competition came from the opening of two new amusement parks, Willow Grove and Woodside.

Today, we may view these financial issues as stemming from the nineteenth-century zoo's self-image as merely a place of entertainment, with resulting marketing problems when faced with competition. No zoo at the time had a fully developed sense of its responsibilities for protecting and conserving species; all were likely to exhibit animals under conditions that later generations would find too restrictive. Yet, in Philadelphia, zoo officials had long reminded the public that their institution offered far more than amusement, and that its scientific study of animals was supremely important.

A *Guide to the Garden of the Zoological Society of Philadelphia* dating from 1886 provides a glimpse of its educational bent. The author was the zoo's second superintendent, Arthur Erwin Brown. In the introduction, he set out Linnaeus's system of classification of organisms. After listing all six divisions by which animals are broadly categorized, he noted that the zoo dealt only with that of *Vertebrata*. The five classes of vertebrates followed, subdivided by orders, then families, genera, and species. Next, the guide described in detail each species of animal exhibited by way of guiding the reader to every stop at the zoo. This ninety-one-page guidebook, which sold for fifteen cents,

Paul Cret's Pachyderm House has been repurposed as the Hamilton Family Children's Zoo and Faris Family Education Center, now augmented by the KidZooU.

clearly was intended to provide basic instruction in biology at the same time it discussed the animals on view.[19] Thomas Jefferson, that shipper of wild animals to Peale's Museum early in the century, no doubt would have approved, both of the exhibits and their educational purpose.

Similarly, the zoo pathologist—or prosector, as this employee was termed originally—issued a report on animal deaths as early as 1876. Henry C. Chapman named improper food, the effects of temperature, and poorly designed cages as the chief factors. He also suspected that many monkey deaths may have been caused by tuberculosis. As a result, the zoo soon pioneered in separating animals from visitors with glass rather than bars. In his 1877 report, Chapman had this to say: "When we consider the unnatural conditions to which an animal is subjected under confinement . . . the wonder is not that the animals die but that they live."[20] Chapman's pioneering activity began what has made the Philadelphia Zoo a world leader in the study of the health of animals held in confinement.[21]

The zoo's Laboratory of Company Pathology, founded in 1901, was the first such research institution in any zoo. Necropsies were performed at the Medical School at the University of Pennsylvania until 1904, when the zoo's own facility, also a first, was built on zoo grounds. In 1911, the first tuberculin testing of primates was performed there. The lab was named for Dr. Charles Penrose (1861–1925), the longtime president of the Zoological Society, in 1935. From its beginning in 1901, the lab has archived the original reports and glass slides produced from its necropsies.

In the 1960s, a study on the longevity of captive mammals used data obtained from the Penrose Laboratory over more than sixty years. The results showed significant increases in the lives of individuals from many species, thanks to changes in their diets in 1935, the effects of larger cages, improved facilities, and the use of antibiotics and vaccines. Today, Philadelphia is one of only eleven accredited zoos in the United States with its own in-house pathology program.

By the third decade of the twentieth century, the Philadelphia Zoo was earning renown for its success with large primates. In 1928, the zoo welcomed the first baby orangutan born in the United States, followed a week later by the first chimpanzee bred in captivity. Dr. Herbert L. Ratcliffe, building on the research of Dr. E. P. Corson-White, developed a formula for a nutritious meal—zoocake—for a large variety of these animals; as a result, within five years, their death rate was cut by more than half. In the same period, the zoo's star attraction, Bamboo, was on his way to becoming the longest-lived gorilla in captivity, dying in 1961 at the age of thirty-three.

Another gorilla, Massa, had joined Bamboo at the zoo in 1936. He bested Bamboo's record, living until hours after his fifty-fourth birthday party on December 30, 1984.[22]

Zoo membership declined precipitously after the Depression hit, and the city's appropriations were cut in half, from $50,000 to $25,000, between 1930 and 1932. The number of animals also declined sharply in that period. But with the coming of the New Deal, the Works Progress Administration (WPA), and other federal agencies that were created to offer jobs to the unemployed brought hundreds of workers to the zoo. As a result, the grounds were replanted and improved. On July 15, 1933, the zoo held its first free day and attracted nearly seventy thousand visitors. In 1940, the WPA constructed a new Pachyderm House that had been designed by architect Paul Philippe Cret in the style of an enormous Pennsylvania Dutch barn.[23]

Zoo attendance climbed again during World War II, partly because of many new wartime jobs in the city. A victory garden was planted on the site of the old Elephant House, its vegetables harvested to feed zoo animals. Within a year after the war ended, in August 1946, the city announced that

This nineteenth-century sculpture, "Mother Lioness Carrying to Her Young a Wild Boar," was moved to the zoo early in the twentieth century after it repeatedly frightened horses in its original location on the river drive. (Photograph by Mark Garvin)

A male silverback gorilla, Jabari, died at the age of twenty-eight in 2013 after living much of his life at the Philadelphia Zoo. (Courtesy of Eric Carlin)

it would commit a million dollars to capital improvements. This sign of better times was in stark contrast to the city's drastic cut in the zoo's appropriation only twelve years earlier.

An attendance record that had held since 1876 was broken in 1951, with the opening of a new Carnivore House. That record of nearly 858,000 visitors was again bested six years later, when the first children's zoo in the country was opened. Nine years after that, on November 2, 1966, zoo attendance for the year reached one million for the first time. That figure has been met or surpassed in nearly every year since then. In 2013, the zoo's president boasted that its 1.2 million visitors made it the second-largest ticketed attraction in Philadelphia, second only to the Phillies. An economic-impact study, using data from 2004 projected through 2014, estimated that the zoo's operations would generate $244 million in total regional economic impact in that ten-year period.[24]

The most traumatic event in the zoo's history occurred in the early morning of December 24, 1995, when a fire in the World of Primates building killed twenty-three animals, all of which died in their sleep from smoke inhalation. Family groups of six lowland gorillas and three orangutans were among the dead, along with four white-handed gibbons and ten lemurs. All were members of endangered species. The tragedy occurred at a moment when major planning and renovations were beginning at the zoo, including construction of a new state-of-the-art Animal Health Center. In the fire's aftermath, the zoo's president, Alexander L. "Pete" Hoskins, asked the board not simply to rebuild the primate house, but to create a much more ambitious, and expensive, facility for its new residents. Some months later, Mayor Edward Rendell emphasized the city administration's strong financial support for the zoo's rebuilding program, urging the board to undertake an aggressive schedule for creating the new Primate Reserve.[25] It was completed and opened for the first time on July 1, 1999. Its new residents represent ten species, including all those killed in the fire.

In recent years, zoo stakeholders have wrestled with major planning decisions, including whether or not the zoo should move to a new, and larger, location. They have decided to stay at the original Fairmount Park site, but to allow exhibition space to grow from 38 to 50 percent of the grounds. Although parking issues were ameliorated when a new, four-story parking garage for 683 vehicles was opened in 2013, even that was not sufficient to accommodate all the parking space needed for peak days of visitors to the zoo. Because little more parking for private vehicles was feasible, zoo officials announced, also in 2013, that they would launch an effort to have a new regional rail station built at Thirty-Fourth Street and Mantua Avenue, a short distance from the zoo's south entrance. Should that come to pass—the cost was estimated at about $60 million—it would return train access of the kind that had been available from the zoo's opening in 1874 until 1902, when it fell victim to Pennsylvania Railroad's expansion.[26]

The zoo's limited size also constrains what it can do. Starting in 2007, its four prized elephants were removed to other institutions because of the growing sense that it was impossible to provide spacious enough quarters to meet contemporary standards for housing some of the world's largest animals.[27] Strategic plans published in 1998 and 2008 have acknowledged the increasing relevance for the zoo of conservation and preventing the extinction of species. In keeping with those goals, the zoo is attempting to make its operations carbon-neutral and is helping to save frogs now endangered by a worldwide viral epidemic.[28]

Yet this emphasis on conservation is by no means the only Philadelphia Zoo story in the early years of the twenty-first century. Its officials continue to recognize how important it is to their institution's financial health to maintain the interest of the zoo-going public. The zoo experience for visitors is changing as the result of continuing evolution in the views of those responsible for determining how zoos ought to function.

"Animal rotation" is one such change. Even though the zoo's grounds cannot grow outward, its inhabitants are nonetheless increasingly able to range farther than ever before through innovative new planning. The idea is to give the animals, to the extent possible, the run of the entire zoo. Since 2011, more than 2,200 feet of long mesh tunnels have been constructed over the heads of visitors so that a variety of climbing animals can take turns exploring the grounds away from their habitats. Among the species visitors now may see overhead are monkeys, lemurs, gibbons, and orangutans. Big cats roam their own elevated crossing, Big Cat Crossing. The Gorilla Treeway was inaugurated in 2014 to provide those great apes with freedom to range more widely. Ground-based trails are being constructed for such earthbound species as giraffes, hippos, rhinos, and zebras. While the residents explore this "Zoo360" trail system, visitors can have unexpected views of the animals. In the words of the zoo's chief operating officer: "It's a little more like your own safari in 42 acres in Fairmount Park."[29]

Other major changes came early in the twenty-first century as the result of the zoo's master plan. A new Big Cat Falls was launched in 2006, opening up the spaces where these animals could roam. Two snow leopard cubs made their public debut in 2011. A pair of African lions arrived at the start of 2012, joining another pride of lions long in residence. In 2013, the children's zoo, much expanded and thoroughly reconceived as KidZooU, opened in and around the old Pachyderm House, permitting much of it to remain open in winter. There, the emphasis is both on teaching children about the vital and fragile interconnections among species and allowing them to interact directly with the animals.[30] The new McNeil Avian Center lets visitors get close to hundreds of spectacular birds in their re-created habitats from across the globe.

The Philadelphia Zoo has long taken pride in being a world leader among zoos for breeding animals known to be difficult to breed in captivity. In an age when zoos are often criticized for what is essential to their existence—incarcerating wild animals—the Philadelphia Zoo has a record of considerable success at sustaining the lives of animals, and of learning from that record. Given the pace of species extinction in the wild, zoos today are in the vanguard of those working to

Big Cat Crossing is one of a growing number of mesh trails at the zoo that allow many species to explore the grounds.

Zoo Databases and the Trouble with Zoos

The ability to generate electronic databases of information today is of huge benefit to the managers of wildlife in zoos. The International Species Information System (ISIS) now receives animal data from nearly 650 zoos and aquariums worldwide. ISIS has become a resource that enhances the cooperative work of zoos across the globe by providing valuable data to ISIS members, studbook keepers, and species program managers. All increasingly rely on such information for their cooperative breeding programs and animal acquisition.

These operations are a clear indication of how much has changed in the lives of zoos since the Philadelphia Zoo opened in 1874. Unlike then, when animals were mostly captured from their natural habitats, almost all zoo animals today come from other such institutions. These are wild animals that have never lived in the wild. They are bred in captivity, where the possibilities for inbreeding are much greater than in nature. But where careful breeding programs are added to better understanding of nutrition and disease, many modern zoos may take justifiable pride in the care they give their residents, and the longevity of some.

Yet, opposition to the confinement of animals—to zoos—does not appear to be waning, and may still be growing in spite of what most would regard as the more humane treatment of zoo animals today than ever before. Both factors are no doubt prompted at least in part by what biologists continue to learn about the complexity of animal brains and their social behavior. An ever more educated public understands that we are linked in a mysterious and complex chain of relationships to the creatures we so casually incarcerate. That produces both better treatment by zoos and more opposition to them.

reverse that process. Species such as the Guam rail and the Micronesian kingfisher, recently extinct in the wild, are thriving in the zoo's McNeil Avian Center. They either have been or soon will be reintroduced back into their native habitats. Projects like these suggest that zoos will continue to have an ever more central role to play in the conservation of animal life everywhere in the world.

The animals always have been the main attraction at the Philadelphia Zoological Garden, but its actual gardens always have been given attention, too. For the Victorians, admiring cultivated nature along with exotic creatures provided a pleasurable leisure time activity. Although it is doubtful that contemporary visitors pay their entrance fees with a primary view to admiring the zoo's gardens, they can now enjoy newly renovated landscaping around what always has been the grounds' centerpiece, The Solitude. Since 2008, the Walter Gray Family Gardens have been developed there as a balance between the historic landscape—with its roots as a mid-eighteenth-century Philadelphia country villa—and a more modern emphasis on the use of indigenous plants. The inspiration of the original landscape is to provide carefully framed views to and from the house, while native plants are meant to promote a local wildlife-friendly habitat.

The Mann Center for the
Performing Arts provides
varied fare during the
summer months from its
site on Georges Hill in West
Fairmount Park. (Courtesy
of Mann Music Center)

Performing Arts in the Parks

The tradition of providing music during the summer months in Fairmount Park goes back at least to the early years of the Philadelphia Zoo's operation, when a substantial piece of its annual budget paid for band concerts in the zoo garden. But that practice was discontinued when revenues dropped off with the decline in visitors to the zoo after the 1876 centennial. In 1888, a music pavilion was built at Lemon Hill, capable of seating two thousand concert-goers.[1] In 1906, another such pavilion was built on the grounds at Strawberry Mansion, the administrators of Fairmount Park having turned the mansion itself into a popular restaurant. Summertime concerts continued there until 1930. Light instrumental music was the order of the day.

In the early decades of providing music in Fairmount Park, the most usual presentations were of small bands typical of those that performed in outdoor bandstands in towns across the country during summer. Serious music making typically took place indoors during the colder months. By the late nineteenth century, Philadelphia boasted three opera houses, including the grand Academy of Music, where the Western Hemisphere premiere of Giuseppe Verdi's opera *Il Trovatore* was a great occasion in February 1857, only a month after the building was dedicated. One orchestra, and sometimes two, performed regularly in the city, although it was not until 1900 that the Philadelphia Orchestra was founded, and soon would find its place among the preeminent symphony orchestras of the world.

Matters musical turned more serious for Fairmount Park in 1922, when the city rebuilt the Lemon Hill Concert Pavilion near its namesake mansion, then sponsored a series of free summer concerts. The fifty-piece ensemble was largely composed of members of the Philadelphia Orchestra. From the start,

The National Sangerfest at Lemon Hill

In its first decades as part of Fairmount Park, the Lemon Hill mansion was mostly used as a beer garden frequented by a largely German clientele. Philadelphia's German Americans had founded the nation's first men's choral society, the Mannerchor, in 1835. Similar groups came together in the first national Sangerfest (singing festival), which was held there in 1850. The seventh annual Sangerfest in June 1857, also in Philadelphia, was a four-day celebration that included a concert at the new Academy of Music. The next day, participants paraded from center city to Lemon Hill for a celebration that included singing, instrumental music, athletic games, and dancing, as well as eating and drinking. Between eight and ten thousand people attended. According to a broadside following the event, participants were so thirsty that some "forty barrels of beer were called into requisition, besides any amount of wine, to supply their guzzling propensities."

An early twentieth-century bandstand near the reservoir in East Fairmount Park held musical groups to provide summer fare. (Courtesy of Steve Lynch)

concerts drew crowds of up to twenty thousand, making clear that a larger facility was needed in Fairmount Park. As a result, in 1930 the city constructed an open-air amphitheater in a natural bowl between two grassy knolls at a site lying north of Strawberry Mansion and below the southern boundary of Laurel Hill Cemetery.[2] The facility provided ten thousand seats, with room for many more to sprawl on the adjoining lawn. It was named Robin Hood Dell in honor of the eighteenth-century Robin Hood Tavern, which once stood nearby on land off Ridge Avenue. Its owners, the Hood family, had donated the land to Fairmount Park.[3]

Summer concerts at Robin Hood Dell would become a Philadelphia institution, but launching them was not easy in the midst of the Depression. With the city's budget depleted, musicians of the Philadelphia Orchestra—eager for work during the summer months when they were not performing at the Academy of Music—took charge of the venture as a cooperative effort. Of the ninety players in the Robin Hood Dell Orchestra, some three-quarters came from the Philadelphia Orchestra. The mission of Robin Hood Dell Concerts, which was incorporated in April 1935, was "to provide summer orchestral concerts, operas, ballets, and other musical events of the highest standards."[4] Twelve thousand people attended the inaugural concert on July 8, 1930. In that first season, concerts were offered seven nights a week for eight weeks. The

Performing Arts in the Parks

players divided up the proceeds at the end of each week. Ticket packages initially were offered to subscribers for twenty-one cents per ticket.[5]

From the beginning, Robin Hood Dell was a preeminent center for summer musical fare in America, attracting the greatest musicians of the day. Both Leopold Stokowski and Eugene Ormandy, then the current and future music directors of the Philadelphia Orchestra, appeared there in the first season and in many seasons to come. So did dozens of the world's leading singers, instrumentalists, and conductors. Among those performing in the Dell's first two decades were Marian Anderson, Kirsten Flagstad, Jascha Heifetz, Fritz Reiner, Artur Rubenstein, and Paul Whiteman, along with Billy Eckstine, Ella Fitzgerald, Dizzy Gillespie, Benny Goodman, and Sarah Vaughan. Judy Garland made her concert debut there in July 1943, with André Kostelanetz conducting members of the Philadelphia Orchestra before a capacity audience of nearly thirty-six thousand.

But throughout the 1930s and the years of World War II, financing the Dell's operations was a constant struggle. Funds were periodically raised to provide adequate pay for the players; yet, even after the noted conductor

From 1930 until 1976, Robin Hood Dell was the venue for orchestral concerts in summer, such as this performance of the Philadelphia Orchestra during the 1950s. (Courtesy of Fairmount Park Historic Resource Archive)

Performing Arts in the Parks

Dimitri Mitropoulos became music director, funding gradually failed. Nor did city officials offer financial assistance to keep the concerts coming. As a result, by 1948, the Dell had to shut down its season two weeks early.

In that same year, a former member of the Robin Hood Dell Concerts Board of Directors returned to take complete charge of the operation. Fredric R. Mann (1903–1987) had made a fortune at a young age as a manufacturer of cardboard boxes. He devised a plan to provide joint support from the City of Philadelphia and concert patrons, who were known as "Friends of the Dell," to allow for free admission to concerts. Contributions by the Friends would be matched by the city. Anyone who mailed in a coupon from a local newspaper would be issued a ticket. The plan was first implemented in the summer of 1949. By the time of Mann's death nearly forty years later, it was estimated that some six million free seats for orchestra concerts had been provided.[6] Throughout that period, his plan also provided the endeavor with financial stability.

Mann was well connected in the world of classical music. He used those friendships and connections to bring many of the world's greatest musicians to Robin Hood Dell.[7] For decades following Mann's initiative, summer concerts at Robin Hood Dell were hugely successful. They notably enriched Philadelphia's cultural life while they supported the livelihood of the members of the Philadelphia Orchestra for an additional six weeks of employment each summer. Crowds of more than twenty-five thousand were not uncommon. Over time, what had begun as a band with a good many musicians who were also members of the Philadelphia Orchestra became largely interchangeable with that organization. Acknowledging that fact in 1970, the Robin Hood Dell Orchestra became the Philadelphia Orchestra at the Robin Hood Dell.[8]

Still, one major problem persisted: because the amphitheater was uncovered, too many performances had to be canceled because of inclement weather. After more than twenty years into his tenure heading the operations at Robin Hood Dell, Mann himself led the campaign to build a new, modern pavilion at another site in Fairmount Park. He rallied support from city officials, as well as private and other public sources. The new facility was opened in the bicentennial year of 1976 at Georges Hill in the west park, at the northwestern edge of the grounds where the centennial had drawn millions exactly a hundred years earlier. The new Robin Hood Dell West, as it was initially named, could seat nearly five thousand people under its expansive roof, with room for nearly that many in uncovered seats at the rear, plus a lawn capable of holding an additional four thousand. In 1979, the pavilion was renamed the Mann Music Center; in 1998, it became the Mann Center for the Performing Arts to reflect its expanding role as a venue for other performing arts organizations in the region.[9]

At Fredric Mann's death in 1987, the orchestra's management assumed some of the responsibilities for concerts at the Mann Center, thanks to declining financial support from the city. Within the next decade, the Mann greatly expanded the number and scope of its presentations. In addition to the season of the Philadelphia Orchestra, performances were offered in many other genres, and were often geared to audiences other than those who had supported classical music.[10] Arts in the Park returned opera to the Mann stage, along with performances of Shakespeare. The Mann's Access the Arts Program provided some fifty thousand complimentary tickets through 350 community service and charitable organizations in the region. A Young People's Concert Series allowed upwards of thirty thousand school children to attend programs of music and dance celebrating diverse cultures. The Mann claims to be the only major summer entertainment venue in the nation with public-access programs on this scale that are free.

In 2012, the amphitheater was reconfigured at the top of the hill. The forty-eight hundred outdoor seats were replaced by two thousand more spacious ones. That left room for construction of the Skyline Stage, where audience members stand or sit on the grass close to the performers. The acts are typically nightclub or cabaret-style productions. The Mann's entrance, box offices, and concession stands were all reconfigured at the same time, and a large dining tent was installed on the top of Georges Hill.

The organizational side of the Philadelphia Orchestra has changed greatly since its first summer season at Robin Hood Dell in 1930. Although the orchestra was unionized from its earliest days, during the 1930s, its players were paid only modest wages for a twenty-eight-week season and received little in the way of pensions and benefits. Many players had long moonlighted in theater orchestras and elsewhere to make ends meet. That made the additional income from summers at Robin Hood Dell appeal to many of them. Through the next decades, the Philadelphians' wages rose and seasons were lengthened.

Then, starting in 1963, the players received a contract guaranteeing them employment for fifty-two weeks a year, including a four-week vacation. It was the first contract of its kind for any symphony orchestra in the nation.[11] That led to a six-week season at the Dell and then the Mann for a number of years. Starting in 1966, it also led to the orchestra becoming a permanent resident of the Saratoga Performing Arts Center in upstate New York for

The view from the
Mann Center's grounds
includes distant views of
downtown Philadelphia.

three weeks every August. Years later, the Philadelphians also became a resident orchestra in summer at the Vail Valley Music Festival in Vail, Colorado. Postseason tours overseas also have become standard.[12]

Meanwhile, cultural shifts nationwide were making the presentation of classical music increasingly problematic for any institution that wanted to remain financially solvent. That gradually brought shifts to programming of summer seasons at the Mann, as it did elsewhere. By 2014, the Mann presented twenty-six programs from May through September. Of these, four were Philadelphia Orchestra programs that catered to popular tastes. One included a screening of *Gladiator*, followed by *West Side Story* and *Star Trek into Darkness*, with the Orchestra playing the scores from the soundtracks. Sponsorship of a fourth concert, "Gospel Meets Symphony," allowed it to be presented free of charge.[13] Other Mann Center presentations that season included such groups as Willie Nelson and family with Alison Krauss, Widespread Panic, Diana Ross, Phish, Yanni, and a young people's concert.

During that same season at the Mann, strains were showing in its relationship with the ensemble for which it had been built. The Philadelphia Orchestra took the unprecedented step that summer of presenting crossover programs, similar to those at the Mann, in its Verizon Hall home in center city. From the point of view of Mann officials, the move was entirely out of character with the spirit of partnership that had always defined the relationship between the two organizations. They urged the orchestra to reconsider, fearing that such competition had the potential to harm them both. Yet the orchestra's management viewed its Verizon concerts as likely to produce "a net positive return," which could not be guaranteed for a classical program.[14]

It seemed clear that, however this dustup might play out in future seasons, it could be traced directly to the continuing decline in audiences for classical music across the nation. That led to the Philadelphia Orchestra's increasingly aggressive effort to compete for new patrons and the Mann's effort to remain solvent, which depended heavily on single-ticket sales. It all marked a striking change from the days when the orchestra filled the Mann's seats with eighteen symphonic concerts in a single summer season.

As part of their effort to bring live performances to underserved segments of the population, officials at the Mann have created major fund-raising events. These include an Annual Golf Tournament and Casino Night, a tour of private gardens to benefit the Mann's Educational and Community Outreach Programs, and Party in the Park, a benefit that includes dinner and entertainment at the Mann Center.

Changing Tastes and Music in the Parks

Many German immigrants contributed to Philadelphia's musical life in its first centuries. During the early decades of Fairmount Park's existence, the neighborhoods around all its major entrances were home to middle-class or, in the case of much of the Chestnut Hill neighborhood of the Wissahickon, wealthy families. The evolution of musical entertainment in the park—from bandstands at the zoo, Lemon Hill, and Strawberry Mansion to symphony orchestras at Robin Hood Dell and the Mann Center—reflected not simply the tastes in those neighborhoods but also the growth in broad-based musical education from the second half of the nineteenth to at least the mid-twentieth century.

In the period from about 1920 to 1950, the Strawberry Mansion and Parkside neighborhoods, just outside the borders of the east and west park, became home to some thirty thousand Jewish residents. Among them were many new immigrants, making Philadelphia the third-largest Jewish settlement in the United States. Many were ardent fans of Robin Hood Dell concerts and avid park users, which may have encouraged their assimilation into mainstream American society.

Starting soon after World War II, large numbers of African Americans migrated to Philadelphia. The same neighborhoods that had been overwhelmingly Jewish became predominantly black. That demographic change bordering Fairmount Park has contributed to the evolution in the entertainment offered as summer fare at Robin Hood Dell and the Mann Center. More important is the large and expanding influence on all of American society of popular music that originated among African Americans—from ragtime to jazz, blues, soul, hip-hop, and more. In Philadelphia's parks as elsewhere in the nation, popular entertainment has become a big business.

Once Philadelphia Orchestra summer concerts moved to what is now the Mann Center, the old Dell continued mainly as a venue for popular performers. Philadelphia natives Bill Cosby and Patti Labelle were among the headliners. In recent years, the Dell has offered eight Essence of Entertainment summer programs that have included the highly regarded Philadelphia-based dance company Philadanco, along with other dance groups and annual festivals for families, as well as the offerings of comedians, rhythm and blues groups, gospel, jazz, funk, doo-wop, folk singers, and musical groups from around the world.

In January 2012, a bill was introduced in the Philadelphia City Council to rename the Robin Hood Dell amphitheater the Georgie Woods Entertainment Center, in honor of the civil rights leader and philanthropist. As a result of negotiations with descendants of the Hood family, it was expected that the facility's site would continue to be known as the Robin Hood Dell.

Since 1976, intimate chamber music concerts have been presented on Sunday evenings during the summer at Laurel Hill mansion. Presented by Women for Greater Philadelphia, the organization that maintains the historic mansion, the concerts are presented for an audience of some sixty people in the octagonal music room, whose windows overlook the Schuylkill.[15]

No history of the performing arts in Fairmount Park during the summer would be complete without mention of the mid-twentieth-century era of the Playhouse in the Park. Starting in 1952, theatrical performances were presented in a facility in the west park near Belmont Mansion Drive. A city-built theater-in-the-round was completed there in 1956, replacing the tent that had served as a performance space during the first three seasons. For twenty-three years, the 1,500-seat playhouse was a popular venue for summer stock companies, whose actors and productions toured such centers throughout the warm months. But by the end of that period, summer stock was in trouble throughout the nation, challenged by the medium of television and changing demands on professional actors.

At the close of the 1979 season, the theater remained empty until 1985, when the Fairmount Park Commission signed a lease of one dollar per year with the Philadelphia Marionette Theater, with the condition that the company pay for the substantial upkeep and repair needed to maintain the building. But the new lessee was unable to raise the needed money and never mounted productions in the playhouse, though it performed in a smaller venue next door. After a twelve-year period in which the commission failed to find a tenant able to restore the building—and while it deteriorated further—the theater was demolished in 1997.[16]

In the 1970s, a resident of Philadelphia's Northeast neighborhood, Edward Kelly, led a grassroots effort to create a summer music festival in its Pennypack Park. The group enlisted the cooperation of the Fairmount Park Commission and Department of Recreation, which led the city to construct a band shell on parkland near the intersections of Rhawn Street and Cresco Avenue. As a public/private partnership, the nonprofit Pennypack Park Festival was able to present free summer concerts for a number of years, featuring the likes of the Tommy Dorsey Orchestra and local groups. By the early 1990s, however, the programs ended when the volunteers charged with administering the summer offerings were unable to continue.

In the winter of 2000, a largely new group of citizens came together to create a plan to revive the festival. Already incorporated as a nonprofit organization, a new Board of Directors was formed, and the City of Philadelphia began work to restore the abandoned shell. By the summer of 2001, the organizers were able to present three concerts featuring Latin, jazz, and big band performers. The season has grown since then, extending from May through September, when programs are usually presented on a Wednesday evening and are free of charge. Both local and nationally known groups are presented. The festival involves young people as an important part of its mission, showcasing high school musical talent in May and developing internships for youths in technical and administrative matters, along with volunteer opportunities.

In addition to the restoration of the Pennypack Park band shell and reconfigurations at the Mann Center early in the twenty-first century, the amphitheater at Robin Hood Dell also was substantially renovated. Not for the first time in its more than eighty-year history, officials were discussing the possibility of roofing over much of the Dell's amphitheater.

Musical fare is available in other Philadelphia parks at various times in summer. The Festival Pier at Penn's Landing is a frequent venue for musical entertainment. In West Philadelphia, Clark Park presents an annual music and arts festival in June. Rittenhouse Square offers free concerts weekly in August. FDR Park provides a music festival in September. The Benjamin Franklin Parkway is the site of Welcome America festivities that include music throughout much of the week surrounding Independence Day. Also on the parkway, the Made in America Festival is now an annual event for the Labor Day weekend.

Since the post–Civil War era, Rittenhouse Square has been an elegant oasis in one of Philadelphia's most desirable residential and commercial neighborhoods.

Penn's Five Public Squares

In 1666, while managing his family's estates in Ireland, the young William Penn heard horrific accounts of the Great Fire of London. When he returned to the capital, he saw for himself how the city's density and crowded conditions had contributed to the damage. Eighteen years later, his utopian plan for Philadelphia was to create a "greene Country Towne" that "will never be burnt, and always be wholesome."[1] He and his surveyor, Thomas Holme, set out plots of land large enough for every owner to be able to plant a small garden. To enhance even further their desire for open space, they embedded five public squares within their map of the city's street grid. One appeared in each quadrant of the rectangular layout of the town between its two rivers, with a fifth at the center.

Yet the privately owned green spaces were quickly filled in when residents subdivided their large plots and sold to new settlers. Among them, tradesmen, workers, and artisans were dominant. They and their families needed the kind of dense and inexpensive housing they had known in the towns they came from, with easy access to others who could pay for their services. Meanwhile, for more than a century, the five public squares remained largely undeveloped green spaces. Several served as grazing commons and burial grounds. The one most distant from the center of population, Northwest Square, became the site of public hangings.

Penn had planned for Centre Square to be bordered by important civic buildings, such as a state house, school, and meeting house, with the square itself presumably left open. But in contrast to Penn's vision for a city that would grow both east and west throughout the grid from Centre Square, the designated central space remained distant from the town's actual settlement,

It took thirty years, from 1871 to 1901, to complete the construction of Philadelphia's City Hall, which stands at the center of William Penn's planned city on land he named Centre Square.

which was crowded along the Delaware for more than a century. In 1781, Rochambeau and his French army camped in what were still the city's outskirts in Centre Square on their march from upstate New York to Virginia and the decisive Battle of Yorktown.

Then in 1799 came the creation of the Centre Square Water Works. When Latrobe's elegant engine house was constructed there in 1799, it actually enhanced the space as a public park. William Rush's sculpture and fountain were installed at the site soon after; the ground was landscaped with trees and walkways and became the locus of public celebrations. But the Centre Square Water Works proved to be short-lived when, early in the nineteenth century, the facility was deemed to be too small. Latrobe's engine house became obsolete within a few years after Philadelphia's waterworks moved to Fairmount, and it was demolished in 1829. In that same year, Rush's fountain and sculpture were taken from Centre Square to the new South Park at Fairmount (Chapter 1).

In 1825, the city officially named each of the five public squares after a prominent historical figure, with Centre Square taking the name of the founder. Penn and his fellow Quakers had refused to name places for individuals, so each had borne the prosaic name of its location within the rectangular grid of the city. After the demolition of the engine house, the recently renamed Penn Square again became a ten-acre open space, while an expanding city began to grow around it. Starting in the 1840s, a nearly thirty-year debate played out before Penn Square was chosen in a referendum as the site of Philadelphia's new City Hall (the long delay in making that decision no doubt tipped the weight of public opinion toward this location and away from Washington Square, which by 1870 was increasingly being left behind by the westward growth of the city). The result would transform Penn Square definitively from a park to the locus of Philadelphia's most grandiose landmark.

Construction of City Hall began in 1871. The massive building in the French Renaissance style by architects John McArthur Jr. and Thomas Ustick Walter was not completed until 1901. This seat of Philadelphia's government contains 750 rooms and 14.5 acres of floor space, making it bigger than the U.S. Capitol. The 250 pieces of sculpture covering its walls are all from the studio of Alexander Milne Calder, and represent the founding and history of Philadelphia and the region. A thirty-seven-foot statue of William Penn, also by Calder, stands at the pinnacle of the clock tower, 548 feet above street level. The clock itself is larger than London's famed Big Ben.

Building City Hall cost more than three times its original budget—$24.5 million, about $7 billion today—thanks to bountiful corruption throughout its construction. Moreover, long before the building was completed, its architectural style had gone out of fashion. In 1885, a headline in the *Evening Standard* proclaimed it the "Biggest and Ugliest Building in America." Some critics proposed tearing it down. In 1924, one architect argued for leaving only the clock tower as a landmark within a traffic circle. That proposal, ironically, came from Paul Philippe Cret, the father of the Benjamin Franklin Parkway, which was then being completed. City Hall may have been spared that fate simply because of the enormous costs of demolition.[2]

As so often happens with architectural tastes, what was vilified originally came to be venerated by succeeding generations. City Hall remains the tallest all-masonry building in the world. This "marble elephant" was cleaned and polished early in the twenty-first century, so that today it gleams again as the visual terminus of the Benjamin Franklin Parkway.[3]

Yet William Penn's vision of a park at the center of his city did not entirely die. Green shoots began to appear at its periphery early in the twenty-first century. That is when the long-vanished park at Penn Square was revived as a slightly displaced piece of its former self in the new space with a spot of green at Dilworth Plaza, now renamed Dilworth Park. The plaza itself was created in the 1960s as a westward extension of City Hall's apron when adjacent property was condemned in an urban renewal project.[4] It was dedicated in 1977 and named in honor of Richardson Dilworth, the reform mayor who led Philadelphia from 1956 to 1962. The original design included a sunken platform with stairs leading to underground transit stations, a solid-surface arrangement that inhibited its attractiveness as a lively public space.

In September 2014, the radically reconfigured plaza reopened as a park with a large green lawn, groves of trees, a café, and a programmable fountain. The new space can accommodate a range of special events, concerts, outdoor markets, and ice skating in winter. Its transit entrances are sloping head houses of transparent glass, designed so that they frame and appear to slide under the central Market Street axis through City Hall's courtyard. The new Dilworth Park contains 120,557 square feet of public space, 21 percent more than was available before the remodeling. The raised lawn is surrounded by bench seating for hundreds of park goers. The architects pay homage to the site's early role as the engine house and water supply system for the city: "The new design recreates [*sic*] this historic use through the collection of on-site rain water, its purification and storage occurring in a reservoir below the plaza lawn. The water is then redistributed to support the irrigation of the plaza landscaping."[5]

The new Dilworth Park holds a final tribute to Philadelphia's urban planners, from William Penn to Paul Cret and Jacques Gréber. It leads directly from Penn's Centre Square at its northwestern edge to LOVE Park and the Benjamin Franklin Parkway, that sliver of Fairmount Park drawn into the heart of the city a century ago.

When city councils in 1825 gave the names of prominent Americans to each of Penn's original squares, the one in the southeast quadrant of the city was renamed for Washington. This square adjoined the eighteenth-century city, its northeast corner diagonally opposite what later became Independence Square once construction began on the State House (Independence Hall) in 1732. Since 1706, this space with two rough roads, a gulch, and a stream me-

andering through it, had been designated a "common and public burial ground." Its deceased occupants were paupers, immigrants, prisoners, and former slaves during a time when upstanding citizens could be buried in churchyards and private plots. In April 1777, John Adams wrote that he had spent a morning here "in the congregation of the dead," whose graves "are enough to make the heart of stone melt away."[6]

When the British occupied Philadelphia during the Revolutionary War, they housed prisoners in the Walnut Street Prison across Sixth Street from the square. Those who died were buried in the square, as were other troops from Washington's army once the British evacuated the city. Pits twenty by thirty feet were dug along Seventh and Walnut Streets, then filled with coffins piled one atop another until space in the mass grave ran out. Then long trenches were dug on the south side. Some two thousand British and

In 2014, a renovated Dilworth Plaza became Dilworth Park, with a green lawn, café, and pool with water jets on land abutting the west side of City Hall near the southeastern terminus of the Benjamin Franklin Parkway.

Penn's Five Public Squares

American soldiers may have been buried there, more than in any other single resting place in America for the victims of the Revolutionary War. The last burials came in the terrible year 1793, when yellow fever swept the city.

In that same year, on January 9, this square in what was then the nation's capital was festive when the first lighter-than-air balloon ascent in America lifted Jean Pierre Blanchard from the courtyard of the Walnut Street Prison at Sixth and Walnut Streets out over an audience that included the president and Mrs. Washington, James Madison, Dr. Benjamin Rush, Stephen Girard, and many other dignitaries gathered on the grounds of the State House. The balloon reached an altitude of more than a mile before Blanchard brought it down in Woodbury, New Jersey. The Frenchman, who spoke no English, reportedly shared a bottle of wine he had brought with curious locals. He also carried with him a *passe-port* letter of introduction from President Washington.[7]

In addition to serving as a graveyard, Southeast Square was a grazing ground for sheep and cattle. From the mid-1790s until 1815, Seventh Street ran straight through the square from north to south ("Little Seventh Street" was the designation for today's Washington Square West), leaving a strip of open land to its west that became a cattle market. By early in the nineteenth century, the square became a gathering place for the city's African Americans, who could often be seen "going to the graves of their friends early in the morning, and there leaving them gifts of victuals and rum," in the words of a nineteenth-century historian. Those ritual acts also led to vibrant festivities. Thousands of black Philadelphians sometimes came to what became known as "Congo Square" to dance and sing, as a white observer put it, "in their native dialects."[8]

By 1825, when it became Washington Square, the city was finally spreading all around it. In 1833, the park was laid out with symmetrical paths and trees in a plan similar to that today. A French botanist, François-André Michaux, selected the original trees. By 1846, the park could be viewed as "a beautiful and fashionable promenade," contributing to the area's development for the first time as a desirable residential district.[9]

City Hall had long been housed in the building directly east of Independence Hall, in cramped space that grew increasingly inadequate. Soon after the Civil War, city officials proposed that Independence Hall be razed to make way for an entirely new and expanded City Hall on that site. The proposal raised such an outcry of opposition that the city then proposed taking Washington Square as the new building site. Irate citizens still were not ap-

Literary Washington Square

For more than a century, Washington Square was the center of publishing in Philadelphia. The Irish immigrant Mathew Carey (1760–1839), arriving in 1784, was the first to establish himself there. While living in Paris, he had met Benjamin Franklin, who recommended him to friends in Philadelphia. Thanks to a gift of four hundred dollars from the Marquis de Lafayette, Carey was able to establish a bookshop and publishing house across from the southeastern corner of the square. Decades later, his son and son-in-law made the firm one of the most prominent publishers in the nation. In 1925, the medical publisher that succeeded them, Lea and Febiger, built an Italianate structure at the site, which is now an art gallery.

J. B. Lippincott established his publishing company in 1836. By the end of the nineteenth century, it was one of the largest and best-known publishers in the world. The business was acquired by Harper and Row in 1978, which became a part of Wolters Cluwer in 1990. Lippincott's Washington Square headquarters were built on Sixth Street in 1900, and were converted to condominium residences at the start of the twenty-first century.

The Pennsylvania Bible Society built its publishing headquarters at the corner of Seventh and Walnut Streets in 1855. Early in the twentieth century, the W. B. Saunders Medical Publishers was established on the northwest corner of Seventh and Locust Streets; its building is now residential. For more than a century, *Farm Journal* magazine was published at its offices across from the southwest corner of Washington Square. The *Farm Journal* building now houses Penn Medicine's cancer center.

In 1910, the massive Curtis Publishing Building rose along the entire block of Walnut Street, opposite the square. This publisher of the *Saturday Evening Post, Ladies Home Journal*, and other popular magazines commissioned a fifty-foot glass mosaic from the studio of Louis C. Tiffany. That mural remains in the Sixth Street lobby of the building that now holds a variety of offices, shops, restaurants, and apartments.

The Athenaeum of Philadelphia was founded in 1814 as a membership library "to disseminate useful knowledge for public benefit." Since 1845, its home across from the square on Sixth Street has been a large Italianate brownstone building designed by John Notman, one of the first in that style in the nation. It was designated a National History Landmark in 1976. Its collection emphasizes the history of American architecture, building, and interior design. Exhibits are open to the public.

peased. Eventually, the Commonwealth legislature interceded by calling for a referendum of Philadelphia voters to determine the location. The resulting vote overwhelmingly approved building the new facility at Penn Square instead. Both Independence Hall and Washington Square were saved.

Back in 1825, when the square was named for Washington, city councils also planned to raise a memorial to the general and to the Continental soldiers buried there. A cornerstone was laid, but no memorial followed. Decades later, after the creation of Fairmount Park along the Schuylkill, the Green Street entrance to the park eventually became the site for Philadelphia's memorial to George Washington. (In 1928, with the completion of the Benjamin Franklin Parkway, the Washington Monument was moved to what today is named the Eakins Oval at the parkway's northwestern terminus.)

FREEDOM IS A LIGHT
FOR WHICH MANY MEN HAVE DIED IN DARKNESS

IN UNMARKED GRAVES WITHIN
THIS SQUARE LIE THOUSANDS
OF UNKNOWN SOLDIERS OF
WASHINGTON'S ARMY WHO DIED
OF WOUNDS AND SICKNESS DURING
THE REVOLUTIONARY WAR

THE INDEPENDENCE AND LIBERTY
YOU POSSESS ARE THE WORK OF
JOINT COUNCILS AND JOINT
EFFORTS-OF COMMON DANGERS,
SUFFERINGS AND SUCCESS.
WASHINGTON'S FAREWELL ADDRESS SEPT. 17, 1796

The Tomb of the Unknown Soldier of the American Revolution was installed in Washington Square in the 1950s. The figure of Washington is a bronze version of the original marble statue done from life by Jean Antoine Houdon.

Not until the mid-twentieth century did a version of the 1825 plan go forward in Washington Square. The Tomb of the Unknown Soldier of the American Revolution was conceived by the Washington Square Planning Committee in 1954, and completed in 1957. The tomb contains the remains of a soldier whose body was disinterred from the square, although it could not be determined whether he was American or British. The focal point of the memorial, designed by G. Edwin Brumbaugh, is a 1922 bronze casting of the original marble statue of Washington created in 1790 by Jean Antoine Houdon. That most renowned portrait sculptor of his time had come from Paris to Mount Vernon at the invitation of Benjamin Franklin to make the only life-size statue of Washington done from life.[10]

In 2005, Washington Square was transferred by the City of Philadelphia to the National Park Service, from which it became a part of Independence National Historical Park (INHP). The transfer was made to assure the park's upkeep at a time when the Fairmount Park Commission's budget was increasingly strained. Since then, many trees have been replanted, bluestone walkways were leveled and secured, the surrounding brick wall was rebuilt, and a long-dormant circular pool and fountain in the center was brought back to life in summertime (Chapter 17).

Visitors to the surrounding historic district of Philadelphia may be only dimly aware of which green spaces are city-owned and which are within the INHP. Since the 1730s, Independence Square, behind Independence Hall, has stood on the northeast corner of the Walnut Street intersection, while Washington Square has nearly touched it across its southwestern corner. Both were once city parks that have long looked as if they should be sisters. The grassy plots of the INHP's Independence Mall extend north between Fifth and Sixth Streets all the way to Race Street, where Franklin Square (city owned) lies at

The northeastern corner of Washington Square, in the foreground, nearly touches (across Sixth Street) the southwestern corner of Independence Square, the tower of its namesake building rising behind.

the northwest corner of the Sixth Street intersection in much the same relation to the mall as Washington Square on the south.

Additional green space belonging to the INHP unfurls for several blocks to the east between Chestnut and Walnut Streets, and surrounds the American Philosophical Society's Library Hall, the Second Bank of the United States, Carpenters' Hall, and other historic buildings. As a stroll through this district reveals, many of these green plots were created when the INHP came into being in 1956. They often replace buildings, long since demolished, that housed governmental offices during the ten-year period, 1790–1800, when Philadelphia was the nation's capital.

Directly to the south, Society Hill is dotted with green spaces, either in private hands, such as churchyards and gardens, or public, as are several playgrounds. Together, all these pieces create a harmonious web of small parks and open spaces, regardless of their ownership.

Franklin (Northeast) Square also had served as an eighteenth-century grazing and burial ground. From 1741 to 1835, the German Reformed Church buried more than 3,100 of its congregants there. A piece of the square had been granted the church for that use by Thomas Penn, the founder's son. After decades in which the City of Philadelphia contested that usage with

Penn's Five Public Squares

the claim that the entire square originally had been intended for public use, the Pennsylvania Supreme Court held with the city and overturned the grant.[11] From 1776 to 1788, the north side of the square held the city's black powder magazine, its gunpowder stored there in a fireproof building. Increasingly surrounded by a largely residential neighborhood, the square also served as a parade and drill ground for soldiers during the War of 1812. A large fountain installed at the center of the park in 1837 is thought to be the oldest of any of those remaining in Penn's original squares.

The arrival of the automobile proved a particular liability for Franklin Square. First came the construction of the Benjamin Franklin Bridge from 1922 to 1926, which hindered access to the park from the east and required many nearby row houses and shops to be demolished. The park's north boundary also was tightly restricted by traffic on Vine Street and, eventually, the Vine Street Expressway. In the 1960s, the creation of Independence Mall to the southeast further eliminated what had been a city neighborhood, transforming the area into an uninhabited open space. By 1961, the urban critic Jane Jacobs accurately described Franklin Square as a "skid row park."[12] That is what it remained throughout the rest of the century, when it was known principally as a refuge for the homeless. Installation in 1976 of the Living Flame Memorial to the city's fallen police and firemen did little to reverse the square's decline.

In the first years of the twenty-first century, the opening nearby of the National Constitution Center made the derelict square more visible to tourists than it had been before. That encouraged the park's complete makeover by the nonprofit organization Historic Philadelphia. In July 2006, to mark the tercentenary of Benjamin Franklin's birth, the park was rededicated as a family-oriented space. Among its new features were a carousel, a miniature golf course marked out by small-scale versions of famous historical landmarks

Black Powder Magazine

From 1776 to 1788, Franklin Square housed Philadelphia's black powder magazine, or storage place, for the city's ammunition that was used during and immediately after the American Revolution. It was of the utmost importance that the powder be stored in a dry and fireproof environment, far enough away from the city's residents in the event of an explosion. The status of the magazine remains unclear during the nine-month period of British occupation (1777–1778). After the occupation, it was reported that the magazine could hold up to eight hundred casks of gunpowder. Eventually, the magazine was moved, and the structure was demolished sometime after 1811. The rubble found in a 1975 excavation is significant, as it is most likely the only remaining Revolutionary War military structure in center city Philadelphia.

Source: INHP sign in Franklin Square.

Franklin Square is today a popular family destination.

in Philadelphia, eating places, temporary exhibits, and a pavilion available for private parties. Three years later, the Delaware River Port Authority announced its intention to renovate and reopen its long-shuttered PATCO (Port Authority Transit Corporation) Speedline subway station beneath the square.[13]

Northwest Square became Logan Square to honor Philadelphia's early mayor and the colony's acting governor, James Logan (1674–1751). Logan had been William Penn's principal assistant and administrator of the colony from shortly after its founding. Until early in the nineteenth century, this space was the site of public executions and used as a burial ground. Development began around it by midcentury—the Cathedral Basilica of Saints Peter and Paul and the Academy of Natural Sciences remain from the mid-nineteenth century. In the same period, Wills Eye Hospital stood at Eighteenth and Race Streets on the square's south side, further demarcating the area as one for public institutions.

For three weeks in June 1864, the square was the temporary site of the Great Sanitary Fair, whose booths, tents, and arcades created a 200,000-square-foot complex where nearly a hundred vendors sold everything from arms and trophies to wax fruit, lingerie, and ale. For men, there was a smoking lounge in a Turkish divan. All proceeds went to buy medicines and supplies for Union troops. President and Mrs. Abraham Lincoln visited the fair, and the president donated ten signed copies of his Emancipation Proclamation, which sold for ten dollars each. By the time it ended, the hugely successful fair had raised more than a million dollars.[14]

When a traffic circle was created within Logan Square with the construction of the Benjamin Franklin Parkway, the former corners of the square remained outside the boulevard. Although these spaces continued to be regarded as parks, they were underused and little appreciated for decades. In 1999, the Central Philadelphia Development Corporation and Center City District headed a project to rejuvenate the parkway with the goal of attracting more visitors, especially pedestrians. Reviving these corner plots of Logan Square was a target.

In 2007, Aviator Park, the wedge of open space between Logan Circle and the western (Franklin Institute) and southern (Moore College) fronts received new sculpture and landscaping. Pedestrian access to that area, as elsewhere around the circle, was improved. Another makeover of the Sister Cities Park was completed in 2012, directly in front of the Cathedral Basilica

The Academy of Natural Sciences and the Franklin Institute

The Academy of Natural Sciences (ANS) of Drexel University is America's oldest natural history institution and today a world leader in biodiversity and environmental research. It was founded in Philadelphia in 1812 by many of the leading naturalists of the young Republic, whose express mission was "the encouragement and cultivation of the sciences." Throughout its two centuries, the academy has sponsored expeditions, conducted original environmental and systematic research, and amassed natural history collections containing more than seventeen million specimens. It has been located on the south side of Logan Square at Nineteenth Street since 1876. The academy became an affiliate of Drexel University in 2011 (www.ansp.org).

The Franklin Institute was established in 1824 and began operations in 1825. Its original Greek Revival building designed by John Haviland, at 15 South Seventh Street, is today the home of the Philadelphia History Museum at the Atwater Kent. The institute moved into its current home, designed by John T. Windrim (whose father, James T. Windrim, had designed the neighboring home of the ANS), on the Benjamin Franklin Parkway at Twentieth Street in 1934. Named after the noted American scientist, statesman, and Philadelphian, the Franklin Institute is one of the oldest centers of science education and development in the United States. The rotunda, which was modeled after the Pantheon in Rome, houses the Benjamin Franklin National Memorial. A twenty-foot-high marble statue of a seated Franklin by James Earle Fraser is the centerpiece (www.fi.edu).

The Cathedral Basilica of Saints Peter and Paul forms the park's backdrop.

of Saints Peter and Paul on Logan's eastern perimeter. A pavilion was created there with a café and visitor center, a children's play area, a boat pond, and an interactive fountain that pays tribute to Philadelphia's ten sister cities around the world. A rocky trail and a miniature creek in one corner are a small reminder of the Wissahickon. In the enthusiastic words of the *Inquirer*'s architectural critic, the park "captures the refined whimsy of Paris' Luxembourg Gardens and packs it into a space a quarter the size of Rittenhouse Square."[15]

Still another wedge of land outside Logan Circle was scheduled for a makeover. Directly in front of the Free Library on the north side, Shakespeare Park—named for Alexander S. Calder's Shakespeare Memorial, which dominates the space—will be considerably enlarged when it is extended to cover the below-grade I-676 and relandscaped. That will largely complete the transformation of the square surrounding Logan Circle into several attractive small parks.

For most of the first century after Thomas Holme laid out his plan for Philadelphia, the area around Southwest Square was heavily forested, and was frequented mostly by hunters and fisherman. As the city grew nearer, Southwest Square remained largely a grazing ground surrounded by brick kilns; a 1777 map shows six brickyards within two blocks of the square.[16] It became Rittenhouse Square in 1825 in recognition of David Rittenhouse (1732–1796), whose ancestral home is the remnant of a village bearing the family name in the Wissahickon.[17] As with the renaming of Penn's other public squares in the same year, the move by city councils, in addition to honoring several deceased notables, represented a first step toward turning the four outlying spaces into genuine parkland (Centre Square had taken on that aspect in 1799, when it became the site of the first waterworks).

The creation of Sister Cities Park in 2012 transformed a strip of Logan Square to the east of its traffic circle into a refreshment area with wading pool and summer playgrounds. (Photograph by Mark Garvin)

Rittenhouse Square was enclosed by a fence in 1816. Soon thereafter, property values in the area began to rise sharply, thanks to the burgeoning growth of Philadelphia. In 1840, the first of many large mansions to come was built on its north side. In that same year, it just missed becoming the site for a new astronomical observatory, proposed as a monument to David Rittenhouse himself. In 1853, the rough board fence that had encircled the plot of land for decades was replaced with one of wrought iron, and three large ornamental fountains were installed inside. Two smaller public drinking fountains and a horse trough stood outside the fence on Walnut Street. These new installations were a mark of the neighborhood's growing prestige. Its development as an enclave of the rich and powerful grew full tilt in the aftermath of the Civil War.

A self-made Irish immigrant, James Harper, led the way in 1840. A successful brick maker from the neighborhood and one of Philadelphia's leading citizens—he served both in city councils and the U.S. Congress—he had acquired lots adjacent to his brickyard, across the street from the square on Walnut Street. There he built his own fine house, along with the one next door for his daughter and son-in-law. He then made a handsome profit selling his other lots to well-to-do newcomers.

Within a few years, other neighbors included some of the nation's most prominent bankers and brokers, railroad builders and executives, international traders, and a distinguished widow who made *Godey's Lady's Book* the leading women's periodical in America. In 1857, the Episcopalian character of the neighborhood was underlined with the construction of the Church of the Holy Trinity at the corner of Walnut and Nineteenth Streets on the square. That church's young rector, Phillips Brooks, both drew and repelled congregants with his abolitionist sermons at the start of the Civil War. He would later write a poem, "O Little Town of Bethlehem," which would become a Christmas classic when set to music by Holy Trinity's organist, Lewis Redner.

By the end of the century, affluent neighbors began to push for the square's complete overhaul. Once plans developed for the creation of a Parisian-style parkway through Logan Square, Paul Philippe Cret, who had been instrumental in the 1907 parkway plans, was hired by the Rittenhouse Square Improvement Association and the Fairmount Park Commission (FPC) to redesign Rittenhouse Square. The Cret plan, which brought renovations that were begun in 1913 and completed in 1918, remains largely unchanged today. Flanked by ornamental balustrades, the park's entrances lead to diagonal walkways that cut across a circular walk near the perimeter.

The central plaza is a long oval set off by low railings, classical urns, a reflecting pool, flower beds, and sculpture. The tone of the whole is classically romantic and a durable setting for the most popular of Philadelphia's downtown squares.

In 1919, Albert Laessle's *Billy* was installed near the southwest entrance to Rittenhouse Square. The lifelike bronze goat has been a favorite of generations of children who love to climb onto its polished back. The sculpture was the gift of Eli K. Price II, who figured so prominently in the construction of the Philadelphia Museum of Art (Chapter 12). According to his grandson, Philip Price Jr.—the most recent member of his family to serve as a Fairmount Park commissioner (his great-great-grandfather, the first Eli K. Price, was responsible for adding most of the park's acreage in the 1870s)—

Rittenhouse Square has remained largely unchanged since its makeover a century ago by Paul P. Cret. (Photograph by Mark Garvin)

The bronze *Billy* near the southwest entrance to Rittenhouse Square is a favorite for children to climb.

the then president of the FPC, Edward T. Stotesbury, at first objected strongly to the idea that so mundane an animal should be featured in a park sculpture. E. K. Price II, who reportedly was not a particularly sociable figure but a quietly tenacious one, simply bided his time until he got his way with the Fairmount Park Art Association.[18]

In the 1950s, the city proposed building a giant underground parking garage beneath Rittenhouse Square. That raised the specter of a disfigured park with ramps spilling thousands of vehicles daily onto elegant and narrow streets. Residents in the neighborhood led the opposition in a campaign that ultimately stopped that project. Although the square is now surrounded by hotels and high-rise apartment buildings, several of the nineteenth-century mansions of the rich remain and have been converted to other uses. The park's lawns, benches, and walkways accommodate thousands daily.

By the second decade of the twenty-first century, Penn's four original squares were perhaps more uniformly prospering and gleaming than they had been at any time in their more than three-hundred-year history. Even their fifth companion, the long-vanished park at the center, was revived as a piece of its former self in the new green space at Dilworth Park. Notable in

Mansions on Rittenhouse Square

During the second half of the nineteenth century and the first decades of the twentieth, Rittenhouse Square was home to a number of Philadelphia's wealthiest citizens. A number of the grandest mansions of that period have been demolished, but several remain, converted to other uses. Since 1924, the Curtis Institute of Music has occupied two stately houses on the southeast corner of Eighteenth and Locust Streets, most notably, that of George W. Childs Drexel on the corner, which dates from 1893. Much of its great hall remains intact. Its Bok room, with ceiling murals by Edwin Blashfield, was the Drexel living room. The connecting house on Eighteenth Street was that of Edward A. Sibley. It retains an elaborately tiled floor designed by Philadelphia architect Frank Furness. The Field Concert Hall to the east on Locust Street was built on the site of the Drexel garden and greenhouse.

Just south of the Square at Eighteenth and Rittenhouse Streets, the freestanding mansion built for Samuel P. Wetherill in 1906 has long been the home of the Philadelphia Art Alliance, the oldest multidisciplinary arts center in the United States, founded in 1915. The house was purchased from the estate of the founder of the Art Alliance, Christine Wetherill Stevenson. Much of its interior, which contains a restaurant and is open to the public, retains features from the time of its construction.

On the northwest corner of Eighteenth and Walnut Streets, the Van Rensselaer mansion, dating from 1896–1898, in recent decades has housed a store selling apparel. In the Beaux Arts style, curved bays emerge from each end of its symmetrical façade on Eighteenth Street. On the second floor, medallion portraits of dozens of Venetian rulers remain on the ceiling of the "Doges' Room."

Two doors to the west, the Beaux Arts façade is all that remains of the Rittenhouse Club, which first moved its headquarters there in 1875 to what had been James Harper's 1840 house. In 1902, the club added the adjacent house, which had belonged to Harper's daughter, and had the new façade created to unify the buildings. After the club vacated the structure in the 1990s, a new thirty-three-story residential building was constructed just behind the Walnut Street address. The architect incorporated the façade while demolishing the rest of the building.

At the southwest corner of the square, three nineteenth-century townhouses were combined in the mid-twentieth century to become the home of a noted art collector and philanthropist, Henry P. McIlhenny. He was first a curator and later chairman of the board of the Philadelphia Museum of Art. Within a two-block radius of Rittenhouse Square are at least a dozen other distinguished houses from the same period. The 1800 block of Delancey Street is particularly notable for the number of residences dating from the period of circa 1850 to 1880.

the revival of each of them was the contribution that private organizations and foundations continued to make for their upkeep and renovation. At a time when taxpayer-based funding for Philadelphia's parks was among the lowest of any large city in the nation, these organizations, usually acting in concert with city agencies (or the National Park Service, in the case of Washington Square), in fact had become essential.[19]

With the creation of the Benjamin Franklin Parkway, Logan Square became the site of the Franklin Institute, which houses the national memorial to the parkway's namesake Philadelphian. (Photograph by Mark Garvin)

The Benjamin Franklin Parkway

In the 1680s, William Penn and his surveyor, Thomas Holme, made their mark as the first urban planners in the British colonies. Their design for Philadelphia in 1683 created a city with a gridiron of streets that would become the model for nearly every other town and city still to be created across North America. The imagined city's boundaries would stretch westward some two miles from the Delaware to the Schuylkill River, and reach roughly a mile from north to south between Vine and Cedar (now South) Streets. But a century later, Philadelphia's population was growing rapidly and soon started to spill over into land beyond those boundaries. In another few decades, new parkland at Fairmount began to develop outside the founder's planned city.

When the new waterworks began attracting increasing numbers of leisure time visitors to Fairmount, starting about 1815, the city's street plan made it awkward to reach the site. Philadelphia's parallel streets and squared-off blocks for building made it a developer's dream, but the layout required everyone in the city, whether riding or on foot, to take a right-angled or a zigzag path to any destination not in direct alignment with the gridiron of streets. Fairmount rose at a forty-five degree angle to the grid about a mile northwest of Centre Square, the hypothetical center (though still, in 1815, at the western edge) of Holme's Philadelphia.

As the century progressed, Fairmount Park grew from its nucleus at the waterworks to a vastly expanded acreage extending north to the new city limits on both sides of the Schuylkill and far up the Wissahickon Valley.[1] When railroads began to transport people from city to suburb, they also broke up the city's street grid by sometimes crossing it with their tracks. New rail lines carried visitors to the park, and were largely responsible for delivering nearly ten million people, some one-fifth of the nation's population, to the Centennial Exhibition within a six-month period in 1876. The exposition grounds were far removed from the park's historic heart, however, and pulled its center of gravity to land that had been almost entirely undeveloped a few years earlier. Even with rail access, all routes from center city remained indirect.

With the park's growth, the Fairmount Park commissioners also puzzled over what they should consider to be its main entrance: the bottom of the South Park beneath Fairmount, the Green Street entrance to the east, the Girard Avenue Bridge, or some other thoroughfare. Many streets ambled into the park; none commanded attention as an entry point. The presence of the grid of streets was only one factor here. Fairmount Park was created piecemeal over some three-quarters of a century. Unlike New York's Central Park, it had no master plan and, therefore, no moment when its major entrances could be determined and rationalized.[2]

Nonetheless, by the 1890s, the Green Street entrance, abutting the base of Fairmount to the east, had come to be viewed as the main portal from the heart of center city to the east park. That was the site chosen for the most important public work of art yet acquired by the park, the Washington Monument. The tribute to the nation's first president was unveiled there by President William McKinley on May 15, 1897.[3]

By then, however, a number of voices had been raised urging the creation of a boulevard or avenue that would connect the east park with Broad Street. As early as 1871, a pamphlet was published by an unknown author advocating such a plan: "If the great park, with which we have undertaken to adorn the city, is to be a place of general resort and to benefit all of our citizens," the writer argued, "it must be brought within the reach of all. It must be connected with Broad Street and with the centre of the city by as short a route as possible." The author suggested that two "grand avenues" might lead to each side of the park. Both would commence on North Broad Street, one at today's Spring Garden Street, the other at Callowhill, and then move diagonally to the eastern and western boundaries of the park, intersecting other imagined radial avenues along the way.[4]

A few years later, City Hall was under construction at Penn (formerly Centre) Square, making it a new focal point.[5] In 1884, that site was proposed as the Broad Street terminus of a grand boulevard running straight from there to the foot of Fairmount. A group of leading citizens began to support the idea with a petition drive, and in 1891, a bill to create such an avenue was introduced into the city councils. The measure was referred to the Department of Public Works, whose director, the architect John H. Windrim (1840–1919), responded with a plan for a parkway in February 1892. Both councils approved, and Mayor Edwin S. Stuart signed it into law on April 12.[6] The route of the parkway was added to the official city map.

Yet, in what would be a recurring theme in the effort to create a parkway, political forces were out of alignment. For most of the period from the end of the Civil War until World War II, the Republican machine dominated Philadelphia politics. Although he was a Republican, Stuart had been elected as a reform mayor, and he had the advantage of a new city charter granted by the state legislature in 1887, which increased the mayor's power. When the financial Panic of 1893 struck, the machine blamed reform elements for the city's resulting economic distress. Mayor Stuart then withdrew his endorsement of the Windrim plan. In July 1894, he vetoed parkway legislation in favor of funding for two essential city projects: rebuilding the city's water supply and improving its Delaware River piers. By December of that year, the proposed new boulevard was stricken from the city map.[7]

For the next two years, the boulevard project remained on hold. Meanwhile, however, Chicago's Columbian Exposition of 1893 was beginning to produce a profound impact on America's vision for its cities. The elegant, if temporary, "white city" that arose around the exposition's central lagoon suggested how the dirty, crowded cities of America could be revitalized through visionary planning. The "City Beautiful" could replace the dowdy industrial metropolis by erecting monumental buildings on broad boulevards and plazas, providing both sunlight and greater ease of movement.

In Philadelphia, one of those inspired by this promise was a young Republican lawyer, James M. Beck (1861–1936), who was clear in linking the goal of creating a parkway with an economic payoff. In an article he wrote for the *Philadelphia Inquirer* in 1894, he reasoned that beauty should be regarded as an investment, attracting developers to invest and spend in the city. "That American city which first appreciates the utility of mere beauty will ultimately lead our Western civilization," he predicted.[8] Beck's bona fides with the Republican machine—he would go on to serve as Warren G. Harding's solicitor general and a bitterly anti–New Deal congressman—reflected how the parkway project was no longer the sole darling of reform politicians. Still, the drive to make it a reality moved at a glacial pace throughout the rest of the 1890s.

At the turn of the century, a rising young architect, Albert Kelsey (1870–1950), took up the cause. He was instrumental in creating a coalition of private groups interested in building a parkway. First came the Art Federation of Philadelphia in 1900; two years later, that group spun off the Parkway Association, which contained a number of the city's wealthiest and most prominent citizens. Included were Alexander J. Cassatt, president of the Pennsylvania Railroad; John G. Johnson, corporate lawyer and art collector; James M. Beck; P. A. B. Widener, the transportation baron; Edward T. Stotesbury, an investment banker; and Mayor Samuel H. Ashbridge (best remembered for having said after his election in 1899: "I shall get out of this office all there is in it for Samuel H. Ashbridge").[9]

The Art Federation began the revival of the parkway project by hiring the architect Wilson Eyre Jr. to prepare a proposal. His plan aligned the southeastern stretch on the dome of the Cathedral of Saints Peter and Paul at Logan Square. The boulevard then continued on a slightly different angle to the park's east entrance near Green Street. But the Park Association's architect, William J. McAuley, straightened that route, and Kelsey redrew it. Meanwhile, the support of important groups and individuals was sustained, and the route returned to official maps of Philadelphia in March 1903.[10]

During this same period, two other organizations played important roles in the parkway effort: the Fairmount Park Art Association (FPAA) and the City Parks Association (CPA). The FPAA had been founded in 1871 to beautify Fairmount Park. Beginning in 1900, it began to turn its attention to other projects meant to improve the quality of life in the city. Leslie W. Miller, the organization's capable secretary for twenty years, helped make it an influential supporter of the parkway project. The CPA had been founded in 1888 to advocate for more parkland in the city. At the same time that Miller became secretary of the FPAA, Andrew Wright Crawford took that position for the CPA. He helped steer the organization toward city planning, arguing for new boulevards. Making the case for their economic benefits became something of a specialty for the CPA, as seen in this comment from one of its annual reports: "If Philadelphia remains rectangular, ugly, uninteresting, it will lose the millions of money that annually pass its doors."[11] The drive to create the parkway evidently was becoming irresistible.

Even so, in 1906, city councils intruded into the plans by modifying its route once more. Again, the axis was broken at Logan Square, as Eyre's plan had done, and the boulevard's terminus returned to the Washington Monument at the Green Street entrance to the park. This move was said to make more economical use of existing routes, requiring less demolition. It no doubt also took account of the financial interests of some of those connected with the machine. Once councils acted, demolition actually began of a modest house on North Twenty-First Street on February 22, 1907.

Less than six weeks later, Mayor John E. Reyburn took office and quickly assumed ownership of the parkway project. Within days after his inaugural, Reyburn was invited by the immensely rich streetcar magnate P. A. B. Widener to visit him at Lynnewood Hall, his baronial mansion in Elkins Park. Since 1893, Widener had been arguing for a new art museum to replace the cramped and distant gallery in Memorial Hall. An 1899 study had shown that the Schuylkill River was irredeemably polluted as a source for Philadelphia's water supply, so the Fairmount reservoirs soon would be useless. Widener had concluded that the best site for a new city gallery was that summit. He urged Reyburn to agree that the best arrangement would be to realign the parkway so that it terminated at the foot of Fairmount. Playing his trump card, he pledged that if that were to happen, he would pay to build the new art museum on the hilltop himself.[12]

Mayor Reyburn happily agreed. The other important advocacy groups also were persuaded. The FPAA commissioned a new architectural plan a mere three weeks after Reyburn met with Widener. They selected the French American architect, Paul P. Cret; Clarence Zantzinger and partners, one of whom, Charles L. Borie Jr., would play an important role also as a member of the FPAA from 1907; and Horace Trumbauer. By July 3, Zantzinger presented a preliminary report to the FPAA, and later in the summer, Cret prepared a bird's-eye view of the plan.[13] Cret's drawing shows a classical, domed art museum atop Fairmount, facing a grand rectangular plaza below. With what appears to be an obelisk at the center and monumental buildings on each side, the influence of the Place de la Concorde in Paris is apparent.[14] A smaller square at the plaza's northeast corner forms the base of a road running straight up the park's east side until it curves back toward the river in front of Boathouse Row. In Zantzinger's comment on this plan, it is "not an extension of Fairmount Park which is being created. It is an avenue in the city giving access to Fairmount Park."[15]

In spite of general enthusiasm for the proposal, its proponents were shocked when they learned that this revised, slightly more southern route, would add some $2 million in demolition costs because of the more expensive properties that stood in its way. A would-be compromise was suggested that would have required building an artificial extension of the hillside on the east side of Fairmount to place the parkway's terminus at a point where some of those demolition costs could be avoided. Finally, however, Mayor

No planner has had a greater impact on Philadelphia's Benjamin Franklin Parkway and other public spaces than this French American architect. A native of Lyon, Cret (1876–1945) came to Philadelphia in 1903 to join the Department of Architecture at the University of Pennsylvania, which he headed for the next thirty years. He was one of the main participants in creating the basic plan for the Benjamin Franklin Parkway for the Fairmount Park Art Association in 1907.

The next year, construction began on his design (with Philadelphia's Albert Kelsey, who earlier had pushed for a parkway in Philadelphia) for the new Pan American Union building in Washington, D.C., which would cement his reputation as a leading architect. While parkway construction was stalled, Cret was asked to prepare new landscaping for Rittenhouse Square. Those plans were completed by 1918, providing the design that Rittenhouse Square still wears today.

Meanwhile, Cret was in France when World War I broke out. He enlisted in the French army and served for the duration of the war, winning both a Croix de Guerre and Legion of Honor for his service. Back in Philadelphia while the parkway was being completed, he soon collaborated with Jacques Gréber on the design for the Rodin Museum. In the 1930s, Cret created designs for the three terraces of the Ellen Phillips Samuel Memorial on Kelly Drive in East Fairmount Park. In addition to other commissions outside the city—the Folger Shakespeare Library in Washington became one of his most acclaimed achievements—Cret left a further legacy in Philadelphia. He designed the Federal Reserve Bank on Chestnut Street, the Benjamin Franklin Bridge, the Barnes Foundation in Merion, Pennsylvania, and the National Memorial Arch at Valley Forge.

Cret received a gold medal from the American Institute of Architects in 1938. He is buried at Woodlands Cemetery, whose ornamental entrance gates he designed.

Reyburn was persuaded that such a scheme would be "ludicrous," and he then campaigned for more than a year on behalf of the more expensive route. In April 1908, voters approved a $1 million loan for the project. Later that year, the mayor personally led councilmen and leading arts advocates to the top of Fairmount to see the view.

Among those converted to the cause that day was Eli Kirk Price II, the president of the City Parks Association, vice president of the Fairmount Park Commission (FPC), and the grandson and namesake of the man who had been principally responsible for the rapid expansion of Fairmount Park in the 1860s and 1870s. In the years to come, in working to complete the parkway and especially the city's new museum of art, he would prove to be every bit as dogged as his grandfather.

On June 8, 1909, for yet a third time, a new version of a parkway was returned to the official map of Philadelphia.[16] For the remaining two-and-a-half years of Reyburn's term as mayor, the parkway project grew more prominent in the public eye. The Third Annual City Planning Conference held its meeting in Philadelphia in May 1911. One of its leading figures, Frederick Law Olmsted Jr., praised Reyburn's effort, saying: "Your city is the farthest ad-

vanced in the country in city planning."[17] The Department of Public Works created a model of the parkway for conference participants—and, afterward, the general public—to inspect.

In 1911, city councils finally passed two ordinances relevant to the Fairmount project. One decommissioned the waterworks and assigned the mayor to transform its buildings into an aquarium. The other gave the reservoirs on Fairmount's summit to the Fairmount Park Commission as the site for a new art museum. In December 1911, Reyburn left office to plaudits as the booster of the parkway and father of the grand art museum project. Yet, if the city was at last ready to accept Widener's generous offer to finance building it there, more than four years had passed since then, and Widener apparently was growing impatient if not disenchanted. Worse, the political omens now turned negative.

Rudolph Blankenburg, a Democrat, succeeded Reyburn as the most prominent champion of the Progressives yet to win office as mayor. Yet in a typically Philadelphian irony, this "Old Dutch Cleanser," as he was known, never was able to obtain the appropriations needed from the machine-controlled city councils to advance parkway construction. Throughout his

By 1911, plans for the parkway produced this model, looking from City Hall toward Fairmount, with a projected new art museum on the summit.

The Benjamin Franklin Parkway

four-year term, the project languished while the model still on display at City Hall grew dusty. Nor did any plan visibly advance—even though architects had been hired—to build a new art museum on Fairmount. At the very end of Blankenburg's term, in November 1915, P. A. B. Widener died, along with any lingering hope that he might finance a new building.[18]

Months before, in May of that year, the state legislature gave all Pennsylvania cities the important new right to control construction within two hundred feet of parkland. Philadelphia's city councils then voted to annex the parkway to Fairmount Park, thereby placing its control in the hands of the FPC. Mayor Blankenburg vetoed the measure; the commission, after all, was run by prominent Republicans, and the mayor was no doubt distrustful of its independent powers. Councils then overrode the mayor's veto.[19] In what may look today like another typically Philadelphian irony, here the forces of reform opposed expanding Fairmount Park, while the political machine, winning again, favored such action.

The Fairmount Park Commission, assessing the auguries, waited until Mayor Thomas B. Smith took office in 1916 before exercising its new powers. Smith's election restored Republican rule to City Hall, which meant a much more favorable climate for deals to be made with machine-connected contractors. Public works projects were suddenly in favor again. The FPC soon drafted land-use regulations for the parkway that differed from those for the city. The new regulations, adopted by the commission on December 13, 1916, in effect created Philadelphia's first zoning plan:[20] "The controls, still in effect today, limit building heights and establish setbacks designed to maintain the narrow connection east of Logan Square in contrast to the broad and more open areas to the west."[21]

Suddenly, parkway demolition proceeded full speed ahead, some ten years after ground was first broken for the project. Although Mayor Smith was twice indicted for election offenses while in office, he pushed parkway construction so quickly that it was nearly completed by the time the United States entered World War I in April 1917. Marines practiced battlefield maneuvers on the rubble. Several buildings that were engaged in war-related work were spared from demolition throughout the conflict. Most prominent of these was the Medico-Chirurgical Hospital between Seventeenth and Eighteenth Streets, which served as a navy hospital before taking in victims of the influenza epidemic of 1918. Still, once a temporary road was laid around the hospital, the parkway was declared fully open on October 26, 1918. Some thirteen hundred properties had been razed at a total cost of $35 million.[22]

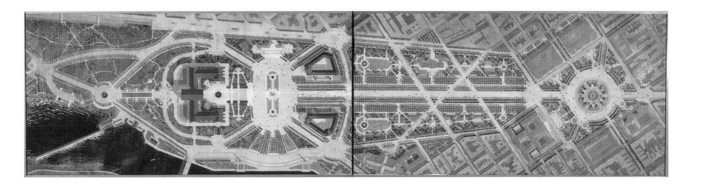

It had been nearly half a century since a parkway was first proposed, some thirty years since the first plans for it actually were laid. It also had been nearly ten years since the Cret-Zantzinger-Trumbauer plan had been adopted for a project not yet under the jurisdiction of the FPC. Given that change and the time that had elapsed since plans were begun, the commission decided to assert its authority by hiring its own consultant to reexamine the earlier design. In March 1917, its members voted to appoint the French landscape architect Jacques Gréber for that task. Gréber was in Philadelphia at the time, designing the grounds for the palatial new mansion of the commission president, Edward T. Stotesbury, who had urged fellow commissioners to choose the Frenchman for this assignment. Gréber spent the next months both in Philadelphia and back in France, preparing many drawings showing his revisions for the parkway.[23] At the behest of Mayor Smith, the Art Jury approved Gréber's plans on January 25, 1918. Five days later, the FPAA exhibited them publicly, and then published them as a booklet.[24]

The most notable change Gréber made to the 1907 plan drawn by Cret was to turn its northwestern stretch into a wedge of parkland reaching down toward the city. Where the original design had placed a rectangular plaza lined with monumental buildings at the foot of Fairmount, Gréber drew a more modest oval somewhat dwarfed by the tree-lined green spaces abutting the great diagonal boulevard. Civic buildings might now arise amid the green space on the parkway rather than cluster about the base of Fairmount. Logan Square, in turn, was transformed into a circle within a square, now enlarged to Twentieth Street, whose northern and western straight sides were intended for public buildings to complement the Cathedral of Saints Peter and Paul on the east and Academy of Natural Sciences on the south side that had been built there between the 1840s and 1870s. Gréber was clear about his intended allusion to Paris's Place de la Concorde and Avenue des Champs-Elysées, noting, as World War I drew to a close,

The Benjamin Franklin Parkway

If by this work the city of Paris may be enabled to bring its sister in America the inspiration of what makes Paris so attractive to visitors, it will be the first opportunity of Paris to pay a little of the great debt of thankfulness for what Philadelphia and its citizens have done for France during the last three years.[25]

Paul Cret, meanwhile, spent the war serving in the French army. From Europe, he grew increasingly unhappy over how his plans for the parkway seemingly had been usurped by a fellow countryman. In January 1919, he wrote of his concerns to Eli Kirk Price II, who responded with a soothing reply. Gréber's work, Price reassured him, had been limited to working out the landscaping of the parkway in keeping with Cret's own original design.[26] That was something of an understatement, although it was true that the 1907 plan was still discernible beneath Gréber's revisions. Price's reassurance no doubt helped Cret to reconcile with Gréber in the postwar period. Together, they designed the parkway's Rodin Museum in the late 1920s. That project, first rejected by Cret because of his unwillingness to work with Gréber, eventually came to pass as the result of the latter's careful cultivation—and praise—of Cret.[27]

(Facing page) From Logan Circle in the foreground to the Philadelphia Museum of Art, the Benjamin Franklin Parkway draws Fairmount Park down into center city.

The Parisian Parkway

The 1907 plan for what would become the Benjamin Franklin Parkway and every architectural iteration that followed paid homage to the most famous boulevard in Paris, the Avenue des Champs-Elysées. Philadelphia's version also would create a broad and tree-lined diagonal slicing across often dingy and congested streets. Its chief original designer, Paul Cret, had been schooled at Paris's Ecole des Beaux-Arts. His plan placed a monumental plaza in the spirit of the Place de la Concorde at the foot of Fairmount, with an obelisk as its centerpiece, surrounded by grand public buildings, much like its Parisian counterpart at the foot of the Champs-Elysées.

Ten years later, when construction of the parkway was finally ready to begin, another French architect, Jacques Gréber, made adjustments to the earlier plan. Gréber turned Cret's plaza into a smaller oval, while making the upper reach of the boulevard a green extension of the park. He also moved Cret's reference to the Place de la Concorde to Logan Square. That tribute became very clear by the time between 1927 and 1941, when two buildings were completed on the north side of the square on Vine Street that were meant to remind passersby of Concorde's two great landmark buildings, the French Maritime Ministry and Hotel de Crillon. The Philadelphia institutions are Horace Trumbauer's Free Library and John T. Windrim's Family Court building, respectively.

In place of the two great fountains and an Egyptian obelisk in Concorde, the focal point of Logan Circle is the immense Swann Fountain. The neoclassic Philadelphia Museum of Art, not the Arc de Triomphe, marks the boulevard's terminus at one end; City Hall, which resembles the Louvre, rises—like its counterpart at the visual end of the Champs-Elysées—at the other.

Nor is that the end of French connections on the parkway. The Philadelphia Museum of Art, the Rodin Museum, and the Barnes Foundation combine to provide along that boulevard one of the world's largest collections of the masterworks of French art.

Philadelphia's Free Library (above) and Family Court (top, opposite) on Logan Square were constructed to resemble landmark buildings on Paris's Place de la Concorde.

The French counterparts to Philadelphia's Free Library and Family Court: the French Maritime Ministry (bottom, opposite) and the Hotel de Crillon (visible, in part, to the left of the fountain).

During the first two decades of the twentieth century, a number of proposals were advanced for buildings and institutions that might line the parkway. Among those that never came to fruition were plans for an Episcopal cathedral, a campus for Temple University, a new building for the Pennsylvania Academy of Fine Arts, and a small art museum to house the collection of John G. Johnson. But during the period from 1920 to America's entry into World War II in December 1941, most of the important parkway buildings familiar to Philadelphians today were constructed, including the Philadelphia Museum of Art, whose birth pains are considered later.

First came the headquarters of the Insurance Company of North America, in 1925, at Sixteenth Street and the parkway, Emlyn L. Stewardson and George B. Page, architects. In 1927, the main branch of the Free Library of Philadelphia opened on the north side of Logan Square, Horace Trumbauer, architect. In 1928, the Fidelity Mutual Life Insurance Company was completed at Twenty-Fifth Street and the parkway, Clarence Zantzinger, Charles Borie, and Milton Medary, architects. The Rodin Museum by Cret and Gréber opened in 1929. In 1930, the Philadelphia Council of the Boy Scouts of America opened its headquarters building at Twenty-Second and Winter Streets, Charles Z. Klauder, architect. In 1932, the School Administration Building opened at Twenty-First and Winter Streets, just to the west of the Franklin Institute, Irwin T. Catherine, architect.

In 1934, after 110 years in other locations, the Franklin Institute officially opened its new building at Twentieth Street and the parkway, John T. Windrim, architect. In 1937, what had been named the Fairmount Parkway was officially changed to the Benjamin Franklin Parkway, and the following year, the Franklin Memorial in the Institute's rotunda was dedicated. Its colossal marble statue of a seated Franklin, by James Earle Fraser, is the focal point of what in 1976 was named the national memorial to Philadelphia's great eighteenth-century citizen. In 1937, sulfur lamps were installed alongside the parkway, illuminating the boulevard at night for the first time. In 1941, the Municipal Court (later, the Family Court) was dedicated on the north side of Logan Square, John T. Windrim, architect.[28] Its design paired it with Trumbauer's 1927 Central Library building across Eighteenth Street.

Two sculptural monuments would dominate the parkway. The Swann Memorial Fountain, the defining landmark and principal ornament of the

This colossal marble statue of a seated Franklin, by James Earle Fraser, dominates the memorial's rotunda. (Photograph by Mark Garvin)

new Logan Circle in the long view from City Hall to Fairmount, was completed in 1924 and named for Dr. Wilson Cary Swann, the founder of the Philadelphia Fountain Society. And in 1928, the Washington Monument was moved from the Green Street entrance to the new oval at the foot of Fairmount, marking the completion of the grand new approach to Fairmount Park.

The Swann Memorial Fountain, formally the *Fountain of the Three Rivers*, portrays Philadelphia's three principal waterways—the Delaware, Schuylkill, and the Wissahickon—as three allegorical figures of Native Americans. They are surrounded by the wildlife that thrives in these streams, principally frogs, turtles, and fish. Swans are present as a pun on the name of Dr. Wilson Cary Swann, for whom the installation was named. Architect Wilson Eyre designed the basin and water jets. The sculpture is the work of Alexander Stirling Calder (1870–1945), the son of Alexander Milne Calder (1846–1923), who had adorned City Hall with his statuary nearly half a century earlier, and the father of Alexander (Sandy) Calder (1898–1976), who would become famous as the creator of the mobile later in the twentieth century.

From a second-story window of the Philadelphia Museum of Art, it is possible to see examples of the work of all three generations of Calders. In the museum's Great Stair Hall, Sandy Calder's *Ghost* hangs from the ceiling. Looking down the parkway, Stirling Calder's Swann Memorial Fountain is visible at Logan Circle. At the far end rises City Hall, whose façade displays the many sculptures of Alexander Milne Calder.

Today, the neoclassic building of the Philadelphia Museum of Art (PMA) may look as if it has reigned through the ages from its Fairmount acropolis. But the history of its construction bears all the marks of an Olympian struggle. The story begins in the aftermath of the Centennial Exhibition, when Memorial Hall became the home of the Pennsylvania Museum of Art and Industry, which at first displayed and collected industrial objects as well as fine and decorative arts, including antique furniture. The model was the South Kensington Museum—today, the Victoria and Albert—in London.[29] But art-minded Philadelphians were critical of the facility from the beginning. They argued that Memorial Hall was both too far from center city and had inadequate gallery space for a first-class art museum. The grounds of Lemon Hill looked to some to be a preferable site for a new museum, although its mansion presumably would have to be demolished.

P. A. B. Widener, who in the post–Civil War period had become one of America's richest men as well as a noted art collector, became the most powerful advocate of a new museum at the Lemon Hill site. In 1894, he served on a

committee of the FPC that reported unfavorably on the alternative some
preferred, which was to enlarge Memorial Hall. Then, at Widener's urging,
the commission voted in 1895 to sponsor an open competition for the design
of a new museum at Lemon Hill. Although a winner was named in December of that year, both the contest and its outcome were met with skepticism
by those who saw bias on the part of the panel of jurors, whose choice of a
New York architectural firm was controversial. At the start of the contest,
however, the city's Franklin Fund offered its support for a new gallery if the
city would add a supplemental appropriation. Some two years later, in 1897,
a referendum approved a loan for the project.

At that point, however, plans came to a standstill. For the next decade,
the project's supporters largely marked time. During the last four years of
the century, Philadelphia's mayor, Charles Warwick, was among those opposed to a new museum. Funds were never appropriated in spite of the 1897
referendum. Widener and his allies no doubt grew increasingly frustrated at
the city's inaction. But by the start of the new century, he and others began
to think about a possible alternative site. One important player, the wealthy
collector John G. Johnson, held out for a site on South Broad Street, where

Alexander S. Calder's
*Fountain of the Three
Rivers,* popularly known
as the Swann Memorial
Fountain, has been the
focal point of the basin
at the center of Logan
Circle since 1924.

he exhibited his own vast collection of early European art in a building next to his opulent residence. In 1906, however, the Broad Street option was taken off the table when it was concluded that the terms of the bequest for the Wilstach collection, the centerpiece of the holdings at Memorial Hall for decades, forbade its being moved from Fairmount Park.[30]

The final straw against a Lemon Hill gallery may have come in March 1907, when the Board of City Trusts withdrew the Franklin Fund offer of a dozen years before. That is when a determined Widener invited the incoming mayor, John E. Reyburn, to his home to press upon him his new preference for Fairmount. From that moment on, with Widener's magnanimous offer in his pocket, Reyburn led the campaign to build the museum where the city's water supply had been stored for a century. But not even that activist mayor's exertions could move the museum project forward. That he failed no doubt had much to do with his comparative success at reenergizing the larger parkway project. Making that boulevard run straight from City Hall to the foot of Fairmount would be frightfully expensive; the museum project would have to wait. Reyburn did devise the strategy, at the end of his term in 1911, which would give the reservoir site to the FPC for an art museum. He also sought to appropriate the $200,000 voted by the people in 1897 to prepare the land and secure a design for the new building. But his official silence on the subject by the end of his term said that Widener's generous offer had been withdrawn.

Meanwhile, Eli Kirk Price II, the vice president of the FPC, had become the art museum's new champion. Once the reservoirs were transferred to the commission, it was Price who chaired the committee that the commission established to secure a design for the building. Studies had been made as early as 1905 for improving the Schuylkill River banks. These showed a new art gallery facing east toward the Green Street entrance to the park on the site of the reservoirs. Price and his committee now turned to a revised coalition of the architects involved in that effort.

The 1905 planning had included the architectural firm of Zantzinger and Borie, Paul Cret, and Horace Trumbauer. In 1911, the FPC named the same team, but without Cret. Trumbauer was known to be the favorite architect of Widener and Stotesbury, and Cret had a known distaste for Trumbauer's work.[31] As plans for the museum were developed, an important member of the team would be Trumbauer's chief designer, Julian Abele, the first prominent African American architect in the nation. For the next two years, the architects developed their designs and waited for the powerful Art Jury's approval and for the needed appropriations for the project to move off the drawing boards.

Yet these were the years when Mayor Rudolph Blankenburg was in office and at loggerheads with the machine-dominated Republicans. That party's majority in councils refused to pass the appropriations the mayor called for to finance the parkway and museum. The stalemate gave the architects little to do except to offer a number of possible designs for the new building. Then contractors concluded that the slope of the Fairmount site required further design changes. In 1914, the building plans were still being revised because of disagreements between the Zantzinger and Trumbauer offices, when the FPC demanded that the design process be brought to a conclusion. At last, on June 24, 1915, the Art Jury approved a compromise design "in principle." Eli Price had a large plaster model set up in City Hall courtyard, where thousands came to see it during the next several months.[32]

Machine rule was restored to City Hall with the election of Thomas Smith as mayor. Early in 1916, Price managed to persuade the new mayor to transfer large items in the Fairmount Park budget to the museum loan. Further architectural advisers were brought in for their suggestions. In January 1917, the mayor criticized the continuing delays. Finally, by March, both the Art Jury and the FPC gave their approval so that construction could begin. The end result was, to put it blandly, a collaborative effort "in response to input from Philadelphia's civic leaders and a host of architects."[33] But once more, the timing was ill-fated. A month later, on April 6, 1917, the United States declared war on Germany. As the war progressed, building materials became increasingly unavailable. Construction never got off the ground until almost the end of the war. After the dismissal of a lawsuit over a construction contract, it began at last in July 1919.

The year 1920 brought to office a new reform mayor, J. Hampton Moore, who placed the parkway projects under scrutiny in his opposition to "contractive rule."[34] The mayor grew increasingly suspicious of building costs at Fairmount, while construction moved at a snail's pace. He demanded an accounting from the commission at a meeting in November 1922. Price reported that more than $5 million in additional funds were needed simply to enclose the museum, which would still leave the interior unfinished. That caused the newspapers to attack the commission, and Price in particular, while the mayor responded by demanding a full report on the contracts that had been awarded. Construction still moved slowly—and expensively—although the FPC did then allow construction bids to proceed more openly. Price convinced his colleagues that they should build the two outer pavilions first, which was his obvious ploy to embarrass the city into coughing up the funds to complete the connecting, central pavilion. In 1924, the architects estimated that finishing

the interior would cost an additional $8.5 million, bringing the total cost to
$17 million.[35]

Again, like a rewound clock, the election of a new mayor with the backing of the machine brought a more workmanlike conclusion to the final four
years in the building saga. From 1924 to 1928, Mayor W. Freeland Kendrick
coaxed the city into providing some $9 million in appropriations. In the autumn of 1925, Fiske Kimball arrived to take charge of the museum's direction; months later, Eli Price was elected its president. Together, they would
steer the renamed Philadelphia Museum of Art into a new age. The nearly
completed building opened to the public on March 26, 1928. It recorded a
million visitors within its first year.

The long, titanic struggle had left its toll, however. Following P. A. B.
Widener's death in 1915, his son and heir, Joseph, both added to his father's
art collection and assumed his mantle in the project for a new art museum—
no longer to be financed by a Widener. He, along with Price, became a member of the Art Jury. In 1918, he promised that the Widener collection would
go to the city provided a satisfactory gallery was built for it. He also took a
personal interest in the collection of his father's contemporary, John G.
Johnson, who had died in 1917. Johnson had refused to bequeath his huge

collection of paintings to the city, but maintained them in a museum next to his own home on South Broad Street. Shortly before his death, he had added a codicil to his will designed to ensure that his collection remain in a home of its own unless some extraordinary circumstance should prevent that. For a time, Widener led the way in persuading city leaders that a second, smaller gallery should be built on the parkway to accommodate the Johnson collection.

But in 1920, the new reformist mayor, J. Hampton Moore, made it plain that he would not ask the city to finance a second new museum when construction of the first atop Fairmount was proving to be so expensive. Widener and the mayor then engaged in "a battle royal," at the end of which Widener resorted to the scorched earth policy of the defeated. In July, he resigned from the Art Jury, which had been entrusted with the Johnson collection, and rescinded his offer to give his own collection to the city.[36] Neither Eli Price nor, later, Fiske Kimball, could persuade him otherwise, although they and others tried for years. Instead, Joseph Widener became a founding benefactor of the new National Gallery of Art in Washington, and the gift of his collection was announced at its 1939 opening by President Franklin D. Roosevelt.

For nearly a century, the Philadelphia Museum of Art has dominated the summit of Fairmount.

The Benjamin Franklin Parkway

The Philadelphia Museum of Art

The Philadelphia Museum of Art opened its new and still unfinished building atop Fairmount to the public on March 26, 1928. The inaugural exhibition presented fine art and crafts from several European countries and America, as well as period rooms alongside the exhibit. Within a year, the PMA undertook the purchase of some two hundred objects from the collection of the French art connoisseur Edmond Folc, the largest single purchase by a museum up to that time.

Today, the museum houses some 230,000 objects dating from the first century A.D. in the Western world, and from the third millennium B.C.E. from Asia. In fact, Asian artifacts were collected from the early days of the PMA's origin as the Museum of Art and Industry at the close of the 1876 Centennial Exhibition.

During the past century, the PMA has become one of the leading art museums in America. The museum has long been strong in its holdings of Medieval European and Renaissance art. The John G. Johnson collection contains some twelve hundred works of pre-twentieth-century European masters. The Kienbusch collection of arms and armor is one of the largest in the Western Hemisphere.

Today, the museum has impressive collections of nineteenth-century work, including that of Cezanne, Monet, Renoir, and Van Gogh. The great Philadelphia painter, Thomas Eakins, is also well represented. The PMA administers the Rodin Museum at Twenty-Second Street and the parkway, which contains the largest collection outside Paris—127 marbles, bronzes, and plasters—of sculpture by Auguste Rodin. That collection was bequeathed to Philadelphia in 1926 by the philanthropist Jules Mastbaum.

Modern and contemporary art is represented in depth by such masters as Picasso, Brancusi, Klee, and Matisse. The Marcel Duchamps collection is the world's largest. The Alfred Steiglitz collection includes work by Georgia O'Keefe, Marsden Hartley, and others from the Steiglitz circle. Jasper Johns, Ellsworth Kelly, Robert Rauschenberg, and Cy Twombley are among many other contemporary artists represented.

Widener's action still left the fate of the Johnson collection unresolved. Its trustees were eventually persuaded that the works might be loaned to the Philadelphia museum if they could be displayed there within a specified period. To comply, some of the Johnson paintings were exhibited in the completed basement of the new building in October 1924. The entire collection finally came to the PMA nine years later. Johnson's bequest reportedly had required that his collection be housed in a fireproof building. In 1933, Orphan's Court was persuaded that Johnson's Broad Street house, unlike the PMA, did not meet that requirement. This constituted the extraordinary circumstance that Johnson's will had specified, which permitted the collection's removal to Fairmount.[37] After more than another half century, the court agreed in 1989 that the paintings need not be displayed separately from the general collection but might be integrated into it. The space on the parkway that had looked for a time as if it might house a Johnson gallery instead became the site of the Rodin Museum in 1929.[38]

From the 1930s until the end of the twentieth century, the only other major change to the Benjamin Franklin Parkway came with the creation of

John F. Kennedy Plaza in the 1960s. That project was the brainchild of Philadelphia's city planner Edmund Bacon and architect Vincent G. Kling. The square sits atop an underground parking garage between Fifteenth and Sixteenth Streets. Its creation was made possible with the demolition just to the south of the Pennsylvania Railroad's old Broad Street Station in 1953, along with the viaduct known as the "Chinese Wall" that carried trains west to the Schuylkill. Named as a memorial to President John F. Kennedy, the square is now familiarly known as LOVE Park for its Robert Indiana sculpture that has become an icon for visitors and a favorite vantage point for viewing the parkway (Chapter 15).

Otherwise, the parkway itself changed little throughout the last half of the twentieth century, apart from the maturing and, starting in 1989, replacement of the trees lining the boulevard above Logan Circle. Trees planted when the parkway was built were increasingly dead or dying by the 1980s. The FPC sponsored the Logan Circle/Parkway Trust for contributions toward replanting. Starting in 1989, 128 red oak trees and the stumps of an additional 90 were removed, along with old building rubble that had interfered with tree health. Long trenches were then dug to accommodate the root systems of the new trees: red maple, sweet gum, and red oaks.

In 1952, a Youth Study Center was built at Twentieth Street on the boulevard's north side, but was demolished in 2010 to make way for the new Barnes Foundation. The Moore Institute (now College) of Art built its school and galleries at Twentieth and Race Streets on the south side of Logan Circle in 1959. In 1969, the Friends Select School replaced its school buildings that had stood on the block between Sixteenth and Seventeenth Streets since 1848 with a coeducational school and office building. In 1965, what would become Eakins Oval was completed around the foot of Fairmount below the Art Museum to facilitate traffic flow. That extended Gréber's smaller oval eastward into a five-acre egg shape. As part of the celebration of the bicentennial of the United States in 1976, a tradition began to fly the flags of many nations on the upper parkway throughout the summer months. This includes some ninety flags that represent countries with significant populations in Philadelphia.[39]

The Central Philadelphia Development Corporation (CPDC), created in 1956, and its later affiliate, the Center City District (CCD), are made up of more than a hundred major Philadelphia companies. In their mission to promote the city's economic development, they have worked since 1999 with city and state agencies as well as other nonprofits to enhance the parkway. Proposing a return to the ideas inspired by Paul Cret in 1907, the goal has

been to induce somewhat more building along the boulevard, as well as improved amenities to encourage more activity.[40]

Fifteen years later, much had been achieved. New pedestrian and architectural lighting was in place, along with improved directional and interpretive signing, rebuilt sidewalks and curbs, benches, improved pedestrian access to Logan Circle, and a central median widened to eighteen feet, as well as new trees, shrubbery, and flowers.[41] In 2008, the relandscaped Three Parkway Plaza at Sixteenth Street became the home of the new Café Cret, which sold light fare and provided an information kiosk for visitors. A more ambitious project, the transformation of Dilworth Plaza into Dilworth Park, has brought the parkway's green ribbon to Penn Square itself for the first time since City Hall was built there in the 1870s (Chapter 11).

The latest grand building on the parkway was opened in May 2012, when the Barnes Foundation relocated its headquarters to Twentieth Street and the parkway from its Cret-designed home in Merion, Pennsylvania. After years of controversy and legal action over the terms of the indenture of Albert Barnes (1872–1951) for his immense collection, the move brought the most important new cultural institution to the parkway since the PMA was opened in 1928.[42] The court's decision allowing the move required that the collection be displayed in exactly the same arrangements that Barnes had decreed before his death in 1951. The architects Tod Williams and Billie Tsien designed an elegant building that re-created the Merion galleries precisely—even to their south-facing windows—while slicing twice through them to make space in between for intervening rooms and an atrium. At a right angle to the main galleries, they also added a separate pavilion for temporary exhibits, administrative space opposite the galleries, and a courtyard between them topped with a lantern or light box that emits gently filtered light (Chapter 18).

The collection, containing more than two thousand objects, is valued at more than six billion dollars today. Its collection of nineteenth- and early twentieth-century French masters is largely unparalleled outside Paris. The Barnes now presents itself as having the largest collection of Renoirs in the world, and more Cézannes than the Louvre.

Meanwhile, the first decades of the twenty-first century initiated significant expansion for the Philadelphia Museum of Art. In 2007, the Ruth and Raymond G. Perelman Building opened directly across the street from the main building between Twenty-Fifth and Twenty-Sixth Streets at Kelly Drive. The original Art Deco structure had begun in 1928, as headquarters for the Fidelity Mutual Life Insurance Company. In transforming it into

(Facing page)
City Hall tower is viewed at the end of the parkway. The fountain marks LOVE Park. (Photograph by Mark Garvin)

The "light box," which allows filtered light into the central hall of the new Barnes Foundation on the parkway.

the Perelman, Gluckman Mayner Architects doubled its size, mainly with the addition of a long, light-filled concourse, galleries, and a café along the back of the original Zantzinger-Medary-Borie building. The Perelman now houses the PMA library in addition to galleries and administrative space.[43]

In the year before the Perelman opened, PMA officials announced plans to expand the main building on Fairmount's summit during the next ten to fifteen years, adding some eighty thousand square feet of public space. New galleries for contemporary art and special exhibitions were to be carved out beneath the central plaza facing the Eakins Oval. Frank Gehry was named as the architect for the comprehensive master plan. The preliminary stage of the expansion was completed in 2009, when a new 440-car garage was created by excavating the hillside just to the northeast of the main building. Its green roof became the site for the new Anne d'Harnoncourt Sculpture Garden, named in memory of the late museum director. The project's second phase was completed in 2012, when the building's original ground-level entrance on the northeast side—facing directly across Kelly Drive to the Perelman's entrance—was reclaimed from its long use as a loading dock (a new 68,000-square-foot art handling facility, also green-roofed, was added below the building's southwest wing).

The reclaimed entrance led directly to an original, five-hundred-foot arcade, which in turn would open into the underground galleries to come. Their creation would be by far the largest part of the project. The new floor beneath the plaza would extend to the iconic steps leading down to the parkway. A possible window cut into those steps would allow views toward City Hall. The plan also would replace the ground floor auditorium with a dramatic new lobby opening into the arcade and then into the new galleries.[44]

The Barnes Foundation lantern also extends over an outdoor courtyard.

The Benjamin Franklin Parkway

A 2014 model of the Philadelphia Museum of Art reveals how Frank Gehry proposed to expand its galleries by creating a new subterranean floor and rearranging its interior.

A new auditorium was to be created below ground on the building's northwest corner.

Within weeks after the Barnes Foundation launched its new building on the parkway, the Rodin Museum reopened next door, in July 2012, after having been restored and its grounds renovated. Arts aficionados began to refer to Philadelphia's new "museum mile," which could now be said to run from the expanding Art Museum down the parkway past the Rodin, the Barnes, and then turn east on Cherry Street to the Pennsylvania Academy of the Fine Arts on Broad Street. In 2011, the academy's two buildings—the 1876 Historic Landmark Building and the 2002 Hamilton Building across the street to the north—were provided with a pedestrian link to the parkway when their shared block of Cherry Street became Lenfest Plaza. Several years earlier, while the Barnes Foundation's move to the parkway was still on the drawing boards, the PMA director, Anne d'Harnoncourt, had speculated that when it came to pass, "Philadelphia would have the largest concentration of French postimpressionist and modernist masterpieces outside of Paris."[45]

With the opening of the Barnes and the completion of improvements and renovations on the lower stretch of the Benjamin Franklin Parkway, the city announced a plan in 2013 to enhance underused space on the upper parkway between Logan Circle and Fairmount. The first phase was meant to be completed within three years, by the end of Mayor Nutter's term in office. It would concentrate on four plots totaling some thirteen acres: Eakins Oval; the perimeter of the Van Colln Memorial playing fields; "Iroquois Park," a strip to the north of the Oval named for Mark di Suvero's sculpture on that lawn; and a long grassy strip on the south side of the parkway in front of Park Towne Place. All of these spaces would be redesigned to attract the ten thousand Philadelphians residing within a ten-minute walk of the parkway.[46]

An initial step eliminates parked cars from Eakins Oval and improves pedestrian access there and at other intersections. The idea is to make the Oval a gathering place for entertainment and temporary art installations (Chapter 18). [47] To the north across the boulevard, Iroquois Park will be reconfigured to make it a neighborhood destination with walking paths and a gated play area for children. The playing field to the south of Spring Garden Street will have enhanced facilities for spectators and landscaped borders to separate the athletic areas from the more formal aesthetic of the parkway itself. Its west end will become the northern gateway to Eakins Oval from the Fairmount neighborhood. The Park Towne strip will be reconfigured as a set of outdoor rooms with a walking path, public art, boccie and volleyball courts, chess tables, and an enclosed play area for children. Refreshment facilities and restrooms will be created at a number of sites.[48]

Cutaway view of the Art Museum expansion.

The Benjamin Franklin Parkway

209

The Rodin Museum
houses the largest
collection of the works
of Auguste Rodin outside
Paris. (Photograph by
Mark Garvin)

In 2014, plans were announced to transform one of the signature build-ings on Logan Square into a luxury hotel. The Municipal (later Family) Court building that is the twin of the Free Library across Nineteenth Street would become vacant with the court's move to new and larger quarters at Fifteenth and Arch Streets. The new hotel's developer was required to pro-tect the building's historical features, including its façade and much of the interior, which includes thirty-seven murals and other details designated as "historically significant."[49] With 199 rooms, a ballroom, meeting and board-rooms, a spa and fitness center, restaurant and bar, the landmark building seemed set to become a public amenity in a way it had never been before.

In 2015, plans were well under way for a complete makeover of JFK Plaza (LOVE Park), the last piece in revitalizing the parkway. The entire plaza is built over underground structures—a parking garage and transit passage-ways—where structural repairs were needed. That prompted city officials to decide to reconfigure the park spanning the roof. With foundation support and public input, the goal was to make the space greener, more flexible, and a thoroughly inviting gathering place for the public at all hours of the day. The reconfigured park also should clarify its place as the end point of the parkway and approach to Dilworth Park and City Hall.[50] Its new water feature will further showcase the importance of water to the city all along the parkway. Visible first at the Fairmount Water Works, that theme continues at Logan Circle's Swann Fountain, then is carried to JFK Plaza and Dilworth Park at the door of City Hall.[51]

All of these recent plans and accomplishments are meant to make the parkway far more of a public park than it has been throughout most of its first century. As these changes have unfolded, increasing numbers of Philadelphians might agree with this observation from the president of the Greater Philadelphia Tourism Marketing Corporation:

> Almost a hundred years ago, the city built a boulevard that became a highway. Over the years buildings went up on it. . . . It's been relighted, replanted, populated with cafes and bicyclists. I look at it and think, we have a mile that is no longer a highway but a boulevard with people strolling on it.
>
> And I think, surely this was what was originally intended.[52]

Near the parkway, Lenfest Plaza links the two buildings of the Pennsylvania Academy of the Fine Arts on Broad Street. (Photograph by Mark Garvin)

The Benjamin Franklin Parkway

The Girard Avenue Bridge provided rail access to the Centennial Exhibition grounds, seen in the distance, while horse-drawn vehicles passed through Promontory Rock on the east side of the Schuylkill. (Courtesy of Steve Lynch; from Frank Leslie, *Illustrated Historical Register of the Centennial Exposition* [Philadelphia, PA: Frank Leslie's Publishing House, 1876])

Parks and Transportation
An Evolving History

Starting in the 1820s, the waterworks and then a growing Fairmount Park were leisure-time destinations for visitors from the city. Fairmount Park took shape at a time when transportation technology was undergoing dramatic change in America, although in the park's first decades, that scarcely mattered. The only parklands were those surrounding the waterworks, which lay little more than half a mile beyond the old city boundary at Vine Street, and so were accessible on foot. But with the growth of the park along both banks of the Schuylkill and the Wissahickon, travel to and through the area had to be addressed.

As early as 1805, at a time when a number of people were experimenting with how the steam engine might be used for transport, a Philadelphia inventor, Oliver Evans, attached such an engine to a hull, mounted it on wheels, and reportedly drove it through the streets of Philadelphia to the Schuylkill.[1] Two years later, Robert Fulton conducted his successful trial of a steamboat on the Hudson, ushering in a new age of waterborne transportation. That would make the Schuylkill a major route for delivering anthracite coal to the port of Philadelphia.[2] It also would allow small, steam-powered pleasure boats to provide access to the park. Soon, regular steamboat service carried visitors up the river from the end of Chestnut or Market Street to the boat basin just below the new dam and adjacent to the forebay. The canal and lock along the western bank allowed boats to move on upstream, where by the late 1830s, passengers might also disembark at Laurel Hill Cemetery. Starting in 1874, with the approach of the centennial, steamboats also stopped below the new Philadelphia Zoo at the Girard Bridge wharf on the western bank.

In Fairmount's early years, those visitors who did not arrive by boat either walked or rode in vehicles pulled by draft animals. Dozens of independently operated horse-drawn streetcar lines created a growing web of public transportation following the city's consolidation in 1854. Meanwhile, railroads were arriving. As early as 1832, the Philadelphia, Germantown, and Norristown Railroad became the first to serve the city. Others began operations later in that decade. Among them were lines that competed with or complemented the horse-drawn trolleys to carry commuters traveling about the city.

By the time of Fairmount Park's dramatic expansion, starting in the late 1860s, railroad lines were already crossing some of that land. Some rail companies attempted to build on parkland without obtaining the approval of the Fairmount Park Commission, which asserted its authority to prevent such efforts.[3] The commission took the initiative to make the park's further reaches accessible to the public. Since the point of the park was to preserve— or re-create—a bucolic landscape, care had to be taken when it came to creating and improving its roadways. The commissioners assured the public that these routes would be "judiciously adapted for pleasant transit, without injury to the natural scenery among which they are located."[4] That was not an impossible task when the only option for "pleasant transit" on the roads was nonmechanized travel, whether on horseback, by horse and carriage, bicycle, or on foot. Because of the park's configuration, long north-south roads were relatively easy to create through the flat terrain along both banks of the river. These and other roads through the park were almost entirely unpaved. Until the last decades of the nineteenth century, only the rare traveler would have walked or ridden by private conveyance the entire length of the park from downtown to the suburban countryside to the north.

In 1871, Fairmount Park's chief engineer, John C. Cresson, reported that tunneling had begun through Sedgley Rock. That outcropping, below today's Girard Avenue Bridge, is also known as Promontory Rock. It extends from the plateau above to the water's edge on the east bank, the only serious obstacle to creating a long road there. (The resulting tunnel remains today as a familiar feature to all who travel by car on Kelly Drive.) In the same year, Cresson also reported that after the Flat Iron had been acquired and its buildings demolished, "directions were given for the immediate opening of provisional drives and rides and walks, upon lines that would admit the public to the knowledge and enjoyment of the many remarkable objects which are found on the eastern bank of the Schuylkill."[5]

In their report of 1870, the Fairmount Park commissioners took evident pride in the varied kinds of transportation they were putting in place to make the park accessible to its citizens:

> The Commissioners have assiduously sought to furnish to the masses of the people every facility of access to, and recreation within, the splendid domain. . . . Steamboats and row-boats have been encouraged to ply on the Schuylkill; wheeled vehicles have been authorized, at moderate rates and with suitable safeguards against imposition, to carry passengers over the grounds; arrangements for cheap fares and frequent trains have been made with the railroads that penetrate the Park, and places for temperate refreshment have been provided.[6]

From our perspective today, those self-congratulations also hint at an inherent contradiction for this and other urban parks: such an abundance of means for gaining access to the park might someday threaten its peace and its very raison d'être.

That contradiction was thrust suddenly to the fore when, a year later, it became official that the nation's centennial would be celebrated in West Fairmount Park. Then the overriding concern became how to transport unprecedented numbers of people to its fairgrounds. Many Philadelphians were skeptical of the venture at the outset, and unsure that their city could—or even should—attempt the first world's fair to be staged in America. This immensely complex project had to be planned and created from the ground up in relatively little time, amid swirling uncertainties about leadership, funding, and logistics. A kind of trial run took place on Independence Day in 1875, some ten months before opening day for the exposition. That day's celebration at Fairmount Park showed serious deficiencies in the city's transportation capabilities. Even though more than 130,000 people had succeeded in getting to the park by public transportation, thousands of others had to walk. As a result, alarms were sounded for exposition planners.

Yet, by the time the great event ended in November of the following year, it had succeeded in providing adequate transportation to millions of visitors.[7] All the local streetcar lines increased their services. Both the Pennsylvania and the Philadelphia and Reading Railroads ran special trains to the Centennial Exposition from center city; excursion trips were added at reduced rates from New York, Baltimore, and Pittsburgh. An open-car, narrow-gauge train made the circuit of the exposition grounds in thirty-five minutes, with stops. For a five-cent fare, it carried nearly four million passengers about the

Horses strain to pull an overloaded car across the Centennial Exposition fairgrounds. (Courtesy of Steve Lynch; from Frank Leslie, *Illustrated Historical Register of the Centennial Exposition* [Philadelphia, PA: Frank Leslie's Publishing House, 1876])

fairgrounds. Rolling chairs also were available for rent, as were horse-drawn carriages from the city. Steamboat rides left from the boat basin above the dam. No previous world's fair had succeeded so well in transporting its visitors.[8]

By this and other measures, the Centennial Exposition had been an enormous success. But it had turned a huge swath of the park into a bustling if temporary city, whose demise had been planned from the start. Only two of its more than two hundred buildings remained after the exposition's close. The temporary hotels constructed just outside the grounds to house centennial guests were demolished. Public transportation in all forms was cut back with the reduction in crowds to the park after November 1876. The west park became a park again, albeit with the rigorous new concourse roads, traffic circle, and imposing Memorial Hall, suggesting to all who followed that a golden city, not a wilderness, had passed from there.

In 1896, the Philadelphia Transportation Company (PTC) began operation of its Fairmount Park Trolley, providing service from Wynnefield to Strawberry Mansion. The company built a power station to generate the necessary electricity below the level of the road where Montgomery Drive begins to rise from the west bank of the Schuylkill; a carbarn was constructed in a ravine above it. The section of the trolley track from Belmont Mansion to the carbarn was laid out in the bed of the 1834 inclined plane built for the Philadelphia and Columbia Railroad. Twenty stone arches, viaducts, and iron bridges were built to avoid grade crossings.

The open trolleys made two loops in summer, both stopping at Woodside Amusement Park, which was built and operated by the PTC. It carried passengers to distant stretches of the park, including Chamounix Lake. The trolley continued its service until 1946, when it was replaced by a bus route that served both the eastern (Forty-Fourth Street and Parkside) and western (Thirty-Third and Dauphin) terminals, but skirted the park. Today, the power station houses the Fairmount Park Building Maintenance Department and the carbarn is the automotive shop for Fairmount Park. Woodside Park was on the south side of Ford Road, just east of its intersection with Monument and Conshohocken Roads.[9]

Only with the dawn of a new century would another great change in transportation begin to impact Philadelphia's parks substantially. At first, the coming of the motorcar may have seemed unthreatening to Philadelphia's parks.

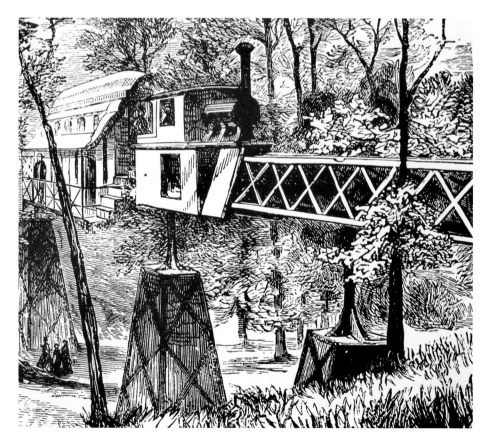

The world's first monorail gave visitors a brief ride across a narrow valley in Fairmount Park. (Courtesy of Steve Lynch; from Frank Leslie, *Illustrated Historical Register of the Centennial Exposition* [Philadelphia, PA: Frank Leslie's Publishing House, 1876])

Parks and Transportation: An Evolving History

Cars ventured into the largest, Fairmount Park, for recreation. That soon led to adapting the new Chamounix Speedway, meant for racing horses in 1901, into a track for racing cars. In 1906, Mount Pleasant became the headquarters of a ladies' automobile club. But within another few years, as car ownership grew rapidly while automobiles grew ever more powerful and speedy, many began to see how much they were disrupting the peace of the park. Car races were soon banned from Chamounix. In 1920, after much dispute, the only road along the banks of the Wissahickon came to be called Forbidden Drive when all automotive traffic was banned from it.

Yet at the same time, motor vehicles were fast becoming everyone's essential conveyance for getting into and around the city. Within a few decades, they had almost completely replaced beasts of burden for transporting people and goods. The long roads on both banks along the Schuylkill were paved and made ideal for automobiles. By the mid-twentieth century, those roads had become convenient thoroughfares through a large piece of the city once citizens of every class became car owners. The East and West River Drives (today's Kelly and Martin Luther King Jr. Drives) soon resembled four-lane highways to speed commuters through a landscape that no driver could take the time to savor. Contemplating nature was out of the question.[10]

Philadelphia, of course, was not the only American city in which park roads became highways. But both Fairmount Park's size and place within the city made its two river drives especially susceptible to speeding traffic. The architects of New York's Central Park, Olmsted and Vaux, had created east-west carriageways elevated and largely hidden from strollers through the park below. Those roads still allow motor vehicles to cross the park with little disturbance to park goers. Fairmount's configuration would not have allowed a similar solution.

The other large parks in the city—most notably, Cobbs Creek, Pennypack, and Tacony—followed the narrow valleys of their namesake waterways where no roads ran. Although each of them was crossed by numerous city streets and highways, none offered much possibility for extended travel by roadway through the parks themselves. It would be another half century before these places would be threatened by other types of vehicular traffic.

The conversion of Fairmount's East and West River Drives into what amounted to highways paled beside the decision to build the Schuylkill Expressway (today's I-76) through the length of West Fairmount Park. Those miles of open land made it a highway builder's dream. By the time its final section was opened in 1960, the expressway seemed to many a reactionary conclusion to what had begun nearly thirty years earlier as an innovative

A postcard from circa 1915 suggests the hazards in traversing Fairmount Park's Wissahickon Creek, where roads were unimproved. (Courtesy of Steve Lynch)

plan to alleviate traffic congestion. Conceived as the "Valley Forge Parkway" in 1932, the original idea was for a cars-only road from Fairmount Park to Valley Forge State Park, similar to parkways then being constructed around New York City. But that plan stalled and was abandoned. In 1947, a more ambitious proposal for an all-vehicle expressway that would connect with the Pennsylvania Turnpike near Valley Forge was approved by city officials. Construction began in 1949.

In the years that had passed between the first proposal for a parkway and the start of construction on a much-expanded expressway, automotive traffic had increased severalfold throughout the nation. By the 1950s, the Eisenhower administration was pouring federal funds into the creation of interstate highways (the Schuylkill Expressway became a part of that system in 1956). Railroads were neglected and failed, while motor vehicles became almost the sole mode of transportation in the United States.

It was in this context that construction of the Schuylkill Expressway beside the river became irresistible, even for Philadelphians who had loudly resisted having it traverse Fairmount Park. What made it so above all was the park's very openness; no city blocks of buildings would have to be demolished to build the road. One of the engineers in charge of designing the highway proposed that for one mile of the route through the park it should be elevated on a hundred-foot-high platform. Although that did not happen, the proposal probably mollified the opposition that many citizens had expressed at the plan to build the expressway through the park.

Parks and Transportation: An Evolving History

The loss to the park was grave. The barrier it created for all who want to move westward from Martin Luther King Jr. Drive at least is penetrable in places, thanks to crossroads beneath the roadbed. But a set of access ramps at Ridge Avenue and Kelly Drive eliminated an easy approach to the Wissahickon from the east park and center city. In the west park, Chamounix Falls was destroyed and Chamounix Lake in the glen below the house was buried under the expressway.[11] Any number of once serene and peaceful plots within the park are now disturbed by the hum and roar of traffic from the expressway.

Richardson Dilworth was Philadelphia's mayor when the expressway was completed through Fairmount Park and Philadelphia's University City neighborhood. Long after leaving the mayor's office in 1962 to run unsuccessfully for governor, he called the expressway project "the worst mistake in my administration."[12] He never again held elective office.

Meanwhile, at the same time a "parkway" was first proposed to slice through Fairmount Park, a plan was launched for a similar thoroughfare through Cobbs Creek Park. In its final form, in 1964, it would have become a five-mile link in a highway system around and through Philadelphia. It would have begun near the Philadelphia International Airport at the Delaware Expressway (I-95), run north through much of the lower part of Cobbs Creek past Mount Moriah Cemetery, and then connect to another motorway at Whitby Avenue in West Philadelphia. That would have brought the loop back across the Schuylkill to Gray's Ferry and the Schuylkill Expressway itself.

No Champ Car Races on the Parkway

Just as the open spaces of Philadelphia's parks have long lured drivers of all kinds of vehicles, so has the Benjamin Franklin Parkway looked to some—including some commuters—like a raceway. In 2005, Philadelphia considered a proposal to hold the Champ Car World Series there. It would have turned the parkway into a 1.8-mile course, from Logan Circle at Eighteenth Street around the Eakins Oval at the foot of Fairmount, and back again. The design would have required an estimated $800,000 in renovation costs, which would have included creating at least four pedestrian bridges and the widening of some streets.

The proposal was supported by at least one member of the City Council, and by actor Paul Newman, co-owner of a racing team. Proponents argued that the event would generate millions of dollars in visitor spending for hotels, restaurants, and shopping.

But the Parkway Council Foundation, whose members included the cultural institutions along the parkway, opposed the idea. In the words of the president of Moore College of Art and Design: "Turning our most beautiful boulevard into a high-speed racetrack goes against everything we want." Suggestions for other sites in the city, including FDR Park in South Philadelphia and Fairmount Park itself, were ruled out as unusable for other reasons.

By the 1960s, the Cobbs Creek proposal was joined in the public mind to plans announced in 1962 for a second Schuylkill Expressway parallel to the first, but running through East Fairmount Park. Opposition to both grew so great that both proposals were finally withdrawn. That marked the end to the "expressway revolts" as they related to the destruction of Philadelphia's principal parks.[13] Although limited-access highways continued to be built, both in the Philadelphia area and across the nation, their costs as well as their benefits in moving people and goods at last had become evident. The costs drew such opposition in Philadelphia that, unlike some cities, only one such expressway was constructed through its heart. But the one the city did build seriously compromised one of the nation's greatest urban parks.

From the time of its completion, studies have shown that the Schuylkill Expressway has been perennially unable to cope with ever-growing traffic demand. Undoubtedly because the section within the west park is unencumbered by nearby buildings, a piece of it was widened to six lanes by 1972. Suggestions are made from time to time to bury and cap at least part of the expressway in the park. As of now, that is more fantasy than realistic possibility, thanks to the

Across the river from the waterworks, the Schuylkill Expressway slashes through West Fairmount Park.

Parks and Transportation: An Evolving History

enormous cost. For the foreseeable future, as for the past half century, Philadelphia will live with the unhealed gash through its largest park.

Just as the impact of automobiles on virtually every aspect of modern life has been profound, so William Penn's original public squares also have been affected (Chapter 11). Franklin Square became a derelict park through much of the twentieth century once its neighborhood of residences was destroyed to make way, first for the Benjamin Franklin Bridge and then the Vine Street Expressway. Rittenhouse Square was threatened, then saved, from the almost certain desecration of having a parking garage constructed beneath it. Logan Square, meanwhile, was given over almost completely to vehicular traffic when it was largely replaced with a traffic circle as part of the construction of the Benjamin Franklin Parkway.

By the last years of the twentieth century, a new vehicular menace was threatening Philadelphia parklands. All-terrain vehicles (ATVs) and dirt bikes (off-road motorcycles) give their drivers the ability to seek automotive thrills on virtually any open land—the less urbanized the land, the greater the adventure. Banned on city streets and parks, their presence nonetheless grew in the city. By 2012, Tacony Park had become a preferred space for ATV users, although they also had done damage to other parks in the city. That October, the commissioner for Parks and Recreation (PPR) reported to City Council that his department had spent $250,000 to repair damage to parks in recent years. Some proposed that a solution would be to create an approved site for the use of these vehicles, similar to that for skateboarders. The commissioner argued that there was insufficient public space in Philadelphia to allow their safe operation. But he did suggest that advocates might look to the private sector to help provide such a space, or spaces.[14]

The controversy over ATVs was in many respects a replay of that over racing cars in the park a century earlier. Both underlined the inherent contradiction in how automotive vehicles can be used: they are the most essential means of general transportation, but have recreational uses as well. Since parks are specifically intended for recreation, they are, for some, obvious venues for that second usage, in spite of the social and environmental disturbances that ensue. The conflicts that result have never been permanently resolved.

Although automobiles remain the centerpiece of transportation modes today, signs have appeared in recent years of a new emphasis both on taming traffic in urban areas and on nonmotorized alternatives, such as bicycling. Early in our century, a federal highway was reconfigured for a nine-mile stretch through Philadelphia's northern suburbs as the Route 202 Parkway, a "shared-use trail." Traffic was slowed by reconfiguring the roadway and

All-terrain vehicles are driven illegally across Fairmount Park's Belmont Plateau while a game of sandlot baseball is in progress. (Courtesy of the *Philadelphia Inquirer*)

installing new traffic lights. A twelve-foot-wide paved trail alongside the road provides nonmotorized transportation and a recreation facility for walkers, runners, skaters, and cyclists.

In the city, similar efforts were under way to calm traffic on both the Benjamin Franklin Parkway and Columbus Boulevard along the Delaware. In both places, the goal was to make the avenue more attractive to pedestrians and other recreational users. The plan for the parkway, announced in spring 2013, captured the goal in its catchphrase, "More Park, Less Way." These moves seemed to be in harmony with the temper of the times. In what was perhaps a sign that America's love affair with automobiles was tapering off nationwide, a smaller percentage of young adults were becoming car owners than ever before.

Not coincidentally, these developments are occurring at a time when bicycles are staging a comeback in urban areas, both for workday commutes and recreation (Chapter 17). In June 2013, the first stretch of the Delaware River Trail was opened from Spring Garden to Ellen Street. Once that trail is completed, in ten to fifteen years, it will connect with a series of bicycle and pedestrian paths meant to expand into a citywide transportation system, as well as the East Coast Greenway, which is projected to run from Maine to Florida and connect to both the Delaware and Schuylkill Rivers.[15]

A bronze sculpture by Jacques Lipchitz, *The Spirit of Enterprise*, dominates the central terrace of the Ellen Phillips Samuel Memorial, which borders the Schuylkill River on Kelly Drive in East Fairmount Park. (Photograph by Mark Garvin)

Public Art in Philadelphia

Philadelphia is home to more than a thousand works of art scattered throughout its parks and other public places. That constitutes the largest number of artworks available for the public to enjoy free of charge in any American city. This legacy would not have been possible without its intimate connection to the history of Fairmount Park for the past 150 years, and specifically to the creation of the Fairmount Park Art Association (FPAA) in 1872. But by 1872, Philadelphia was already nearly two hundred years old, with a public art tradition that had taken root in the previous century.

In the first decades of the new Republic, Philadelphia was home to skilled portrait painters—Charles Willson Peale, Gilbert Stuart, and Thomas Sully among them. Although none of these artists produced work to be exhibited publicly out of doors, all created popular art in the sense that they sought to capture the likenesses of statesmen and other notables of their time. Many of their works, such as Stuart's portraits of Washington, became enduring popular icons. Peale deserves a special nod, both for his effort to record and display the faces of as many contemporary leaders as possible, and for his appeal to popular taste in the exhibits that he created for his own natural history museum. His many portraits of American military and political leaders at the time of the Revolution are owned by the City of Philadelphia and housed in the Portrait Gallery of the Second Bank of the United States in Independence National Historical Park.[1]

During the same period, likenesses of the nation's first heroes were being created as busts and statues for public display. The French sculptor Jean-Antoine Houdon made portrait busts of several prominent Americans when

14

A tribute to Benjamin Franklin was Philadelphia's first public monument in 1792. This 1950s copy is displayed on the façade of the American Philosophical Society Library on Fifth Street.

they were in Paris—Franklin, Jefferson, and John Paul Jones among them. After Franklin proposed it, Houdon traveled to Mount Vernon in 1785 to create a life portrait of General Washington. The marble original of Houdon's standing figure of Washington went to Virginia's capitol in Richmond about 1790. In the 1950s, a bronze casting of that work was made and installed in Philadelphia's Washington Square. In 1792, Philadelphia's first public monument was mounted in a niche over the entry to the Library Company's building on Fifth Street. The figure, by Francesco Lazzarini, was of the city's own Benjamin Franklin, dressed in a classical pose complete with toga, his right elbow resting on a pile of books.[2]

Yet neither Houdon nor Lazzarini was an American. It was a Philadelphia wood-carver, William Rush (1756–1833), who became the nation's first distinguished sculptor. Beginning as a carver of ship mastheads, Rush came from the early American tradition in which fine craftsmanship led to fine art, as we now recognize was also the case with Philadelphia's distinguished furniture- and cabinetmakers of the period. Rush was first called on to adorn Latrobe's waterworks at Centre Square in 1809. After the new pumping station was built on the riverbank below Fairmount, Rush was commissioned to create the two figures in his *Allegory of the Schuylkill*, followed in 1829 by his *Mercury*. In 1824, he carved the figures for the great Civic Arch made in honor of Lafayette's triumphal return to Philadelphia. Those figures, *Wisdom* and *Justice*, then were displayed in the engine house at the waterworks once its steam engines were made obsolete by the conversion to water power at Fairmount. His *Water Nymph and Bittern* fountain also was moved from Centre Square to Fairmount's South Garden.[3]

At the time of his death, Rush was recognized as a major and unique figure in American art. He had successfully blended the neoclassicism or "correct style" of his day with the folk appeal of his own early work as a ship's carver. The examples of his artistry at the waterworks no doubt registered in the minds of Philadelphians as an appropriate precedent for public art.

William Rush's two figures, *Schuylkill Freed* (shown) and *Schuylkill Chained*, were installed at the Fairmount Water Works in 1825. (Photograph by Mark Garvin)

Schuylkill Chained, one of the two figures in William Rush's *Allegory of the Schuylkill*. (Photograph by Mark Garvin)

Starting in the 1830s, the development of Laurel Hill Cemetery north of Fairmount soon would lead to a veritable explosion of public art in its funerary monuments.[4] Like the other rural garden cemeteries that followed it in Philadelphia—Cathedral, Woodlands, and Mount Vernon—Laurel Hill was effectively a public park before the public grounds at Fairmount extended beyond several acres at the waterworks. Attracting thousands of visitors to stroll there in fine weather, Laurel Hill gradually filled up with a forest of monuments created by distinguished architects, with statuary commissioned from leading sculptors.

Among these was an immigrant from France in 1850, Joseph Alexis Bailly (1825–1883). Like Rush, he began as a wood-carver and would soon become a popular and accomplished figurative sculptor in his adopted city. He created a number of pieces as memorials at Laurel Hill and, in 1869, a marble likeness of George Washington that was installed in front of Independence Hall.[5] Important sculptures by other artists at Laurel Hill include James Thom's *Old Mortality* near the cemetery's main entrance, as well as work by both Alexander Milne Calder and his son, Alexander Stirling Calder.[6] The Twiggs tomb, commemorating the lives of a father and son who died in the Mexican War, is by Richard Graff, son of the elder Frederick Graff, the designer of the Fairmount Water Works.

The landscape and sculptural adornment of Laurel Hill make plain the Romantic ideal of the time in which the cemetery was conceived and the sturdy moralism of the Victorian period in which it grew. Individuals were honored in death through their heroic likenesses in stone or bronze; so were representations of the principles meant to guide each generation, such as honor, faith, chastity, humility, and perseverance.

With the growth of industry in Philadelphia following the Civil War, the fading of what seemed a simpler, perhaps a more principled and civilized era brought a call to action in the early 1870s. Two local young men from the city's political and social elite decided to take action against what they saw as "the universal standardization of machinery . . . stamping out the artistic soul of the individual." Young as they were, these two succeeded in acquiring enough support from the social circles they moved in to form the Fairmount Park Art Association (FPAA), which was chartered by the Commonwealth in 1872.

Charles H. Howell (1848–1902), a member of the First City Troop, would become an active friend and contributor to many charities. Henry K. Fox (1847–1930) was the son of the then mayor of Philadelphia, Daniel M. Fox. Howell served on the FPAA Board of Trustees from its inception, as secretary from 1886 to 1900 and as president for the last two years of his life. Fox was also a trustee and later vice president of the association.

Thirteen additional prominent men consented to act as temporary officers and trustees. A constitution and bylaws were drawn up, with a preamble specifying that members were obligated to make annual contributions for a fund "devoted to and employed in the adorning of Fairmount Park with works of art, either of a memorial nature or otherwise."[7] The financier and philanthropist Anthony J. Drexel became president and held that position until his death in 1893. Some two hundred subscribers became charter members of the association, making it the nation's first private nonprofit organization dedicated to providing public art. It would be a citizens' organization intended "to increase the appreciation and love of art in our midst, to add to the number of its votaries, promote the refinements of life . . . and encourage artists in the practice of their profession."[8]

Although it was initially created to enhance Fairmount Park with sculpture, the FPAA soon expanded its concerns to consider public art projects throughout the city. That practice was not formalized until 1906, when the FPAA amended its charter to "promote and foster the beautiful in the city of Philadelphia, in its architecture, improvements and general plan."[9] More than a century later, after its long experience as the leading organization in promoting, guiding, and providing public art projects throughout the city, the FPAA formally changed its name to reflect what had been its role from its infancy. Now the Association for Public Art (aPA), it describes itself as the first such organization "dedicated to integrating public art and urban planning."[10] The FPAA/aPA cannot be credited for all the public art in Philadelphia today. But its hand is visible in virtually everything that has been displayed to the public since the early 1870s.

The term "urban planning" was virtually unknown when the FPAA was formed in 1872. Yet a dominant aesthetic was clearly present to guide the organization in its artistic choices for the park and, eventually, for the rest of Philadelphia. Not surprisingly, that aesthetic has shifted through the years in keeping with changing artistic tastes and social values. No doubt the FPAA has more often reflected each era's aesthetic mainstream than it has acted as an artistic vanguard. But it also has been a consistent watchman to ensure high levels of taste and sensibility in Philadelphia's public art.

For many years, figurative work dominated the choices for art in the public sphere. Allegorical themes were in style, as much of the statuary in Laurel Hill makes clear. The very first gift to the FPAA, Edward Stauch's *Night* in 1872, is such a work. Other examples include Moses Jacob Ezekiel's *Religious Liberty* of 1876, commissioned by the American chapter of B'nai B'rith and today installed on Independence Mall in front of the American Jewish

Ezekiel's *Religious Liberty* of 1876 now faces Independence Mall in front of the American Jewish Museum.

Museum; and Daniel Chester French's circa 1880 grouping, *Law, Prosperity, and Power*, originally at the U.S. Post Office at Ninth and Chestnut Streets and now on Georges Hill above the Mann Center for the Performing Arts.

At the moment the FPAA came into being, the immense new City Hall was rising on Penn Square. By the time it was completed in 1901, its façade was heavily decorated with more than 250 pieces of sculpture, almost all of which came from the studio of Alexander M. Calder. There is no evidence that the FPAA had a direct hand in guiding the decoration of City Hall, whose sculptural program continued from 1873 to 1893. But Calder and his studio cannot have been unaware of the association's purpose, and FPAA members surely were supportive of Calder's work there.

The *Fountain of Orestes and Pylades* was acquired for Fairmount Park in 1884.

The City Hall sculptures are, above all, a collective tribute to the founding of Pennsylvania, as is evident from the colossal statue of William Penn towering over the city from his perch atop the clock tower. Allegorical themes abound, revealing Philadelphia's history and government, as well as more abstract ideas such as justice, liberty, fame, industry, peace, prayer, science, and repentance. Its central pavilions include representations of the four continents with the heads of animals native to each among the dormers. On the eaves of the clock tower, four bronze figures below Penn represent European settlers to the region and Native Americans; between them are four bronze eagles. As Philadelphia's Historical Commission noted in 1981, the building is "as much a work of art as an architectural and engineering wonder."[11]

References to classical sculpture were also very much the fashion when the FPAA began its work, with such Athenian virtues as democracy and liberty having long been associated with republican America. Early acquisitions for Fairmount Park include the 1884 *Fountain of Orestes and Pylades*; a bronze casting of the ancient work attributed to Praxiteles, *Silenus and the Infant Bacchus*, installed in 1885 in the east park north of Fairmount Avenue; and, in the same year, the reproduction of the Greek *The Wrestlers*, which was donated by A. J. Drexel.[12]

Sculptural depictions of heroes were very much in vogue, as they had been from the time when Washington and Franklin were so honored. By the 1870s, the martyred

Abraham Lincoln was the subject of an impressive monument installed on Kelly Drive at Sedgley Drive. While the place of these individuals in the pantheon of American history seemed secure, changing views of other historical figures could sometimes alter the power of their monuments over time.

For example, a statue of Christopher Columbus was dedicated on the Centennial Exhibition grounds on October 12, 1876, the anniversary of his first landing in the Americas. A century later, it was relocated to Marconi Plaza on South Broad Street. That relocation placed the statue in the heart of a traditionally Italian American neighborhood. But it also seemed to mark the explorer's demotion at a time when his "discovery" of the New World was increasingly challenged by Native Americans and other non-Europeans.

Nor have all the other non-American historical figures memorialized in Philadelphia retained their charisma over time. Yet, they were often created as a tribute to, and with the support of, relevant immigrant communities. In the 1870s, Philadelphia's German citizens provided the funds for a sculptural likeness of the great German polymath Alexander von Humboldt, which was dedicated as part of the centennial celebration of 1876. At the time of his death in 1859, Humboldt was hailed as one of the greatest figures of the age, although few who pass his likeness in West Fairmount Park today are likely to recognize his accomplishments. Emmanuel Frémiet's *Joan of Arc*

In 1885, a reproduction of *The Wrestlers* from Classical Greece was a gift to the Fairmount Park Art Association. (Photograph by Mark Garvin)

was unveiled in 1890, with members of the city's French community participating in a ceremony that included orations in French and English, and the Girard College band playing "La Marseillaise."[13] While the Maid of Orleans remains universally known, in France, her symbol today has come to be associated with extreme right-wing politics.

Public monuments inevitably reflect the status of the individual being honored at the time they are created. A Philadelphia leader, Morton McMichael, who had served both as mayor of Philadelphia and the first president of the Fairmount Park Commission, was given his own bronze likeness in the park only two years after his death in 1879. Within the next few years, Pennsylvanians remembered as Civil War heroes also were memorialized; the north plaza of City Hall holds equestrian statues of Lancaster's major general John Fulton Reynolds and Philadelphia's general George McClellan. Another Philadelphian, General George G. Meade, who in retirement had been an important member of the Fairmount Park Commission, is shown astride his horse in a tribute north of Memorial Hall that was created by Alexander M. Calder.

Also from the early days of the FPAA, perhaps reacting to a romantic nostalgia for what was fast disappearing, public art in Philadelphia revealed a strong interest in portraying both wild animals and indigenous people. An early purchase was Edward Kemeys's 1872 work, *Hudson Bay Wolves Quarreling over the Carcass of a Deer*. It has been joined at the Philadelphia Zoo by several other depictions of wild animals from the same period, as well as more recent tributes to zoo residents. The French animaliers, led by Antoine Louis Barye, came to be regarded as pathbreaking in their naturalistic depiction of animals. An 1885 casting of Barye's earlier *Lion Crushing a Serpent* has long had an honored place in Rittenhouse Square.

A bit later in the nineteenth century, at a moment when the culture of Native Americans had been nearly extinguished, *The Medicine Man* and *Stone Age in America* provided noble and nostalgic depictions of the lives of native people. A few years later, Frederic Remington's *Cowboy* glorified that figure at a time when it was fading into romance. Yet, *Stone Age in America* was moved to a more prominent site on Kelly Drive in 1985, after it had stood for a century near Strawberry Mansion. By the latter date, indigenous cultures were receiving perhaps less romantic treatment, but somewhat greater respect, than had been the case a century earlier.

Frederic Remington selected the site for his *Cowboy* on today's Kelly Drive.

Not far from Remington's *Cowboy*, a mother and her children from *Stone Age in America* look toward the river.

The 1876 Centennial Exhibition in Fairmount Park brought an unprecedented number of sculptures to Philadelphia from throughout Europe and America. Most of the 675 pieces received by the Art Department were displayed in Memorial Hall and its annex. But outdoor sculpture also was scattered throughout the fairgrounds. Most prominent were the two *Pegasus* figures that still stand in front of Memorial Hall. At the time of the centennial, the French artist Frédéric Auguste Bartholdi was at work on a lighthouse for New York's harbor, the colossal *Statue of Liberty*. Its enormous arm with torch was displayed on the exhibition grounds, and terra-cotta models of the complete work were sold to raise money to finish the project.[14]

In the late nineteenth century, new and important public sculptures in Philadelphia were typically dedicated with great public celebrations. That was the case with the presentation of the Meade Monument when, on October 18, 1887, some thirty thousand people watched the general's grandsons unveil the statue in Fairmount Park.[15] In 1895, the dedication of a statue memorializing President James A. Garfield—who had been felled by an assassin's bullet before he could leave any real mark on the nation—was accompanied by parades and an illuminated pageant and flotilla on the Schuylkill, including naval and military ceremonies. When this work was unveiled, a thousand red flares were lit along the riverbanks and under the bridges.[16] Four years later, dedication of the equestrian memorial to President Ulysses S. Grant was turned into a citywide victory celebration for the recently concluded Spanish-American War.[17]

With bold new ideas spreading across the globe about what art should be in the twentieth century, Philadelphia and its rather conservative artistic tastemakers were seldom in the forefront. Yet while the Philadelphia Museum of Art was built in the most chaste and neoclassic of styles, an important collection of art from a bold and innovative sculptor was about to find its home in the 1929 Rodin Museum on the Parkway. The Philadelphia collector, Jules Mastbaum, had amassed the most important collection outside France of the work of Auguste Rodin (1840–1917). By the time Mastbaum gave his collection to Philadelphia, the sculptor, while still controversial, was increasingly recognized as having launched an important transformation in the way human subjects would be portrayed in three dimensions. Acknowledged for his naturalism and humanism, Rodin placed his figures at eye

James A. Garfield is among the American presidents memorialized on Fairmount Park's Kelly Drive, in a portrait bust by Augustus Saint-Gaudens. (Photograph by Mark Garvin)

The equestrian memorial to President Ulysses S. Grant, by Daniel Chester French.

level rather than elevating them on pedestals, the better to reveal their common humanity, as in *The Burghers of Calais*; revealed the frailties of their flesh, as in his nude study of Balzac; and depicted his own very personal vision of the human condition in such work as *The Gates of Hell*.[18] These are among 130 of the artist's works that are on view at Philadelphia's Rodin Museum.

Nor was the public arrival of the Rodin collection in Philadelphia the only mark of a modernist presence in Philadelphia's built landscape. In 1932, the Pennsylvania Savings Fund Society (PSFS) building, the first high-rise building in the United States in the new international style, was completed at Twelfth and Market Streets.[19] But if these were modernist "victories" in early twentieth-century Philadelphia, they by no means marked the defeat of the traditional. In the decades that encompassed both world wars, and in every facet of cultural and artistic life in America, conflicts raged between the old and the new, between the traditional view of public art as celebrating recognized—and recognizable—heroes, and the modern insistence on a broader exploration of ideas that reached beyond a predetermined canon,

(Facing page) A massive bronze door fronting the Rodin Museum depicts the sculptor's conception of *The Gates of Hell*.

Rodin's "The Burghers of Calais" stands in the museum's courtyard. (Photograph by Mark Garvin)

sometimes simply to celebrate the forms, materials, colors, and textures their makers had created. Decades passed before some trends, at least, were clear.

The realistic depiction of historical figures as heroes went into a decline from which it has not yet recovered. From the second half of the twentieth century, only a handful of such examples can be found in Philadelphia. The best known are probably Harry Rosin's portrayal of baseball great Connie Mack, *Mr. Baseball*, at Lincoln Bank Park and that of Mayor Frank Rizzo in front of the Municipal Services Building by Zeno Frudakis—neither of which is without its critics. The most popular example, of *Rocky* beside the Art Museum steps, is, after all, of a fictional film character and derided as more a film prop than important art. Still, its popularity says something about the unchanging role of public art, which is to appeal to the public.[20]

For a time, allegorical representations of heroic or historical themes were a substitute for realistic portrayals. The clearest indication in Fairmount Park of that transitional period is seen in the Ellen Phillips Samuel Memorial terraces on Kelly Drive. The eighteen monumental pieces of sculpture that were installed there between 1933 and 1961 reflect, as a group, the unsettled views of the time as to what monumental tributes to America's heritage should be. While all of the pieces may be seen as allegorical, those that most clearly represent human figures are not heroic in any earlier understanding of that term, while those that are most abstract may seem the most heroic.

At about the same time as the Samuel Memorial was being created, the fate of other sculptural work reflected a shift in public attitudes toward the nation's early luminaries. In 1890, a legacy from William M. Reilly called for a memorial featuring heroes from the Revolutionary War to be placed in front of Independence Hall. But by 1938, when the will's financial conditions finally made action possible, the decision was made to place the *Terrace of Heroes* on the slope behind the Philadelphia Museum of Art instead. In the intervening years, accomplishments of those depicted—all heroes of the Revolutionary War—had no doubt faded still further from the public mind. No doubt, too, the overseers of the project and city officials were increasingly wary of the likely demands from other groups to have their heroes' likenesses planted at the nation's birthplace. In any case, the installation was not completed until 1957, nearly seventy years after Reilly had made his bequest, and long after it had been fashionable to install such heroic statuary at historic sites.[21]

If the military figures portrayed in the Reilly Memorial are no longer appreciated by all Americans, this is surely even more the case with two nineteenth-century notables memorialized on the north plaza of City Hall. Not many passersby today would recognize the achievements of either

(*Facing page*) Noguchi's *Bolt of Lightning* was installed in 1976 on the Benjamin Franklin Bridge's terminal plaza beside the Delaware to honor one of the eighteenth-century Philadelphian's most famous accomplishments.

Matthias Baldwin (locomotives) or John Christian Bullitt (Philadelphia politics). The cruel tendency of time's passage to erase the public's memories of one-time high achievers no doubt also helps to account for a decline in such memorials today.

By the mid-twentieth century in Philadelphia, more overtly abstract sculpture was finding a place in its public art. By the century's end, many dozens of abstract works had been installed throughout the city. A cross-section includes Tony Smith's *We Lost* in the University of Pennsylvania's Blanche Levy Park; Robinson Fredenthal's *Water, Ice, Fire* at 1234 Market Street; Seymour Lipton's *Leviathan* at Penn Center Plaza on Sixteenth Street; William P. Daley's *Helios* at the Germantown Friends School on Coulter Street; George Rickey's towering *Two Lines* on the grounds of the Morris Arboretum; and Isamu Noguchi's *Bolt of Lightning* memorial to Benjamin Franklin, which greets visitors entering Philadelphia from the Benjamin Franklin Bridge.[22]

In spite of this record, all of Philadelphia's public sculpture by no means has been abstract for the past half century and more. Among many other representational works, the human form is recognizable in, for example, the portrayal of a seventeenth-century Boston Quaker, Mary Dyer, at the Friends Center on Fifteenth and Cherry Streets; in Leonard Baskin's allegorical grouping at Society Hill Towers at Third and Locust Streets; and in Arlene Love's *Face Fragment* at 3500 Market Street. Similarly, animal forms are clearly represented in such works as Henry Mitchell's Bodine Fountain on the campus of Thomas Jefferson University, in which otters play. Although they include comparatively literal representations, none of these would be mistaken for pre-twentieth-century statuary; all of them, like many others from this period, reflect their time.

Claes Oldenburg's creative translation of familiar and mundane objects into monumental sculpture has won him great popularity throughout the world as a public artist. Philadelphia now has installed four of his works where they enliven prominent civic spaces. His *Clothespin (The Kiss)* from 1976 stands across from City Hall at Fifteenth and Market Streets; *Split Button*, 1981, is on the campus of the University

(Facing page)

Claes Oldenburg's

Clothespin across from

City Hall is among four of

the artist's works that

command public spaces

in Philadelphia.

of Pennsylvania; *Giant Three-Way Plug: Cube Tap* was installed in 2010 in the Anne d'Harnoncourt Sculpture Garden behind the Philadelphia Museum of Art; and *Paint Torch*, 2011, looms over the Broad Street sidewalk at Lenfest Plaza next to the Pennsylvania Academy of Fine Arts.

Philadelphia's public art of the past sixty years is far too diverse for simple generalizations. In its variety and quantity, it forms an artistic cornucopia—to steal from the title of Red Grooms's delightful *Philadelphia Cornucopia* of 1982, another example of the period's artistic variety.[23] Grooms's playful depiction of the city's history first exhibited for Philadelphia's three-hundredth birthday is largely molded in papier-mâché, a rather ephemeral medium for a civic monument, though typical of Grooms's semicartoonish yet stylish work. That pop art sense of transience, too, is a characteristic of much of the art of our time.

The 1976 Bicentennial of the United States

The huge success for Philadelphia of the 1876 Centennial Exposition was not to be repeated a century later for the nation's bicentennial. A congressional commission determined in 1973 that it would designate no city as the exclusive host of the 1976 celebration, but instead encouraged towns and cities across the nation to develop their own festivities. Philadelphia planned a number of activities, and highlights included visits by Britain's Queen Elizabeth and Prince Philip, as well as all-star games for the National Basketball Association, the National Hockey League, and major league baseball. The city also hosted the National Collegiate Athletic Association (NCAA) Final Four. But far fewer visitors came than had been anticipated, and a new illness, Legionnaires' disease, infected 231 American Legion conventioneers at the Bellevue-Stratford Hotel, which resulted in thirty-four deaths, as well as that of the venerable and grand hotel.

Nonetheless, the nation's two-hundredth birthday celebration did inspire an impressive amount of new public art for Philadelphia. At least a dozen new projects were either directly or indirectly conceived for the bicentennial. In addition to Oldenburg's *Clothespin* at Penn Center and Indiana's *LOVE* in JFK Plaza, these include Walter Erlebacher's *Jesus Breaking Bread*, which stands in front of the Cathedral Basilica of Saints Peter and Paul at Logan Circle; Alexander Calder's mobile, *White Cascade*, and Beverly Pepper's *Phaedrus*, both at the Federal Reserve Bank on Independence Mall; John Rhoden's *Nesaika* at the Afro-American Historical and Cultural Museum; Louise Nevelson's *Bicentennial Dawn* at the William J. Green Jr. Federal Building; Charles Searles's large painting, *Celebration*, in the interior of the Federal Building; the sculptural *Ghost Structures* by Venturi and Rauch to suggest the plan of

Benjamin Franklin's lost house at its original site on Market Street; Al Held's two black-and-white murals, *Ascension/Descension* and *Order/Disorder*, in the interior of the Mid-Atlantic Social Security Service Center; and Joe Brown's monumental figures engaged in their sports, *Punter, Batter, Tackle* and *Play at Second Base* at the sports complex, Broad and Pattison Streets.

The FPAA also conceived an International Sculpture Garden for Penn's Landing to "celebrate the impact of other cultures on the American experience." That garden eventually included pre-Columbian, ancient Indian, Javanese, and Korean sculpture, as well as a totem from America's Northwest.* The 1976 gift of Greece, *The Charioteer of Delphi*, also came to the foot of Fairmount in that year.

*At the time of this writing, most of those pieces were in storage with plans under way to redesign the garden, perhaps at a different location.

Another of Oldenburg's sculptures is *Giant Three-Way Plug* at the Philadelphia Museum of Art. (Photograph by Mark Garvin)

The temporary quality of some art has been made explicit in several major works in recent years in and around Fairmount Park. In 1970, the artist Christo wrapped the staircase in the Art Museum's great hall with fabric, turning the space into a temporary exhibition. In 1972, Gene Davis's huge *Franklin's Footpath* was painted on the pavement of the Benjamin Franklin Parkway near its terminus at Eakins Oval. Its six miles of stripes in fifteen colors, all of identical width, were filled in by school students enlisted for the project, which was meant to fade from view gradually through weathering.[24] On the slope behind the Art Museum that leads down toward Boathouse Row, a work of floral art was installed in 2012. *Lines in Four Directions in Flowers* realized a design created in 1981 by Sol LeWitt. Each of the four flower beds measured 4,400 square feet. The four color quadrants together contained more than seven thousand plantings. Each color palette displayed four to five plants that bloomed sequentially. The installation was intended to last through two years' growing seasons.[25] Also in 2012, the temporary *Open Air* exhibit created by Rafael Lozano-Hemmer pierced the night sky over the

Benjamin Franklin Parkway. For several weeks in early autumn, dramatically changing beams of light could be voice activated by viewers.

Because public art is meant to appeal to the public, it emerges from and becomes part of the local political and social fabric. In Philadelphia, many of the tributes to public figures that were dominant among early installations were intended to inspire sentiments of patriotism, along with admiration for the subject's sterling qualities. So it is that Philadelphia, like every other city in America, displays statues of the veterans of distant conflicts—especially the Civil War—whose names are little known today. That these representations have gone out of fashion may reflect growing awareness of how such sentiments can change over time, dimming with the memory of the honored individual.

Rather than praising individuals, public art may salute specific religious or ethnic communities as a way of acknowledging their contributions to society. Irish immigrants to Philadelphia have been honored in the 1876 *Catholic Total Abstinence Union Fountain* (Chapter 3), commemorating prominent Irish Catholic figures from the time of the American Revolution in a paean to abstinence from strong drink, and the 2003 *Irish Memorial* at Penn's Landing, which memorializes the famine of 1845–1850 as well as the millions of Irish immigrants to the United States. Italian, German, French, African American, and Scottish immigrants also have their monuments.[26]

Public art also can serve in public rituals. Nathan Rapoport's *Monument to Six Million Jewish Martyrs* at Sixteenth Street and the parkway was commissioned by the Association of Jewish New Americans and donated to the city in 1964, with the support of the Federation of Jewish Agencies of Greater Philadelphia. Since then, it has served as the focus of Holocaust remembrance ceremonies. Far more lighthearted rituals, including photographs with subjects in obligatory poses, take place daily at both the *LOVE* sculpture in JFK Plaza and the *Rocky* statue below the Art Museum. Both sites are among the most photographed tourist stops in Philadelphia today.

The history of *Rocky* reflects what may be another trend: periodic contention between the city's artistic establishment, as represented in the FPAA, and popular tastes. The statue was commissioned by actor Sylvester Stallone in 1982, and was placed at the top of the Art Museum steps for the filming of *Rocky III*. Its advocates wanted it to remain there permanently, but the FPAA, arguing that it was not a genuine work of art, called for it to be moved to the sports complex in South Philadelphia. After years of controversy, the city agreed in 2006 to install the piece on a grassy spot near the bottom of the Art Museum steps, where it attracts a stream of visitors. This history is in some sense unique because of the association of the statue with an iconic cinematic scene. But it is also a reminder that American popular culture knocks on the door of the cultural establishment more loudly today than in earlier generations. In the past, there were sometimes criticisms from the public of the art chosen by the FPAA, but few assumed that popular tastes should overturn its judgment.[27]

The FPAA (today's aPA) has been instrumental for 150 years in the immense collection of public art that is visible throughout Philadelphia. But since 1959, its effort has been abetted by other initiatives. Just as the founders of the FPAA fought against the dehumanizing impact of the industrial age on their city, in 1959, a new generation took action against the stripped-down barrenness of much modernist architecture. In that year, Philadelphia's City Council was persuaded to enact a "percent for art" ordinance, the first of its kind in the nation. It mandated that a percentage of construction costs of city projects be set aside for fine arts. Months earlier, the city's Redevelopment Authority had required redevelopers to allocate 1 percent of their construc-

This mural at Thirteenth and Locust Streets is among several thousand throughout the city that have been created under the direction of the Mural Arts Program.

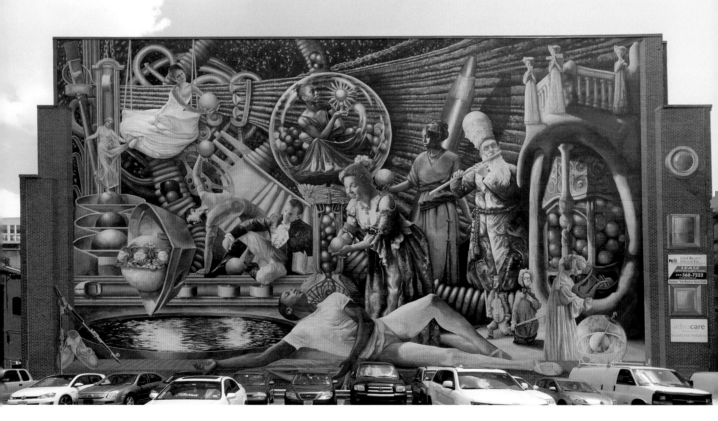

tion costs for fine arts. Since then, other governmental agencies, civic and private groups, nonprofit institutions, and individuals also have contributed to what is now a commonplace assumption, not just in Philadelphia, but throughout America: that great new buildings demand great public art.[28]

These requirements sometimes bring conflict between architects and artists, especially when artists seem to be brought aboard a project at the end to "decorate," as the architect may see it, what is already a fully refined work of art. Those responsible for artistic tastemaking also may encounter opposition from those in the community who find a particular work of art jarring or incomprehensible. Older Philadelphians remember such a reaction from then mayor Frank Rizzo in 1976 to Jacques Lipchitz's *Government of the People*, which, said the mayor, looked to him like a load of wet plaster. Yet the Lipchitz, like so much of the other public art in Philadelphia, is meant to commemorate an event, an idea, and an immensely important historical development. Ironically, a statue of Rizzo was unveiled several years after his death only steps away from *Government of the People*.

This survey of the history of public art in Philadelphia focuses mostly on some of the most prominent in Philadelphia's park system. A great many more are to be seen in and around major buildings and in other civic spaces. They are the legacy of the FPAA/aPA, the city's percent for art program, the work of its Art Jury/Art Commission, and private organizations.

In 1986, Mayor Wilson Goode created the Anti-Graffiti Network to attack the blight of graffiti scrawled on surfaces throughout the city. In 1994, that effort was expanded into the Mural Arts Program, which continues to engage neighborhoods to help define the locations and subject matter for new mural projects on walls that otherwise might be targets for graffiti artists, many of whom are enlisted to help create the new murals. The result has been a stunning success, both at eliminating graffiti and creating a great deal more public art. Philadelphia now exhibits several thousand murals spread through every section of the city.[29]

In 2014, two murals were installed in Fairmount Park on the concrete supports of the Girard Avenue Bridge, the first such venture of the Mural Arts Program into the park. These hundred-foot-long paintings of rowers on the river would be visible to all who walked, hiked, or cycled along both the east and west riverbanks. Those who advocated placing these murals there argued that they simply added to the store of art already scattered throughout the park. Critics feared that they opened the door to further intrusions into the park's bucolic spaces from a program whose goals were largely social rather than artistic.[30]

The Mural Arts Program

From its beginning as an antigraffiti project, a more ambitious goal led to the Mural Arts Program in 1996, when it was placed under the oversight of the Philadelphia Recreation Department (today's Parks and Recreation Department). It is now an independent city agency operating as a major public art program. By 2014, it had produced some 3,600 murals in public places throughout the city.

Mural Arts seeks to involve members of the community in determining what kind of public art they would like to see in their neighborhood, then to engage local artists to create the design for the murals and young people—especially those at risk—to carry them out. Some fifteen hundred youth participate annually in these projects. Philadelphia Mural Arts Advocates, a nonprofit organization, raises private funds to support this work. The Mural Arts Program also promotes art as a part of criminal and restorative justice by sponsoring educational programs in local prisons.

Although criticism sometimes accompanies the murals this program produces, its leaders strive to provide art of high quality while involving the neighborhood in the decisions that lead to it. Thanks to Mural Arts, many eyesores and derelict sites have been beautified throughout Philadelphia, and the plague of public graffiti largely eliminated. Still, where murals brighten many neighborhoods today, there once stood functioning shops, homes, and other buildings.

The Museum Without Walls audio tour was launched by the FPAA in 2010. It provides a narrative for fifty-one works of public art in a series of thirty-five stops starting on the parkway at City Hall and continuing to the rowing grandstands on Kelly Drive. At each stop, signs are posted for dialing instructions for listening via cell phone. The tour can also be downloaded as a mobile app or accessed online.[31]

When, in 2012, the Fairmount Park Art Association changed its name to the Association for Public Art, it did so with the argument that, after 140 years, the time had come to adopt a name that more clearly reflected what in fact had long been the organization's mission. That was, and is, to promote the inclusion of public art wherever possible throughout Philadelphia. The move followed the reorganization of the Fairmount Park system beginning in 2009, which we examine in Chapter 16. Both changes reflected an evolving view of how public space should be regarded within the ever-changing metropolitan area of Philadelphia.

(*Facing page*)
A mural at Eleventh and Walnut Streets in Philadelphia.

Carl Milles's *Playing Angels*
are castings from a larger
original grouping that
overlooks Stockholm's harbor.

Fairmount Park
The Outdoor Museum

Philadelphia's outdoor museum encompasses far more public art than is confined to its parks. But because the parks have long served as the base for it, we now highlight some of the most notable of that art, especially in the east and west parks beside the Schuylkill. It has accumulated there in all styles and represents the many changes in artistic taste over 150 years. We begin next to City Hall on the Benjamin Franklin Parkway, and proceed toward the park, with digressions, as an indefatigable walker might view the highlights of the outdoor collection.[1]

Directly north across the street from City Hall, in the Municipal Services Plaza, stands the Lipchitz work, *Government of the People*. Commissioned in 1965, the project was taken over by the Fairmount Park Art Association (FPAA) after the artist's death in 1973. Two other monumental bronzes by Lipchitz are in Fairmount Park. His *Prometheus Strangling the Vulture*, from 1953, stands in front of the east entrance to the Philadelphia Museum of Art (PMA) at the opposite end of the parkway. *The Spirit of Enterprise* was installed in the Samuel Memorial's north terrace on Kelly Drive in 1960. Both the PMA and the Barnes Foundation have additional works by Lipchitz in their collections, making the city one of the largest depositories of his sculpture in the world.

John F. Kennedy Plaza at Fifteenth Street is now familiarly known as LOVE Park thanks to the work by Robert Indiana that overlooks the plaza from its southeastern corner. Indiana's 1964 painting of the same design had become a cultural icon of the 1960s, appearing on jewelry, posters, and finally a postage stamp. After the artist created this painted aluminum and stainless

15

steel version of *LOVE*, he loaned it to the city for the 1976 bicentennial celebration. Two years later, when an effort to sell it to the city failed, it was removed to a New York gallery and an outcry erupted in Philadelphia. Soon thereafter, F. Eugene Dixon, then the chair of the Philadelphia Art Commission, purchased the work and donated it to the city.[2] Since reinstalled at JFK Plaza, it remains a popular and iconic Philadelphia landmark.

At Sixteenth Street on the parkway stands Nathan Rapoport's bronze *Monument to Six Million Jewish Martyrs*. In a tangle of anguished human limbs, flames, fists, and clutching daggers, a pair of hands holds a Torah aloft. In contrast to the passion expressed in this memorial is the quiet sculpture almost directly across the street, Henry Moore's *Three-Way Piece Number 1: Points*. When it was acquired in 1964, it was placed in JFK Plaza and then moved to this location in 1990. The points of the title are the resting places on granite for the free-form bronze, which may or may not seem to evoke for the viewer a range of natural or animal forms.[3]

(*Facing page*) *Prometheus Strangling the Vulture* is one of a number of sculptures by the French artist Jacques Lipchitz at the Philadelphia Museum of Art and elsewhere in Fairmount Park. (Photograph by Mark Garvin)

Robert Indiana's *LOVE* sculpture has become a much-photographed icon, creating a backdrop for viewing the length of the Benjamin Franklin Parkway. (Photograph by Mark Garvin)

Fairmount Park: The Outdoor Museum

On the parkway at Eighteenth Street, this sculpture honoring the five hundredth anniversary of the birth of Copernicus was installed in 1972. (Photograph by Mark Garvin)

At Seventeenth Street and the parkway, Dame Barbara Hepworth's large *Rock Form (Porthcurno)*, pierced by two openings, is a bronze work from 1964. Donated to the Association for Public Art (aPA) in 2012, it was installed there in that year. At the next intersection at Eighteenth Street, an enormous stainless steel ring represents the earth in orbit around an inner sphere, the sun. It was installed in 1972 to commemorate the five hundredth

anniversary of the birth of Mikolaj Kopernik (Nicolaus Copernicus), who was the first to declare that the earth revolves around the sun. The sculpture by Dudley Talcott was the gift of Polish Americans.[4]

The central concourse of the Benjamin Franklin Parkway is Logan Circle, and its expansive center is marked by the glorious *Swann Fountain* by Alexander Stirling Calder and Wilson Eyre, its architect (Chapter 12). Officially titled *The Fountain of Three Rivers*, Calder said: "It was my fancy to imagine the three great decorative bronze figures enclosing Philadelphia; the Delaware represented by the male Indian, the Schuylkill (or gentle) river, by a female figure, and the Wissahickon (for hidden creek) another female figure to the west."[5] The fountain was unveiled to the public on July 23, 1923, the eve of the hottest day of the year. According to contemporary reports, more than ten thousand sweltering people tangoed around the fountain to the music of the police band.[6]

Henry Moore's "Three-Way Piece Number 1: Points" stands near Sixteenth Street and the Cret Café. (Photograph by Mark Garvin)

Fairmount Park: The Outdoor Museum

In Logan Square across from the Franklin Institute, the *All Wars Memorial to Colored Soldiers and Sailors* honors African American war veterans. (Photograph by Mark Garvin)

A second work by A. S. Calder stands directly in front of the Free Library on the north side of Logan Circle. This six-foot-high bronze was dedicated on Shakespeare's birthday in 1929 and depicts tragedy and comedy. Hamlet leans his head against a knife while Touchstone, the jester, sits at his feet. Inscribed on the base is a quotation from *As You Like It*: "All the world's a stage and all the men and women merely players." Just to the east of the Shakespeare Memorial is the Beaux Arts–style monument to General Galusha Pennypacker, who, at age twenty-two, was the youngest general to serve in the Civil War. Created by Albert Laessle, the bronze on a granite base was installed there in 1934.[7]

Fairmount Park: The Outdoor Museum

On the west side of the square, facing the Franklin Institute, the *Aero Memorial* inspired the name Aviator Park for the rejuvenated wedge of parkland lying outside the circle itself. Created by Paul Manship as a tribute to the aviators who died in World War I, the bronze sphere illustrates the signs of the zodiac and is inscribed with the Latin names of constellations and planets. Nearby stands J. Otto Schweizer's 1934 *All Wars Memorial to Colored Soldiers and Sailors*, which was relocated there in 1994 from a more obscure location near Memorial Hall. Honoring African Americans who served the United States in war, it stems from an appropriation by the Pennsylvania legislature to construct "a lasting record of their unselfish devotion to duty."[8]

At Twentieth Street and the parkway, two massive marble works, which together form the *Civil War Soldiers and Sailors Memorial*, flank the boulevard and present a grand entrance to the western end of the parkway and the beginning of Fairmount Park. The twin pylons, one depicting soldiers, the other sailors, were designed by Herman Atkins McNeil in 1927. Ellsworth Kelly's *The Barnes Totem* towers over a reflecting pool near the entrance to the new Barnes Foundation, on the north side of the parkway above Twentieth Street. A forty-foot, lightning-like, broken column of polished steel, it was the gift of philanthropist Joseph Neubauer to the Barnes at its opening in 2012.[9]

The Thinker has brooded before the Rodin Museum's Meudon Gate since the building was opened in 1929.

Between Twenty-First and Twenty-Second Streets, the 1929 Rodin Museum and garden were restored in 2012. That restoration returned to their original outdoor placements a number of the works of French sculptor Pierre Auguste Rodin (1840–1917) that had been removed over the years to preserve them. But *The Thinker* has stood there for more than eighty years before the Meudon Gate, where *Adam* and *The Shade* were reinstalled in its arches. Past the gate and the garden behind it, visitors can view *The Gates of Hell* in the portico of the museum itself (Chapter 14). *The Thinker* was originally the small central figure in that complex work (which Mastbaum had cast in bronze for this museum), but Rodin enlarged the brooding man in 1904, and then exhibited it in Paris. *The Age of Bronze* and *Eve* were returned to niches on each side. *The Burghers of Calais* (Chapter 14) were placed in the east garden. *Three Shades* in the west. Inside are more than a hundred additional examples of Rodin's work.[10]

The 440-foot *George Washington Monument* rises within the Eakins Oval at the base of Fairmount and the Philadelphia

The fountain in the foreground is dedicated to Eli Kirk Price II. Behind it, the elaborate *Washington Monument* has dominated the open space at the foot of Fairmount since the Art Museum opened above it in 1928.

Museum of Art. The bronze and granite statue by the Berlin artist Rudolf Siemering was unveiled by President William McKinley in 1897 at the Green Street entrance to Fairmount Park. It was moved to its present location with the completion of the Art Museum in 1928. It took Siemering a staggering sixteen years to model and cast the monumental work, but it had taken the Society of the Cincinnati, which had commissioned the work, almost seventy years to raise the necessary funds. The monument is constructed in three zones, each representing a different concept. Washington, the hero, sits at the top; allegorical figures depicting his time are on the middle level; and on the bottom are the flora and fauna of North America, with representative human figures. A large bison and an elk meditate on the perpetual traffic jam amid jets, pools, and competing fauna.[11]

On each side of the Washington monument are two large circular fountains designed by Horace Trumbauer. One is dedicated to Eli Kirk Price II, the Fairmount Park commissioner who was principally responsible for the completion of the Philadelphia Museum of Art. The other is dedicated to Captain John Erickson, an inventor and engineer, and a direct descendent of

Fairmount Park: The Outdoor Museum

Leif Ericson. In a grassy lawn on the north side of Eakins Oval, a red-painted steel construction, *Iroquois*, was installed in 2007. It is the first Philadelphia work of the abstract expressionist, Mark di Suvero, who regards his approach to his work as painting in three dimensions, "with the crane as my paintbrush."[12]

Flanking the steps to the PMA are cast copies of two works by German artists: Albert Wolff's 1858 *The Lion Fighter* and Auguste Kiss's *Mounted Amazon Attacked by a Panther*, dating from 1837. The originals were installed in the mid-nineteenth century as companion pieces on the steps of the National Museum in Berlin. In 1889, the Fairmount Park Art Association acquired plaster casts for both works, displaying them in Memorial Hall. Eventually, the FPAA had copies cast in bronze, although they only came to their current sites after completion of the PMA in 1929.[13]

A gilded likeness of *General Anthony Wayne* stands on the PMA terrace in front of the east wing. A gift of the Pennsylvania Society of the Sons of the Revolution, it commemorates Pennsylvania's foremost military hero in the American War of Independence. The statue was created by John Gregory and installed there in 1937. Down the hillside below the museum's northeast corner is the 1977 cast of *The Charioteer of Delphi*, whose original dates from the fifth century B.C.E. and is displayed in Delphi's museum. This duplicate was a gift from the Greek government to the Philadelphia Museum of Art in honor of the American bicentennial. Considered one of the finest surviving sculptures from Greek antiquity, the left arm, chariot, horses, and two grooms are missing, as in the original.[14]

On Kelly Drive at Twenty-Fifth Street stands Emanuel Frémiet's golden tribute to *Joan of Arc*, mounted for battle. This work was moved there from its original site at the east end of the Girard Avenue Bridge after the FPAA had it gilded in 1960. The statue was purchased from the artist in 1889 by the French community in Philadelphia with support from the FPAA. The contract stipulated that the artist would cast only three editions of the work; the other two are displayed on the Rue de Rivoli outside the Louvre in Paris, and in Nancy, France. A tragic coincidence attends the story of this memorial to the French heroine who was burned at the stake in 1431. In his search for a young girl to pose as Joan, Frémiet discovered

The Charioteer of Delphi was created in Greece in the fifth century B.C.E. This copy was a gift to the Philadelphia Museum of Art at the time of the American bicentennial in 1976.

Frémiet's *Joan of Arc* was purchased for Philadelphia by the local French community in 1889, and moved to Kelly Drive at Twenty-Fifth Street in 1960.

Valerie Landeau, a fifteen-year-old country girl whose fine features the artist admired. Sixty-two years later, Landeau, still in Paris, lighted her lamp one night and it exploded, burning her to death.[15]

Back atop Fairmount at the museum's west entrance, two mid-twentieth-century works flank the door. On the left is Jacob Epstein's *Social Consciousness.* Its five figures depict consolation and succor attending to the afflicted on each side of a central seated figure, Eternal Mother. The twelve-foot work on a granite base was installed there by the FPAA in 1954. Facing this work is that of Louise Nevelson, *Atmosphere and Environment XII.* A work made of eighteen thousand pounds of Corten steel on a granite base, it was erected in 1970.[16]

Across from the west entrance, steps lead down toward Boathouse Row. At the top are monuments to two important figures in the nation's history who may be little remembered today. *Stephen Girard* (1750–1830), the French-born American, was a merchant, financier, and philanthropist who saved the U.S. government from financial collapse during the War of 1812. He left a substantial legacy for the founding of Girard College, located half a mile northeast of the monument. The other statue represents Major General *Henry M. Muhlenberg* (1711–1787), patriarch of the Lutheran Church in America. Commissioned by the German Society of Pennsylvania, its proposed placement was for a site at Sixteenth and Arch Streets. Park commissioners rejected that location on grounds that their approval would invite every other religious body to ask for a memorial on the parkway then under construction.[17]

The Anne d'Harnoncourt Sculpture Garden was created in 2010 with the completion of a parking garage for PMA visitors that was dug into the slope of Fairmount near the museum's west entrance. The green roof of the garage, comprising more than 195,000 square feet, holds the garden. Exhibits are intended to change over time. Several works by Isamu Noguchi were featured when the garden opened, as well as two concrete block sculptures by Sol LeWitt, and works by Scott Burton, Thomas Schutte, and George Gund. Claes Oldenburg's *Giant Three-Way Plug (Cube Tap)* was a gift dedicated to the memory of d'Harnoncourt, the late director of the PMA. A 2012 addition to the garden's lower terrace is Franz Westin's *Lips*, three playfully contorted columns in pale shades of green, blue, and pink, which can also serve as seating for visitors.[18]

Down the steps past the *Terrace of Heroes*, the *Fountain of the Seahorses* marks the approach to Boathouse Row (Chapter 16). It was a gift to the city of Philadelphia from the Italian government in 1926 in commemoration of the American sesquicentennial, although it arrived too late to be a part of that celebration. It is a replica of the *Fontana dei Cavalli Marini*, circa 1740, in the Borghese Gardens in Rome.[19] Nearby, two sculptures of wild animals look out over the Azalea Garden. *Tiger at Bay*, by the Sardinian-born artist Albino Manca, was exhibited at the Pennsylvania Academy of the Fine Arts before the FPAA had it installed at its current location in 1965. Nearby stands William Zorach's black marble *Puma* on a granite base.[20]

Across Kelly Drive at its intersection with Sedgley Drive stands the massive statue of *Abraham Lincoln* by Randolph Rogers. Funds were raised in just more than a year after Lincoln's assassination, and the piece was dedicated in 1871 before a crowd of some fifty thousand. The martyred president is shown seated, quill in hand, after signing the Emancipation Proclamation. The monument was moved to its current location in 2001 from an adjacent traffic circle when the road was reconfigured.[21]

The William M. Reilly Memorial, *Terrace of Heroes*

Reilly's 1890 legacy largely funded this project, although its construction did not actually get under way until 1938 and was not completed until 1957. The heroes depicted are all military figures from America's Revolutionary War.

Freidrich von Steuben (1730–1794), by Warren Wheelock, portrays the Prussian nobleman and military expert who joined the American forces as inspector general in 1778. He settled in New York after American independence.

John Paul Jones (1747–1792), by Walker Hancock, depicts the Scottish-born naval hero famed for capturing the British ship *Serapis* in 1779 and for declaring, when asked to surrender, "I have not yet begun to fight!"

Casimir Pulaski (1748–1779), by Sidney Waugh, shows the Polish nobleman who served under George Washington at Brandywine and Germantown. He lost his life in the siege of Savannah.

Richard Montgomery (1738–1775), by J. Wallace Kelly, honors the Irish-born patriot. A brigadier general, he was successful in the Canadian campaign until his failed assault on Quebec, when he died in the field.

Nathanael Greene (1742–1786), by Lewis Iselin Jr., is the only native-born hero honored in the memorial. Scion of a Rhode Island Quaker family, late in the war, he commanded forces in the South that drove the British back toward the coast of Charleston. For this campaign, he became known as "the man who saved the South."

Marquis de Lafayette (1757–1834), by Raoul Josset, portrays the most famous of the foreign heroes of the American Revolution in a flamboyant mode.*

*Warren Wheelock (1880–1960), Walter Hancock (1901–1998), Sidney Waugh (1904–1964), J. Wallace Kelly (1894–1978), Lewis Iselin Jr. (1913–1990), Raoul Josset (1899–1957).

This depiction of the young Marquis de Lafayette is one of six figures honored in the *Terrace of Heroes* lining the western slope of Fairmount.

The Pilgrim, by Saint-Gaudens, originally installed at City Hall, was moved to its current site on Kelly Drive in 1920.

At the end of Boathouse Row stands Einar Jonsson's 1918 bronze work of *Thorfinn Karlsefni*, the Icelandic hero who, according to the saga of Eric the Red, may have visited American shores as early as 1004. Opposite, across Kelly Drive, is the nine-foot-high bronze *The Pilgrim*, created in 1904 by Irish-born Augustus Saint-Gaudens, and presented to the city as a gift from the New England Society of Pennsylvanians. The figure wears a buckled hat, and holds a Bible in one hand and a cane in the other, his cape surrounding him. The pilgrim was moved to its present location from the south plaza of City Hall in 1920.[22] Farther along the drive, *Stone Age in America* represents a commemoration of North America's indigenous people at a time, 1887, when ever fewer of them remained (Chapter 14).[23]

The *Ellen Phillips Samuel Memorial* is both a stunning collection of mid-twentieth-century sculpture—it holds seventeen monumental pieces in all, by fifteen artists—and the product of a unique undertaking in Philadelphia's

The Samuel Legacy and the Sculpture Internationals

In her legacy to create a sculptural tribute to America's history in Fairmount Park, Ellen Phillips Samuel asked for the project to be made known to sculptors around the world. In response, the FPAA organized three Sculpture Internationals, held in 1933, 1940, and 1949. Once artists submitted photographs of their work, shipping costs and insurance were paid by the association for work selected for display in Philadelphia.

For the first International, 364 works by 105 leading sculptors from America and Europe were exhibited at the PMA from May through September. Attendance at the museum doubled. Six artists were named by the selection committee to produce finished work for the memorial. Not one of them had been among the popular favorites on the basis of a straw vote conducted by the *Public Ledger*.

By the time of the second International in 1940, World War II prevented the work of many European artists to travel to Philadelphia. As a result, many pieces were loaned by American dealers, collectors, and museums for the exhibition. Among the 431 pieces on display, Alexander (Sandy) Calder's mobiles were sensational and, to some, puzzling examples of how traditional conceptions of sculpture were being exploded.

Four artists were commissioned to create work for the second terrace. None was regarded then or since as a member of the avant-garde. Four sculptors not chosen nonetheless were soon commissioned to create works for the Reilly Memorial's *Terrace of Heroes* (see feature above).

In 1949, the third and final International produced an exhibition at the PMA of 252 works and drew unprecedented

crowds. A photograph in *Life* magazine of seventy participating artists showed them arrayed on the steps of the PMA's great hall, with several pieces of their sculpture visible. Four artists of varied nationalities were chosen to create the work for the north terrace. The FPAA purchased several additional works, including Gerhard Marcks's *Maja*, which now stands on the Art Museum's east terrace.*

*The bequest from Mrs. Samuel (1849–1913) became operative after the death of her husband in 1929. Bach, *Public Art in Philadelphia*, pp. 91–100, provides a thorough account of the Sculpture Internationals. For the perspective of a member of the selection committee, see R. Sturgis Ingersoll, "The *Ellen Phillips Samuel Memorial*," in *Sculpture of a City*, pp. 250–257.

The *Ellen Phillips Samuel Memorial* includes seventeen works of sculpture on three connected terraces beside the Schuylkill on Kelly Drive, all dating from the middle decades of the twentieth century. In this photo, Jacques Lipchitz's *The Spirit of Enterprise* is in the foreground. Works by Heinz Warneke, Maurice Sterne, and Helene Sardeau are in the background. (Photograph by Mark Garvin)

artistic history. Its three connected terraces were built, and the sculpture installed, by the FPAA between 1933 and 1961 on a strip of land between the Schuylkill and Kelly Drive. The project was in response to a bequest from Ellen Phillips Samuel, a descendant of the earliest Sephardic Jewish settlers in America and a member of the FPAA. She asked for a series of sculptures representing American history from the time of its earliest settlers to the modern period. Paul Philippe Cret and his firm created the designs for the three terraces.

The FPAA determined that the figures should be allegorical, expressing ideas and movements in American history, rather than of specific individuals. The central terrace was the first to be created. Its theme is America's westward expansion, emancipation of slaves, and immigration. Artists and their works originally represented are Robert Laurent (France), J. Wallace Kelly (United States), John B. Flannagan (United States), Heinz Warneke (Germany-United States), Helene Sardou (Belgium), and Maurice Sterne (Russia-United States). Their pieces include two bronzes, each showing two figures in symbolic action; the other four are of crouching individuals carved in limestone. *The Spirit of Enterprise* by Jacques Lipchitz (Lithuania-France-United States) also has stood in the center of this terrace since 1986, when it was moved from the north terrace, where it had been placed after having been commissioned at the time of the third (1949) International.

The south terrace is the product of the second International in 1940. It represents the founding of the nation and the birth of independence. There, the work is by Wheeler Williams (United States), Harry Rosin (United States), Henry Kreis (Germany-United States), and Erwin Frey (United States). Two of the sculptures contain limestone groupings of figures shown in relief against walls; the others depict two sets of roughly life-sized individuals standing alone.

Robert Laurent's *Spanning the Continent* was the first to be installed, in 1938.

The north terrace, created after the 1949 International, depicts the spiritual, intellectual, and physical forces that shaped America. Works displayed are by Waldemar Raemisch (Germany), José de Creeft (Spain), Koren der Harootian (Armenia), and Ahron Ben-Shmuel (North Africa-United States). These four granite figures are nearly life-sized representations of four distinctive types who helped shape the nation. Works by Jacob Epstein and Jacques Lipchitz were originally intended for this terrace, but because of their much-larger size, both eventually were placed elsewhere, as indicated earlier.

The *Samuel Memorial* reflects a time of transition in the world of art. Its site also underwent drastic change from the time Mrs. Samuel chose it in 1907 to its completion in 1960. At the earlier date, the drive alongside it was used mostly by horse-drawn pleasure carriages, runabouts, four-in-hand coaches, and occasionally tandem dogcarts. The rare automobile was subject to a twelve-mile-an-hour speed limit. By the time the FPAA began work on the terraces, horses had disappeared, and the drive itself had become a blacktop highway for speeding automobiles. The sculpture can still only be explored on foot, whether or not today's visitors arrive by car, bicycle, or as a rest stop in the midst of a jog.

Directly across Kelly Drive stands a bronze bust of President James A. Garfield by Saint-Gaudens. Commissioned by the FPAA in 1889, the artist and his associate, the architect Stanford White, picked the site for the monument. There were differences of opinion on the part of the artist and the committee as to what the finished work should be; a standing figure was the committee's preference, but Saint-Gaudens prevailed in finally creating a bust of the martyred president above an allegorical figure of the Republic with the symbolic representations of soldier and statesmen in her shield, wreath, and sword[24] (Chapter 14).

Farther along Kelly Drive, Frederic Remington's *Cowboy* reins in his horse at the edge of a rocky ledge (Chapter 14). It is Remington's only large bronze, and his last major work before his death the following year. It was commissioned by the FPAA and installed there in 1908. The site, chosen expressly by the artist after a drive through the park, became the clear inspiration for the pose of horse and rider.[25] Past the Remington near the riverbank stand three whimsical *Playing Angels* by Carl Milles. These delicate angels make music atop three twenty-foot pillars, dancing and blowing horns. These are castings from a group of five originals in Stockholm's Millesgarden, where they have overlooked that city's harbor since the 1950s. These three were purchased by the FPAA and installed at their current location in 1972.[26]

Almost directly across the road, at the intersection of Fountain Green Drive, is the imposing equestrian statue of *General Ulysses S. Grant* by Daniel Chester French and his former student, Edward C. Potter (Chapter 14). The five-ton bronze-and-granite work towers more than thirty feet above the roadway. The FPAA created a fund for a memorial shortly after Grant's death, then awarded the commission to French from among seven artists who had been invited to prepare sketches. The sculpture, which depicts the general surveying a battlefield, was dedicated on April 27, 1899, the seventy-seventh anniversary of Grant's birth.[27] An additional work by French in Fairmount Park is his *Law, Prosperity, and Power*, circa 1880, now at South Georges Hill Drive above the Mann Center. The work was originally placed at the Post Office Building at Ninth and Chestnut Streets. When that building was demolished in 1937, the sculpture was given to the city and relocated to Georges Hill.

The grounds of the Philadelphia Zoo hold seven sculptures of wild animals. Two of these, *The Dying Lioness* and *Hudson Bay Wolves Quarreling over the Carcass of a Deer*, were among the first acquisitions of the FPAA. Auguste Cain's *Lioness Carrying to Her Young a Wild Boar*, was acquired in 1886, and later moved from its original site on the river drive because, according to a contemporary newspaper account, its "realistic pose . . . terrified many horses" (Chapter 9). Albert Laessle's bronze *Penguins* was placed at its current location in 1917; the black granite *Bear and Cub*, by Joseph J. Greenberg Jr., arrived in 1957. Heinz Warneke's *Cow Elephant and Calf*, probably the largest freestanding single-block sculpture in the United States, was installed in 1962. That year also brought Henry Mitchell's *Impala Fountain*, which captures the explosive flight of a herd of impalas. They leap across ten powerful water jets while a doe and her calf, unaware of the danger the rest of the herd has sensed, stand quietly to the side.[28]

The gateway to the west park is the *Smith Memorial Arch*. Although it forms a grand entrance to the Centennial District, it was not conceived until twenty years after the close of that exhibition, nor completed until 1912. It is a monument to the military heroes of the Civil War, nearly as ambitious in its scope as the *Samuel Memorial* decades later. It was the result of a bequest from the Philadelphia entrepreneur Richard Smith (1821–1894), who left the design and construction to the architect James H. Windrim and the choice of artists to the FPAA. A committee of the association awarded commissions to fourteen sculptors to prepare portrait busts, colossal figures, equestrian statues, and decorative sculpture. Within a year, some artists' models were approved, others rejected. Quarrels and a withdrawal ensued. Deadlines were

Among the first acquisitions of the Fairmount Park Art Association, *The Dying Lioness* has long stood before the entrance to the Philadelphia Zoo. (Photograph by Mark Garvin)

missed and contracts nullified. As a result, by the time the memorial was dedicated in 1912, little fanfare accompanied it. Still, in the century since then, the *Smith Memorial* has taken its place as one of the high points of decorative art of its period, as well as a grand landmark in West Fairmount Park.

For those with an interest in America's art history, the difference between the *Smith Memorial* (1898–1912) and the *Ellen Phillips Samuel Memorial* (1933–1961) is instructive. Although one can see stylistic differences among the sculpture of the earlier work, they are extremely minor when compared to those in the latter groupings. Traditionalism still reigned while the earlier monument was being created. By the time the *Samuel Memorial* was completed some half a century later, modernism had called nearly all the established truths about art into question.

In front of Memorial Hall, a major double work first exhibited there in 1876 remains in place. The winged horse-god *Pegasus* is shown in two figures, each accompanied by a muse. They were created in 1861 by Vincenz Pilz (1816–1896) for Vienna's Imperial Opera House but, once installed there, were thought to be out of scale. Although the Austrian government ordered them to be melted down, they were instead allowed to be purchased by a Philadelphia businessman, Robert H. Gratz. He offered them to the Fairmount Park Commission, which had them installed there in time for the centennial.[29]

Not far to the north is the Horticultural Center, built on the footprint of the original Horticultural Hall. That "permanent" exhibition building from the centennial was destroyed by a hurricane in 1964; its smaller replacement was constructed in the 1970s. Inside are works by two prominent women sculptors: Margaret Foley (1820–1877) and Beatrice Fenton (1887–1983). As a student in Rome, Boston-born Foley began by sculpting large medallion portraits in marble. Her work here, *Centennial Fountain*, was originally conceived as a large bronze for a Chicago park. After the Great Chicago Fire of 1871, she released the project's subscribers and translated the work into marble for the 1876 centennial. Fenton's *Seaweed Girl Fountain* won the Widener Gold Medal in 1922 and a bronze at the 1926 sesquicentennial. Originally on Lemon Hill

The *Smith Memorial Arch*

In December 1897, a committee of the FPAA sent a circular to seventy-three prominent sculptors, notifying them of their plan to construct a monument to Pennsylvania's military heroes of the Civil War, in keeping with the terms of Richard Smith's bequest. Fifty-nine artists responded with bids. In May 1898, the committee awarded commissions to fourteen. But one artist soon angrily withdrew over what he considered a too-meager offer to pay for the first step, modeling the busts. It would be the first of a number of contentious developments. Some fourteen years passed before the memorial's dedication.

The monument actually forms an enormous open gateway framed by two walls that curve toward the central opening on either side, each wall containing an arch. Those approaches—with their two towering pillars that soar from the tops of the walls on each side of the central gate—hold the sculpture. Atop each pillar stands a figure: General George Gordon Meade, by Daniel Chester French, and Major General John Fulton Reynolds, a work by Charles Grafly. Rising from the projecting end of each arched wall are the equestrian statues of General George McClellan by Edward C. Potter and Major General Winfield Scott Hancock by John Quincy Adams Ward.

Another full-length figure, of the benefactor Richard Smith, stands on a bracket at the base of the pillar on which Reynolds soars far above, to the right of the central opening. In niches around the walls are the busts of fourteen individuals—five military figures and three civilians—created by seven sculptors. Two were women: Bessie O. Potter and Katherine M. Cohen. The male artists were Grafly (who did two busts in addition to his standing figure of Reynolds), A. S. Calder, George E. Bissell, Samuel Murray, and Moses Jacob Ezekiel.

John Massey Rhind added further decoration with two eagles and globes acting as sentinels. Angels beckon from the tympanum above the columns that support each arch, while in the cornice above them are incised the names of all the Pennsylvanians honored in the memorial. The work remains, in the words of an observer in the 1970s, "one of the most visually striking public monuments erected at the turn of the twentieth century."

Source: Lewis Sharp, "The Smith Memorial," in *Sculpture of a City*, pp. 168–179, quotation p. 170. Bach, *Public Art in Philadelphia*, p. 208.

Generals Meade, Reynolds, McClellan, and Scott are the four most prominent Union heroes of the Civil War honored on the *Smith Memorial Arch* in West Fairmount Park.

Drive, the fountain was moved to its current location for the bicentennial. Fenton was a member of the Philadelphia Ten, a group that promoted the work of female artists.[30]

A number of other works are scattered near the Horticultural Center. As a grouping, they are a wonderfully eclectic mix of the kinds of figures earlier generations chose to honor. Here are included a reverence for the ancient past, distinguished nineteenth-century composers, an important clergyman-statesman, German literary greats, and allegorical figures. *The Wrestlers* is a circa 1885 cast of a Roman marble copy of a stunning ancient Greek work of art whose realism excited Victorian viewers[31](Chapter 14). For more than a century, the work stood in front of Memorial Hall. Stolen from there in 1991, it was soon recovered, but had to be repaired after a hand was hacked

off while still in storage. Once restored, it was installed at its current location. Nearby, the biblical story of *Rebecca at the Well* is depicted in a brass relief by John J. Boyle.[32]

Close by is *Night*, a mysteriously hooded figure that was the first gift to the FPAA in 1872. The Presbyterian leader and patriot John Witherspoon is depicted in bronze by Joseph Alexis Bailly, whose casting of George Washington stands in front of Independence Hall.[33] Nearby are portraits of three composers: *Franz Schubert* by Henry Baerer, 1891; *Franz Joseph Haydn* by Idusch and Son, 1906; and *Giuseppe Verdi* by G. B. Bashanellifusi, 1907. The great literary figures *Goethe* and *Schiller*, both by Heinrich C. J. Manger, dating from the 1890s, are neighbors. Not far away, Lindsay Daen's modernist work from 1975, an elongated *The Journeyer*, strides across the lawn.

(*Above, left*)
At the Horticultural Center, *Centennial Fountain* remains from Philadelphia's Centennial Exposition.

(*Above, right*)
The bronze *Seaweed Girl Fountain* was a feature at the 1926 sesquicentennial.

The memorial to Charles Dickens was installed in Clark Park in West Philadelphia when the park opened in 1895.

At the end of the Avenue of the Republic, almost directly in front of the Mann Music Center, sprawls the impressively odd *Catholic Total Abstinence Union Fountain*. It was commissioned, as its name suggests, by the Catholic Total Abstinence Union of America at the time of the centennial to commemorate prominent Catholic figures from the period of the American Revolution— John Barry, Archbishop John Carroll, and Senator Charles Carroll—along with the contemporary temperance advocate, Father Theobald Mathew. The central figure is Moses, gesturing toward heaven. A number of prominent Catholics who participated in the Revolutionary War are pictured in medallions in the wall surrounding the immense circular fountain (Chapter 3). The artist, Herman Kirn, worked for the Fairmount Park Commission, and later created the *Toleration* figure overlooking the Wissahickon.[34]

Two other commemorative pieces can be found on Martin Luther King Jr. Drive on the Schuylkill's west bank. Johann Heinrich Drake's *Alexander von Humboldt* was a gift from Philadelphia's German American community to commemorate the nation's centennial. Nearby is a bronze of *St. George and the Dragon* that was rescued from storage in the basement of the PMA in 1975, and installed at this location in time for the bicentennial. The artist is unknown, but the work once stood atop the headquarters of the Society of the Sons of St. George in a neoclassic building at Thirteenth and Arch Streets. It was then out of sight for three-quarters of a century after the society building was demolished in 1901.[35] Its survival and resurrection at its current location are a reminder that Philadelphia has sometimes been overwhelmed by the sheer amount of its public art, but, fortunately, also has produced both official and volunteer groups of citizens who strive to maintain and preserve it.

One additional piece of sculpture outside Fairmount Park proper deserves mention here because it has largely identified the park in which it sits since the end of the nineteenth century. It is the statue of Charles Dickens, a seated bronze in University City's Clark Park, with his beloved creation, Little Nell, standing against his pedestal. The park, which covers just more than nine acres, is bordered by Forty-Third and Forty-Fifth Streets, and Baltimore and Woodland Avenues. The *Dickens* was created by Francis Edwin Elwell in 1890, and won two gold medals at the Columbian Exposition of 1893 before it was installed in this newly created park in 1895. The park recently has been renovated and the figure of Nell, which had been vandalized in 1989, restored.[36]

The *Fountain of the Sea Horses*, below the west face of the Art Museum near the waterworks, was a gift from the government of Italy to the United States in 1926.

The Parks' New
Governance System

On November 4, 2008, Philadelphia voters approved an amendment to the
city's Home Rule Charter, which transformed the way Philadelphia's parks
had been governed since 1867, when the Fairmount Park Commission (FPC)
was created. For the first time in its history, administration of the park system
was combined with that for recreation. The result was a merged Philadelphia
Parks and Recreation Department (PPR). The Fairmount Park Commission
was replaced with a new Commission on Parks and Recreation (PaRC), appointed by the mayor and advisory to the PPR.

Support for the amendment had focused largely on two arguments. The
first was that it would make the new commission more politically accountable than the old one had been, largely by giving its appointive power to the
elected mayor of the city rather than the unelected and more politically removed Board of Judges of the Court of Common Pleas. The second was that
it would reflect the actual, indivisible relationship that had grown up over
time between the city's parks and its recreational facilities scattered throughout Philadelphia. Opponents of the measure expressed concern that the new
commission, unlike the old, would have advisory powers only, rather than
the authority to take independent action. Some feared that this, combined
with the mayor's new power to appoint its members would undercut its ability to act independently.

The public discussion of the charter change proposal was extensive and
full in the months leading up to the November poll. A report commissioned
by the city from an independent consultative firm generally supported a
merger. Among the weaknesses of the park system, it found a confusing
governance system, the lack of accountability of the FPC, and the lack of

adequate funding. Other "good government" groups generally supported the charter change as well.[1]

We consider first the history of the FPC's accountability, the related charge of elitism, and the feared loss of independence for the parks' governors. Clearly, in 1867, the decision to vest the appointive power for the FPC in the Court of Common Pleas was an attempt to remove the commission from Philadelphia's combative political arena by giving it independent authority. Commissioner's terms were for five years, with reappointment permitted. Only six years earlier, mayoral terms had been extended from two to three years, and single terms would remain more the norm than the exception for decades to come. At the time, city government contained two councils, select and common, which together wielded considerable independent power. Nor had the concept of a municipal department for recreation under the authority of a mayor been invented. In that context, it was thought that an independent and somewhat politically detached authority might best protect and develop what was still a new urban park.

Even so, from the time the FPC was born, it did not shut out political interests. The commission's first president, Morton McMichael, was also the city's mayor, and at first an ex officio member of the FPC. Regardless of his dominant position as a political figure in the city—or perhaps because of it— McMichael proved a vigorous and effective advocate for Fairmount Park. He remained as FPC president until his death in 1879, far past the end of his ex officio membership as mayor ten years earlier. The commission's first vice president, General George G. Meade, was a public hero, if not a political figure, by virtue of his recent victory at Gettysburg. With those two officers and a third member appointed by the court, the well-connected real estate lawyer Eli Kirk Price, the FPC began its work with leaders possessing real prowess in the public sphere.

Still, the commission's ostensible removal from the political fray meant that it was always vulnerable to the charge of elitism. That was a charge first heard, in fact, even before the FPC came into being, when it was lodged at city officials responsible for creating the beginnings of Fairmount Park. Those charges never entirely disappeared across more than a century of the commission's existence as an independent body. Nor were they always groundless.

The most egregious efforts to tie private interests to park development came early in the twentieth century when a few of the richest men in the city—all members of the FPC at one time or another—made their public legacies dependent on having their will prevail with the commission and the

The Parks' New Governance System

Fairmount Park Art Association. When they failed, it was because they came into opposition with elected officials who viewed themselves as protecting the city's financial interests against the egoistic demands of a few.[2] Yet, because the battles were over would-be gifts to the city, whatever the strings attached, many would think the real losers in such cases were the citizens of Philadelphia.

Nor were outcomes such as these ever the result of a simple division between high-minded elected officials and unaccountable, and unelected, members of the FPC. From shortly after the Civil War until World War II, City Hall was mostly dominated by the Republican machine, which in turn was dominated by the newly rich. Members of the FPC, in contrast, tended to be patricians unwilling to engage in the crass patronage deals dispensed from City Hall. Nonetheless, they did grow accustomed to looking the other way while their fellow Republicans in elected offices procured the contracts for park projects. The ironic result was that on rare occasions when a reformist mayor unexpectedly came to power, he was so at odds with the machine, as well as the usual majorities in city councils, that public works projects slammed to a halt. As the thirty-year effort to complete the Benjamin Franklin Parkway and the Philadelphia Museum of Art made clear, only when the machine was in power did the graft-filled work get done.[3]

By the second half of the twentieth century, other factors began to change the way the Fairmount Park Commission was seen by the public. Now the charge was less of elitism than of its lack of accountability. The fact that its members were a remove or two away from elected officials once had been partially offset by the sheer civic stature of many of the leaders of the FPC. But in Philadelphia, as in other cities throughout the country, the traditional WASP establishment of civic leaders went into a gradual decline. Less and less did a listing in the social register, a hallowed family name, or even a vast fortune denote one's unquestioned place as a civic leader. While noblesse oblige gave way to society's greater democratization, Democrats replaced Republicans as the dominant political force in the city. Women and minority groups increasingly came to the fore. Some among them found their way to the FPC.

Without the huge fortunes of such earlier members as Widener or Stotesbury to dangle as prizes before public officials, the commission's prominence—its power and authority—as a Philadelphia institution began to slip. Questions were increasingly asked about the qualifications of those chosen as commissioners, particularly because the whole process by which they were selected through the Board of Judges remained opaque. Then the cry began to be heard that the appointees were *too* politically connected, if not chosen out of political correctness, since for some critics there seemed no other good explanation for their appointments. Moreover, throughout the decades when Philadelphia was shedding population, its parks budget either remained stagnant or actually shrank. The result, not surprisingly, was decline in the upkeep of public land and very little in the way of long-term planning to reverse that trend.[4]

By the start of the twenty-first century, it could reasonably be argued that "lack of appreciation for this remarkable asset [Fairmount Park], combined with an historically elitist and later politicized Park Commission, left the park system starved of money and leadership."[5] The *Philadelphia Daily News* was scathing in opposing the FPC's claim that a bigger budget would solve its problems. It provided this anecdote to bolster the newspaper's argument for charter change:

> In fact, increasing its budget sometimes *became* the problem, as was the case with a 1997 grant of $26.6 million from the William Penn Foundation. The money was originally intended for building environmental centers in four parks, but the Fairmount Park Commission found itself in the embarrassing position of ending the grant period without having spent the grant as it had been intended and ultimately had to forgo about a third of the money.[6]

Park officials dispute this account, arguing that the money in question was simply repurposed to restore other parkland when then mayor Rendell refused to allocate money to staff the new centers.[7] Yet, a growing drumbeat of criticism was convincing much of the electorate that the Fairmount Park Commission was no longer the most effective or appropriate authority to govern the parks. Its independence and autonomy had brought it respect for much of its history, but by the time of the charter change vote, those factors were widely viewed as liabilities.

The second major argument in 2008 for changing how the park system was governed related to the intimate relationship that had grown up between parks and recreation, both as a matter of administration and in the public mind. That perception had been widespread for many years, though it probably did not register at all in 1867, when Public Law 547 created the Fairmount Park Commission.

At that time, the ex officio members of the commission were the mayor, the presidents of select and common councils, and two park engineers. No recreation official was named, since neither the activity's civic face nor the

concept that a city officer might play a role in it existed. Parks were not yet regarded as places for active recreation, but as open spaces where city dwellers might find escape to enjoy fresh air and admire the beauties of nature.[8] School playgrounds and playing fields were meant for more physical activities. The idea that parks might be places for organized recreational use built slowly and gradually through the last decades of the nineteenth century, and did not become dominant until well into the twentieth century.[9]

By the end of the nineteenth century, the park on either side of the Schuylkill had grown to some three thousand acres and distant plots of parkland had been brought under the jurisdiction of an entity named, however confusingly, the Fairmount Park Commission. New city charters in 1919 and 1951 left the structure and responsibilities of the FPC largely in place.

The 1951 Philadelphia Home Rule Charter, which remains the city's constitutional document today, did incorporate the Fairmount Park Commission

Mario Lanza Park in the Queen Village neighborhood of Philadelphia honors the singer whose boyhood home was nearby.

Along Cobbs Creek Bridge, a 1941 painting by Edmund Martino, provides a glimpse of the city's largest park in West Philadelphia. (Private collection)

into the city's governmental structure, at least on paper. Yet, even though it was designated for the first time a departmental commission of the Department of Recreation, the FPC remained largely independent of departmental control. It remained apart from the charter's strong mayoral system by virtue of the fact that its ten citizen members continued to be appointed for five-year terms by the Board of Judges of the Court of Common Pleas. While the commissioner of recreation, in whose department the FPC resided, was selected by the mayor, the appointed members of the FPC were, formally speaking, still beyond the mayor's reach.[10] Here was a nod to the importance of recreation in modern urban parks, but with no corresponding move to curb the FPC's apparent independence.

Meanwhile, almost every other major city in the country had united its parks with its public recreation authority. That added to the argument that Philadelphia was out of step in an era when ideas about urban parks had evolved well beyond those prevalent when city parks remained a novelty in America.[11] In a time of increasingly tight budgets, the efficiency argument also drew attention. Critics could point to possible bureaucratic overlaps while parks and recreation management remained in separate spheres, or the converse, lack of coordination between the management of parklands and their recreational use.

The Parks' New Governance System

The Philadelphia Parks Alliance

The mission of this nonprofit advocacy organization is to champion the public interest in outstanding parks, recreation, and open space in Philadelphia. It regards itself as the leader in moving citizens to help shape policies for the city's public parks and to drive their restoration. In addition to its role as advocate, the Parks Alliance seeks to be an important information resource, providing statistics, facts, and studies about municipal parks.

The alliance spearheaded the movement that led to a 2008 amendment to Philadelphia's Home Rule Charter, resulting in the creation of a new Department of Parks and Recreation. Its "Trust for Public Land" study showed that Philadelphia's parks and recreation facilities bring hundreds of millions of dollars in annual income and savings to Philadelphia and its citizens (www.philaparks.org).

In November 2008, the amendment to the city charter passed with 73 percent approval. That was a remarkable accomplishment for the administration of Mayor Michael Nutter, who had been in office for less than a year, and the Philadelphia Parks Alliance, which had led the campaign. For more than a decade previously, the attempt to merge the Fairmount Park Commission with the Department of Recreation had foundered, with many park supporters concerned that their interests would not be as well represented under a combined authority.[12]

Neither of Mayor Nutter's immediate predecessors—first, Edward G. Rendell, then John F. Street—had made the parks or a reordering of their governance structure a high priority. But Mayor Nutter came to office with a reputation gained as a friend of the parks while he served as a councilman. He had represented the Fourth District, which includes some 60 percent of the Fairmount Park system, and had often made his voice heard as a parks advocate. Several months before the public was asked to vote on the charter change, the mayor no doubt helped the cause when he announced a nearly $20 million initiative to reinvigorate the Benjamin Franklin Parkway and to develop a new green space, Hawthorne Park, at Twelfth and Catharine Streets. He was joined in that announcement by then governor Rendell and a number of other officials, as well as representatives from funding agencies and relevant community organizations.[13]

The new PaRC is now the main advisory body to the PPR.[14] Mayor Nutter named Michael DiBerardinis as the first commissioner of Philadelphia Parks and Recreation in the merged department. DiBerardinis brought a wealth of relevant experience to the position. He was a prominent community activist when he was first appointed to public office by then mayor Rendell in 1992. From that year to 2000, he had served as recreation commissioner in the Rendell administration, and was credited with expanding the department's

The Commission on Parks and Recreation (PaRC)

PaRC replaced the 142-year-old Fairmount Park Commission in July 2009, following the passage of an amendment to the Home Rule Charter. The new commission has fifteen members, nine of whom are appointed by the mayor from a list of nominations submitted by City Council from applications that interested residents offer to council. Appointments are made at the beginning of each mayoral term, and are meant to be determined on the basis of the individual's demonstrated skills and knowledge about park and recreation matters. Ex officio members include the president of City Council and the executive director of the City Planning Commission or their designees, the water commissioner, the streets commissioner, the public property commissioner, and—the most important of these six thanks to this individual's portfolio—the parks and recreation commissioner.

PaRC's charge is to create written, enforceable standards relevant to the use of Philadelphia's park and recreational land and facilities, recommend how revenue might be enhanced, and assist in promoting parks and recreational programs and facilities.

PaRC holds six public meetings a year, on the third Wednesday of every other month (January, March, and so forth). Citizens are invited to provide comments and information to the commission. The Philadelphia Parks Alliance provides information regarding the time and location of public meetings (www.philaparks.org).

activities and services. He was simultaneously a Fairmount Park commissioner. In 2003, after Rendell was elected governor of Pennsylvania, he appointed DiBerardinis secretary of the Department of Conservation and Natural Resources (DCNR) for the Commonwealth. He left that post in 2009 to begin his term as leader of Philadelphia's newly merged department under Mayor Nutter. As a deputy mayor for environmental and community resources, DiBerardinis is also a member of Nutter's cabinet and oversees the Free Library of Philadelphia.

The first deputy commissioner of parks and facilities is Mark Focht, who was named by Mayor Street as executive director of the FPC in 2005. The latter position was abolished with the merger, and Focht now is responsible for implementing the policies and decisions of the commissioner of the PPR rather than the FPC. He reports to the commissioner and, through him, to the mayor. PaRC, which has no staff, is charged with advising the mayor directly.

The new governance structure was meant to bring a renaissance for Philadelphia's park system, allowing the city "to recapture its position as the nation's leader in the park and recreation field."[15] In anticipation of the charter change vote, Mayor Nutter had earlier in 2008 persuaded City Council to increase the city's parking tax with the plan to use some of the additional revenue to help provide for $8 million in new funding for the city's parks. But by the time that vote came, the nation's massive economic downturn began to herald drastically reduced tax revenues for the city. As a result, the mayor ordered the new parking tax fees to go into the general budget instead of to programs in the newly merged department.[16] This setback was a sharp reminder of the fact that the PPR had been granted no greater source of independent funding than had the FPC. Also like its predecessor, the new department had no dedicated funding stream. (See Chapter 18 for a fuller exploration of contemporary efforts to fund the parks.)

The Fairmount Park Conservancy

The Fairmount Park Foundation was incorporated in 1998 as a fund-raising organization operating independently of the FPC to raise monies for the parks. In 2001, its name was changed to the Fairmount Park Conservancy. Several of its directors also serve on PaRC. Pennsylvania's governor is a member ex officio. The conservancy regards itself as a leader and steward of signature capital projects that support the Fairmount Park system. It actively seeks partnerships with other organizations to promote funding for the parks.

The conservancy also is engaged in environmental education to develop the next generation of park stewards. Its partners are the Philadelphia Water Department and the PPR. The program brings local students to the park's environmental centers while offering teachers the option of lessons in their classrooms. Fairmount Park environmental educators teach by using local parks as the focal ecosystem.

During the first decade of the twenty-first century, a committee of the conservancy, Women for the Water Works, raised $5 million to restore the waterworks at Fairmount (Chapter 2). The conservancy also undertook the designation of the Centennial District along with the refurbishment of the Horticultural Center there.

All of these projects have been made possible by private gifts and grants from the nonprofit and for-profit sectors. For details, see www.fairmountparkconservancy.org.

The Fairmount Park Historic Preservation Trust

The trust was chartered as a nonprofit corporation in 1992 to address the city of Philadelphia's significant historic properties that were abandoned and underutilized in Fairmount Park. It helps the PPR to restore, rehabilitate, and manage the historic properties, largely by identifying public and private organizations able to restore and maintain sites through long-term leases. A number of properties now have been restored and are financially self-sufficient.

In 1997, the trust created the Conservation Program in which architectural conservators assess the conservation needs of the historic properties and create appropriate treatments.

The Historic Properties Fund was created in 2002 with a five-year gift from the Dorrance H. Hamilton Charitable Trust. It is administered in partnership with the trust on a matching grant basis. It engages in restoration and repair of some of the more than two hundred properties in the Fairmount Park system. Stewards of these properties are encouraged to leverage additional funding for their care. Among others, the trust and fund have completed restoration projects at Chamounix, Lemon Hill, Ohio House, Mount Pleasant, the John Bartram House, Valley Green Inn, and Historic Rittenhouse Town. In 2015, the Fairmount Park Historic Preservation Trust merged with the Fairmount Park Conservancy, which became the name of the combined organization.

A child's treehouse was the inspiration for Martin Puryear's "Pavilion in the Trees," which was installed in West Fairmount Park's Lansdowne Glen in 1993, a commission of the Fairmount Park Art Association.

For the short run, therefore, the hopes that park advocates had held for major new funding initiatives were not borne out in the first years of the governmental change. A new property tax overhaul looked to be a promising source of new revenue, but that had not yet been put in place by the time the first stage of the parks and recreation merger was done in 2012.[17] That prevented an additional $2.5 million from going to the PPR, although by the end of that year, City Council approved a midyear transfer ordinance to increase the department's operating budget for the following year by $2.675 million. Even with that boost, the department's budget was actually lower than it had been four decades earlier, having suffered a 30 percent decrease since 2009.

Yet economic growth was slowly returning to the city and the nation. Property tax reform came about in 2013, and started to produce some additional revenues for the city. During each of the next two years, slight increases occurred in the budget for the PPR. In mid-2014, City Council approved two funding increases proposed by Mayor Nutter for fiscal year 2015, which together added another $1 million to the PPR's budget. Such moves at last suggested a somewhat more hopeful trend for funding Philadelphia's park.

At about the time the mechanics of the merger were completed in 2012, the commissioner and his deputy suggested that it might take a decade before its outcome could be evaluated fully. With comparatively little data on public-sector mergers of this kind, integration was proceeding carefully "to find the right synergies," in the words of Commissioner DiBerardinis. What he called "cultural integrity" would have to be built in the merged department. That intangible goal would demand assessments of the quality of performances over time.[18]

Two events in particular had produced serious controversies in the last years when the Fairmount Park Commission was still the governing authority for the parks. Together, they had a clear impact on the success of the movement for charter change.

In 2004, the FPC agreed to an initiative from the School District of Philadelphia (SDP) to provide a parcel of Fairmount Park land near Forty-First Street and Girard Avenue for the construction of a new high school for nearly eight hundred students. The project, dubbed the "School of the Future," was inspired by an offer from the Microsoft Corporation, which offered laptop computers and software to teach low-income and at-risk students by emphasizing project-based learning, technology, and community involvement. The parkland was essential, went the argument from the SDP and its allies, both because it was near the target population of students in the Parkside neighborhood of Philadelphia and because of the greater ease in starting construction quickly than if private land had to be acquired elsewhere in the city. In return, the School District agreed to donate money to the parks and make other improvements.[19]

At the time, criticism of the FPC's action in allowing a school to be built on parkland was somewhat tempered by the argument from its proponents— led by the administration of Mayor Street and the then CEO of the School District—that the school would be a shining model for a new era in education. They argued that to build the school on a greensward rather than in a decrepit urban neighborhood was important to its attractiveness and, therefore, its success. The FPC was persuaded and the school was built. Students were selected by lottery. The school's opening in September 2006 was featured on television talk shows.[20]

But the high expectations some had for the project were dashed by the time the first class was preparing to graduate three years later. Three School District superintendents had come and gone, along with four school principals. Test scores of students remained low, as were graduation rates. Nor was the new building filled to capacity. Promised technology often did not materialize.

During the next several years, the project still found advocates who called for patience, arguing that it would ultimately provide more-positive results.[21] Yet initial disappointments no doubt fueled renewed criticisms of the FPC for giving up parkland in the first place.

The FPC approved another move to lease parkland the next year. In 2005, the commission agreed to the plan of the Fox Chase Cancer Center to expand onto some nineteen acres of Burholme Park in Philadelphia's northeast. It would grant the medical institution an eighty-year, renewable lease in return for payment of $2.25 million plus additional fees as Fox Chase constructed new buildings. According to the FPC, most of those funds would be used to improve Burholme Park. After the plan became public, neighborhood groups and park advocates joined to oppose it. Nevertheless, City Council approved the transfer, and lawsuits followed. Here was as clear an example as any throughout the park's history of the FPC acting not independently of City Hall but in tandem with it.

The transaction was finally stopped by a judge of Philadelphia's Orphans' Court, who ruled in December 2008 that the FPC had no authority to sell land left to the city in accordance with the 1896 will of Robert W. Ryerss, owner of the Burholme estate. Ryerss had specified that he bequeathed the land "to the citizens of Philadelphia to be used as a park forever."[22] The issue of Fox Chase's expansion eventually was resolved when Temple University Health Systems agreed to merge with Fox Chase. With its ownership of Jeanes Hospital on land adjoining Fox Chase, Temple agreed that Fox Chase personnel would have access to those facilities. Officials from both institutions anticipated an eventual cancer treatment hub on forty-seven acres owned by Temple that surrounds Jeanes Hospital.[23]

Both experiences, those involving the School of the Future and Fox Chase expansion, prompted action by park advocates at the time the 2008 charter amendment was approved. Almost the first order of business for the newly created PaRC was to develop an ordinance to protect park and recreation land in Philadelphia. Mayor Nutter made clear his support for such legislation. In the words of PaRC's chairperson: "Up to now, there have been no formal, consistent guidelines to follow when there has been a desire to transfer park or recreation land to a new use. The . . . [Open Lands Protection] ordinance establishes a predictable and transparent process for everyone to follow."[24] Requiring public participation in a proposed conveyance was a key component of the legislation. Once adopted by PaRC, it was unanimously approved by City Council and signed into law on April 15, 2011.[25]

The School of the Future project became the catalyst that made the merger of parks and recreation get to the ballot when it did. The Fox Chase experience spurred both the merger and the campaign to create legislation that sets out protections for the city's parkland. That action was possible, however, only because of the support for such legislation from both the mayor and the members of City Council. We may wonder how far PaRC's power only to advise will carry should it propose a measure not endorsed by the city's elected officials. Nonetheless, at a moment when the new governance system is still in its infancy, it appears to have started life vigorously— or as vigorously as possible given the thin gruel of its funding. Concerns that

Monoshone Creek in the Wissahickon Valley for centuries powered the Rittenhouse paper mill.

The Parks' New Governance System

charter change would weaken the hand of park authorities have largely dissipated, at least for the present.[26]

In 2012, Temple University sought approval from PaRC to build a new facility for its rowers near Strawberry Mansion Bridge. That became the first test for the new Open Lands Protection Ordinance. Opposition was voiced, both from the commission and the public, to building a large new structure on what had been picnic grounds without a comparable acquisition of new parkland. Temple at first agreed to consider PaRC's suggestion that, as an alternative, it should pay to renovate the nearby East Park Canoe House, which had once housed the university's rowers. However, in December 2013, citing the costs of such renovation, the university announced a much more draconian move: it would eliminate seven of its varsity athletic programs—five for men, two for women—including both men's and women's rowing teams.

That brought a huge outcry of opposition, especially from the rowing community. Two months later, in February 2014, Temple reversed some of its earlier decision. The university's president announced that both rowing programs would be reinstated and, after all, the university would renovate the East Park Canoe House for their teams. That reversal was accompanied by a commitment by the city to make $1 million in repairs to a retaining wall at the site that had collapsed into the river, as well as a $2.5 million contribution toward renovating the boathouse. A Temple board member pledged an additional $3 million through his foundation. This promised a happy ending to what at first had been a clear division between park supporters and Temple officials, an outcome made possible once both groups found a financial solution that would protect and restore park property while maintaining a well-regarded varsity program.[27]

The officials who first headed the PPR point to programmatic advantages they already have seen with the merger of parks and recreation. New recreational activities are now possible because parkland for the first time is perceived as available for their use; rock climbing and kayaking are examples. Youth triathlons also are now sponsored by the city, and were not considered by the old Recreation Department because they too need park resources.[28] To the extent that activities such as these remain popular and well administered in the city's parks, they can only deepen public awareness of the work of the PPR and appreciation for its responsiveness to the recreational needs of its citizens.

Much has been made about the greater transparency in the way PaRC must conduct its business as opposed to the apparent lack of it in the FPC. Yet, an irony lurks here, one that may come into view over time. Members of the old FPC were chosen by the Board of Judges of the Court of Common Pleas, whose composition was largely unknown to the public, as were the criteria the judges used in making their appointments. Mayors always could argue—when they, or the public, disagreed with the FPC's action or inaction—that they had no control over the commission.[29] The new PaRC is appointed from a list of citizen volunteers, all of whom are allowed to present their candidacies before City Council. The council then creates a list of twenty-five nominees to present to the mayor, who names nine from that list. The process is clearly more open than in the old days, and the members are now directly accountable to the mayor.

Yet, because the new commission is only advisory while the old had the power to act on its own, PaRC in fact may need to do less of its business in public than the old FPC did. The new agency provides minutes of its meetings, while the old one created complete verbatim records of its proceedings. PaRC is required to meet in public session six times a year, whereas the FPC held ten such meetings. Starting in 2002, when the plan was proceeding for the Barnes Foundation to move to the parkway, public hearings were held at each stage of the process for a total of five during the next several years.[30] The old FPC was in charge of that process. It remains to be seen how fully PaRC will include the public in major plans that come before it in the future.

The Race Street Pier juts into the Delaware River almost directly beneath the Benjamin Franklin Bridge. It has been a popular destination for joggers and other pedestrians since it was completed in 2011. (Photograph by Mark Garvin)

The Greener City

The general approbation that greeted the new governance system, which incorporated a revised Commission on Parks and Recreation (PaRC) into a new Parks and Recreation Department (PPR), no doubt stemmed partly from the way it was seen to harmonize with other recent public initiatives for Philadelphia. The most important may be Mayor Nutter's green initiative. In his January 2008 inaugural address, Nutter pledged to make Philadelphia the greenest city in America; shortly thereafter, in spring 2009, he created an Office of Sustainability, which produced a plan to accomplish that. Greenworks Philadelphia set fifteen ambitious targets for improving the city's environment, reducing energy use, creating jobs, and enhancing the quality of life.[1]

Within a few years, it became clear that the greening of Philadelphia should endure as an important part of Philadelphia's government. In November 2014, Philadelphia voters elected to make the Office of Sustainability a permanent part of city government, following a trend in other cities.

Philadelphia's Office of Sustainability serves to implement its Greenworks Philadelphia Plan (2009). Its officials argue that "for the first time in decades, changes beyond our borders—primarily rising energy prices, but also climate change and an emerging green economy—are increasing the value of our urban assets." The office has created partnerships with relevant federal, regional, and state, as well as private nonprofit and for-profit organizations to fund the projects it supports.

As a result of this initiative, one piece of legislation now requires that all new construction and major renovation of large city government buildings must meet the Leadership in Energy and Environmental Design (LEED)

17

standards set by the U.S. Green Building Council. Another requires cool roofs that meet Energy Star roof standards for all new construction in the city. Additionally, Philadelphia has partnered with the U.S. Department of Energy to develop local solar energy initiatives to displace the use of fossil fuels. The goal is to transform the local market for solar energy, making solar technologies cost-competitive, and to develop 57.8 megawatts of solar power for the city by 2021.

Other green initiatives included replacement of thousands of traffic signals with LED lights, the creation of hundreds of miles of bicycle lanes, and the purchase of several hundred hybrid buses for the Southeastern Pennsylvania Transit System (SEPTA).

The Greenworks Plan's Target 9 relates most directly to the work of the PPR. It is "to provide walkable access to park and recreation resources for all Philadelphians." More specifically, it set out to provide those resources within a ten-minute walk for 75 percent of residents. That led to the formulation of a plan called Green 2015 by the PPR in collaboration with the urban planning organization, Penn Praxis.[2] They found that, in 2010, some 80 percent of Philadelphians actually did enjoy walkable access to open space, although that still left some 202,000 residents outside the range of a ten-minute walk. As a result, Green 2015 set three broad goals to be achieved by that target year.

The first was to add five hundred acres of "publicly accessible space" throughout the city. In other words, the space need not necessarily be city owned, but should nonetheless be accessible to the public. An example is Penn Park, which was created in 2011 on twenty-four acres of land owned by the University of Pennsylvania along the west bank of the Schuylkill between Walnut and South Streets. It remains university property, but is available for the recreational use of the public at large. Within the next several years, additional green spaces had been acquired or planned across the city. The goal was to hit a target of 10,800 acres of parkland by 2015.

The second goal was to convert many facilities, such as school playgrounds and parking lots, from asphalt to permeable, green surfaces. In 2011, the PPR partnered with the Trust for Public Land (TPL), a national, nonprofit land conservation organization, and the Philadelphia Water Department (PWD) to support a green play spaces pilot program. The idea was to work with community groups to identify and redevelop open space where it was most needed.[3] Some of that space would be created by removing pavements from streets and lots where it was no longer required, and then planting them. To create green school yards, the PPR joined with the PWD, the School District (SDP), and the Mural Arts Program. Making playgrounds

and other hard surfaces permeable also assists the city in its larger goal of creating additional storm water management capacity. As of 2012, Philadelphia was the only city in the nation to win approval from the U.S. Environmental Protection Agency for its storm water management.[4]

The third goal was to plant 300,000 new trees by 2015, and to do so in a way that would increase tree coverage to 30 percent of the land area in all neighborhoods. The budget for tree planting throughout the city more than quadrupled during Mayor Nutter's first four years in office, from $350,000 to $1.5 million annually. The program, undertaken jointly by the PPR and the Fairmount Park Conservancy, is meant to provide free trees for planting on private property in areas where they are scarce. A substantial amount of the funding is contributed by Wells Fargo Bank.[5]

These green initiatives, along with any number of others in Philadelphia and elsewhere, flow from what may be a historical paradigm shift in how our cities are perceived. That shift, in turn, springs from the growing realization that our postindustrial age demands a transformed worldview. We

Washington Square is an original open space in the affluent Society Hill neighborhood of Philadelphia. The Tomb of the Unknown Soldier of the American Revolution is visible to the left of the central circle.

Early in the twenty-first century, Hunting Park, a part of the Fairmount Park system since 1871, was revitalized through a public-private partnership. Team Vick Field is now a state-of-the-art facility.

have left the time, in the words of one critic, "when we thought industrialization was the end goal, waste was growth, and wealth meant a thick haze of air pollution."[6] After a half century of decline and loss of population, Philadelphia, like other old rust belt cities of America, has made the transition to a postindustrial future, and is no longer seen as locked in a losing competition with its suburbs, as was the widespread assumption in recent decades. For the first time in fifty years, the city's population increased in the first decade

Revitalizing Hunting Park

This eighty-seven-acre park in North Philadelphia is on land once owned by James Logan, William Penn's secretary, Philadelphia's mayor, and acting governor of the colony of Pennsylvania early in the eighteenth century. His manor house, Stenton, is three-quarters of a mile to the northwest (Chapter 6). Hunting Park came under the jurisdiction of the Fairmount Park Commission in 1871. Its neighborhood grew increasingly impoverished in the second half of the twentieth century, and the park declined to the point that safety became a concern.

In 2009, the Fairmount Park Conservancy partnered with the PPR and then consulted with neighborhood residents and community groups to produce a master plan for renovating and revitalizing Hunting Park. It called for $20 million in funds, to be raised from both public and private sources, with the project to be carried out in stages. The first phase had largely been completed four years later. To rectify the paucity of fresh food sources in the neighborhood, a farmer's market, operated by the Food Trust, was created to serve the community one day each week through the warmer months. Two new playgrounds were installed. A state-of-the-art baseball field was opened in a project partially funded by the family foundation of Ryan Howard of the Philadelphia Phillies. The diamond soon attracted a huge increase in Little League Baseball.

Team Vick Field, launched with a gift from Philadelphia Eagles quarterback Michael Vick, created a state-of-the-art football field for the North Philly Aztecs. A community garden provided plots for neighbors to grow their own food. Renovated tennis courts were put in place. An upgrade in the lighting of the park's peripheral streets also made the park safer and more attractive than it had been in years.

The Greener City

of the twenty-first century; that pace then accelerated early in the following decade.[7]

In part, Philadelphia's renewed population growth simply reflects global trends. For the first time in history, more than half the world's people now live in cities, and cities can be—will have to be—capable of sustainable growth if the planet is to remain habitable. Political leaders in societies that are most advanced economically increasingly see their cities as leading the way. In America, growing numbers of city dwellers are beginning to understand that urban density, walkability, and a shrinking carbon footprint through improved public transportation facilities and the reduction of fossil fuels all make both good economic and environmental sense. By improving the livability of cities, such policies help them to remain places of innovation, entrepreneurship, and opportunity.

In the first dozen years of the twenty-first century, urgency may have been added to the sustainability movement by the increase in dramatically destructive storms across the continent.[8] Throughout the first two centuries of its history, Philadelphia, like many other American cities, systematically reconfigured its many small streams into drainage conduits. These often became combined sewers to carry sewage as well as storm water. The result has

Philadelphia's modern skyline forms the backdrop for a view from West Fairmount Park's Belmont Plateau.

increasingly meant that, in times of flood, these sewers often discharge directly into nearby rivers and streams, thereby contributing in a major way to the pollution of urban waterways. The Philadelphia Water Department has begun a decades-long project to keep storm water out of sewers, partly by encouraging the creation of permeable surfaces throughout the city as part of an increasingly green infrastructure.[9]

An obvious component of a greener urban area is the health of its parks. Not only are they green in the literal sense, but parks also underpin sustainable goals. They are an essential recreational substitute for the private yards and gardens that are at a premium in closely built neighborhoods, and therefore an alternative to increased suburban sprawl. They can raise property values nearby, as has been demonstrated in a number of American cities in recent years. More intangibly, their tree canopy absorbs the carbon dioxide that contributes to global warming. According to the U.S. Forest Service, the trees in Philadelphia remove almost 500,000 metric tons of carbon from the air, at an estimated value close to $10 million.[10]

Further recent initiatives in Philadelphia also assist in the city's greening, including adding to its parkland. Some of these are outside the purview of the city's parks system, but are developing in ways that should advance both a parks agenda and green goals for the city.

Historically, the Delaware River waterfront in the heart of Philadelphia has largely been excluded from the Fairmount Park system. While parks throughout the city were added to the Fairmount Park Commission's (FPC's) authority from an early date, only two small plots along the Delaware—Penn Treaty Park and Pulaski Park—came under its jurisdiction. Penn Treaty Park, the legendary site of a possibly legendary peace treaty between William Penn and the leaders of the indigenous Lenni-Lenape people, became a part of Fairmount Park in 1894. In those two centuries after Penn, the site near the end of Shackamaxon Street had become increasingly surrounded by the factories of industrial Philadelphia.[11] More than a century after that, those industries have all but disappeared, just as they have along most of the riverbank within Philadelphia's city limits. On a similar stretch of the river to the north, Pulaski Park is a small green space at Allegheny Avenue, serving the Port Richmond neighborhood.

After years of little city planning and fits and starts of disjointed redevelopment, Philadelphia at last has created a long-range plan for how the six-mile stretch through the central part of the city—from Oregon Avenue on the south to Allegheny Avenue on the north—should be developed. The initial agent for the plan was Penn Praxis, which during 2006–2007 engaged with some four thousand citizens and fifteen civic associations from neighborhoods along the central Delaware riverfront. From those exchanges came an Action Plan in 2008 that served to outline a civic vision and a guide to how that vision should be implemented over the next decades.[12]

Within the next several years, implementation was well under way. A new master plan for the central Delaware was fleshed out almost entirely from the 2008 set of proposals; a new management agency, the Delaware River Waterfront Corporation (DRWC) was created, replacing a discredited Penn's Landing Corporation; and a new zoning code was adopted to ensure that development would take place that was consistent with current land use and settlement patterns.[13]

Much of the plan for the central Delaware was informed by, or helped to inform, the green initiatives undertaken by the city, in large part through its Parks and Recreation Department. All these agencies share the goal of creating parks within a ten-minute walk of every home and neighborhood. One of the city's first completed projects on the Delaware was the creation of the Race Street Pier from a derelict structure jutting into the river nearly under the Benjamin Franklin Bridge. When the new little park was opened in 2011, its handsome sloping boardwalk, benches, and planted spaces provided a delightful destination for pedestrians. Soon after, completion of a well-lighted connector allowed walkers to move easily from Second and Race Streets under the I-95 expressway to the pier. That connector was intended as a model for another of the master plan's objectives, which was to reconnect and continue the grid of Philadelphia's streets to the waterfront wherever possible, thereby providing public access to the river over extended streets.

Along the riverfront itself, the goal is to create a recreational trail for walkers and cyclists. Since much of the land is privately owned, the process of securing such a trail must proceed bit by bit, through discussions with property owners and developers. There were fears that city authorities would fail to hold the line: The hundred-foot buffer first recommended by the Action Plan and many others gave way to a proposed fifty-foot zone after strong objections to the wider corridor from developers. Even that narrower band remained an issue of contention between environmentalists and developers throughout much of 2012. Late in that year, City Council finally approved a bill enshrining the fifty-foot buffer into the new zoning code.[14]

In keeping with sustainability goals, the riverbank is to be returned to its natural state wherever possible. A completed project is the Washington Avenue Pier. It became a public park in 2014 at the site of the station where, from 1870 to 1910, more than a million immigrants were processed when they entered the United States through Philadelphia. Spearheaded by the DRWC, Pennsylvania's Department of Conservation and Natural Resources, and the William Penn Foundation, the pier provides a boardwalk promenade above wetlands and a sculpture, *Land Buoy*, in the form of a stainless steel mast and spiral staircase for views of the river and the city.[15] The next such conversion was under way further south, at pier 68, where in 2015 a park was created containing a native tree grove featuring picnic areas and hammocks, walking paths, and fishing areas along the water, and an opening in the pier for visitors to observe fish and aquatic plants below. The new park restores the natural habitat at a postindustrial site and continues creation of the Delaware River Wetlands Park.[16]

To the north, another short section of the riverfront path—the Penn Street Trail—was completed in June 2013, from Spring Garden to the parking lot of the SugarHouse Casino. Two more connectors beneath the I-95 expressway from neighborhood to riverfront were being created at Spring Garden Street and Columbia Avenue.[17]

The parklike centerpiece of the Action Plan was to replace the concrete plaza and ramps at Penn's Landing with open space and grassy lawns. That publicly owned parcel along the waterfront, between Walnut and Market Streets, has for decades been configured into a semicircular amphitheater used in warm months for entertainment. Next to part of that stretch, I-95 is sub-

The Washington Avenue Pier also became a park in 2014; its *Land Buoy* sculpture is a reminder of the millions of immigrants who first entered the United States from there. Its creator, Jody Pinto, raises her hand at the top of the staircase; Philadelphia Mayor Michael Nutter is at the top left of the pole.

(*Above, right*)
A piece of Penn's Landing on the Delaware was transformed into a summertime destination, Spruce Street Harbor Park, in 2014.

merged and covered. But between the expressway and the plaza, scissor ramps provided vehicular access from Market Street down to Columbus Boulevard, at ground level. Now the intent is to extend the I-95 cover so that it slopes across both roadways down to the river's edge. That would allow a broad lawn and gathering place on the riverbank that is easily accessible on foot from center city.[18]

In spite of the many obstacles that lie in the way of fully implementing the vision for the central Delaware, the plan itself and the new initiatives it has already spawned hold much promise. Nor is this the only stretch of the river now preparing for a greener future. North of Allegheny Avenue, the PPR is partnering with the private, nonprofit Delaware River City Corporation (DRCC) to extend the ribbon of parks and green spaces to the city limit. That is an additional nine miles of riverfront bordered by seven neighborhoods.

Back in the heart of the city, two crosstown greenways are also in the planning stages. The one at Spring Garden Street was being designed in 2012. The second, at Washington Avenue, was expected to follow within a few years. They would incorporate new green pedestrian and bicycle paths within the two major streets that now demarcate the northern and southern boundaries of an expanding center city. Each would create a green ribbon stretching from the Delaware to the Schuylkill, connecting the waterfronts and parklands that increasingly help to define Philadelphia.

It is worth remembering that both the Schuylkill River and Wissahickon Creek were lined with industries before they became parkland in the nineteenth century. We do not suggest that a comparable strip of the Delaware waterfront will, or should, become public land. But powerful long-term trends in economic, social, and environmental spheres are converging to suggest that the future belongs to green and sustainable cities. It is no longer hard to imagine that all three of the city's riverine shores will play the central role in allowing Philadelphia to lead the way there.

The Natural Lands Trust

From its origins as a private group of local conservationists in 1953, the Natural Lands Trust (NLT) is now the largest and most comprehensive conservation organization in the greater Philadelphia region. Its first important initiative was to oppose dumping landfill in the Tinicum marshes along the Delaware, land now preserved as the John Heinz National Wildlife Refuge.

The NLT works primarily in two ways to save open space in eastern Pennsylvania and southern New Jersey. One is by acquiring and managing a growing number of private nature preserves; today they number forty-one with a total of more than 21,000 acres over thirteen counties in the two states. The second is by executing conservation easements for private landowners, who maintain full title to their property while prohibiting its development in the future. The NLT funds these initiatives by partnering with government agencies and nonprofit organizations.

The NLT's staff members also act as stewards in providing leadership in the ways to manage natural resources to conserve them for the future. They assist in restoration of wetlands and other resources, and advise communities in the creation of new parklands (www.natlands.org).

The Trust for Public Land

Soon after the first Earth Day in 1972, the Trust for Public Land (TPL) was founded as a national organization to bring business expertise to conservation. Lawyers, real estate professionals, and finance experts have been involved from the beginning. Headquartered in Washington, the TPL has been an important lobbying group for conservation and park issues nationwide. The trust has stimulated the growth of the land trust movement, in particular, to protect open space for communities across the West.

The TPL also has provided financing to help communities organize and pass conservation ballot measures. Its Washington office assists groups in finding relevant funding sources at the federal and state levels. At present, the trust claims to have completed more than 5,200 park and conservation projects nationwide (www.tpl.org).

A new boardwalk extends this section of Schuylkill Banks Park out over the river, thereby providing walkers, runners, and bicyclists with a parkway from the South Garden at Fairmount through center city to the South Street Bridge and beyond. (Photograph by Mark Garvin)

The City in a Park

In America, urban parks are born and live in counterpoint to urban density. When William Penn laid out Philadelphia in the 1680s, he anticipated such a relationship in his careful placement of five squares about his plan for the city. His new settlement quickly thrived, growing to become the largest in the thirteen British colonies by the time of the Revolution. Even so, it was home to only about thirty thousand people in 1776, with perhaps another ten thousand in neighborhoods adjacent to the confined city. Philadelphia's population was largely restricted to a single mile along the Delaware riverfront and somewhat less than that extending west to the vicinity of Southeast (Washington) and Northeast (Franklin) Squares, six blocks from the river.

Yet those planned open spaces, like their counterparts in the other quadrants of the town, were only minimally landscaped. Throughout the eighteenth century, they were used to graze animals and as places to bury the dead. In the summer of 1781, several thousand French troops set up camp at the undeveloped Centre (Penn) Square on their march from New England to Virginia and the decisive battle of Yorktown. No sense of civic urgency existed to transform any of the five squares into manicured parks because any able-bodied Philadelphian could have access to the countryside at the end of a ten-minute walk. In 1752, Benjamin Franklin had famously conducted his kite experiment in open land just to the north of the city limits.

By the dawn of the next century, Centre Square, still at the far western edge of settlement, began to be transformed into a genuine park when Latrobe's engine house for the city's new waterworks was started in 1801. Landscaping, walkways, and the installation of public art soon followed. During the next several decades, the other four of Penn's original squares also were renamed and landscaped as genuine public parks. By the 1860s, when the no-longer-distant Rittenhouse Square was furnished with an elaborate iron fountain and horse trough, Philadelphia's newly consolidated population had soared to more than half a million.

Not coincidentally, with urban growth came its counterpoint. That was also the time when Fairmount Park began its rapid expansion along both banks of the Schuylkill and up the Wissahickon Valley. In Philadelphia, as elsewhere in the nation, the unprecedented growth and industrialization of cities spawned bold new initiatives in the creation of urban parks. The reach of railroads and horse-drawn trolleys allowed citizens to escape their dense residential quarters for more distant and expansive pleasure gardens than had been thought possible a century earlier. Meanwhile, those same developments in transportation allowed people of means to begin to build their private domains at greater distances from the congested city; the Pennsylvania Railroad's Main Line stretching west from Philadelphia is a prime example.

That gradual removal of many of Philadelphia's wealthiest citizens from actually living in the city may also help explain why the further expansion of the Fairmount Park system gradually slowed starting at about the same time, following the huge acquisition of land that was concluded by 1876. Nonetheless, the city's population more than doubled, from 674,000 in 1870 to more than one-and-a-half million by 1910, while park acreage grew very little. By the latter year, the focus of park proponents had shifted to the creation of a grand public boulevard, today's Benjamin Franklin Parkway, as a project that would improve access to the park while creating an unprecedented ornament of the city. The parkway added comparatively little to the park's acreage, but what it did add would be a prime public asset in every sense of the term.

Philadelphia continued to grow into the 1950s to a peak population of more than two million, although the rate of growth slowed in each of the decades after 1880. The 1960 census was the first to show loss, a trend that continued through the census of 2000. The shrinking population—the most drastic loss of more than 260,000 came in the decade between 1970 and 1980—reduced the city's size by some half a million people during the second half of the twentieth century. Meanwhile, the metropolitan area more than compensated for that loss by adding some 1,580,000 residents in the same period. But those beyond the city limits were not contributing substantially to the city's tax coffers, and hence to its parks budget, even though at least some of them undoubtedly made use of Philadelphia's parks.[1]

This first-ever decrease in the ratio of Philadelphia's population to its parks spelled trouble for the park system, making it increasingly difficult for the city's shrinking population to support the counterpoint of parkland. The parks' growing budgetary woes were part and parcel of the enduring struggle by City Hall to reconcile generally decreasing tax revenues with the need to provide essential services to the people of Philadelphia. In the absence of effective efforts to quantify the economic benefit of parks to the city, they could too easily be regarded as nonessential to the life of the community, making them a target for budget cuts. By early in the twenty-first century, the result of that long, slow shrinking of park funds could be phrased in various ways, all of them dire.

In 2012, four years after the start of the Great Recession, the budget for Philadelphia's Parks and Recreation Department was lower than it had been forty years earlier, having decreased by 30 percent over the previous three years.[2] But the recession was not solely responsible for those cutbacks. A 2008 study had concluded that, when adjusted for inflation, Philadelphia's parks budget in that year was already less than half what it had been only twenty years before, well after decline had begun.[3]

By virtually any measure, Philadelphia lagged behind almost every other major city in the country in the amount it spent on its parks (see Table 18.1). In 2010, for example, Philadelphia's operating and capital expenditures for its parks was almost $100 million. When considered as the amount spent on a per capita basis, that came to $64 per resident, placing the city in thirteenth place out of fourteen cities in park spending. In contrast, those cities at the top of the list—San Francisco, Seattle, and Minneapolis—spent respectively $280, $272, and $200 per resident for their parks. Among East Coast cities, New York, at $158, and Boston, at $103, also far outdistanced Philadelphia in per capita park spending.[4]

At last, civic leaders began to recognize that new initiatives were required to stem the drift. Several more hopeful signs and trends began to appear on the horizon. One was the effort to leverage additional funding for the parks from public and private agencies beyond City Hall.

In 1992, the Fairmount Park Historic Preservation Trust was created as a nonprofit corporation to address the problems of historic properties that were either abandoned or underutilized throughout the park system (Chapter 16). Its mission was to enlist private and nonprofit groups to contribute to the upkeep of park properties. Starting its work at a time after a number of such sites had been badly damaged or destroyed, the trust has been successful in the restoration of neglected park houses, and leasing them to organizations committed to maintaining them. Rockland and the Sedgley Porter's House in East Fairmount Park are two recent examples.[5]

Table 18.1
How Much Cities Spend on Parks (Fiscal Year 2010)

	Population	Park Spending*	Spending per Resident
San Francisco	815,258	$228,285,744	$280
Seattle	616,627	$167,541,163	$272
Minneapolis	385,378	$79,932,406	$200
Sacramento	466,676	$75,014,463	$161
New York	8,391,881	$1,329,673,995	$158
Cincinnati	333,012	$51,964,588	$156
Chicago	2,851,268	$379,504,652	$133
San Diego	1,306,300	$152,711,954	$117
Boston	645,169	$66,742,851	$103
Cleveland	431,369	$44,115,668	$102
Pittsburgh	310,037	$30,797,363	$99
Phoenix	1,593,659	$125,004,725	$78
Philadelphia	**1,547,297**	**$99,627,494**	**$64**
Baltimore	637,418	$36,797,232	$58

*Includes operating and capital expenditures, but excludes stadiums, zoos, museums, and aquariums. If a city has multiple park agencies, their expenditures have been consolidated.
Source: Center for City Park Excellence, Trust for Public Land, Philadelphia Parks Alliance.

A more ambitious effort began in 1998. Since then, the organization now known as the Fairmount Park Conservancy has become the leader in raising money for Philadelphia's parks beyond that appropriated by the city. Created as a nonprofit organization committed to an effective development program for the parks system, its proclaimed goal is to make Fairmount Park "a national model for urban revitalization, sustainability, and civic engagement."[6] The conservancy seeks partnerships with other organizations to promote park funding, and has become the principal steward of major capital projects. Some of its directors also serve on the Parks and Recreation Commission. In recent years, the conservancy has led in the relighting of Boathouse Row, the restoration of the Fairmount Water Works, South Garden, Cliffside Walk, and of Hunting Park, Penn Treaty Park, and the Centennial District. In 2015, the conservancy became the clearinghouse for a grant of $11 million from the William Penn and Knight Foundations to help fund five new park projects.[7]

A second and related trend in the effort to boost park funding can be seen in more focused and effective efforts at advocacy. For years, many had argued that Fairmount Park was an important economic driver for Philadelphia, while polls also revealed that residents typically described the park as the city's chief asset. Finally, an important study commissioned by the Philadelphia Parks Alliance (PPA) and funded by the Lenfest Foundation began to quantify those claims. The 2008 report by the Center for City Park Excellence of the Trust for Public Land addressed the question, "How much value does the city of Philadelphia receive from its parks and recreations system?" The astonishing answer was that total cost saving factors for citizens were estimated to be more than $1 billion annually. As the Philadelphia Parks Alliance put it in its own introduction to the final report, "that's not a bad return on investment" since it amounts to about one hundred times the amount that the city spends on parks each year."[8]

The report's authors acknowledged that not every aspect of a park system can be quantified, citing as examples the mental health value of a walk in the woods or a way to value the carbon sequestration of a city park. But they enumerated seven major factors that could be evaluated, at least roughly: clean air, clean water, tourism, direct use, health, property value, and community cohesion. They then divided their findings into categories, two for city government, and two relevant to citizens. See Table 18.2 for their summary findings:

Table 18.2
Estimated Annual Value of Philadelphia Park and Recreation System

Revenue-Producing Factors for City Government	
Tax Receipts from Increased Property Value	$18,129,000
Tax Receipts from Increased Tourism Value	$5,177,000
Estimated Total Municipal Revenue-Producing Factors	**$23,306,000**
Cost-Saving Factors for City Government	
Storm Water Management Value	$5,949,000
Air Pollution Mitigation Value	$1,534,000
Community Cohesion Value	$8,600,000
Estimated Total Municipal Cost-Saving Factors	**$16,083,000**
Cost-Saving Factors to Citizens	
Direct-Use Value	$1,076,303,000
Health Value	$69,419,000
Estimated Total, Citizen Cost-Saving Factors	**$1,145,722,000**
Wealth-Increasing Factors to Citizens	
Property Value from Park Proximity	$688,849,000
Profit from Tourism	$40,263,000
Estimated Total, Wealth-Increasing Factors	**$729,112,000**

Source: Philadelphia Parks Alliance, "How Much Value Does the City of Philadelphia Receive from Its Park and Recreation System? A Report by the Trust for Public Land's Center for City Park Excellence for the Philadelphia Parks Alliance," 2008, p. 3.

The effort to place dollar amounts on the many factors that bring benefits from urban parks is still in the early stages. As the report makes clear, that is largely because cities typically have not invested much in gathering data on park facilities, their use, spending on their behalf, and the effects on property around parks.[9] As a result, the specific amounts listed in the previous table are no doubt open to question. But there can be no debate about the fact that the cost savings and wealth production of Philadelphia's parks are very large. Whether or not they outweigh their costs to the city as much as a hundredfold, their costs are comparatively trivial compared to the benefits they bring.

This kind of engagement in quantifiable cost/benefit analysis is unprecedented for Fairmount Park. It is credibly based on rigorous methods rather than hunches. It also suggests that more refined empirical analysis will be the standard for the future. Park advocates should celebrate both its findings and the methods used to arrive at them. Yet, however persuasive the conclusions in this report, they do not and cannot address the question of how even so good an investment is to be maintained when tax revenues are not more robust.

Strong advocacy by the PPA was also instrumental in the passage, later in 2008, of the charter amendment that merged Fairmount Park with recreation, as described in Chapter 16. At this writing, it is too soon to conclude definitively whether that merger will produce a substantial and sustained increase in park funding, as its supporters argued. In his February 2008 budget address, Philadelphia's newly installed mayor, Michael Nutter, said: "I want to make this Park the best in the country, bar none. To do that we must give it the resources it's been denied for years."[10] That ringing commitment seemed to launch 2008 as a banner year for Fairmount Park. A few months later, publication of the parks report appeared with its impressive conclusions about the parks' benefits for the city. In November came the decisive referendum on the merger, which was championed as a way to produce greater revenue for parks and recreation than in the past. But then, with the onset of the Great Recession in the same year, Mayor Nutter's push for more resources soon was effectively reversed, and budget increases stalled.

By the start of 2012, the nation's economy was making a slow recovery. Philadelphia's parks budget had not. Although there were modest signs of help when $2.675 million was transferred to Parks and Recreation near the end of that year—a boost of nearly 3 percent to its budget—the city's overall spending on parks and recreation still kept it near the bottom among large American cities. And the toll in too many years of deferred maintenance continued to mount. A tour in that summer of some of the smaller parks and recreation centers throughout the city revealed broken doors and equipment, leaking roofs, nonfunctioning air-conditioning, unusable toilet facilities, and much more. As a member of one recreation center's neighborhood volunteers noted, at their worst, such places seemed ready to revert to nature. Because deferred maintenance almost inevitably would mean higher bills when repairs were eventually undertaken, costs could only mount. In the words of the executive director of the PPA: "We're turning $500 problems into $500,000 problems."[11]

Happily, during the next three years, budgets for Philadelphia's parks increased on the order of half a million dollars each year. However positive that trend, it still left the Philadelphia Parks and Recreation Department (PPR) some five million dollars short of what Mayor Nutter had promised near the start of his term. Yet, in spite of funding that perpetually fell short of what park advocates pressed for, there also had been areas of remarkable progress and promise in the parks system during the early years of the current century. Early in 2015, an article in the *New York Times* proclaimed that Philadelphia ranked third among more than fifty places it named throughout the world for travelers to visit. The rationale for the city's high ranking flowed almost entirely from the pleasures provided by its new parks, green spaces, and other public amenities, especially along both the Schuylkill and Delaware Rivers.[12]

In that same year, some of the most iconic features of the Fairmount Park system shone with a brilliance that seemed almost miraculous in light of budgetary woes. Philadelphia's parks bore a remarkable likeness to Charles Dickens's *Tale of Two Cities* in the best and worst of times. One of the most dramatic examples of the best of times was the complete restoration of the Fairmount Water Works, along with the adjacent South Garden and Cliffside Walk. After decades of work, these places now look much as they did at their prime in the nineteenth century, when they were renowned internationally and attracted hordes of leisure-time visitors. True, the waterwheels no longer turn and the forebay has long since become a grassy lawn. But the old mill house now beckons visitors to the Fairmount Water Works Interpretive Center, the engine house is home to a fine restaurant, and the gardens, pavilions, and walkways invite exploration. Nearby, the *Fountain of the Seahorses* has undergone a complete renovation; and the Philadelphia Museum of Art has created a sculpture garden near Fairmount's summit and is undertaking the largest expansion of its galleries in its history.

Boathouse Row flourishes, creating what may be Philadelphia's most romantic vista from the Schuylkill's west bank. For decades, the picturesque

Early in the twenty-first century, the esplanade below the Fairmount Water Works was renovated. Along with descriptions of the commercial history of the Schuylkill, this metal fisherman was reinstalled in 2004 after having been lost in the river during a 1999 hurricane.

buildings, many dating from the nineteenth century, have been outlined in twinkling lights at night, their reflection glimmering in the water. The addition of Lloyd Hall in 1998 brought an attractive new public facility to the row of private boating clubs. In 2002, St. Joseph's University and St. Joseph's Prep opened a new home farther upriver, the first new boathouse on the Schuylkill in a century. In 2014, Temple University announced that its men's and women's rowing teams would be headquartered in a renovated East Park Canoe House near Strawberry Mansion Bridge. That would both restore a historic city-owned boathouse and reverse Temple's earlier decision to eliminate its rowing programs in a cost-cutting measure.[13]

Meanwhile, Penn's public squares were all more beautifully buffed and polished than they had been for generations. Washington, Rittenhouse, and Logan Squares had never looked more lush, trim, and beckoning. Franklin Square, the last to be refurbished, had undergone a makeover that made it popular with families. Even City Hall at Penn Square had undergone a multiyear cleaning that left it glowing. Dilworth Plaza on its western face had been transformed into Dilworth Park, a grassy gathering place as well.

By 2012, the Benjamin Franklin Parkway at last was fulfilling the promise held out for it when it was created a century earlier. There were both new and refurbished destinations for art lovers, as well as major expansions under way or planned for other public buildings. Just as important, a number of efforts had been completed to make the parkway friendlier to walkers, and a

The City in a Park

destination in its own right, than it had ever been before. Cafés were created, along with play spaces and imaginative landscaping for underused plots. New art was installed. Improvements even extended to the thoughtful placement of benches. Further to the east, when the Pennsylvania Academy of the Fine Arts created its block-long Lenfest Plaza, it provided what could someday become the first phase of a new connector from North Broad Street to the Parkway. LOVE Park was about to be redesigned to make it a more welcoming link between Dilworth Park and the parkway. In addition to its namesake sculpture, it was expected that a new piece of public sculpture would be installed in the reconfigured LOVE Park.

Less dramatic, but also important, has been the gradual restoration and reuse of several of the park's historic villas. The greatest of the houses have generally been well preserved since the 1920s, but a number of others have been lost to neglect or vandalism through the decades in which there was

Dilworth Park next to City Hall has become a spot to relax and socialize where the old Broad Street Station once disgorged thousands of passengers daily. (Photograph by Mark Garvin)

The City in a Park

insufficient funding to maintain them properly. Even with those losses, these houses still make Fairmount unique among America's urban parks in their number as well as their architectural and historical importance. In recent years, the Fairmount Park Historic Preservation Trust has been effective in partnering with organizations willing and able to restore a number of these properties and maintain them.

The key to the success of the Preservation Trust and its more wide-ranging sibling, the Park Conservancy, has helped bring about many of these other accomplishments as well. It has required looking beyond the city's budgetary allocations to cement partnerships with others in both the public and private spheres. Without question, to continue and expand such partnerships will remain an important key to the health of Philadelphia's park system. Both the trust and the conservancy have proved their worth with every new dollar they have leveraged. The Parks Alliance has become the park system's invaluable publicist to would-be funders and the community at large.

But there are hazards here. As the current "best" and "worst" lists make clear, those able and willing to help fund Philadelphia's parks are typically more interested in supporting new capital projects than they are in paying

Among recent changes to the Benjamin Franklin Parkway is the new Barnes Foundation. (Photograph by Mark Garvin)

for maintenance and routine upkeep of existing facilities. Nor is that tendency confined only to Philadelphia and its parks. It is a phenomenon well understood by fund-raisers throughout the country, and it means that the agency receiving the funding often must pay for the resulting maintenance from its own pocket.

Eakins Oval has been transformed into a leisure-time destination in summer.

An unfortunate example for Fairmount Park came when it was unable to complete the environmental centers intended by a 1997 grant from the William Penn Foundation. Once the centers were built, they would have to be staffed out of the park budget. But the idea of increasing the park's staff— and presumably, the city's allocation—hit a brick wall of opposition from Mayor Edward Rendell. However attractive the foundation thought the capital project to be, its maintenance could only come with the compliance of financially constrained public officials.[14] It was not the first time, and surely will not be the last, when the laudable desire to create a new public facility had to be balanced against the added cost of maintaining it. That conflict occurred when the Fairmount Park Commission (FPC) still functioned independently from the mayor's office. One may hope that with the 2008 charter change, which made the FPC's successor (the Commission on

Parks and Recreation, or PaRC) a body appointed by the mayor, the potential for that kind of standoff has been reduced.

Regardless of these caveats, nonprofit support for capital projects is doing very good things for Fairmount Park. Because so many of the park's star features are now restored and gleaming, they are able to attract the kind of grateful attention from the public that should itself boost park revenues over the long run. That may be the most hopeful prospect for the renovation and maintenance of the multitude of less-glamorous facilities throughout the city. That they are less glamorous does not mean they are of lesser value to those in their neighborhoods or to the city as a whole. Nowhere is that more clear than in the introduction by the PPA to the 2008 report by the Center for City Park Excellence:

> In their present state, the city's parks generate $18 million in added property tax revenue and $689 million in increased equity for homeowners near parks. Improved parks could triple those numbers.
>
> . . . Philadelphia's parks already bring in $40 million in tourist revenue. Picture how they might perform when fully equipped with functioning restrooms, water fountains, restored historic homes, repaired picnic tables and upgraded trails.
>
> . . . Philadelphians already save $70 million in medical expenses by using parks. That number would rise if the city's parks were cleaner, safer, and stocked with amenities like bikes to rent and water ice to slurp.
>
> . . . Our more than 10,000 acres of parks, woods, riverbeds, and open space already provide at least $7 million worth of storm water and air pollution control each year. Every new tree fights asthma. Every new trail fights obesity. Every cleared streambed dries out a basement and unclogs a storm drain.[15]

That same 2008 report also suggested that Fairmount Park might earn as much as 40 percent of its budget through concessions and fees. Shortly thereafter, the parks system was reorganized and consolidated. Then, in 2011, two local consulting firms were tapped by PPR officials to assess the obstacles to more effective concessions projects, and make recommendations. Their report, "Generating Future Revenues through Concessions in Fairmount Park," found rich opportunities for expanding concessions in ways that could significantly improve the experience of park users and generate additional income. Possibilities included adventure sports in the park's wooded ravines and family attractions around Memorial Hall's Please Touch Museum.[16]

Just as steamboats once carried visitors from above the Fairmount Dam up the Schuylkill, so pleasure boats on park lakes and water taxis on the river might return to serve park goers in summer. Excursion boats on the Schuylkill were operating most summers after 2006. A new vendor was chosen in 2013 by the Schuylkill Development Corporation, which oversees the recreational area there. Passengers could board a replica of a 1920s small commuter yacht on the river at Walnut Street for cruises south to Bartram's Garden or, in the evening, north to the Philadelphia Museum of Art to view the architecture of prominent buildings and bridges.[17]

A central recommendation was for park officials to concentrate concessions around so-called "gateways," entry points to parks from a variety of neighborhoods where amenities should be clustered to include adequate parking, restrooms, improved signage, and refreshment facilities. The goal of such a focus would be to enliven the parks and their surrounding neighborhoods, and—here is the intended payoff—generate revenue that would be returned to the parks themselves. One example was the concession for bike rentals at Lloyd Hall at the end of Boathouse Row. In the words of the executive director of the Parks Alliance, Loren Bornfriend, that concession "is not only drawing new users to nearby trails, but has produced thousands of dollars for trail maintenance that might otherwise have had to wait."[18]

Park officials soon began to embrace a number of the study's ideas, indicating their willingness to be more responsive to the needs of concessionaires and the interests of park users. They also were considering a possibly greater role for the Fairmount Park Conservancy in the development and promotion of concessions opportunities.[19] The Parks Alliance's director called the PPR's response an intelligent strategy, but noted these warnings: concessions development should not be restricted to "tourist-rich" parks near center city, but needed to take place in outlying parks as well; concessions must not be allowed to spoil the parks' natural beauty or negatively impact their use; and, most important, the goal of returning concessions' earnings to the PPR should not be used as an excuse to cut the parks and recreation budget. She also called for community groups to be effectively engaged in planning, and for a thoroughly transparent process for picking concessionaires.[20]

In 2014, the PPR released a new plan meant to provide a guide for investment in the park during the next several decades.[21] For the near future, the plan focused on how to improve access to Fairmount Park along both banks of the Schuylkill. It proposed a number of ways in which trails can be upgraded for more direct and easy passage through the park's hinterlands to the river. It also called for a public boathouse on the river's west bank, making it an anchor for a new Boathouse Row. Even today, rowing on the Schuylkill is not accessible to the masses; membership in a private club has been a prerequisite for rowers since the mid-nineteenth century. Yet, this plan did not include providing equipment for noncompetitive activities on the river, such as rowboats, canoes, and sailboats.[22]

However, in 2015, the announcement of a multimillion-dollar grant from two foundations revealed a strong commitment to improve park amenities for neighborhoods that had missed out on recent economic growth in the city. Five projects were designated: A "Centennial Commons" to sprawl across the lawn between the Please Touch Museum and the School of the Future, providing an innovative playground with a spray park and ice skating in winter; refurbishing of the Lovett Memorial Library and Lovett Park in Mount Airy; adding "Bartram's Mile" to the Schuylkill Banks Trail to wind north from the gardens and give residents in that southwest neighborhood of the city greater access to the river; development of a special program for wilderness skills by Audubon and Outward Bound at the nature preserve near the reservoir in East Fairmount Park; and, finally, commencing work on the long-awaited Reading Viaduct Park.[23]

That last project, first proposed more than a decade earlier, will turn the obsolete viaduct of the old Reading Railroad into a high-line park. That structure makes a slice like a giant check mark through one of Philadelphia's oldest and most depressed industrial districts, running in a diagonal southwest from Poplar east of Tenth Street to Vine Street, then curving back to the northwest to Noble just east of Broad Street. Construction began in mid-2015 on the first stretch of Reading Viaduct Park, that between Callowhill and Thirteenth and Noble Streets, where one of three access routes would connect directly to Broad Street. This portion is owned by SEPTA, Philadelphia's urban transit system, so it is under the city's jurisdiction. Design work supported by the William Penn Foundation and Poor Richard's Charitable Trust was conducted by two private firms for the Center City District, which acted in partnership with the city and its departments of Commerce and the PPR. Turning this spur into a park will cost an estimated $8.6 million.[24]

The city has not yet been able to take control of the main branch of the viaduct from the Reading Company, which still owns it.[25] City officials hope that once the initial phase is completed, the ownership issue will be resolved. If it proves to be as popular and attractive as they expect, it may induce additional funding to complete the project along the viaduct to the

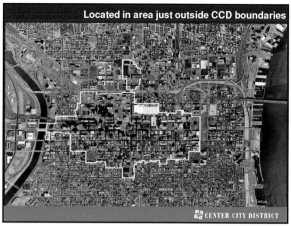

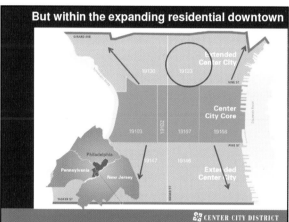

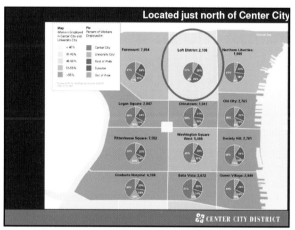

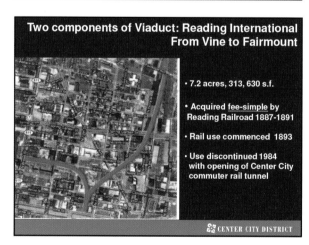

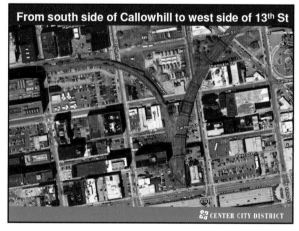

Reading Viaduct Park will transform an unused railroad viaduct into an elevated pedestrian park in a district directly north of Vine Street and center city. (Courtesy of Center City District)

east. They cite the popularity of New York's High Line as a model. To the extent these hopes and plans are realized, they will create a peaceful strip of green where it is very much needed. Such a park also will surely help revitalize much of the area where the viaduct has long been a barrier and an eyesore. It will give a boost to what some have named the Loft District, conceivably transforming the area more completely than could be done by any amount of rehabbing of old industrial buildings.

Much of this potential no doubt depends on a continued influx of residents to central Philadelphia. But with the proximity of Chinatown and center city's business district to the south, and the gentrification of such neighborhoods as Northern Liberties to the east, it may not be fantasy to imagine a growing tax base here that someday could help pay for the park's maintenance.

Somewhat more fantastic as of this writing is the proposal to create a "low-line" park in the trench for the old Reading line that continues west from the viaduct after moving underground below Broad Street. Supporters see it as the logical third phase of the viaduct project, one which could transform a below-grade corridor into a new green path connecting to the Benjamin Franklin Parkway behind the Barnes Foundation. Together with a completed Reading Viaduct Park, that green path would stretch for 3.7 miles along the northern edge of center city. As the *Philadelphia Inquirer*'s architectural columnist argued, this "Viaduct Greene," as it was dubbed, "would almost certainly ignite development in the triangle between Temple University, Northern Liberties, and Spring Garden."[26] In 2012, the Community Design Collaborative of the American Institute of Architects sponsored a team of local designers to create a design that could make the case for a low-line park.

Meanwhile, however, a new city plan had designated the Reading trench as the location for a high-speed bus route to connect a number of cultural attractions in West Fairmount Park—the Mann Center, the zoo, and the Please Touch Museum—to a downtown loop around the Convention Center. With no prospect that such a route would soon be put in place, even some SEPTA officials suggested that plans for a park should go ahead. The tunnel, wide enough to hold four parallel railroad tracks, might even share its green path with a bus route in the future.[27]

We began by noting the connection between urban density and the need for, and likely viability of, a city's parks and green spaces. Throughout most of the second half of the twentieth century, Philadelphia's population and its tax base declined, which resulted in declining funding for its parks. The early

New glass headhouses lead to public transit at Dilworth Park next to City Hall. (Photograph by Mark Garvin)

years of the twenty-first century have seen the city's population stabilize, and even grow a bit. While that has by no means reversed the shrinkage in the city's parks budget, it has brought something else, something we believe is connected to the ways that cities like Philadelphia are changing to serve society's needs today and tomorrow.

That is, first of all, adaptation to a postindustrial future, one in which some kinds of industry still may thrive, but in a context in which the nineteenth-century model is gone forever. This postindustrial city is home—or increasingly will be home—to a better-educated population, one with more leisure time and greater demands for the amenities that go with extra leisure. These include venues for active recreation, as well as outlets for other kinds of pleasure, whether it be the high culture of museums and concert halls, fine dining, or the simple restorative pleasure of walking through a nearby park.

Here is one example of these shifting priorities in our current century: Reliance on private transportation grew in Philadelphia, as elsewhere, throughout most of the twentieth century. One symptom was the loss in 1902 of the train station serving the Philadelphia Zoo, thus ending the most efficient mode of public transport there throughout the rest of that century. But in 2013, zoo officials announced that they wished, in effect, to move full circle back to the earlier time by aggressively pursuing the construction of a new city rail line there.[28]

If they are to thrive, Philadelphia and cities like it will have to lead in ways such as this toward a more sustainable way of human life and a greener future than the recent past has been. The density of cities can make them leaders in this respect, but only when their infrastructure—from mass transit to waste management, watershed and sewage control—all work as efficiently as possible for the public good, and when their carbon dioxide emissions are countered as much as possible by abundant swaths of green. For these reasons, the leading cities of the future almost certainly must increase the ratio of parks and open spaces beyond what has seemed adequate before now. Our health and our lifestyles demand it.

Now that many jobs no longer are tied to a particular place, a good number of new and especially younger residents are attracted by a city's quality of life. The new arrivals then stimulate additional economic activity and new

Dilworth Park is a new gathering place in the heart of the city. (Photograph by Mark Garvin)

jobs—the reverse of the traditional pattern.[29] Philadelphia's leaders seem increasingly to understand how quality-of-life issues matter to the city's future. That helps explain some of the most exciting moves connected to the expansion and improvement of its green space in recent years.

To accomplish any of the visions touched on here will require dedication on the part of city officials and the continued enlistment of entrepreneurs and others in the for-profit sector. But it also will demand of those who are custodians of the public spaces to keep them at their public best. They must take care to prevent private interests from dominating these spaces even while they encourage private enterprises, as a matter of self-interest, to invest in Philadelphia's parks for their own and the public's good. From our vantage point today, it seems certain that the ratio of green space will increase in relation to Philadelphia's population—and that it should do so if Philadelphia is to remain among the nation's premier cities. Philadelphia's livability will depend more than ever before on a rich and expanding counterpoint of attractive parks, waterfronts, and playgrounds. With continuing effort, particularly to maintain a still-growing park system, Philadelphia, well positioned to meet the future, is fast becoming a city in a park.

For more than two centuries, the temples of the Water Works have drawn pleasure-seekers to Fairmount, the entry to Philadelphia's incomparable park. (Courtesy of Rodney Miller)

Appendix
Philadelphia's Parks, Squares, and Playgrounds

The Philadelphia Home Rule Charter was amended following a popular vote in November 2008 to transfer the duties of the Fairmount Park Commission (FPC) to a new Department of Parks and Recreation. The FPC was then reconstituted as the Commission on Parks and Recreation (PaRC). That name change at last integrated the management of Philadelphia's public parks with its playgrounds and made that authority more accountable to elected officials and the public. (For a fuller analysis of the implications of the new governance system, see Chapter 16.) This directory of more than a hundred such green spaces is expected to grow still larger in years to come.

Aviator Park

Bounded by Race Street, Twentieth Street, and the diagonal of the Benjamin Franklin Parkway where it leaves the Logan traffic circle, this park constitutes the western triangle of Logan Square. Within it, permanent installations of sculpture pay tribute to the nation's war veterans. Moore College provides temporary exhibits. A farmer's market sells produce on Wednesdays during warm weather months.

Bardascino Park

At Tenth and Carpenter Streets in the Bella Vista neighborhood, this small park was created after the demolition on this site of the Community Hospital in 1968. Free summer concerts and boccie court (www.bardascinopark.org).

Barkan Park

Created in 1971 at Fiftieth and Spruce Streets in West Philadelphia, it is named for its neighborhood advocate, Ben Barkan. This small green space is the site of community activities throughout the year (http://universitycity.org/barkan-park).

Barnes and Loney Park

In the Fox Chase neighborhood in Philadelphia's Northeast, this small park is at 7966 Oxford Avenue.

Boone Park

At Churchview and Tower Streets in Philadelphia's Manayunk section, this small park, a section of Manayunk Park, is nearly adjacent to Pretzel Park to its west.

Buckley Park

At the intersection of Hartwell and Germantown Avenues in Chestnut Hill, this park was dedicated in 1973 as a memorial to Charles Buckley, a U.S. marine killed in the Vietnam conflict, "and other Americans who gave their lives in the Republic of Vietnam."

Buist Park

In the Elmwood section of Southwest Philadelphia between Sixty-Eighth and Hobson Streets on Buist Avenue NS (www.phila.gov/recreation/parks/Buist_Park .html).

Burholme Honor Square

At the intersection of Cottman, Oxford, and Rising Sun Avenues in Burholme.

Burholme Park

On Cottman Avenue in the Fox Chase neighborhood, this sixty-five-acre park was given to the city through a bequest from the Ryerss family, whose mansion is open to the public (Chapter 6). The park contains several baseball diamonds and football and soccer fields, as well as a wooded area. Also on-site are the Burholme Park Driving Range and a miniature golf course (www.phila.gov/parksandrecreation).

Campbell Square

In the Port Richmond section of Philadelphia, at the intersection of Allegheny and Belgrave Avenues. In 1998, the Friends of Campbell Square were formed and spearheaded the park's renovation (www.phila.gov/recreation/parks /CampbellSquare.html).

Carroll Park

Between Fifty-Eighth and Fifty-Ninth Streets on Girard Avenue in West Philadelphia. Assisted by the Carroll Park Neighbors Advisory Council, it is the site of summer concerts, a garden club, and summer camp for preschool children. There is a walking track around the perimeter (www.phila.gov/recreation/parks /Carroll_Park.html).

Cedar Park

A small triangular park at the intersection of Baltimore Avenue and Catherine and Fiftieth Streets in West Philadelphia. It takes its name from the neighborhood at the western end of the larger University City District of West Philadelphia (http://universitycity.org/cedar-park).

Cianfrani Park

At Eighth and Carpenter Streets in the Queen Village neighborhood. The Friends of Cianfrani Park meet on the first Tuesday of every month in the park, weather permitting, or at the Palumbo Recreation Center, Tenth and Fitzwater Streets. There are concerts during the summer months, as well as holiday events (http://cianfranipark.com).

Clark Park

This nine-acre park in Philadelphia's Spruce Hill neighborhood is the largest green space in West Philadelphia. Bounded by Baltimore and Woodland Avenues, Forty-Third and Forty-Fifth Streets, Clark Park was created in 1895 when a local developer, Clarence Howard Clark, gave the land to the city. It holds an 1890 statue of Charles Dickens, whose character, Little Nell, is depicted at his feet. The park now hosts a basketball court and playground, as well as an open field where a theater company performs Shakespeare in Clark Park during the summer months. A year-round farmer's market is also an important feature (www.friendsofclark park.org).

Clarkson Park/Chevchenko Park

At Broad and Somerville in the Logan/Fern Rock section of North Philadelphia, Clarkson Park borders Chevchenko (Schevchenko) Park, which was named for the Ukrainian poet and patriot, Taras Schevchenko, in 1921. To the west is Wistar's Woods Park; nearby are Girls' High School and Central High, and the campus of LaSalle University.

Clearview Park

At 7600 Buist Avenue in the Elmwood section of Southwest Philadelphia, this park contains a softball field.

Cliveden Park

In the Germantown and Mount Airy sections of Philadelphia, this park runs between Cliveden and Johnson Streets and from Musgrave to Chew. It contains a walking path, bridge, and playground.

Cobbs Creek Park and Golf Course

See Chapters 8 and 16 and www.fairmountpark.org/CobbsCreekPark.asp.

Connell Park

At the corner of Elmwood Avenue and Sixty-Fourth Street in West Philadelphia, this little park serves its neighborhood as a family-centered gathering place and playground.

Conshohocken-Windemere Park

This park at 3910 Conshohocken Avenue serves mainly as a playground for the nearby residents of Wynnefield Heights. It is located close to the western boundary of West Fairmount Park.

Coxe Park

At Beechwood and Cherry Streets in west center city, south of the Benjamin Franklin Parkway.

Daly Park

At Twelfth, Sedgley, and Clearfield Streets in North Philadelphia.

Delancey Park (Three Bears Park)

In the Society Hill neighborhood of Philadelphia, this little playground sits between Delancey and Cypress, Third and Fourth Streets. It abuts the garden of the Physick house, an elegantly furnished eighteenth-century residence, neoclassic and freestanding, that is open to the public. A sculpture of three bears in the playground gave the park its nickname. (For another house connected with Dr. Philip Syng Physick, see Laurel Hill in East Fairmount Park, Chapter 5.)

Diamond Park
At Eighteenth and Diamond Streets, near Temple University in North Philadelphia.

Dickinson Square Park
In the South Philadelphia neighborhood of Pennsport, this park is bounded by Moyamensing Avenue and Fourth, Tasker, and Morris Streets. From 1821 to 1896, this was the site of the stockyard for the Pascal Iron Works. After the plant ceased operations, the land was deeded to the city and became a public park in 1900. It was named for John Dickinson, an important participant in the Constitutional Convention and a governor of Pennsylvania. The park's playground was a model for such facilities when the park was created. Today, the Friends of Dickinson Square maintain it as a playground and sponsor a farmer's market during the summer months (www.dickinsonsquare.org).

Dilworth Park
See Chapter 12.

Disston Park
In the Tacony section of Northeast Philadelphia, this park ranges for several blocks from Keystone to Levick to Princeton Streets near the Delaware waterfront. It was named for the family that for nearly a century ran the world's largest handsaw factory there (www.recreationparks.net/PA/philadelphia/disston-park -philadelphia).

Drexel Park
Across from Drexel University at Thirty-Second Street and Powelton Avenue, the green space was completed in 2008 on a former industrial site. It serves the community and Drexel students as a recreational facility (http://universitycity.org /drexel-park).

Eastwick Park Playground
At Eightieth and Mars Streets, near the city limits in the Elmwood section of Southwest Philadelphia.

Eighty-Second and Lyons
In the Eastwick neighborhood of Southwest Philadelphia, near the airport.

Elmwood Park
In the southwest section of Philadelphia, this block-square park takes its name from its neighborhood. Bounded by Seventy-First and Seventy-Second Streets and Buist and Dicks Avenues, Elmwood Park has been completely renovated in recent years. The Friends of Elmwood Park worked with the Pennsylvania Horticultural Society and the Association for Public Art to raise the funds to install, in October 2010, *The Labor Monument: Philadelphia's Tribute to the American Worker*, by John Kindness.

Fairhill Square
Between Fourth and Fifth Streets and Lehigh and Huntingdon Avenues in North Philadelphia.

Fitler Square
Located between Pine and Panama, Twenty-Third and Twenty-Fourth Streets in center city, this neighborhood oasis was named in 1896 to honor Edwin H. Fitler

(1825–1896), mayor of Philadelphia from 1887–1896. A re-created Victorian fountain was installed in the middle of the square in the 1970s. In summer, a farmer's market occurs on Saturdays (www.fitlersquare.org).

Fotteral Square

Between Eleventh and Twelfth and Cumberland and York Streets in North Philadelphia, it contains a playground with swings for young children, basketball and baseball fields, and picnic tables. This park is on a piece of the land where an early horticulturalist laid out his garden at the start of the nineteenth century. Its owner, Bernard McMahon, published the first extended seed list in the United States.

Frankford and Pennypack

At Frankford and Pennypack Avenues in the Frankford section of Philadelphia.

Franklin Square

See Chapter 11.

Gilbert Stuart Park

At 5132 Germantown Avenue in Germantown.

Gold Star Park

This small park in the Passyunk Square neighborhood is on Wharton between Sixth and Seventh Streets. Originally called the John Hay Playground, it was built on the former site of a school by that name. After World War II, it was renamed for the Gold Star families, who displayed gold stars on banners in their windows in memory of family members lost during that war.

Gorgas Park

On Hermitage at Ridge Avenue in the Roxborough section.

Grable Post

At Third and Moyamensing in Philadelphia's Southwark neighborhood.

Gray's Ferry Crescent

See Chapter 17 and www.schuylkillbanks.org/projects/grays-ferry-crescent.

Hamilton Plaza

At Butler and Rising Sun Avenue in North Philadelphia.

Harrowgate Park

At Tioga Street and Kensington Avenue between the Juniata Park and Port Richmond sections of Philadelphia.

Howard and Reed

At the intersection of these streets near the Delaware waterfront in South Philadelphia.

Howell Park

At 5215 Greene Street in Germantown, it contains what is claimed to be the largest Chestnut Oak tree in Pennsylvania.

Hunting Park

This nearly eighty-seven-acre park in North Philadelphia runs from Ninth Street to Old York Road, and from Luzerne to Hunting Park Avenue (Chapters 6 and 17 and www.fairmountparkconservancy.org/ . . . /RevitalizingHuntingPark.php).

Jefferson Square

This early nineteenth-century park named for the nation's third president is situated between Washington Avenue, Federal, Third, and Fourth Streets in the Southwark section of South Philadelphia. It was used as a camping ground for Union forces during the Civil War. Later in the nineteenth century, the park was relandscaped on a plan similar to that for Rittenhouse Square. Its character remains that of a classic nineteenth-century strolling park (www.jefferson squarepark.org).

Jerome Brown Park (Kenderton Park)

At Twentieth and Ontario Streets in the Tioga section of North Philadelphia.

John F. Byrne Golf Course

In Philadelphia's Torresdale neighborhood, at 9500 Leon Street. The Torresdale Creek winds through the fairways.

John F. Kennedy Plaza (LOVE Park)

This plaza, at Fifteenth Street and John F. Kennedy Boulevard, was created adjacent to City Hall at the end of the Benjamin Franklin Parkway in the mid-twentieth century. In 1976, at the time of America's bicentennial, Robert Indiana's *LOVE* sculpture was installed here. Indiana's original work on this theme was his earlier painting, which he transformed into sculpture in 1964. Since its installation there, it has become the informal name of this plaza (Chapter 15).

Julian Abele Park

This neighborhood park, at Twenty-second and Montrose Streets, was created in 2008 to honor Julian Abele, one of the principal architects of the Philadelphia Museum of Art and the first African American to graduate from the University of Pennsylvania's Department of Architecture. Abele is depicted in a mural at the site. Jazz concerts and a farmer's market appear in summer (www.julianabelepark .org).

Juniata Park

See *Tacony Creek Park*.

Kahn Park

This vest-pocket park at center city's Pine and Eleventh Streets was created in honor of Louis Kahn, the noted twentieth-century Philadelphia architect.

Kelly Park

At Pechin and Parker Avenues in the Roxborough section of Philadelphia.

Konrad Square

At Tulip and Dauphin Streets in the Kensington section of Philadelphia.

Lindbergh Park

At Sixty-Third and Lindbergh Avenue in Southwest Philadelphia's Elmwood neighborhood.

Logan Square (Logan Circle)

See Chapters 11–12.

Lovett Park

At Germantown and Sedgwick Avenues in Philadelphia's Mount Airy neighborhood.

Malcolm X Park

Formerly known as Black Oak Park, bounded by Fifty-First and Fifty-Second and Larchmont and Pine Streets in West Philadelphia, this well-tended park has towering oak trees and a playground for children.

Manayunk Park

In the city's Manayunk section, this neighborhood park extends from Roxborough Avenue along Tower and Churchview Streets (see *Boone Park*, *Pretzel Park*).

Marconi Park (Marconi Plaza)

Straddling South Broad Street between Oregon and Bigler near the sports complex, this has long been a popular gathering place for those in the nearby Italian American neighborhood. This park includes a bocce court.

Mario Lanza Park

This neighborhood park in Philadelphia's Queen Village is at 200 Queen Street. It was named for the tenor, who grew up nearby (Chapter 16).

Market Square

At Germantown Avenue and School House Lane, this was the town square for Germantown when it began as a municipality separate from Philadelphia.

McMichael Park

Dating from 1929, this East Falls park at Midvale Avenue and McMichael Streets honors the Philadelphia mayor, Morton McMichael, who led in the development of Fairmount Park after the Civil War (www.eastfallscommunity.org).

McPherson Square

In the Port Richmond neighborhood at Indiana and Clearfield Streets and between E and F Streets.

Merritt Square

Between Glendale and Carey-Dungan Streets in the Port Richmond/Frankford section of Philadelphia.

Mifflin Square

Between Wolf and Ritner Streets, west of Fifth Street in South Philadelphia.

Morris Park

Connected to Cobbs Creek Park from City Line to Lansdowne Avenue, the park surrounds Indian Creek and Indian Run.

Muhammed Park (Clara Muhammed Square)

Between Forty-Seventh and Forty-Eighth Streets on Lancaster Avenue in West Philadelphia, this 3.6-acre park was renovated in 2011.

Nicetown Park

At Eighteenth Street between Germantown Avenue and Cayuga in the Nicetown neighborhood of North Philadelphia.

Nichols Park

In West Philadelphia, at Race and Conestoga Streets.

Norris Square

At Hancock and Diamond Streets in North Philadelphia between Front and Second Streets.

Northwood Park

On Castor Avenue at Arrott Street in Philadelphia's lower northeast.

Overington Park

In Philadelphia's Frankford neighborhood, at 4600 Leiper Street.

Paine's Park

See Chapter 7.

Palumbo Park

A 2.8-acre recreational facility between Ninth, Tenth, Bainbridge, and Fitzwater Streets in the Queen Village/Bella Vista section of the city. It contains sports fields and two basketball courts.

Paolo Park

At Sixth and Sears Streets in the Bella Vista/Southwark area of South Philadelphia.

Pastorius Park

In Philadelphia's Chestnut Hill, at Lincoln Drive and Abington Avenue, this sixteen-acre park was established in 1915 to honor Francis Pastorius, the seventeenth-century leader of the German immigrant community to this area. The park contains a pond and an amphitheater. The Chestnut Hill Community Association sponsors summer concerts there.

Penn Park

A University of Pennsylvania development of athletic and recreational facilities at the eastern edge of its campus. The grounds, which are open to the public, extend from Walnut to South Street below the Schuylkill Expressway on the river's west bank. The park contains turf fields, a softball stadium, and tennis courts (http://universitycity.org/penn-park).

Penn Treaty Park

This park is on the presumed site of Penn's 1683 treaty with the Lenape Indians, whose Shakamaxon village stood there at the time. It is located on the Delaware River at Columbia Avenue and Beach Street in the Fishtown neighborhood of Philadelphia. A statue of William Penn stands near the north entrance.

Pennypack Park

See Chapter 8, www.foxchasefarm.com, and www.pennypackpark.com.

Pleasanthill Park (Fish Hatchery)

This three-acre park and public boat launch is in the East Torresdale neighborhood of Philadelphia, at Linden and Delaware Avenues. It was recently renovated to make the boat launch more accessible and the facility more environmentally friendly.

Poquessing Creek Park

This park comprises parts of the watershed of the 21.5-mile Poquessing Creek, which empties into the Delaware at Glen Foerd between the Torresdale and Andalusia neighborhoods of Philadelphia. It was assembled by the Fairmount Park Commission in the 1970s, after the nearby prison farm was converted to an industrial park. European settlement at this site predates William Penn's claim to the land in 1682.

Powers Park

In the Kensington/Port Richmond area of Philadelphia, at Ann and Almond-Mercer Streets.

Pretzel Park

At Silverwood and Rector Streets in the Manayunk neighborhood. Officially a part of Manayunk Park, its popular name derives from the sculpture of a pretzel there.

Pulaski Park

At Allegheny Avenue and the Delaware River between Kensington and Port Richmond.

Race Street Pier

A derelict pier almost directly beneath the Benjamin Franklin Bridge on the Delaware waterfront was transformed and inaugurated as a public park in 2011. It provides a walkway, seating, and green space along the water's edge. The landscaped pier is one of the first initiatives completed in implementation of Philadelphia's Master Plan for the central Delaware through the heart of the city (Chapter 17).

Reyburn Park

A neighborhood park in Northwest Philadelphia, at Lehigh Avenue between Twentieth and Twenty-Second Streets.

Rittenhouse Square

See Chapter 11.

Roosevelt, Franklin D., Park

See Chapter 7.

Ross Park

At 1000 Glenwood Avenue, in the Tioga section of North Philadelphia.

Saunders Park Greene

This small park at Thirty-Ninth Street and Powelton Avenue is the joint project of the nearby Penn Presbyterian Medical Center, the People's Emergency Center, CDC, Saunders Park Neighbors, and the Philadelphia Horticultural Society. It holds picnic tables and benches, and hosts neighborhood events (http://university city.org/saunders-park-greene).

Schevchenko Park

See *Clarkson Park*.

Schuylkill Banks Park

See Chapters 8 and 18.

Schuylkill River Park

See Chapters 8 and 17.

Schuylkill River Trail

See Chapters 8 and 17.

Seventy-Fifth and Chelwynde

In the Elmwood neighborhood of Southwest Philadelphia.

Sherwood Park

At Fifty-Seventh Street and Baltimore and Washington Avenues in West Philadelphia.

Sister Cities Park

See Chapter 12.

Starr Garden

This sports area and playground is on Lombard between Sixth and Seventh Streets at the edge of both the Society Hill and Queen Village sections of the city, and may be the oldest public playground in the city. Many activities are available for children, as are limited facilities for picnics. The Starr Garden Neighbors help to maintain it.

Stenton Park

At Seventeenth and Courtland Streets in the Logan section of North Philadelphia, this park is part of the James Logan estate, where his circa 1740 house, Stenton, is located (Chapter 6).

Stinger Square

At Thirty-Third and Reed Streets in South Philadelphia near the east bank of the Schuylkill River.

Tacony Creek Park

This large park follows the course of Tacony Creek from Cheltenham and Melrose Park, suburbs north of Philadelphia, as it flows southeasterly between the Olney and Rhawnhurst neighborhoods. The park ends at Juniata Park, which contains the Juniata Golf Course.

Triangle Park

At 601 Christian Street in the Queen Village/Passyunk neighborhood of South Philadelphia.

Twenty-Second and Ontario

In the Tioga section of North Philadelphia.

Vandergrift Park

At Eighth Street and York and Germantown Avenues in the Northern Liberties neighborhood of Philadelphia.

Vernon Park

At 5818 Germantown Avenue, north of Chelten, in the Mount Airy neighborhood.

Walnut Lane Golf Course

In the Wissahickon Valley section of Fairmount Park, this is the shortest of the Philadelphia public golf courses. Opened in 1940, it is approached from 800 Walnut Lane.

Washington Green

Dedicated in 2010 on the Delaware waterfront at the base of Washington Avenue, this new green space on the river was a step toward creating a walking trail along the river through Philadelphia. Under the jurisdiction of the Delaware River Waterfront Commission, it is in keeping with the thirty-year Master Plan for the central Delaware (Chapter 17).

Washington Square

See Chapter 11.

Weinberg Park

At Sixth and Jackson Streets in South Philadelphia, near Mifflin Square.

Welcome Park

This small park was created in 1982 for the three-hundredth anniversary of the founding of Pennsylvania by William Penn, and is named for his ship, *The Welcome*. It stands on the site of Penn's Philadelphia residence from 1699 to 1701, the Slate House, which was demolished in 1867. On Second Street, north of Walnut Street in center city, the park presents a time line of Penn's life, including directives he set down for Pennsylvania, such as religious liberty and civil freedoms, which would greatly influence the heritage of the future United States of America.

Wharton Square

In South Philadelphia's Point Breeze neighborhood, between Twenty-Third, Twenty-Fourth, Wharton, and Reed Streets.

Wissinoming Park

At Frankford and Comly Streets in Philadelphia's Tacony section.

Wistar's Woods Park

See *Clarkson Park/Chevchenko Park*.

Wolf Park

In Philadelphia's Mount Airy neighborhood, at 7018 McCallum Street.

Womrath Park

Between Frankford and Kensington Avenues and Adams Street in Philadelphia's Frankford neighborhood.

Notes

Introduction

1. The Arthur Frommer travel organization's list of the world's ten best cities for parks includes four in the United States. In addition to Philadelphia, they are Chicago, New York, and San Francisco. The others are in Barcelona, London, Paris, Melbourne, Munich, and Tokyo. Available at www.frommers.com.

2. As cited by David Schuyler, *The New Urban Landscape: The Redefinition of City Form in Nineteenth-Century America* (Baltimore, MD: Johns Hopkins University Press, 1986), p. 65.

3. One exception was Munich's Englishcher Garten, which was the first public garden on the European continent, dating from the eighteenth century. It is still the largest city-owned park in Europe.

4. As cited by Schuyler, *The New Urban Landscape,* p. 65.

5. The Fairmount Park Art Association, established in 1872, was renamed in 2010 as the Association for Public Art to reflect the fact that its interest in promoting and providing public art extends to the entire city.

6. See www.phila2035.org for the Philadelphia City Planning Commission's plan for the city to 2035; and *Philadelphia: The State of the City: A 2012 Update* (Philadelphia: The Pew Charitable Trusts, Philadelphia Research Initiative, 2012).

Chapter 1: In the Beginning, Clean Water

1. Latrobe's Bank of Pennsylvania was the first example of the Greek revival style in the United States. It remained a Philadelphia landmark until it was demolished in 1870. In the view of one recent scholar, Latrobe's "Centre Square Water Works is a perfect example of a small Villa Rotunda [à la Palladio] set in the fifth square of William Penn's 'Greene Country Towne.'" Sign at the Fairmount Water Works Interpretive Center, quoting Arthur S. Marks, "Palladianism on the Schuylkill," *Proceedings of the American Philosophical Society* 154, no. 2 (June 2010): 201–257.

2. In 1803, President Thomas Jefferson appointed Latrobe surveyor of public buildings. After the Capitol was burned in the War of 1812, Latrobe was engaged to rebuild it.

3. The Rush fountain, *Water Nymph and Bittern,* was carved in wood and stood more than seven feet tall, the water spouting high in the air from the bird's beak.

4. Philadelphia was the largest city in the United States at the time of independence, with almost thirty thousand residents, to be surpassed by New York within the next decade. Still, it grew very rapidly, doubling and redoubling during the first half of the nineteenth century. The 1854 Act of Consolidation that greatly expanded the city's boundaries brought its population to well over four hundred thousand, then to more than one million by 1900.

5. Just as Latrobe had done at Centre Square, Graff disguised "an aesthetically pleasing building to house a potentially dangerous function." Jane Mork Gibson, "The Fairmount Waterworks," Philadelphia Museum of Art, *Bulletin* 84, nos. 360–361 (Summer 1988): 12.

6. Gibson, "Fairmount Waterworks," p. 15. She has concluded that "it took ten cords of oak wood in 20 hours to raise 100 gallons 98 feet at each stroke, at 24-3/4 strokes per minute; the capacity was confirmed to be 3,556,401 gallons in 24 hours." See www.workshopoftheworld.com/fairmount_park/water.html.

7. The dam's length is stated on interpretive signs currently installed in Fairmount Park. The film shown at the Fairmount Water Works Interpretive Center gives the length as 1,712 feet. Gibson, "Fairmount Waterworks," states its length as 1,204 feet. The discrepancy probably resulted from earlier observers' failure to recognize that the mill house and the canal's retaining wall were part of the structure of the dam. The mound dam at the eastern end was replaced by the new mill house when the facility was expanded in 1851 to accommodate new and larger turbines. Also, the dam has been rebuilt a number of times over the years, possibly at varying lengths. A 2,008-foot length is currently acknowledged by the Water Department.

8. Scholarship dating from 2010 argues that Graff's design for the mill house was based on a bridge by Palladio, which may have come to Graff's attention earlier by way of Latrobe, whose library contained Palladio's most famous work, *I quattro libri dell'architectura*. See Marks, "Palladianism on the Schuylkill."

9. Charles Dickens, *American Notes for General Circulation* (London and New York: Chapman & Hall, 1842; reprint, New York, 1985), p. 89.

10. The parenthetical shorter names were those given by the public. Rush's bill of March 1825 reads as follows:

> Corporation City Philada. Dr.
> Wm. Rush & Son.
> to carving two figures for water work fair Mount
> One male figure Emblematic river Schuylkill in its
> improved state
> One female Ditto Emblematic of the water works
> $450.

Watering Committee Papers; Common Council Minutes, May 5, 1825, with concurrence of Select Council, 283, Philadelphia City Archives, as cited in Charles Coleman Sellers, "William Rush at Fairmount," in *Sculpture of a City: Philadelphia's Treasures in Bronze and Stone*, Fairmount Park Art Association (New York: Walker, 1974), p. 11. Today, the figures above the mill house entrances are in fact fiberglass copies of the originals, which were carved in pine and painted white, and are on display atop Fairmount in the Philadelphia Museum of Art. The copies were made in 1978–1979 to celebrate the 300th anniversary of the founding of Philadelphia by William Penn. The Philadelphia Museum of Art owns a bronze cast of *Water Nymph and Bittern*, made from the original pine in 1872. Afterward, the original was returned to its place in the forebay until around 1900, when it was finally removed. *Mercury* is also now in the museum's collection.

11. Gibson, "Fairmount Waterworks," p. 23.

12. Frances Trollope, *Domestic Manners of the Americans* (London: Whittaker, Treacher, & Co., 1832), vol. 2, pp. 74–75, as cited in Gibson, "Fairmount Waterworks," p. 28.

13. Sellers, "William Rush at Fairmount," p. 14. The *Wisdom* and *Justice* figures are now on view at the Pennsylvania Academy of Fine Arts in Philadelphia.

14. Gibson, "Fairmount Waterworks," p. 29.

15. *Historic American Buildings Survey: Fairmount Park*, (Washington, D.C: National Park Service, U.S. Department of the Interior, documentation completed after 1968), vol. 1, p.3. Pratt's practice from the beginning of the century of opening the Lemon Hill gardens to the public already had established the idea that the area should be treated as parkland.

Chapter 2: A Park Grows from Fairmount

1. *Historic American Buildings Survey: Fairmount Park* (Washington, D.C.: National Park Service, U.S. Department of the Interior, documentation completed after 1968), vol. 1, p. 7. In the words of contemporary observers unhappy at the city's lack of action at Lemon Hill, "the tenants settled like incubi upon the spot." *Lemon Hill: The Papers of Charles S. Keyser and Thomas Cochran* (Philadelphia: Horace J. Smith, 1856), p. 6.

2. Meanwhile, however, Frederic Graff Jr. resigned his post as superintendent of the waterworks in 1856. He would return to serve again from 1867 to 1872, this time as a commissioner of the newly created Fairmount Park Commission, which he joined as the newly appointed chief engineer of the Water Department. The chief engineer's post had been created, along with the renamed Water Department, by the 1854 Act of Consolidation. Other changes in name, authority, and reporting structure followed until 1951, when the new city charter enacted in that year created today's Water Department.

3. *Historic American Buildings Survey*, vol. 1, p. 9.

4. Ibid., pp. 9–10. Landing Avenue later became Twenty-Ninth Street, running on a north–south axis to the east of Lemon Hill. East–West Coates Street was renamed Fairmount Avenue in the early 1870s.

5. Graff quit as chief engineer in 1856 because of differences with the recently consolidated city government. In the years when he was out of office, 1856 to 1867, three men served brief terms as chief engineer: Samuel Ogdin, Henry P. M. Birkinbine, and Isaac S. Cassin. Jane Mork Gibson, "The Fairmount Waterworks," Philadelphia Museum of Art, *Bulletin* 84, nos. 360–361 (Summer 1988): 38. It was Birkinbine who designed the new mill house.

6. Ibid., pp. 35–36.

7. Ibid., p. 31.

8. *First Annual Report of the Commissioners of Fairmount Park* (Philadelphia: King and Baird, 1869), p. 6.

9. Gibson, "Fairmount Waterworks," p. 38. Since 1876, the city's public art museum had been housed in Memorial Hall in West Fairmount Park, as had been intended from the time that building was constructed for the centennial celebration. But for years, many had called for a new art museum nearer center city. The Fairmount summit was officially designated as the new site in the 1911 ordinance.

10. William E. Meehan, "Building an Aquarium for Philadelphia," *Transactions of American Fisheries Society* 43, no. 1 (1914): 179–181; and *The Fairmount Park Aquarium: Its History and Maintenance* (Philadelphia: Fairmount Park Commission, 1929).

11. Gibson, "Fairmount Waterworks," p. 39.

12. *Commissioners of Fairmount Park, 88th Annual Report* (Philadelphia: City of Philadelphia, 1955), pp. 25–26. The aquarium superintendent reported that "on four separate occasions the entire freshwater collection died." Moreover, two hurricanes in 1955, on top of Hurricane Hazel in 1954, had caused extensive flood damage.

13. Ernesta Drinker Ballard (1920–2005) also was a founding member of the Fairmount Park Conservancy, which was created in 1998 as a fund-raising organization operating independently of the Fairmount Park Commission. Her work on behalf of the preservation effort is memorialized in an urn at the foot of the recently restored Cliffside Walk on Fairmount. The Fund for the Water Works remains available for future maintenance.

14. The Philadelphia Water Department, with a grant from Pennsylvania's Coastal Zone Management Program, placed the statue beside the esplanade in 1989. It was swept into the river during Hurricane Floyd in 1999, but was recovered some five years later.

15. The re-created Mercury Pavilion is at the summit of Fairmount, nearly across from the northwest entrance to the Philadelphia Museum of Art, which holds the Rush figure in its collection. Yet historical accounts describe Rush's *Mercury* as having been placed atop a "rustic pavilion" halfway up the hill. An 1838 print shows that pavilion as a lattice-roofed structure that more nearly resembles today's reconstructed Mercury Pavilion at the summit than it does the 1860s Rustic Pavilion and its current reinterpretation in steel.

Chapter 3: The Nineteenth-Century Park

1. All figures are from the reports of the United States Census Bureau for the decades of the nineteenth century.

2. *First Annual Report of the Commissioners of Fairmount Park* (Philadelphia: King and Baird, 1869), p. 6.

3. For an example of how the practical requirement and the recreational goal coincided, it was understood when the dam was built, it would create a pool of water behind it that would be suitable for boating in summer and ice skating in winter. See Jane Mork Gibson, "The Fairmount Waterworks," Philadelphia Museum of Art, *Bulletin* 84, nos. 360–361 (Summer 1988): 17–18.

4. "For Emerson and his followers, nature—attunement with it, contemplation of it, immersion in it—was thought to train the spirit. The softened popular version of the transcendentalist ideals attributed virtue to things found in nature like trees and meadows that could be transplanted or duplicated by human ingenuity and paved the way for park propaganda and park design theory." Galen Cranz, *The Politics of Park Design: A History of Urban Parks in America* (Cambridge, MA: MIT Press, 1982), p. 7.

5. George Thomas, "The Statue in the Garden," in *Sculpture of a City: Philadelphia's Treasures in Bronze and Stone*, Fairmount Park Art Association (New York: Walker, 1974), p. 37. Thomas's essay remains an excellent interpretation of the artistic inheritance of Laurel Hill Cemetery. For more on the rise of rural cemeteries in America and their impact on the creation of urban parks, see David Schuyler, *The New Urban Land-*

scape: *The Redefinition of City Form in Nineteenth-Century America* (Baltimore, MD: Johns Hopkins University Press, 1986), esp. chap. 3.

6. As cited by John W. Reps, *The Making of Urban America: A History of City Planning in the United States* (Princeton, NJ: Princeton University Press, 1965), p. 326.

7. Alexander Jackson Downing, "A Talk about Public Parks and Gardens," *Horticulturalist* 3 (October 1848): 157.

8. As early as 1851, Frederic Graff Jr. had proposed creating a continuous loop of parkland on both sides of the river. *Historic American Buildings Survey: Fairmount Park* (Washington, D.C: National Park Service, U.S. Department of the Interior, documentation completed after 1968), vol. 2, p. 6.

9. *Lemon Hill: The Papers of Charles S. Keyser and Thomas Cochran* (Philadelphia: Horace J. Smith, 1856), p. 14, as cited in *Historic American Buildings Survey*, vol. 2, p. 6.

10. *Historic American Buildings Survey*, vol. 1, pp. 9–10. The plan was that of Charles Sidney and Andrew Adams, partners from 1858 to 1860, with an office at 520 Walnut Street. Sandra L. Tatman and Roger W. Moss, *Biographical Dictionary of Philadelphia Architects 1700–1930* (Boston: G. K. Hall, 1985), p. 717.

11. Nicholas B. Wainwright, ed., *A Philadelphia Perspective: Diary of Sidney George Fisher Covering the Years 1834–1871* (Philadelphia: Historical Society of Pennsylvania, 1967), p. 409, as cited in *Historic American Buildings Survey*, vol. 2, p. 10.

12. *Historic American Buildings Survey*, vol. 1, p. 11.

13. The commission's organization remained largely unchanged for 142 years, even with new city charters in 1919 and 1951. In April 1951, the Fairmount Park Commission (FPC) was incorporated as a part of the Philadelphia city government with the adoption of the Philadelphia Home Rule Charter and designated a departmental commission of the Department of Recreation. Under the twentieth-century charters, the six ex officio members of the FPC were the mayor, president of City Council, the commissioner of public property, the recreation commissioner, the water commissioner, and the chief engineer and surveyor of the Department of Streets.

In July 2009, following passage by the electorate of an amendment to Philadelphia's Home Rule Charter, a new Department of Parks and Recreation was created. The Fairmount Park Commission was reconstituted as the new Commission on Parks and Recreation (PaRC). It consists of fifteen members, nine of whom are appointed by the mayor at the beginning of his or her term from nominations made by City Council. Six are ex officio members; they include the president of City Council and the executive director of the City Planning Commission or their designees, the water commissioner, the street commissioner, the public property commissioner, and the parks and recreation commissioner (www.fairmountpark.org/pdf/PaRC_Statement_.pdf). For more on the implications of these institutional changes, see Chapter 16.

14. In his May 1872 monthly report, Samuel Lightfoot Smedley, chief engineer for Fairmount Park, noted that "an average force of 147 men have been worked 21 days" at that task (www.fairmountpark.org/HistoryPart3.asp). Much of the former Flat Iron district is today the site of the azalea garden.

15. Minutes, Fairmount Park Commission meeting of October 14, 1867. For a fuller account of Boat House Row and rowing on the Schuylkill, see Chapter 7.

16. J. Thomas Scharf and Thompson Westcott, *History of Philadelphia: 1609–1884* (Philadelphia: L. H. Everts, 1884), vol. 3, p. 1855, as quoted in *Historic American Buildings Survey*, vol. 1, p. 12. The Lansdowne estate had been that of John Penn, who built

it in 1773 when he was governor of the colony. His widow sold it after her husband's death in 1795. See Chapter 6.

17. Scharf and Westcott, *History of Philadelphia*, p. 1856, quoting from the committee's report, as cited in *Historic American Buildings Survey*, vol. 1, p. 13.

18. Fairmount Park Commission, Archival Records: 149.1, Board of Commissioners Minutes (1867–1995).

19. Theo B. White, *Fairmount: Philadelphia's Park* (Philadelphia: Art Alliance Press, 1975), p. 24.

20. Ibid., p. 25. Today, only two such structures remain: the Valley Green Inn and Wissahickon Hall, a one-time tavern that has long served as a park police barracks.

21. Ibid., p. 21. The Georges' land had come down to them from an ancestor of the same name, "who owned it on the settlement of the province under William Penn." *First Annual Report of the Commissioners of Fairmount Park* (Philadelphia: King and Baird, 1869), pp. 21–22.

22. Eli K. Price, "Journal," July 1, 1876, unpublished, as quoted in Timothy Long, "The Woodlands" (master's thesis, University of Pennsylvania, 1991), p. 295.

23. From the earliest years in the life of the Fairmount Park Commission, its authority extended to additional green spaces distant from the waterworks and the Schuylkill. On May 15, 1871, Hunting Park was brought under the commission's jurisdiction, having been a city park from July 10, 1856.

24. *Historic American Buildings Survey*, vol. 2, quoting the Fairmount Park Commission Annual Report, 1871.

25. As quoted by White, *Fairmount*, p. 39, without disclosing his source. Schuyler, *New Urban Landscape*, p. 214n15, quotes similar language in letters from Copeland to Olmsted and to Frederick Knapp.

26. *Report of the Committee on Plans and Improvements of the Commissioners of Fairmount Park upon the Extension of the Park* (Philadelphia: King and Baird, 1868), p. 11. In a lecture on April 9, 2012, at the Philadelphia Athenaeum entitled "Fairmount Park, Olmsted and Vaux," Elizabeth Milroy argued that the 1868 plan for the park was probably by Hermann Schwarzmann, and that John C. Cresson, Philadelphia's chief engineer, blocked the 1871 proposal by Olmsted and Vaux.

27. Philip Pregill and Nancy Volkman, *Landscapes in History: Design and Planning in the Western Tradition* (New York: Van Nostrand Reinhold, 1993), p. 408.

28. See *Historic American Buildings Survey*, vol. 1, pp. 15–16, 18, for a discussion of correspondence between Olmsted and Vaux and the FPC, which eventually resulted in the commission's declining to accept the team's plans for the park. See also Minutes of the Commissioners of Fairmount Park, January 27, 1872.

29. Fairmount Park Commission Minutes, June 20, 1868, p. 249.

30. *Historic American Buildings Survey*, vol. 2, pp. 32–33. See also Schuyler, *New Urban Landscape*, pp. 107–108.

31. *Historic American Buildings Survey*, vol. 2, p. 27.

Chapter 4: The Post–Civil War Period

1. The scheduled April opening was pushed into May because of construction delays.

2. James McClelland, "1876 Centennial Craze Sweeps into Philadelphia," *Pennsylvania Heritage: Quarterly of the Pennsylvania Historical and Museum Commission and the Pennsylvania Heritage Society* 32, no. 2 (Spring 2006): 16–17.

3. Robert W. Rydell, *All the World's a Fair: Visions of Empire at the American International Expositions, 1876–1916* (Chicago: University of Chicago Press, 1984), pp. 10–11. Rydell (p. 236) depicts centennial authorities as "loathing" the honky-tonk amusements built just outside the fairgrounds, many of which were condemned and removed.

4. *Third Annual Report of the Commissioners of Fairmount Park, Appendix I* (Philadelphia: King and Baird, 1872), p. 57.

5. Ibid., p. 49.

6. John Maass, *The Glorious Enterprise: The Centennial Exhibition of 1876 and H. J. Schwarzmann, Architect-in-Chief* (Watkins Glen, NY: American Life Foundation, 1973), pp. 34–36. For Schwarzmann's role in creating the Philadelphia Zoo, see Chapter 9.

7. Ibid., p. 36.

8. George B. Tatum, preface to Hatfield, Martin, & White (architects), *A Plan for the Adaptation of Memorial Hall* (Philadelphia: Fairmount Park Commission, 1958). On the very same day, April 11, 1874, that Schwarzmann's plan for the grounds was approved, he "commenced to prepare plans for Memorial and Horticultural Halls, outside of the competitive designs, no decision having been reached at the time." H. J. Schwarzmann, "Report of the Chief Engineer, etc.," in *U.S. Centennial Commission: International Exhibition of 1876, Report of the Director-General* (Philadelphia, 1874). City of Philadelphia, Records Department, City Archives, RG 230, United States Centennial Commission.

9. Maass, *Glorious Enterprise*, pp. 35–36.

10. Ibid., p. 50, and figs. 14–15 following p. 96, for two views of the Escalier plans and their resemblance to Schwarzmann's Memorial Hall.

11. McClelland, "1876 Centennial Craze," p. 22.

12. Hatfield, Martin, and White, *Plan for the Adaptation of Memorial Hall*.

13. *Historic American Buildings Survey: Fairmount Park* (Washington, D.C: National Park Service, U.S. Department of the Interior, documentation completed after 1968), vol. 1, p. 20.

14. McClelland, "1876 Centennial Craze," p. 23.

15. Ibid.

16. *Historic American Buildings Survey*, vol. 2, p. 36.

17. Ibid., vol. 1, p. 21.

18. See Chapter 14 for the role of the Fairmount Park Art Association.

19. *Ordinances 1871*, Select and Common Councils of the City of Philadelphia, January 24, 1871, p. 8.

20. See www.fairmountparkconservancy.org/project/centennial.php. The master plan was funded with support from the William Penn Foundation and the Lenfest Foundation.

Chapter 5: The Country Houses of Fairmount Park

1. John Cornforth, *Country Life*, January 4, 1973, as quoted in Joan Church Roberts, "The Schuylkill Villas," Philadelphia Antiques Show catalog, 2006.

2. Mary Maples Dunn and Richard Dunn, "The Founding, 1681–1701," in *Philadelphia: A 300 Year History*, ed. Russell F. Wiegley, Barra Foundation (New York and London: W. W. Norton, 1982), p. 7.

3. Penn's Philadelphia residence, the Slate Roof House, was on Second Street, north of Walnut. See note 9.

4. Roger W. Moss, *Historic Houses of Philadelphia*, Barra Foundation (Philadelphia: University of Pennsylvania Press, 1998), p. 90.

5. E. Howitt, *Selections from Letters Written during a Tour through the United States in the Summer and Autumn of 1819* (Nottingham, Library Company of Philadelphia); James Boyd, *A History of the Pennsylvania Horticultural Society 1827–1927* (Philadelphia, 1929), p. 433.

6. Michael W. Fazio, *The Domestic Architecture of Benjamin Henry Latrobe* (Baltimore, MD: Johns Hopkins University Press, 2006), p. 275.

7. For a contemporary account of Eaglesfield, see Kathleen A. Foster, *Captain Watson's Travels in America: The Sketchbooks and Diary of Joshua Rowley Watson, 1772–1818* (Philadelphia: University of Pennsylvania Press, 1997), p. 40.

8. Lewis Mumford is credited with the aphorism: "Every generation revolts against its fathers and makes friends with its grandfathers." *The Brown Decades: A Study of the Arts in America, 1865–1895* (New York: Harcourt Brace, 1931), p. 3.

9. *Second Annual Report of the Commissioners of Fairmount Park* (Philadelphia: King and Baird, 1870), pp. 5–6. During the same period when the Sedgley and Lemon Hill mansions were meeting different fates, William Penn's Slate Roof House on Second Street in Philadelphia was demolished (1867). The effort to save it marked the first concerted effort at historic preservation in Philadelphia. It failed when its would-be rescuer, the Historical Society of Philadelphia, found its members divided over whether it would be an appropriate use of the society's funds to purchase the building as a house museum. Moss, *Historic Houses*, p. 8.

10. Letter from Fiske Kimball to Charles E. Peterson, November 24, 1954, Fairmount Park Office Archives, "Mount Pleasant" file.

11. Moss, *Historic Houses*, pp. 94–96.

12. Horace Mather Lippincott and Harold Donaldson Eberlein, *The Colonial Homes of Philadelphia and Its Neighborhood* (Philadelphia: J. B. Lippincott, 1912), p. 113.

13. Roberts, "Schuylkill Villas," p. 128, citing Martha Crary Halpern, "Information Memo to Park House Guides," 1997.

14. In 1872, Fairmount Park's chief engineer, John C. Cresson, reported: "The mansion at Mount Pleasant has been restored nearly to its original aspect, which it was deemed right to preserve as a fine specimen of Roman [*sic*] architecture." *Third Annual Report, Fairmount Park Commission, Appendix I* (Philadelphia: King and Baird, 1872), p. 43.

15. Roberts, "Schuylkill Villas," p. 106. The author notes that Macpherson's estate had orchards, grazing fields, and a walled garden in which "he grew such luxuries as asparagus, strawberries, and artichokes," p. 104.

16. Ibid., pp. 108–109.

17. William Rawle became a prominent Philadelphia lawyer, serving as chancellor of the Philadelphia Bar Association. In 1783, he established his own law office, which descended in his family and eventually became Rawle and Henderson, the oldest law firm today in Philadelphia. Roberts, "Schuylkill Villas," p. 109.

18. Moss, *Historic Houses*, p. 99.

19. Ibid., pp. 104–107; and Roberts, "Schuylkill Villas," pp. 120–122.

20. Roberts, "Schuylkill Villas," pp. 100–102.

21. Samuel Breck, "Recollections," 1830 manuscript, from Breck Collection, Historical Society of Pennsylvania.

22. Moss, *Historic Houses*, p. 82; and Roberts, "Schuylkill Villas," pp. 117–119.

23. Two other domestic structures also have been moved to the park. The Letitia Street House, circa 1713, which in the nineteenth century was incorrectly thought to have been built for William Penn, was moved from its original location in Philadelphia to Fairmount Park in 1883. Similarly, Hatfield House, which had been constructed in 1750 at a Nicetown farm, was moved to Fairmount Park in 1930.

24. Moss, *Historic Houses*, pp. 86–88; Roberts, "Schuylkill Villas," pp. 98–99.

25. *First Annual Report of the Commissioners of Fairmount Park* (Philadelphia: King and Baird, 1869), p. 13.

Chapter 6: Historic Structures in Philadelphia's Parks

1. The number of historic site museums in the Philadelphia area runs into the hundreds. See Roger W. Moss, *Historic Houses of Philadelphia*, Barra Foundation (Philadelphia: University of Pennsylvania Press, 1998), p. 11; and Charles F. Jenkins, *The Guidebook to Historic Germantown* (Philadelphia: Germantown Historical Society, 1973). The Germantown section of Philadelphia is particularly rich in historic houses, and its Historic Society led the way early in the twentieth century in the preservation effort.

2. Lorett Treese, *The Storm Gathering: The Penn Family and the American Revolution* (University Park: Pennsylvania State University Press, 1992), pp. 187–199.

3. Marie G. Kimball, "The Furnishings of Lansdowne, Governor Penn's Country Estate," *Antiques* 19 (June 1931): 450–455. Moss, *Historic Houses*, p. 65, describes Lansdowne's loss as "one of the great tragedies of American architecture."

4. Moss, *Historic Houses*, pp. 66–69.

5. Quoted in *Pennsylvania Magazine of History and Biography* 12 (1888): 454.

6. Efforts continue to document the property's involvement in the Underground Railroad, that pre–Civil War network of stations north of the Mason-Dixon Line, where volunteers assisted runaway slaves to escape into freedom.

7. 2000 Reservoir Drive. 215-763-2222.

8. Moss, *Historic Houses*, p. 71. 3810 Mt. Pleasant Drive.

9. 33rd Street near Girard Avenue.

10. 200 Chamounix Drive.

11. 3250 Chamounix Drive.

12. Fairmount Park Commission, Chamounix file, quoted in Jessica A. Sloop, "Chamounix Mansion Structure Report," paper, Historic Preservation Program, University of Pennsylvania, 1994.

13. Kendall Brown, as quoted by Virginia A. Smith, writing for the Philadelphia Inquirer, March 30, 2012, p. D3.

14. Horticultural and Lansdowne Drives. 215-878-5097.

15. Martin Luther King Jr. Drive.

16. David Contosta and Carol Franklin, *Metropolitan Paradise: The Struggle for Nature in the City, Philadelphia's Wissahickon Valley, 1620–2020* (Philadelphia: St. Joseph University Press, 2010), vol.1, pp. 120–124.

17. 206 Lincoln Drive. 215-429-5711.

18. Quoted by Moss, *Historic Houses*, p. 74.

19. Since 2009, management of the property has been in cooperation with the Parks and Recreation Department as the result of the new governance system that came into effect that year (Chapter 16).

20. 54th and Lindbergh Avenue. 215-729-5281.

21. Moss, *Historic Houses*, p. 72.

22. 20th and Pattison Streets. 610-664-8456.

23. 5001 Grant Avenue. 215-632-5330.

24. Moss, *Historic Houses*, p. 72.

25. 7300 Central Avenue. 215-745-3061.

26. Moss, *Historic Houses*, p. 146.

27. 4601 N. 18th Street. 215-230-7321.

28. See www.fairmountpark.org./HistoricSites.asp. See also note 11.

Chapter 7: Boating and Playing in the Park

1. *Historic American Buildings Survey: Fairmount Park* (Washington, D.C: National Park Service, U.S. Department of the Interior, documentation completed after 1968),vol. 1, p. 7.

2. J. Thomas Scharf and Thompson Westcott, *History of Philadelphia, 1609–1884* (Philadelphia: L. H. Everts, 1884), vol. 1, p. 646. See also Jefferson Moak, "National Registry of Historic Places Inventory-Nomination Form," National Register of Historic Places, National Park Service, U.S. Department of the Interior, p. 669.

3. *Historic American Buildings Survey*, vol. 1, p. 8.

4. Scharf and Westcott, vol. 3, p. 1871.

5. *Historic American Buildings Survey*, vol. 1, p. 8.

6. Scharf and Westcott, vol. 3, p. 1871. See also *Historic American Buildings Survey*, vol. 1, p. 8. In 1868, only the houses for the Pacific Barge Club (today, the Fairmount Rowing Association), the Bachelors Barge Club, and the Skating Club were left standing. Lloyd Hall, No. 1, opened in September 1998, replacing the nineteenth-century Plaisted Hall, which was razed in 1993 after falling into disrepair.

7. See www.philadragonboatfestival.com.

8. Anne C. Lewis, *Scrapbook: Memories of the Homes of Grandma Lewis Written for Her Grandchildren* (Philadelphia: Library Company of Philadelphia), from online exhibition, "Ice Skating in 19th Century America, A Pictorial View," available at www.librarycompany.org/skating/iceskating.htm. See also www.pschs.org for the history of the Philadelphia Skating Club and Humane Society, which now has its headquarters in Ardmore, Pennsylvania.

9. The winter of 1856 was so severe it allowed ice skating on the Delaware at Philadelphia for one of the few times in the city's history.

10. The leading designer of urban parks, Frederick Law Olmsted, was adamant in insisting that recreation should not take place there, arguing that it would detract from "pleasant contemplation of natural scenery." David Schuyler, *The New Urban Landscape: The Redefinition of City Form in Nineteenth-Century America* (Baltimore, MD: Johns Hopkins University Press, 1986), p. 186.

11. Galen Cranz, *The Politics of Park Design: A History of Urban Parks in America* (Cambridge, MA: MIT Press, 1982), p. 5.

12. *Second Annual Report of the Commissioners of Fairmount Park* (Philadelphia: King and Baird, 1870), pp. 23–24.

13. *Third Annual Report of the Commissioners of Fairmount Park* (Philadelphia: King and Baird, 1871), p. 30.

14. Ibid., pp. 43–44.

15. See http://smithkidsplayplace.org.

16. See http://www.fairmountpark.org/Courts.asp.

17. See http://www.fairmountpark.org/Stables.asp.

18. Annual Report of the Captain of the Park Guard, *Sixth Report of the Commissioners of Fairmount Park* (Philadelphia: King and Baird, 1899), p. 94.

19. "Proposed Speedway in Fairmount Park, Philadelphia 1901," Chamounix Speedway File, Fairmount Park Archives, Fairmount Park Office, Philadelphia.

20. Letter to Fairmount Park Commissioners from the Quaker City Motor Club, July 20, 1909, Fairmount Park Archives.

21. Inga Saffron, "Changing Skyline: Common Ground," *Philadelphia Inquirer*, May 17, 2013, p. D1. See Chapters 12 and 17 for other recent improvements to the parkway.

22. Cranz, *Politics of Park Design*, p. 12.

23. *Second Annual Report of the Commissioners*, p. 16.

24. In the words of Cranz, *Politics of Park Design*, p. 98: "The quality of experience in a reform park was markedly different from that in a pleasure ground. Rather than quiet and serene, it was noisy and organized."

Chapter 8: Rest and Recreation

1. The landscape of the Wissahickon already had been altered by the presence for centuries of Lenni-Lenape Indians who periodically burned the forest's understory, especially to encourage the growth of chestnut trees, whose nuts were an important part of the Native Americans' diet. David Contosta and Carol Franklin, *Metropolitan Paradise: The Struggle for Nature in the City, Philadelphia's Wissahickon Valley, 1620–2020* (Philadelphia: St. Joseph's University Press, 2010), vol. 1, pp. 58–59.

2. Wissahickon Hall and Valley Green Inn are the only public houses of this period to survive in the valley. The former was occupied by the Fairmount Park Guard until that body was abolished in the 1970s. The Philadelphia Police Department's 92nd District then based its headquarters in the structure until 2008. After the police moved out in that year, marking the end of the city's park-based police districts, the hall was renovated to house the city's Urban Forestry Division.

3. Contosta and Franklin, *Metropolitan Paradise*, p. 176.

4. Since the 1930s, the Valley Green Inn has been under the joint care of Fairmount Park and a nonprofit group, the Friends of the Wissahickon.

5. Eunice Story Ullman, "Valley Green Inn" (unpublished typescript, May 26, 1970, p. 6), Wissahickon Collection, Chestnut Hill Historical Society.

6. Contosta and Franklin, *Metropolitan Paradise*, vol. 2, p. 10.

7. Penny Balkin Bach, *Public Art in Philadelphia* (Philadelphia: Temple University Press, 1992), pp. 167–169, 256.

8. Contosta and Franklin, *Metropolitan Paradise*, vol. 2, p. 296.

9. Maria Panaritis, "New Schuylkill Walkway," *Philadelphia Inquirer*, October 3, 2014, pp. B1, B5.

10. Julie Zauzmer, "Schuylkill Trail Link for Grays Ferry," *Philadelphia Inquirer*, June 11, 2012, pp. B1, 4.

11. Inga Saffron, "Nonprofits to Fund High-Line Park Plan," *Philadelphia Inquirer*, March 16, 2015, pp. A1, 8. Bartram's Mile was one of four new projects supported by grants from the William Penn and Knight Foundations (Chapter 18). See also Linda Loyd, "Opportunity on the Schuylkill," *Philadelphia Inquirer*, May 27, 2012, pp. C1, 4.

12. Zauzmer, "Schuylkill Trail Link," citing both Joseph Syrnick, CEO of the Schuylkill River Development Corporation, and Harris Steinberg, executive director of Penn Praxis, the program of the University of Pennsylvania's School of Design for developing planning projects with the city.

13. Inga Saffron, "Rx for a Neighborhood?" *Philadelphia Inquirer*, July 6, 2012, pp. D1, 3. Nineteen months later, however, critics were alarmed that the enormous garage podium proposed as the base for the new towers would effectively block the adjacent neighborhood from access to the river. See Inga Saffron, "Wall of Garages Threatens Schuylkill Bank, *Philadelphia Inquirer*, March 28, 2014, pp. D1, D6; and the response of affected community groups in Nicole Contosta, "CHOP's Expansion to the Schuylkill Banks Could Pose Threat to Bicyclists and Cause Gridlock," *Weekly Press*, February 12, 2014, pp. 1–2.

14. See www.pecpa.org/eastcoastgreenway/58th-street-greenway-under-construction.

15. The Eakins Oval plan was part of the proposal, "More Park, Less Way," announced at a public meeting on February 4, 2013. The plan was sponsored jointly by the Nutter administration and Penn Praxis (http://planphilly.com/praxis-projects/benjamin-franklin-parkway).

Chapter 9: The Philadelphia Zoo

1. As quoted by Clark DeLeon, *America's First Zoostory: 125 Years of the Philadelphia Zoo* (Virginia Beach, VA: Donning, 1999), p. 34.

2. Camac's grandfather owned an estate in North Philadelphia known as "Camac's Woods," which gave its name to Camac Street in Philadelphia.

3. Philadelphians with an interest in natural history were a presence as early as the eighteenth century. Many were brought together as members of the American Philosophical Society, founded in 1743 by Benjamin Franklin as America's first learned society.

4. Nigel Rothfels, *Savages and Beasts: The Birth of the Modern Zoo* (Baltimore, MD: Johns Hopkins University Press, 2002) provides an excellent account of this history.

5. As quoted by DeLeon, *America's First Zoostory*, p. 35.

6. Ibid.

7. Theo B. White, *Fairmount: Philadelphia's Park* (Philadelphia: Art Alliance Press, 1975), p. 46. Beginning with thirty-three acres, the Zoological Garden grew to fifty acres, then to forty-two after 1930, when some land was given to the Pennsylvania Railroad in exchange for the railroad's funding of major renovations. For more on The Solitude, see Chapter 6.

8. As quoted by DeLeon, *America's First Zoostory*, p. 38.

9. Ibid. See also John Sedgwick, *The Peaceable Kingdom: A Year in the Life of America's Oldest Zoo* (New York: Fawcett Crest, 1988), p. 60, who does not include the word "forever" in his citation of the Cope loan. Nonetheless, he notes that more than a century later, that prohibition prevented the society from what might have been a profitable source of income.

10. Sedgewick, *The Peaceable Kingdom,* pp. 38–39.

11. Of these original buildings, the Furness gatehouses remain unchanged. Many of the others have been demolished or, like George Hewitt's 1876 Antelope House and Cret's 1940 Pachyderm House, adaptively reused. For Schwarzmann's role in the Centennial Exhibition, see Chapter 4.

12. Thompson would last only until April 1876, when he was replaced by Arthur Erwin Brown, a twenty-six-year-old herpetologist. Brown would remain as superintendent until 1910 when, at age sixty, he died of a heart attack while working in the gardens (DeLeon, *America's First Zoostory*, p. 46). Superintendents who followed were Robert D. Carson (1910–1917), C. Emerson Brown (1918–1935), Roderick Macdonald (1935–1936), Freeman H. Shelly (1936–1966), Roger Conant (1966–1973), Ronald Re-

uther (1974–1978), William V. Donaldson (1980–1991), Alexander L. "Pete" Hoskins (1993–2006), and Vikram Dewan (2006–present). Starting with Donaldson's appointment, zoo heads have been named presidents rather than superintendents.

13. White, *Fairmount*, p. 54.

14. Ibid., p. 56.

15. DeLeon, *America's First Zoostory*, p. 46.

16. Sedgwick, *Peaceable Kingdom*, pp. 62–63. DeLeon, *America's First Zoostory*, p. 48, cites somewhat lower figures for 1875, though still more than 400,000 visitors. It was at about this time when the word "zoo" came into usage as the common abbreviation for "zoological gardens." According to DeLeon (p. 15), a popular British song of 1877 contained the lyrics: "Walking in the zoo is an OK thing to do."

17. At about the same time, in 1878, Dr. Camac stepped down from the zoo's presidency and left the board the following year. Some years later, he returned from a lengthy trip in which he had taken his family up the Nile to discover that the person he had left in charge of his finances in Philadelphia had embezzled most of his fortune. He was in his seventieth year when he died at his son's home in 1900 and was buried in Christ Church Burial Ground. His memory is honored by the Zoological Society in the William Camac Founder's Award, which is presented to a Friend of the Philadelphia Zoo who best exemplifies Camac's generosity of spirit and enthusiasm for the institution he was instrumental in creating.

18. DeLeon, *America's First Zoostory*, pp. 57–58.

19. Arthur Erwin Brown, *Guide to the Garden of the Zoological Society of Philadelphia (Fairmount Park)*, 4th ed. (Philadelphia: Allen, Lane, and Scott, 1886). There is little difference in how the zoo presents its animals today. See "Meet Our Animals" on the zoo's website, available at www.philadelphiazoo.org.

20. As quoted by DeLeon, *America's First Zoostory*, p. 55.

21. L. J. Lowenstine, "To Keep Them Alive: A History of Zoo Pathology," November 13, 2004, International Veterinary Information Service, November 13, 2004, available at www.ivis.org.

22. DeLeon, *America's First Zoostory*, pp. 74–76.

23. Construction of the Pachyderm House was funded by a bequest from a former zoo director, Wilson Catherwood (DeLeon, *America's First Zoostory*, pp. 110–111). Later in the century, the leading Philadelphia architects Venturi and Rauch designed the new tree house by remaking the Hewitt-Furness Antelope House, and the primate center that burned in the Christmas Eve fire of 1995. After zoo officials retired their elephants starting in 2007, the Cret-designed Pachyderm House became the centerpiece of the new children's zoo, dubbed "KidZooU," which opened in 2013.

24. Vikram H. Dewan, "Philadelphia Zoo's New KidZooU Passes Torch of Environmentalism," *Philadelphia Inquirer*, April 21, 2013, p. C5. That projected $244 million included $61.3 million in tax revenue and $117 million in construction labor, consulting services, and materials.

25. DeLeon, *America's First Zoostory*, pp. 166–169.

26. Paul Nussbaum, "Zoo Wants a SEPTA Stop," *Philadelphia Inquirer*, April 2, 2013, pp. B1, B7.

27. Eric Karlan, "Recent Changes at America's First Zoo," *Pennsylvania Magazine* 35, no. 4 (July/August 2012): 44–48. The oldest of the three African elephants died at age fifty-two before that move could be made.

28. *Philadelphia Zoo Strategic Plan, 2008–2013* (available at www.philadelphiazoo.org).

29. Dr. Andrew Baker, as quoted in Linda S. Kabada, "Just Close Enough to a Tiger," *Philadelphia Inquirer*, June 6, 2014, p. W16. For more on today's zoo, see also Joann Greco, "Where the Wild Things Are," *Philadelphia Style* (Late Spring 2013), pp. 127–129; Jane M. Von Bergen, interviewing zoo president Vikram H. Dewan, "Where Every Day Can Be an Adventure," *Philadelphia Inquirer*, May 5, 2014, p. C8; Sandy Bauers, "Cat Walk," *Philadelphia Inquirer*, May 7, 2014, pp. A1–2.

30. The KidZooU was officially the Hamilton Family Children's Zoo and Faris Family Education Center, named for two major contributors to the project, Richard K. Faris and Dorrance "Dodo" Hamilton.

Chapter 10: Performing Arts in the Parks

1. *Sixth Report of the Commissioners of Fairmount Park* (Philadelphia: King and Baird, 1899), p. 8. The music pavilion was erected at a cost of $10,000; the first concert there was on June 29, 1889. See also Joan Church Roberts, "The Schuylkill Villas" catalog, Philadelphia Antiques Show, 2006, p. 122.

2. Richard E. Rodda, "75th Anniversary of the Incorporation of the Robin Hood Dell Concerts, Predecessor of the Mann Center for the Performing Arts," available at http://manncenter.org.

3. "East" was added to the name of the old Robin Hood Dell after it was superseded by the Mann Center in 1976 (that facility was originally named Robin Hood Dell West). For the 2012 move to rename the Dell's concert facility for Georgie Woods, see Miriam Hill, "Heard in the Hall," *Philadelphia Inquirer*, January 29, 2012, p. A3, and March 6, 2012).

4. Rodda, "75th Anniversary."

5. Daniel Webster, "The Musicians," in *The Philadelphia Orchestra: A Century of Music* (Philadelphia: Temple University Press, 1999), p. 165.

6. Tom Page, "Fredric R. Mann, Arts Patron," *New York Times* Obituary, February 27, 1987.

7. Rodda, "75th Anniversary."

8. Recordings even had been made under the label of the Robin Hood Dell Orchestra. See Webster, "The Musicians," p. 166.

9. Mann had emigrated with his family from Russia to the United States at the age of two. He had aspired to become a concert pianist as a youngster, but after a car accident while a teenager, he gave up that dream. He attended Yale and the Wharton School at the University of Pennsylvania before founding his own company soon after graduating (Rodda, "75th Anniversary").

10. For example, the Mann president and CEO, Catherine M. Cahill, said of the 2013 season: "We believe if we can get families into the Mann to experience what we have, it will get people to consider coming back and trying something else." Peter Dobrin, "Cue Nemo, Zelda, Merrill Reese," *Philadelphia Inquirer*, April 13, 2013, pp. H1, H7.

11. Herbert Kupferberg, "The Ormandy Era," in *Philadelphia Orchestra*, pp. 84–86.

12. Webster, "The Musicians," p. 166. Starting in 1990, the conductor of the Orchestre Symphonique de Montréal, Charles Dutoit, who was long a favorite with Philadelphia Orchestra audiences, became director of the summer seasons at both the Mann Center and Saratoga, a position he held until 2010. From 2008 to 2012, he was chief conductor of the Philadelphia Orchestra.

13. See www.manncenter.org/events/list.

14. Peter Dobrin, "Orchestra and Mann Not in Sync This Summer," *Philadelphia Inquirer*, May 27, 2014, p. B1. The quotation is from the orchestra's executive vice president, Ryan Fleur.

15. "Where Music Lives: High Above the Banks of the Schuylkill," available at www.wrti.org. For the history of Laurel Hill, see Chapter 5.

16. Larry Fish, "City Demolishes the Vacant Playhouse in the Park: A Last-Ditch Effort to Find Someone to Salvage Fairmount Park's Theater in the Round Failed," September 12, 1997, available at http://articles.philly.com/1997-09-12/news/25550905_1 _marionette-theater-city-demolishes-park-amenities.

Chapter 11: Penn's Five Public Squares

1. "Instructions of William Penn to the Commissioners for Settling the Colony, 30 7th Mo, 1681," in *The Papers of William Penn, 1680–1684*, ed. Mary Maples Dunn and Richard S. Dunn (Philadelphia: University of Pennsylvania Press, 1982), p. 121.

2. Cret's vision for turning Penn Square into a traffic circle may have been inspired by Jacques Gréber's 1918 plan that did the same for Logan Square. No massive buildings stood in the way of the Gréber proposal, however, which was realized with the building of the Benjamin Franklin Parkway (Chapter 12).

3. See www.phil.gov./virtualch/.

4. The names "Centre Square" and "Penn Square" are confusingly combined starting in the 1950s, in the development of "Penn Center" to the west of Dilworth Plaza, which was created in the same period (along with JFK Plaza). Penn Center was the project of the executive director of the City Planning Commission, Edmund Bacon (1910–2005), and Mayor Joseph S. Clark (mayor, 1952–1956) following the demolition of the Broad Street Station of the Pennsylvania Railroad at Broad and Market Streets in 1953. That brought an office complex to a neighborhood that had long been cut in two by the railroad's "Chinese Wall" of its elevated viaduct that ran west to the Schuylkill.

5. "Transforming Dilworth Plaza (2011–2013)," Center City Reports, April 2011, available at www.CenterCityPhila.org. For the park's opening in September 2014, see Chris Hepp, "New Look, Name: Dilworth Park," *Philadelphia Inquirer*, August 20, 2014, pp. A1, A8; and Inga Saffron, "A Granite Prairie," *Philadelphia Inquirer*, September 7, 2014, p. A3. The project was funded by federal, state, and local grants, as well as from the John S. and James L. Knight Foundation, the William Penn Foundation, and the Center City District. Architects and engineers were Kieran Timberlake, OLIN, Urban Engineers, and CVM.

6. National Park Service sign in Washington Square, 2012. See also http://www .ushistory.org/tour/washington-square.htm.

7. Lynn H. Miller and Annette H. Emgarth, *French Philadelphia: The French Cultural and Historical Presence in the Delaware Valley* (Wayne, PA: Beach Lloyd, 2006), p. 45.

8. National Park Service sign in Washington Square, 2012.

9. "In 1853, landscape architect Andrew Jackson Dowling's *Rural Essays* praised Washington Square, reporting that it had more well grown specimens of forest trees than any similar space of ground in America." National Park Service sign, Washington Square.

10. The marble original remains in the rotunda of Virginia's capitol in Richmond.

11. According to a Fairmount Park sign in Franklin Square, 2012. The congregation— now known as the Old First Reformed Church—remains active today at its eighteenth-century church building at Fourth and Arch Streets.

12. Jane Jacobs, *The Death and Life of Great American Cities* (New York: Random House, 1961), p. 96.

13. The station was first opened in 1936, and then closed because of insufficient traffic. Reopened again for the 1976 bicentennial, it closed again in 1979. In July 2009, the Delaware River Port Authority approved an initial plan to renovate and reopen the station for a third time. Yet nearly six years later, when a report estimated the costs of such a project would be 50 percent higher than anticipated, it appeared that action again would be postponed. Paul Nussbaum, "$18.5M Cost to Reopen PATCO Stop," *Philadelphia Inquirer,* March 17, 2015, pp. B1, 5.

14. The project also was known as the Great Central Fair. William Y. Thompson, "Sanitary Fairs of the Civil War," *Civil War History*, no. 4 (March 1958): 51–68; Russell F. Weigley, "The Border City in Civil War, 1854–1865," in *Philadelphia: A 300-Year History* (New York: W. W. Norton, 1982), p. 412.

15. Inga Saffron, "A Delightful Oasis on Logan Square," *Philadelphia Inquirer*, May 25, 2012, p. D3.

16. Nancy M. Heinzen, *The Perfect Square: A History of Rittenhouse Square* (Philadelphia: Temple University Press, 2009), p. 5. Most of the surrounding area belonged to the Penn family; hence, its popular name was the "Governor's Woods."

17. David Rittenhouse was the nation's first notable astronomer, the first director of the United States Mint, and an early president of the American Philosophical Society. For a recent history of Rittenhouse Square, see Heinzen, *Perfect Square*.

18. From the authors' conversation with Philip Price Jr., January 23, 2013; see also Heinzen, *Perfect Square*, pp. 110–113.

19. Rittenhouse Square may have profited longest from the involvement of neighborhood groups in its protection and upkeep. The Rittenhouse Square Improvement Association was largely responsible for the park's makeover a century ago. Since 1976, the Friends of Rittenhouse Square have played a vital role. More recently, public-private partnerships have worked to restore and rejuvenate Washington, Franklin, and Logan Squares. A Washington Square plaque acknowledges seven nonprofit and four government agencies for the restoration done there from 1991 to 2002. A comparable combination (seven nonprofit, five governmental) is listed in Franklin Square for the work done in 2006.

Chapter 12: The Benjamin Franklin Parkway

1. Those city limits were established with the Act of Consolidation, making the city of Philadelphia coterminous with Philadelphia County, in 1854.

2. See Sara Cedar Miller, *Central Park: An American Masterpiece* (New York: Henry N. Abrams, 2003), passim.

3. *Sixth Report of the Commissioners of Fairmount Park*, December 31, 1899, p. 12. The memorial was commissioned by the State Society of the Cincinnati of Pennsylvania and presented to the city. It had taken the society almost seventy years to raise the money for the project, and another sixteen years before the artist, Rudolph Siemering, was able to complete the work.

4. *Broad Street, Penn Square and the Park* (Philadelphia: John Penington and Son, 1871), p. 10. Although the author of the Penington pamphlet is unknown, it is possible he was Lewis M. Haupt (1845–1937), who went to work as a topographical engineer for Fairmount Park in 1869. In about 1877, he published a book entitled *On the Best Arrangement of City Streets*, which approved of diagonal boulevards. John A. Gallery calls

Haupt the earliest advocate in Philadelphia for diagonal roads to be superimposed over the grid, although he does not propose Haupt as the author of the 1871 pamphlet. John Andrew Gallery, *The Planning of Center City Philadelphia: From William Penn to the Present* (Philadelphia: Center for Architecture, 2007), p. 20.

5. The author of the 1871 pamphlet was strongly opposed to building City Hall on Penn Square, which no doubt explained why he terminated his proposed grand avenues well to the north on Broad Street. David B. Brownlee, *Building the City Beautiful: The Benjamin Franklin Parkway and the Philadelphia Museum of Art* (Philadelphia: Philadelphia Museum of Art, 1989), catalog, p. 15.

6. Ibid., pp. 16–17.

7. Ibid., and Gallery, *Planning of Center City Philadelphia*, p. 21. Brownlee, *Building the City Beautiful*, p. 14, notes that reformers who wanted to build the parkway were "dependent on the longest-lived political machine in the nation. Their nemesis was the Republican Party's alliance of contractors, public transportation interests, utilities, and the Pennsylvania Railroad."

8. "A Boulevard Will Beautify the City," *Philadelphia Inquirer*, April 15, 1894, p. 5.

9. Ashbridge's term as mayor was from 1899 to 1903.

10. Brownlee, *Building the City Beautiful*, pp. 18–20; Gallery, *Planning of Center City Philadelphia*, p. 22.

11. *Twenty-Fourth Annual Report of the City Parks Association of Philadelphia (1912)*, p. 29. See also Brownlee, *Building the City Beautiful*, pp. 20–21.

12. Brownlee, *Building the City Beautiful*, p. 22; Gallery, *Planning of Center City Philadelphia*, p. 23.

13. Paul P. Cret, Horace Trumbauer, and Zantzinger and Borie, *Parkway Plan as Prepared for the Fairmount Park Art Association*, bird's-eye perspective from east, 1907. Inscribed P. P. C. Horace Trumbauer, C. C. Zantzinger, Paul P. Cret, Philadelphia Museum of Art, Archives, No. 90.1.

14. The Parisian influence was a strong component of the City Beautiful movement, which looked to Baron Haussmann and his transformation of the French capital during the reign of Napoleon III. Moreover, Cret and several of his colleagues were graduates of the Ecole des Beaux-Arts.

15. *Fairmount Park Art Association: Report of the Commission Employed by the Association to Study the Entrance of the Philadelphia Parkway into Fairmount Park, as Presented at the Thirty-Sixth Annual Meeting of the Art Association, December 12th, 1907* (Philadelphia, Fairmount Park Art Association, 1908), p. 15.

16. Brownlee, *Building the City Beautiful*, pp. 25–26.

17. As quoted by Brownlee, *Building the City Beautiful*, p. 27.

18. Ibid., p. 45, who says of Widener that "his great promise to Reyburn had been tacitly withdrawn long before that."

19. Ibid., p. 29.

20. Ibid.

21. Gallery, *Planning of Center City Philadelphia*, p. 24.

22. Ibid., p. 23; Brownlee, *Building the City Beautiful*, p. 30.

23. Brownlee, *Building the City Beautiful*.

24. Fairmount Park Art Association, *The Fairmount Parkway: A Pictorial Record of Development from Its First Incorporation in the City Plan in 1904 to the Completion of the Main Drive from City Hall to Fairmount Park in 1919* (Philadelphia: Fairmount Park Art Association, 1919).

25. *Department of the Art Jury, Eighth Annual Report* (Philadelphia: Department of Records, 1918), p. 8.

26. Brownlee, *Building the City Beautiful*, p. 35.

27. Ibid., p. 77.

28. See www.parkwaymuseumsdistrictphiladelphia.org.

29. See www.philamuseum.org.

30. Brownlee, *Building the City Beautiful*, pp. 40–42.

31. According to Brownlee, *Building the City Beautiful*, p. 45: "Cret may have let it be known . . . that he did not desire to be teamed with Trumbauer again."

32. Ibid., pp. 57–60.

33. See www.philamuseum.org.

34. Brownlee, *Building the City Beautiful*, p. 63.

35. Ibid., pp. 66–67.

36. Ibid., p. 77.

37. Scott Jefferys, "A Distant Mirror: John G. Johnson and the Art Museum," August 14, 2007, available at www.broadstreetreview.com.

38. The museum was created thanks to a bequest by Jules Mastbaum (1872–1925), a theater magnate and philanthropist. With the intent of establishing a museum, he collected nearly 130 sculptures and casts by Pierre August Rodin, and left them to the city of Philadelphia at his death (Chapter 14).

39. See www.parkwaycouncilfoundation.org for a map of the current layout of country flags.

40. Gallery, *Planning of Center City Philadelphia*, p. 45. See also www.centercityphila .org. The *Philadelphia Daily News*, June 15, 2004, had published a special twenty-page section in which a number of prominent advocates called for parkway rejuvenation (pp. R2–R22).

41. The driving force behind the most recent improvements has been the 1999 plan by the Center City District, Paul R. Levy, executive director, "Completing the Benjamin Franklin Parkway." Also important was the Parkway Council Foundation, composed of major cultural organizations on the parkway, as well as the Four Seasons Hotel. They joined with city officials in 2005 in opposing a proposal to hold the Champ Car World Series for racing cars on the parkway. Anthony S. Twyman, "Critics Say Races Would Steer Parkway Off Course," *Philadelphia Inquirer*, August 17, 2005, p. A1.

42. The controversy is accounted for in John Anderson, *Art Held Hostage: The Battle over the Barnes Collection* (New York: W. W. Norton, 2003). A highly critical view of the move can be seen in the 2009 documentary film with which Barnes officials refused to cooperate, *The Art of the Steal*, directed by Don Argott. For assessments of the new building, the collection, and the controversy, see David B. Brownlee, *The Barnes Foundation: Two Buildings, One Mission* (New York: Skira/Rizzoli, 2012); Martin Filler, "Victory!" *New York Review of Books* 59, no. 12 (July 12, 2012): 14–18; *Philadelphia Inquirer*, special sec. Q, May 6, 2012.

43. See www.philamuseum.org/perelman.

44. Robin Pogrebin, "Philadelphia Museum Job Sends Gehry Underground," *New York Times*, October 19, 2006; Inga Saffron, "Polishing the Masterpiece," *Philadelphia Inquirer*, May 18, 2014, pp. A12–A13.

45. Quoted by Carrie Rickey, "A 'Museum Mile' Is Adding Luster to the Parkway," *Philadelphia Inquirer*, p. Q4.

46. The proposal, entitled "More Park, Less Way," was launched at a public meeting on February 4, 2013, by the mayor; the deputy mayor and commissioner of parks and recreation, Michael di Berardinis; and Penn Praxis (http://planphilly.com/praxis -projects/benjamin-franklin-parkway).

47. In the summer of 2013, with parking banned from it, the Oval became the site of a temporary "pop-up" park, complete with a sandy beach, chairs, umbrellas, and refreshment stands. Inga Saffron, "Changing Skyline: Pop-Up Parks Perk Up Dull City Spots," *Philadelphia Inquirer*, July 12, 2013, pp. D1, D3. That marked the first of what were intended to be a succession of events and activities planned for the Oval.

48. Ibid. See also Miriam Hill, "City Planning Leaders Air Parkway Proposal," *Philadelphia Inquirer*, February 5, 2013, p. B5; and Harris Steinberg, "Philly's Renewed Urbanity," *Philadelphia Inquirer*, July 11, 2013, p. A16.

49. Jennifer Lin, "Luxury Hotel Set for Family Court Site on Logan Sq.," *Philadelphia Inquirer*, February 18, 2014, pp. B1–B2.

50. Differing visions for remaking LOVE Park had preceded the agreement announced by Mayor Michael Nutter and City Council president Darrell L. Clarke in February 2014. See Troy Graham, "Harmony on Park Plan," *Philadelphia Inquirer*, February 11, 2014, pp. A1, A10. The renovations to come were assisted by grants from the William Penn Foundation. Penn Praxis directed the civic engagement process (www .planphilly.com/lovepark); Hargreaves Associates and Kieran Timberlake were the landscape consultants and architectural firms in charge of the new design.

51. According to Deputy Commissioner Mark Focht, PPR, at a public meeting announcing design alternatives for a renovated JFK Plaza, March 24, 2015. See also Julia Terruso, "LOVE Park Redesign Plans Are Unveiled," *Philadelphia Inquirer*, March 25, 2015, pp. B1, B2.

52. Rickey, "'Museum Mile,'" quoting Meryl Levitz.

Chapter 13: Parks and Transportation

1. Evans's *Oruktor Amphibolos* (Amphibious Digger) had been commissioned by the Philadelphia Board of Health to dredge and clean its dockyards. Never a success, the Oruktor was eventually sold for its parts. Steve Lubar, "Was This America's First Steamboat, Locomotive, and Car?" *Invention and Technology* 21, no. 4 (Spring 2006): 16–24.

2. The Schuylkill Navigation Company was chartered in 1815 to build a series of new improvements on the river. By 1827, it had completed a waterway reaching 108 miles from Philadelphia to Port Carbon outside Pottsville, which included a number of canals and other connections along the river. That ushered in an era in which the Schuylkill was the main avenue for hauling anthracite from the hard coal region to the port of Philadelphia. Increasingly, the water route fell victim to competition from railroads and was largely disbanded late in the nineteenth century. Several of its locks have been restored in recent years.

3. *Third Annual Report of the Commissioners of Fairmount Park* (Philadelphia: King and Baird, 1871), pp. 17–18.

4. *First Annual Report of the Commissioners of Fairmount Park* (Philadelphia: King and Baird, 1869), p. 35.

5. *Third Annual Report of the Commissioners of Fairmount Park, Appendix I*, Report of Chief Engineer, John C. Cresson (Philadelphia: King and Baird, 1871), p. 14, 40–41.

Cresson said that the work referred to awaited a "general plan" for the east park being prepared by "Olmsted and Vance" [*sic*], i.e., "Vaux" (Chapter 2).

6. *Second Annual Report of the Commissioners of Fairmount Park* (Philadelphia: King and Baird, 1870), p. 16.

7. Dorothy Gondos Beers, "The Centennial City, 1865–1876," in *Philadelphia: A 300-Year History*, ed. Russell F. Weigley, Barra Foundation (New York: W. W. Norton, 1982), p. 468.

8. Ibid. *United States International Exposition, Report of Director General*, Report of the Chief of the Bureau of Transportation (Washington, D.C.: Government Printing Office), vol.1, pp. 342–346.

9. See www.workshopoftheworld.com/fairmount_park/transport.html.

10. The stretch of the Schuylkill chosen for the Ellen Phillips Samuel sculptures on Kelly Drive was traversed by slow-moving vehicles when that site was chosen in 1907. By the time the plazas were completed more than fifty years later, speeding passersby could only glimpse the art displayed there (Chapter 15).

11. In place of the waterfall and lake at Chamounix, today's park goers may "explore the trails below the house to find remnants of the Fairmount Park trolley bridges . . . with outstanding brick arches and stone walls" (www.historic-details.com/places/pa /phila/fairmount-park-houses/Chamounix-mansion).

12. See www.phillyroads.com/roads/schuylkill/.

13. Those revolts also prevented completion of the Mid-County Expressway (locally known as the "Blue Route") through Philadelphia's suburban Delaware and Montgomery Counties for many years. That highway, the southernmost twenty-mile stretch of I-476 to its connection with I-95, was begun in 1969 and not completed until 1991, thanks to years of controversy and opposition from those whose neighborhoods were to be most affected. Its completion at last created a wobbly oval of a beltway around the outskirts of Philadelphia.

14. Alex Wigglesworth, "City Council: 'Ultimate Goal' Is to Build a Legal ATV Park in Philly," October 3, 2012, available at www.metro.us/local/city-council-ultimate -goal-is-to-build-a-legal-atv-park-in-philly/tmWljc—22hE09Y73mxbc.

15. Summer Ballentine, "Part of Riverfront Bike Trail Opens," *Philadelphia Inquirer*, June 18, 2013, pp. B1, B5.

Chapter 14: Public Art in Philadelphia

1. One of Peale's most iconic works, especially for Philadelphians, is his self-portrait beckoning visitors to enter the Peale Museum, then housed at Independence Hall. That painting, *The Artist in His Museum*, is in the collection of the Pennsylvania Academy of Fine Arts.

2. The twentieth-century bronze casting of Houdon's Washington stands before the Tomb of the Unknown Soldier of the American Revolution in Washington Square. The Lazzarini marble of Franklin now is visible in a window beside the entrance to today's Library Company headquarters at 1314 Locust Street. It had deteriorated after more than a century in its outdoor niche across from Independence Hall. When the American Philosophical Society built its new library in 1956 on the old site, it reproduced the façade of the original Library Company building, and replaced the Lazzarini sculpture with a copy.

3. See Chapter 1 for the history of the Rush sculptures.

4. See Chapter 3 for more on the cemetery and its influence on Fairmount Park.

5. Bailly's marble of Washington was moved inside City Hall in 1908 and replaced at Independence Hall with a bronze casting. Bailly also did a monumental sculpture of Franklin, now in the lobby of the former Public Ledger building on South Sixth Street across from Independence Square, as well as twelve commemorative busts for the Great Sanitary Fair held at Logan Square in 1864.

6. One commentator has called the 1911 tomb of Henry Charles Lea "a summa of Philadelphia's funereal monuments, combining a significant architectural composition with an important piece of sculpture." The figure is of a seated Cleo, muse of history, by A. S. Calder. The tomb was designed by the firm of Zantzinger and Borie, who would play a major role in the design of the Philadelphia Museum of Art. See George Thomas, "The Statue in the Garden," in *Sculpture of a City: Philadelphia's Treasures in Bronze and Stone* (New York: Walker, 1974), pp. 36–44.

7. Theo B. White, *Fairmount, Philadelphia's Park* (Philadelphia: Philadelphia Art Alliance Press, 1975), p. 94.

8. Penny Balkin Bach, *Public Art in Philadelphia* (Philadelphia: Temple University Press, 1992), p. 43. The author has been the longtime executive director of the Fairmount Park Art Association (now the Association for Public Art).

9. Ibid.

10. See http://associationforpublicart.org.

11. As quoted by Bach, *Public Art in Philadelphia*, p. 202. See also George Gurney, "The Sculpture of City Hall," in *Sculpture of a City*, pp. 94–103; and Gurney "William Penn," in *Sculpture of a City*, pp. 104–109.

12. *Sixth Report of the Commissioners of Fairmount Park* (Philadelphia: King and Baird, 1899), pp. 12–16.

13. *Sculpture of a City*, p. 142; Bach, *Public Art in Philadelphia*, p. 68.

14. David Sellin, "The Centennial," in *Sculpture of a City*, pp. 78–93.

15. Bach, *Public Art in Philadelphia*, p. 206.

16. John Dryfhout, "Garfield Monument," in *Sculpture of a City*, pp. 180–187.

17. Michael Richman, "Ulysses S. Grant," in *Sculpture of a City*, pp. 188–195.

18. Bach, *Public Art in Philadelphia*, pp. 82–84.

19. Architects were the Swiss William Lescaze and his Philadelphia partner, George Howe.

20. Apart from the figures at the *Terrace of Heroes* and the Rizzo and Connie Mack statues, almost no other literal representations of historical figures have been installed in public places in the city since 1960. One of the few is Walter Erlebacher's *Jesus Breaking Bread* of 1976, which has been displayed near the Cathedral Basilica of Saints Peter and Paul at Eighteenth and Race Streets since 1978. Yet quite a number from the 1930s through the 1950s are visible throughout the city.

21. Letter from the Fairmount Park Commission by Dick Nicolai, Information Officer, to Philadelphia City Councilman Joseph Zazcyzny, dated February 9, 1977. See also Chapter 15.

22. See Bach, *Public Art in Philadelphia*, pp. 232–259, for descriptions of these and other public sculptures installed in Philadelphia from 1950 to 1992.

23. Ibid., p. 172. At this writing, the Grooms work remained in storage.

24. Ibid., p. 149.

25. Philadelphia Museum of Art, *Developments* 21, no. 2 (Spring/Summer 2012): 6–7.

26. The *Total Abstinence Fountain* was the creation of Herman Kirn; the *Irish Memorial*'s artist was Glenna Goodacre. Italian immigrants are represented by the Columbus

Monument; Germans by Humboldt; the French by Joan of Arc; African Americans by John Rhoden's *Nesaika*, and the Scots near the *Irish Memorial* at Penn's Landing in the *St. Andrews Memorial.*

27. Other "popular" works sometimes derided by establishment critics include *Mr. Baseball*, the *Irish Memorial*, and *Frank Rizzo.*

28. Bach, *Public Art in Philadelphia*, pp. 130–135.

29. See http://muralarts.org. Jane Golden has been the director of the program from the start.

30. Inga Saffron, "Mural Arts Crosses a Boundary," *Philadelphia Inquirer*, March 21, 2014, pp. D1, D4.

31. Dianna Marder, "The Latest Words on Art," *Philadelphia Inquirer*, June 11, 2010, pp. W18–W19. The Museum Without Walls audio tour can be accessed online at www .museumwithoutwallsaudio.org.

Chapter 15: Fairmount Park

1. See Penny Balkin Bach, *Public Art in Philadelphia* (Philadelphia: Temple University Press, 1992). Bach's more comprehensive presentation ends in 1992. See also *Sculpture of a City: Philadelphia's Treasures in Bronze and Stone* (New York: Walker, 1974); and Roselyn F. Brenner, *Philadelphia's Outdoor Art*, 3rd ed. (Philadelphia: Camino Books, 2002).

2. Bach, *Public Art in Philadelphia*, p. 242. What began as the Philadelphia Art Jury in 1907 is now the Philadelphia Art Commission. It reviews all city-owned construction projects and works of art to set a positive example for the private sector. As noted in its 1927 Annual Report, "the purpose of the Art Commission is to be helpful to the public in preventing the ugly and creating the beautiful" (available at www.phila .gov/commerce/rep/oac/ac_history.htm).

3. Bach, *Public Art in Philadelphia*, p. 234.

4. Ibid., p. 238.

5. Victoria Donohoe, "The Swann Fountain," in *Sculpture of a City*, p. 234. Photos of Swann Fountain appear in the Introduction and Chapter 12.

6. Thomas Hine, "The Swann Fountain's Big Splash," *Philadelphia Inquirer*, June 10, 1990, p. 1F.

7. Bach, *Public Art in Philadelphia*, pp. 217, 226. Albert Laessle (1877–1954) also was the artist for the popular *Billy* sculpture in Rittenhouse Square and *Penguins* at the Philadelphia Zoo.

8. Ibid., p. 229. Paul Manship (1885–1966) is also represented in Rittenhouse Square with his early work, *Duck Girl*. He used similar spheres in other work, including the memorial to Woodrow Wilson in front of the former League of Nations, now the European headquarters of the United Nations, in Geneva, Switzerland. His *Prometheus* in front of New York's Rockefeller Center is perhaps his best-known work. J. Otto Schweizer (1863–1955) was a German-born sculpture who worked in Philadelphia. His bronze of General Peter Muhlenberg stands near the west entrance of the Philadelphia Museum of Art. See Bach, *Public Art in Philadelphia*, p. 226.

9. Kelly (born 1923–) is also represented in a Philadelphia public site by a much earlier work (1957) for the lobby of the Transportation Building at Seventeenth above Market Street, 6 Penn Center. Aluminum panels are arranged on a double-bar grid in four rows. For more on the Barnes Foundation, see Chapter 12 or www.barnesfoundation .org.

10. Philadelphia Museum of Art, *Developments* 21, no. 2 (Spring/Summer 2012): 8–9. See also www.rodinmuseum.org. The works that have been reinstalled outdoors are now protected to preserve their surfaces.

11. John Tancock, "The Washington Monument," in *Sculpture of a City*, pp. 132–141; Jim McClelland, *The Fountains of Philadelphia* (Harrisburg, PA: Stackpole Books, 2005), p. 25.

12. Jeffrey Fuller, "Public Art: *Iroquois*, by Mark di Suvero," *Philadelphia Magazine*, September 2007.

13. In its early years, the Fairmount Park Art Association (FPAA) placed a number of bronze reproduction casts of works by European artists in Fairmount Park. That practice continued even after its 1878 decision to commission new work from American artists in order to support them financially. See Bach, *Public Art in Philadelphia*, pp. 61 and 197.

14. Ibid., p. 245.

15. Ibid., p. 207; Brenner, *Philadelphia's Outdoor Art*, p. 63.

16. Jacob Epstein (1880–1959) was first commissioned to do this work for the *Samuel Memorial* on Kelly Drive. But when it took shape, it was deemed too large for that site and was installed at its current location instead. Philadelphia acquired a second piece by Louise Nevelson (1899–1988) in 1976, her *Bicentennial Dawn*, in painted wood, which is in the lobby of the James A. Byrne Federal Courthouse at Sixth and Market Streets.

17. *Public Ledger*, January 1, 1917. The Girard work is by John Massey Rhind, who also created *Tedyuscung* in the Wissahickon Valley (Chapter 8) and a portrait statue of Henry Howard Houston at Lincoln Drive and Harvey Street. The *Muhlenberg* is by J. Otto Schweizer; see also Schweizer's *All Wars Memorial to Colored Soldiers and Sailors* in Aviator Park at Logan Square.

18. See www.philamuseum.org/sculpturegarden/.

19. Bach, *Public Art in Philadelphia*, p. 217. See Chapter 16 for a view of the *Fountain of the Seahorses*.

20. Manca (1897–1976) spent the latter part of his career in the United States. Zorach (1887–1966) was part of the mid-twentieth-century movement to revive direct carving. Bach, *Public Art in Philadelphia*, pp. 88–89.

21. The American artist Randolph Rogers lived from 1825 to 1892. He also designed nine relief panels, *Columbus Doors*, for the U.S. Capitol. Bach, *Public Art in Philadelphia*, p. 199.

22. Einar Jonsson (1874–1954) was commissioned by J. Bunford Samuel to create this tribute to a possible Icelandic visitor to America. The Saint-Gaudens work is a variation on his earlier monument, *The Puritan*. See Bach, *Public Art in Philadelphia*, p. 211, for the artist's comment on how he altered that work for *The Pilgrim*.

23. Ibid., p. 206. The artist was a Philadelphian, John J. Boyle. Photo appears in Chapter 14.

24. John Dryfhout, "Garfield Monument," in *Sculpture of a City*, pp. 180–187. For a photo of the monument, see Chapter 14.

25. David Sellin, "*Cowboy*," in *Sculpture of a City*, pp. 196–204. Photo appears in Chapter 14.

26. Ibid., p. 297; Bach, *Public Art in Philadelphia*, p. 230.

27. Michael Richman, "Ulysses S. Grant," in *Sculpture of a City*, pp. 188–195; Bach, *Public Art in Philadelphia*, p. 208. Photo appears in Chapter 14.

28. Bach, *Public Art in Philadelphia*, p. 233.

29. Bach, *Public Art in Philadelphia*, p. 199; David Sellin, "The Centennial," in *Sculpture of a City*, p. 79. The Pegasus bronzes are visible in Chapter 4 (image of Memorial Hall).

30. Bach, *Public Art in Philadelphia*, p. 201, 215.

31. Ibid., pp. 191–204. *The Wrestlers* is one of three castings of classical works in the park. See Chapter 14 for a photograph. *Silenus and the Infant Bacchus* is on Kelly Drive across from the Azalea Garden. Near Thirty-Third and East Park are two Greek youths depicted in discourse. Photo appears in Chapter 14.

32. Boyle's work in Philadelphia also includes *Stone Age in America* and portrait statues of *Benjamin Franklin* on the campus of the University of Pennsylvania, and of *John C. Bullitt* outside City Hall.

33. Bailly's original marble of Washington was initially at Independence Hall. It was reinstalled in City Hall's Conversation Hall in 1983.

34. Bach, *Public Art in Philadelphia*, p. 201. See Chapter 8 for more on public works of art in the Wissahickon.

35. Ibid.

36. See www.friendsofclarkpark.org.

Chapter 16: The Parks' New Governance System

1. *Fairmount Park Strategic Plan: A Bridge to the Future*, prepared in 2004 for Fairmount Park and the City of Philadelphia by Leon Young and PROS Consulting (www.prosconsulting.com). For years, the *Philadelphia Daily News* had led a full-throated campaign in favor of such a charter change, starting with its "Acres of Neglect" series of editorials in 2001. By 2008, the Philadelphia Parks Alliance was lobbying hard for the amendment; the watchdog group, the Committee of Seventy, also became a supporter, as did other public-interest groups.

2. See Chapter 12 and the account of Commissioner P. A. B. Widener's offer and accompanying demands for a new art museum, and of his son Joseph's 1920 battle with Mayor J. Hampton Moore. That led to the Widener art collection going not to the Philadelphia Museum of Art as originally promised, but instead to the National Gallery in Washington, D.C. Also, the terms of John G. Johnson's will almost prevented his vast art collection from going to the Philadelphia Museum of Art. Only a very expansive interpretation of the will after Johnson's death allowed the city to obtain it.

3. See Chapter 12 and the contrasts in parkway and museum construction during the mayoral terms of Samuel Ashbridge, John Reyburn, and Thomas B. Smith on the one hand and reformers Rudolph Blankenburg and J. Hampton Moore on the other. For a full assessment of Philadelphia's political corruption in the late nineteenth- and early twentieth-centuries, see Lloyd M. Abernethy, "Progressivism, 1905–1919," in *Philadelphia: A 300-Year History*, ed. Russell F. Weigley (New York: W.W. Norton, 1982), pp. 524–565.

4. From 1975 to 2005, the parks' budget remained at about $13.5 million, according to a longtime member of the FPC. That left it, by the end of that period, with little more than 25 percent of its funding in real dollars from thirty years earlier. Philip Price Jr., "What Really Ails the City's Parks," *Philadelphia Daily News*, October 28, 2005.

5. David Contosta and Carol Franklin, *Metropolitan Paradise: Philadelphia's Wissahickon Valley, 1620–2020, The Struggle for Nature in the City* (Philadelphia: St. Joseph's University Press, 2010), vol. 1, p. 17.

6. "How Park Wrecks Became Parks and Rec," *Philadelphia Daily News*, June 9, 2001.

7. This defense of the FPC comes from the authors' conversation with Mark Focht, first deputy commissioner of parks and facilities for the PRR, on November 26, 2012. He argued that the 1997 grant from the William Penn Foundation was never intended exclusively for the new environmental centers. As evidence that the commission complied with the terms of the grant, Focht noted that the foundation gave the parks an additional $2.5 million in 2003–2004.

8. As late as 1894, one of the leading proponents of public parks as places for the public to enjoy fresh air and glimpses of nature was strongly opposed when a Philadelphia official recommended that the city should provide more playgrounds and pay less attention to purely ornamental parkland. C. S. Sargent, "Playgrounds and Parks," *Garden and Forest* 17 (June 6, 1894): 221.

9. Galen Cranz, *The Politics of Park Design: A History of Urban Parks in America* (Cambridge, MA: MIT Press, 1982).

10. Just as in 1867, the 1951 charter also made city officials ex officio members of the FPC. In addition to the mayor and president of City Council, those named in the 1951 document reflect something of how the perception of city parks, as well as the role of city government, had evolved. Others were the commissioner of public property, the recreation commissioner, the water commissioner, and the chief engineer and surveyor of the Department of Streets.

11. The major cities along the Northeastern Seaboard—Boston, New York, Philadelphia, and Baltimore—all had established city parks by the post–Civil War period. Those beyond the Appalachians were not far behind, though by the time major cities grew in the far west, the idea of combining parks with recreational facilities was already the norm.

12. See, for example, the testimony opposing the merger by the longtime executive director of the FPC, William E. Mifflin, Re: Bill No. 050753, Committee of the Whole, Council of the City of Philadelphia, December 14, 2005.

13. Press release, "Mayor Nutter Announces Almost $20M to Reinvigorate Parkway and Neighborhood Green Space," City of Philadelphia, Office of the Mayor, July 17, 2008. The public/private partnership included the City of Philadelphia, the Commonwealth of Pennsylvania, the William Penn Foundation, Pew Charitable Trusts, and the Knight Foundation. The city would provide $6.4 million out of a total of $17.1 million for parkway improvements, with $6.45 million from the Commonwealth, $2 million from Pew Charitable Trusts, $1.25 million from the Knight Foundation, and $1 million from the William Penn Foundation. For Hawthorne, in addition to $1.1 million from the Pennsylvania Department of Conservation and Natural Resources, Councilman Frank DiCicco and State Representative Babette Josephs both contributed several hundred thousand dollars from their capital budgets. See Chapter 12 for details on refurbishing the parkway.

14. See www.fairmountpark.org/FpcCommission.asp.

15. Ibid.

16. Miriam Hill, "Parks, and Wreck," *Philadelphia Inquirer*, June 13, 2012, pp. B1, B6.

17. Miriam Hill, "Tax-Plan Delay Hits Parks Agency," *Philadelphia Inquirer*, July 15, 2012, p. A3.

18. Views we attribute to Commissioner DiBerardinis were expressed to the authors in an interview on October 4, 2012.

19. Meris Stansbury, "School of the Future: Lessons in Failure," *School News*, June 1, 2009, available at www.eschoolnews.com/2009/06/01/school-of-the-future-lessons-in-failure/. The parcel in question is in West Fairmount Park, only a few hundred yards to the east of Memorial Hall and the *Smith Memorial Arch*, which marks the main entrance into the park's Centennial District.

20. Dale Mezzacappa, "High School 2.0," available at http://educationnext.org/high-school-2-0/.

21. Ibid.

22. That decision, by Judge John W. Herron, was upheld a year later on appeal to Commonwealth Court. See Linda Lloyd, "Fox Chase Loses Appeal to Use Burholme Park," *Philadelphia Inquirer*, December 17, 2009.

23. Scott Maiken, "Fox Chase Cancer Center to Merge into Temple Health System," December 15, 2011, available at www.newsworks.org.

24. Nancy Goldenberg, as quoted in a press release, Philadelphia Parks and Recreation, Thursday, September 12, 2010.

25. The Open Lands Protection Ordinance amended Chapter 15–100 of the Philadelphia Code: "Parks and Outdoor Spaces."

26. One legislator from Philadelphia, State Representative Mark Cohen, threatened to sue the city soon after the charter change vote in November 2008. Cohen challenged the city's right to dissolve the Fairmount Park Commission on grounds that its appointment by the Board of Judges made it a state agency. His specific concern was that the new commission would be unable or unwilling to prevent the sale of parkland. See Sandra Shea, "Park Size Matters, but So Do Other Things," *Philadelphia Daily News*, July 13, 2009. However, Cohen took no such action, possibly because of the passage in the next year of the Open Lands Protection Ordinance.

27. Mike Jensen, "Mixed Vote on Temple Sports," *Philadelphia Inquirer*, February 25, 2014, pp. A1, A8. The Canoe House had been home to Temple's teams for a dollar a year in rent until it was condemned in 2008 for its dilapidated state. The city and Temple had earlier argued over which was responsible for repairs to the building. See editorial by Debra Wolf Goldstein, chair of the Land Use, Planning, and Design Committee of the PPR, *Philadelphia Inquirer*, January 12, 2014, p. E6; Mike Jensen, "For the Lack of a Boathouse," *Philadelphia Inquirer*, December 15, 2013, pp. E1, E9; and Susan Borschel, "Temple Didn't Have to Cut," *Philadelphia Inquirer*, February 2, 2014, p. C4.

28. From our interview of Commissioner DiBerardinis and First Deputy Commissioner Mark Focht, October 4, 2012.

29. Mayor Rendell was reportedly furious when he learned in 1997 that the FPC had applied for and received a substantial grant from the William Penn Foundation to be used in part to create new environmental centers in the park. He was unwilling to budget for the additional staff necessary to maintain those facilities. See note 6.

30. Focht interview, October 4, 2012.

Chapter 17: The Greener City

1. See www.phila.gov/green/PDFs/GW2012Report.pdf for the first annual progress report. For a 2012 interview with Mayor Nutter and profiles of several members of his administration concerned with sustainability, see *Grid* (Philadelphia: Red Flag Media, 2012), pp. 29–35.

2. Both Greenworks and Green 2015 were created in conjunction with a new citywide comprehensive plan (Philadelphia 2035) and zoning code adopted by Philadel-

phia in 2011. Green 2015 was supported by grants from the William Penn Foundation and the Lenfest Foundation and engaged, in addition to Penn Praxis, the Pennsylvania Horticultural Society and the Penn Project for Civic Engagement. Penn Praxis is the clinical arm of the University of Pennsylvania's School of Design that is engaged in applied research in urban design.

3. Editorial, "City Life's Better with Fewer Paved Surfaces," *Philadelphia Inquirer*, May 8, 2012, p. A18. Both the William Penn Foundation and Pennsylvania's Department of Conservation and Natural Resources provided resources in support of the initiative. See also Michael DiBerardinis, "Working Together to 'Green' Philadelphia," *Philadelphia Inquirer*, July 7, 2014, A14.

4. According to Commissioner DiBerardinis, in a conversation with the authors, October 4, 2012.

5. See www.phila.gov/green. The 2014 progress report for Greenworks Philadelphia showed that 10,442 acres of parks and open space had been secured by that year, and that 100,000 new trees had been planted. See also www.treephilly.org.

6. Alex Steffen, "Build Green Cities," *Foreign Policy* 191 (January/February 2012): 72.

7. Harris Steinberg, "We've Come a Long Way, Philly," *Philadelphia Inquirer*, May 8, 2012, p. A19.

8. Among the worst storms affecting major American cities along the East Coast were three hurricane-related disasters, those spawned by Katrina in 2005, Irene in 2011, and Sandy in 2012.

9. The Philadelphia Water Department's (PWD's) program to lessen the overflows of combined sewers was mandated by the U.S. Environmental Protection Agency and also includes such measures as reconstructing wetlands, creating rooftop gardens, and other water-collecting structures along streets and in parks, all in the attempt "to mimic the natural cycle that existed before the city was built." Adam E. Levine, "A Post-Sandy Look at How Philadelphia Streets Flood," *Philadelphia Inquirer*, November 4, 2012, p. D5. The PWD provides useful information about its greening programs at www.phillywatersheds.org.

10. See www.planphilly.com/vision/parks. Michael DiBerardinis, "The Green Country Town," *Philadelphia Inquirer*, October 4, 2013, p. A19.

11. See www.penntreatypark.org.

12. "An Action Plan for the Central Delaware," May 8, 2008, is a partner of the preliminary "Civic Vision for the Central Delaware." For more information, see www.planphilly.com/actionplan. The website grew out of the riverfront planning process and remains an up-to-date source of relevant information. Today, a coalition of more than twenty civic and nonprofit organizations, the Central Delaware Advocacy Group (CDAG) is the principal public voice of the central Delaware communities. Its website is available at www.centraldelawareadvocacy.com.

13. Steinberg, "We've Come a Long Way, Philly," May 8, 2012.

14. Jim Kenney, "City's Rivers Need Relief," *Philadelphia Inquirer*, October 24, 2012, p. A19. Kenney was a Philadelphia councilman who favored the fifty-foot buffer when he wrote this article. For other attempts by City Council to change the new zoning code, see Inga Saffron, "New Zoning Code, but Old Philadelphia Ways," *Philadelphia Inquirer*, November 9, 2012, pp. D1, D10. The bill establishing the buffers was passed by City Council on November 29, 2012. It allows four riverfront uses—marine-related industry, marinas, utilities, and city-owned factories—within the buffer without zoning approval, but bans other commercial uses.

15. See www.centraldelawareadvocacy.com. The *Land Buoy* artist, Jody Pinto, was also the creator of *Fingerspan* in the Wissahickon (Chapter 8).

16. Lydia O'Neal, "City Park Is Set to Rise from Old Pier on Delaware," *Philadelphia Inquirer*, June 27, 2014, pp. B1, B5.

17. Ashley Hahn, "Penn Street Trail Taking Shape," April 26, 2013, available at www.planphilly.com/issues/riverfronts-waterfronts.

18. In April 2013, the DRWC hired a landscape architecture firm to develop a set of conceptual designs for bridging the chasm created by I-95 through center city. The architects were to focus on four strategic points along the waterfront: the existing cap over I-95 between Chestnut and Walnuts Streets, the Market Street scissor ramps, the pedestrian bridge at South Street, and the land around the marina basin. Inga Saffron, "A First Step to Link City, Waterfront," *Philadelphia Inquirer*, April 5, 2013, pp. B1, B8.

Chapter 18: The City in a Park

1. That was not true for nonresidents who worked in Philadelphia. Starting in 1939, everyone employed in the city, regardless of their residence, has been subject to a wage tax, with the rate differing for city residents and nonresidents. At its highest in 1984, residents were taxed at 4.96 percent of their wages, while the rate for nonresidents was 4.3125 percent. During the early years of the twenty-first century, rates were gradually reduced. As of 2015, residents are taxed at 2.8377 percent and nonresidents at 3.0790 percent. The rate paid by residents has gradually been brought below that for nonresidents.

2. Miriam Hill, "Tax-Plan Delay Hits Parks Agency," *Philadelphia Inquirer*, July 15, 2012, p. A3.

3. Philadelphia Parks Alliance, "How Much Value Does the City of Philadelphia Receive from Its Park and Recreation System?" A Report by the Trust for Public Land's Center for City Park Excellence for the Philadelphia Parks Alliance," 2008, p. i.

4. Miriam Hill, "Parks and Wreck," *Philadelphia Inquirer*, June 13, 2012, pp. B2, B6. The article shows Baltimore as the only city ranking below Philadelphia, putting it in fourteenth place with $58 in per capita spending on its parks.

5. See www.fairmountpark.org/HistoricPreservationTrust.asp and Chapter 6.

6. See www.fairmountparkconservancy.org/project/ and Chapter 16.

7. Inga Saffron, "Nonprofits to Fund High-Line Park Plan," *Philadelphia Inquirer*, March 16, 2015, pp. A-1, 8. See also text at note 22, this chapter.

8. Philadelphia Parks Alliance, "How Much Value?" p. i. Since early in this century, the Philadelphia Parks Alliance has itself become the principal booster for Philadelphia's parks. This study did not include the value to the city of Independence National Historical Park (INHP), which is administered by the National Park Service. A 2013 report revealed that INHP drew some 3.59 million visitors in 2011, who generated about $150 million in spending, supporting just over two thousand jobs in the region. Stephen Salisbury, "Study: Park a City Boon," *Philadelphia Inquirer*, February 27, 2013, p. B4.

9. Ibid., p. 3n1.

10. Ibid., p. i.

11. Hill, "Parks and Wreck," p. B2, quoting Lauren Bornfriend.

12. Attractions cited include Dilworth Park, the Delaware River Waterfront, Spruce Street Harbor Park, Race Street Pier, Schuylkill Banks Boardwalk, new public art, and the city's bike share program. See Nell McShane Wulfahrt, "Philadelphia," available at www.nytimes.com/interactive/2015/01/11/travel/52-places-to-go-in-2015.html.

13. Mike Jensen, "Mixed Vote on Temple Sports," *Philadelphia Inquirer*, February 25, 2014, pp. A1, A8. See also Chapter 16.

14. See Chapter 16 and www.fairmountparkconservancy.org/project/ for details.

15. Philadelphia Parks Alliance, "How Much Value?" pp. i–ii.

16. Bill Hangley Jr., "Dawn of a New Era: Park Officials Hope that a New Concessions Strategy Can Revive the Relationship between Parks and Neighborhoods," report for the Philadelphia Parks Alliance. The text of the report is available at www.philaparks.org. It suggests that 15 percent of the parks budget might come from a revamped concessions strategy, whereas the 2008 report had added fees to concessions when it proposed as much as 40 percent of the budget might come from those two sources.

17. See Miriam Hill, "River Tours Come Back," *Philadelphia Inquirer*, April 15, 2013, pp. B1, B8.

18. Loren Bornfriend, executive director, Philadelphia Parks Alliance, in her introduction to Hangley, "Dawn of a New Era."

19. Hangley, "Dawn of a New Era," p. 1.

20. Bornfriend, www.philaparks.org.

21. Harris M. Steinberg, "Polishing Philly's Crown Jewel," *Philadelphia Inquirer*, May 23, 2014, p. A19.

22. Saffron, "Nonprofits to Fund High-Line Park Plan."

23. Inga Saffron, "Fairmount Park Plan Falls Short," *Philadelphia Inquirer*, May 13, 2014, p. A6.

24. Troy Graham, "The Elevated Park Gets on Track," *Philadelphia Inquirer*, April 6, 2014, pp. B3, B12. The design firms of Studio Bryan Hanes and Urban Engineers created the plans for this first phase. Studio Bryan Hanes also was responsible for the design of Sister Cities Park (Chapter 11). In 2014, two groups advocating for creation of Reading Viaduct Park merged to form Friends of the Rail Park, http://therailpark.org.

25. Editorial, "Callowhill's Turn," *Philadelphia Inquirer*, April 14, 2014, p. A19; Inga Saffron, "Tempting Twin Visions," *Philadelphia Inquirer*, November 16, 2012, pp. D1, D5.

26. Saffron, "Tempting Twin Visions," p. D5. In October 2014, tours of the three-mile route of the proposed rail park were offered by DesignPhiladelphia, the annual event sponsored by Philadelphia's Center for Architecture.

27. Saffron cites SEPTA's strategic planner, Byron S. Comati, "Tempting Twin Visions."

28. Paul Nussbaum, "Zoo Wants a SEPTA Stop," *Philadelphia Inquirer*, April 2, 2013, pp. B1, B7.

29. Larry Eichel, "The new feeling of Philadelphia," *Philadelphia Inquirer*, March 24, 2013, pp. C1–C2. The author directs Philadelphia research at the Pew Charitable Trusts. He cites the Pew report, "Philadelphia 2013: The State of the City," available at www.pewtrusts.org/philaresearch.

Index

James McClelland is a freelance writer whose work focuses on the arts. He is Executive Director Emeritus of the Philadelphia Art Alliance and the author of *The Martinos: A Legacy of Art*, *Fountains of Philadelphia: A Guide*, and more than two hundred articles published in national magazines.

Lynn Miller is Professor Emeritus of Political Science at Temple University. He is the author of, among other works, *Global Order: Values and Power in International Politics* and *Crossing the Line* (a novel) and the co-author (with Annette H. Emgarth) of *French Philadelphia: The French Cultural and Historical Presence in the Delaware Valley*.